Margaret Morris

*Portrait of a Decision*

*EUROPE after the First World War*

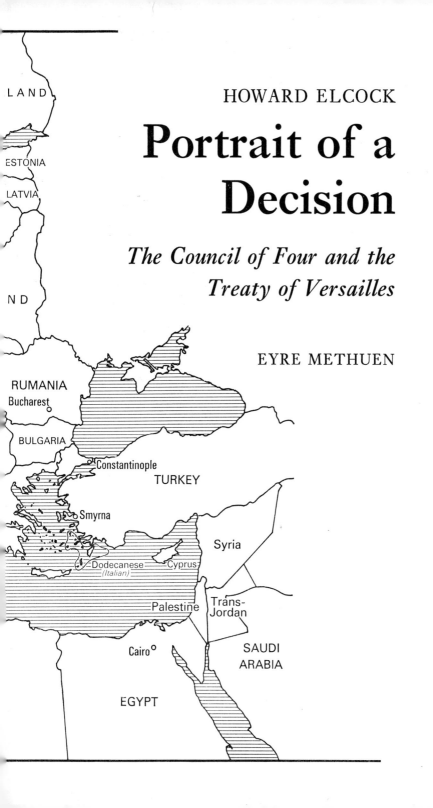

HOWARD ELCOCK

# Portrait of a Decision

*The Council of Four and the Treaty of Versailles*

EYRE METHUEN

*First published 1972*
*by Eyre Methuen Ltd*
*11 New Fetter Lane, EC4P 4EE*

*Printed in Great Britain by*
*Willmer Brothers Limited*
*Birkenhead, Cheshire*

*SBN 413 28370 4*

To my Mother, and my Father
*who fought in the War to end War*

# *Contents*

# *Illustrations*

MAPS



CARTOONS

# *Acknowledgements*

I am grateful to the following for permission to quote from copyright material for which they are responsible: Ernest Benn Ltd, the First Beaverbrook Foundation, Curtis Brown Ltd, the Royal Institute of International Affairs, Macmillan and Co. Ltd, and the St Martin's Press. I am also grateful to Methuen and Co. Ltd, the State Department of the United States of America, and the Director of Publications of Her Majesty's Stationery Office, London.

For permission to quote from unpublished material I am indebted to the First Beaverbrook Foundation, C. and T. Publications Ltd, the Keeper of Manuscripts at the British Museum, and the Marquess of Lothian.

In respect of the illustrations I am indebted to Punch Publications Ltd for permission to reproduce cartoons from the 1919 volumes of *Punch*.



A*

# *Preface*

The signing of the Treaty of Versailles on 28 June 1919 can be regarded both as the signal for the end of the nineteenth-century international system, resting on the polyglot Empire of Austria-Hungary, the monarchies of Russia and Germany, and the French Republic, and as the beginning of the contemporary world of fragmentary and fractious nation states, an inherently unstable situation in Central Europe which has plagued the world ever since, the acceptance of the right of nations to govern themselves even where they would be better off in a multi-national state, and the entrance of the first 'Third World' states into the councils of international relations. The Treaty has been much criticised. It is supposed, by its unwisdom, to have sowed the seeds for the outbreak of the Second World War, especially by 'balkanising' the whole of Central Europe, and it is alleged that the League of Nations which the Treaty established was doomed from the outset to failure by the faults written into its Covenant and by the circumstances in which it came into being. In view of all the denunciations which have been levelled at the Treaty drawn up at Paris in the first six months of 1919, it is meet that we should look again at the men who conducted the negotiations and the ways in which they proceeded, in order to see whether they were such knaves or fools as is often alleged by those who have the assistance of hindsight. This task has become both easier and more important because many collections of documents and papers relevant to the Paris Peace Conference have become available in recent years, which considerably increase our knowledge of what went on there.

The negotiators at Paris had to reach decisions relating to the whole future of the world, by a process of discussion, investigation and inevitably compromise, against a background of war, starvation, pestilence and unrest which made them all feel that their time was limited. If peace and prosperity were not restored quickly, Europe would succumb to Bolshevism and anarchy. Their task was not made any easier by the fact that, in addition to their own strong opinions, they were the servants of democratic Parliaments and electorates who were making extreme demands which, inevitably, the statesmen could not entirely satisfy. Yet they believed that no possible successors could do better. These were, perhaps, the most important background factors.

In what follows, we shall look at the events leading up to the Peace Conference, and at the course of the negotiations themselves, in the spirit of Professor Michael Oakeshott's statement that the historian 'loves [the past] as a mistress of whom he never tires and whom he never expects to talk sense'; it is my hope to make some sense of the Paris negotiations, and to reveal something of the motives, personalities and actions of the chief participants: above all of the members of the Council of Four. I have adopted no sophisticated methodological framework; to do so would be absurd, since the writing of a simple analytical account will produce complications enough; it would also be a mistake to force the facts into a conceptual strait-jacket.

During my work on this subject I have been sustained and stimulated by many people and have thus incurred many debts of gratitude, but first among these must be the debt I owe to Dr R. A. C. Parker, Fellow of The Queen's College, Oxford, who supervised my work on the papers of the Conference while I was a research student there, and was then and has been since an unfailing source of wisdom, friendship and encouragement. At a later stage, my colleagues in the Department of Political Studies at the University of Hull listened to an early draft of some of my ideas and were helpfully critical. In my searches for material I owe an especial debt of gratitude to Miss Margaret Nicholson and Mr David Shaw, of the Brynmor Jones Library at the University of Hull; without them, my task would have been slower and more laborious than it was. My good friend Dr Robert Baxter, of the University College of Wales, Swansea, besides preparing the maps, gave me much encouragement, especially when my spirits were low. Mrs Rosalind Scarrott typed the manuscript, and her patience and ingenuity in deciphering my proverbially illegible handwriting have been remarkable indeed.

In respect of access to documents, I owe a large debt of gratitude to the Trustees of the Beaverbrook Library, the Keeper of Manuscripts at the British Museum, the Keeper of the Public Records, and the Director of the Scottish Record Office. I must also thank the staff of these institutions for their help and advice.

None of these people or bodies bears any responsibility for the faults of what follows; these are entirely my own. Without them, however, whatever there may be of value herein would never have seen the light of day.

Hull, Summer 1971 Howard Elcock

# 1 Prelude: *1915-1918*

The statesmen of the First World War are not remembered today with the same reverence as their successors in the Second War. Perhaps the conduct of the Second World War was more competent, or at least less incompetent, than the conduct of the First, but one of the reasons for the difference in our attitude to Churchill and Roosevelt as compared with our attitude to Lloyd George, Woodrow Wilson and Georges Clemenceau is that Roosevelt and Churchill were spared the task of preparing a peace treaty. From the time of its signing to the present day, the terms of the Treaty of Versailles have been an object of execration and ridicule. Within a year of the Treaty signing at Versailles, J. M. Keynes published his brilliant indictment, *The Economic Consequences of the Peace*,[1] whose theme was the condemnation of the statesmen at Paris for having ignored the real problems of the peace:

> To what a different future Europe might have looked forward if either Mr Lloyd George or Mr Wilson had apprehended that the most serious of the problems which claimed their attention were not political or territorial but financial and economic, and that the perils of the future lay not in frontiers or sovereignties but in food, coal and transport.[2]

Keynes opened his book with apposite but malicious sketches of the characters of the three principal negotiators. Of Clemenceau, Keynes wrote that 'One could not despise Clemenceau or dislike him, but only take a different view as to the nature of civilised man, or indulge, at least, a different hope',[3] and who 'felt about France what Pericles felt about Athens – unique value in her, nothing else mattering. . . . He has one illusion – France; one disillusion – Mankind, including Frenchmen and his colleagues not least.'[4] Then we see Wilson, the 'Presbyterian minister', bamboozled into accepting a Carthaginian peace, allowing his Fourteen Points to become 'a document for gloss and interpretation and for all the intellectual apparatus of self-deception, by which, I dare say, the President's forefathers had persuaded themselves that the course they thought it necessary to take was consistent with every syllable of the Pentateuch'.[5] Finally, in an essay not published as part of the original book, we have Keynes' portrait of his own Chief, Lloyd George, the 'Welsh witch', of whom he asks,

> How can I convey to the reader, who does not know him, any just impression of this extraordinary figure of our time, this syren, this goat-footed bard, this half-human visitor to our age from the hag-ridden, magic and enchanted woods of Celtic antiquity? . . . Lloyd George is rooted in nothing; he is void and without content.[6]

Lloyd George was without principle, indulging in the game of compromise and of bamboozling the President merely for the fun of the thing.

Keynes left us not only these thumb-nail portraits of the chief characters but also an account of the drama itself. He said that 'The President, the Tiger and the Welsh witch were shut up in a room together for six months and the Treaty is what came out.'[7] In his book, Keynes explained how the intimacy of the Council of Four led to the President's downfall:

> . . . it is impossible month after month in intimate and ostensibly friendly converse between close associates to be digging the toes in all the time. . . . Day after day and week after week he [Wilson] allowed himself to be closeted, unsupported, unadvised, and alone, with men much sharper than himself, in situations of supreme difficulty, where he needed for success every description of resource, fertility and knowledge. He allowed himself to be drugged by their atmosphere, to discuss on the basis of their plans and of their data, and to be led along their paths.[8]

Thus the method of decision-making at the Conference, coupled with the characters of the three principal negotiators, was to blame for the defects of the Treaty. In a brilliant summary of his view of the nature of the negotiations, Keynes says that

> Prince Wilson, sailing out from the West in the barque *George Washington*, set foot in the enchanted castle of Paris to free from chains, oppression and an ancient curse, the maid Europe, of eternal youth and beauty, his mother and his bride in one. There in the castle is the King, with yellow parchment face, a million years old, and with him an enchantress with a harp, singing the Prince's own words to a magical tune. If only the Prince could cast off the paralysis which creeps on him and crying to Heaven, could make the sign of the Cross, with a sound of thunder and crashing of glass the castle would dissolve, the magicians vanish, and Europe leap into his arms. But in this fairy tale the forces of the half-world win and the soul of Man is subordinated to the spirits of the earth.[9]

In the intimacy of the Council of Four, Keynes believed that the defects in the characters of these three men and Vittorio Orlando were multiplied together to produce a monstrosity – the Carthaginian peace.

The appearance of Keynes' book helped to ensure the Treaty's defeat by the American Senate, and was followed by a flood of personal reminiscences and analyses of the characters of the statesmen, especially Wilson, most of which appeared to confirm the rightness of Keynes' view. Much was made of a memorandum prepared by Isaiah Bowman, a member of the American delegation, which purported to record Wilson's table-talk during the Atlantic crossing on the *George Washington*; it included such remarks as Wilson's warning that 'The world will be intolerable if only arrangements ensue: this is a Peace Conference in which arrangements cannot be made in the old style,' and his declaration that he and his colleagues must fight for the New Order 'agreeably if we can, disagreeably if we must'.[10] Many writers have been at pains to stress Wilson's essential arrogance: Sigmund Freud, for example, wrote of Wilson that

> I must . . . commence my contribution to this psychological study of Thomas Woodrow Wilson with the confession that the figure of the American President, as it rose above the horizon of Europeans,

> was from the beginning unsympathetic to me, and that this aversion increased in the course of years the more I learned about him and the more severely we suffered from the consequences of his intrusion into our destiny. . . . As everyone knows, the hostile camp during the war also sheltered a chosen darling of providence: the German Kaiser. It was most regrettable that later on the other side a second appeared. No-one gained thereby: respect for God was not increased.[11]

In collaboration with William C. Bullitt, a former member of the American delegation at the Conference, Freud wrote an analysis of Wilson's arrogance and other personality defects which argued that these defects were the result of Wilson's relationship with his mother. In deference to the feelings of Wilson's widow, this study was not published until 1967, after her death. No view of the negotiations which significantly modified or refuted the view inspired by Keynes appeared until 1963, when a Canadian scholar, Professor Harold Nelson, wrote a study of the drawing of Germany's frontiers at the Conference in which he draw attention to Wilson's hostility to Germany, quoting, for example, a letter from Wilson to Smuts dated 16 May 1919, in which Wilson declared that

> I feel the terrible responsibility of this whole business but inevitably my thought goes back to the very great offence against civilisation which the German state committed, and the necessity for making it evident once for all that such things can lead only to the most severe punishment.[12]

Wilson knowingly and willingly consented to a severe Treaty, and Lloyd George was the member of the Council of Four most concerned with procuring a lasting peace. Philip Kerr declared that Lloyd George sought to determine 'the permanent political realities', and Professor Nelson says that he 'possessed a keen sense of the general interest'.[13] Only Keynes' portrait of Clemenceau survives more or less intact, but Professor Nelson was concerned chiefly with British policy.

One other interpretation must be mentioned. In his massive work, *The Politics and Diplomacy of Peacemaking*,[14] which deals chiefly with the attempts of the statesmen at Paris to deal with Bolshevism in Russia and elsewhere, Professor Arno J. Mayer paints a Tolstoian picture of the members of the Council of Four as the tools of a struggle between 'the forces of movement' and the 'forces of resistance'. The true arbiters of the peace treaty were the advances and reverses suffered by Bolshevism on the one hand, and counter-revolutionary forces on the other, in the various countries of Europe, and above all in Russia. Certainly the existence and activities of Bolshevism were major preoccupations of the peacemakers and other political leaders in 1919. However, the Conference never succeeded in taking any effective measures in Russia. The major significance of Bolshevism and the Russian Civil war for the Conference was the way it increased the pressure for a speedy settlement, although it was an important part of the background to the negotiations. Apart from this, Russia was a side-line; an important and time-consuming one, but not the most important influence upon the actual terms of the Treaty.

These, then, are two of the most important historical controversies relating to the Peace Conference of Paris: the interpretation of the characters of the principal participants, and the importance to be attached to Bolshevism. But first it is important to consider some of the limiting factors imposed upon the negotiators by various circumstances, arising either from past history or from conditions in the Europe whose destiny they were to attempt together to settle.

The Conference was held to determine the terms of the peace after a war more horrible by far than any the world had then known. Much has been written of the horrors of the trenches, the mindless slaughter in pointless offensives, the gas attacks, unrestricted submarine warfare and so forth. Photographs and film have survived, as well as contemporary official and newspaper reports, to show us the full extent of the devastation of both people and countries.[15] This terrible war occurred in a Europe which in 1914 had not seen a major conflict on its own territory for ninety-nine years, and its impact could scarcely be exaggerated.

The importance of this for the Peace Conference was increased by the fact that all the three major victorious powers were now Parliamentary democracies. France had been a democratic Republic since 1875, and in Britain progress towards a democracy based on universal suffrage had been continuous since 1832, and in 1918 all men over twenty-one years of age, and some women, had been given the vote. The United States had, of course, been a democratic Republic since its foundation.

The best known and most discussed intervention of the democratic process in the making of peace was the British General Election of December 1918, when Lloyd George's coalition government was returned to office with a massive majority, allegedly on a platform of 'Hang the Kaiser' and 'Make Germany Pay'. Certainly various members of the Government and coalition parties had proclaimed their intention to see that Germany was fully punished for her crime in fighting the war, the most notorious of all such proclamations being Sir Eric Geddes' promise to 'squeeze the lemon until you can hear the pips squeak'. Lloyd George devotes several pages in his memoirs to showing that he himself was never fully party to these promises, pointing out that although he said in an election speech that 'as far as justice is concerned we have an absolute right to demand the whole cost of the war from Germany . . . we propose to demand the whole cost of the war', he went on to say that they 'must exact it in such a way that it does not do more harm to the country that receives it than to the country which is paying it', [16] so suggesting that full compensation might not be forthcoming. Be that as it may, for many electors and for many MPs the Government's mandate was to make a Carthaginian peace, and later Members of Parliament, incited by Lord Northcliffe's newspapers, were to do their best to ensure that the Treaty, and especially the Reparations Chapter, was severe.

Apart from the British General Election and the Parliament it produced – the Parliament, as Baldwin put it, of 'hard-faced men who look as if they have done well out of the war'[17] – democracy was to have other effects upon the course of the negotiations. Pressure from the President of France, Raymond Poincaré, and the Chamber of Deputies was to limit Clemenceau's freedom of action and make his position difficult at crucial points in the proceedings of the Conference; notable men such as Foch and Poincaré, who disliked Clemenceau's moderate policy by French standards, were to embarrass him by making direct appeals to the other statesmen and to the French people over Clemenceau's head. So incensed did Clemenceau become by Poincaré's activities that in May 1919 he whispered to Lloyd George. 'I wish you would lend me your George V', and later was to explain sardonically to Lloyd George the meaning of Poincaré's name: 'Point – not, carre – square. Not square.'

Perhaps the statesman least affected by the pressures of democracy was President Wilson. His essential arrogance served as an insulation, no doubt: 'America has taken much from me. She will take this also,' he is reputed to have declared, and he took few Congressmen and no Republicans with him to Paris. Nonetheless his party had been defeated in the mid-term elections, a fact of which everyone at Paris was aware, and ultimately, of course, the result was the defeat of the Treaty by the Senate. At times, too, Wilson was obliged to reject suggestions made by others out of deference to Congressional opinion, especially where the League was concerned; for example, he was compelled to reject a French request for a League of Nations General Staff on the ground that Congress would regard this as an attempted usurpation of their power to declare war, a usurpation which they would not accept.

It seems important to mention the impact of representative democracy at this early stage, because it is this above all else which renders comparison with previous peace conferences irrelevant. The Congresses of Vienna in 1815 and Berlin in 1878 had been attended chiefly by the representatives of Kings and autocratic Empires – Austria–Hungary, Russia, Prussia and so forth. The constitutional monarchy of Britain was an odd man out, and she was not as democratic even in 1878 as she was in 1919. Only some sixty per cent of adult British males were enfranchised in 1910,[18] as compared with all men and some women in 1918. A Peace Conference between democracies was a novelty. At the level of ideals, Wilson had proclaimed that democracy should be carried into international relations by the negotiation of 'Open covenants openly arrived at' as the first of his Fourteen Points, but no-one realised before the Conference opened what the effects of Parliaments and an inflamed public opinion watching the peace-makers' every move was to be.

A problem of a different kind was to be created by commitments entered into during the war, which many participants in the Conference were still to consider binding, often despite circumstances so vastly changed as to render them irrelevant. Equally, efforts by statesmen to shuffle off wartime agreements which were now an embarrassment to them were to cause many difficulties. The embarrassment was increased by the publication of many of these secret agreements by the Russian Bolshevik Government in 1918, as their contribution to the doctrine of 'Open covenants openly arrived at'. In this discussion of the circumstances of the Conference, we must mention some of the most important of these commitments.

Many were entered into either to secure the adhesion of a further

Power to the Allied cause, or to procure increased effort from an already belligerent country. Thus the Italians in effect auctioned their support to the highest bidder, in terms of the territorial gains each side was prepared to promise in the event of victory. In the end Italy knocked herself down to the Allied Powers* in exchange for the Treaty of London, by which she was promised part of the Austrian Tyrol and a frontier on the Brenner Pass, as well as the islands and most of the coastline of the Adriatic Sea; thus a large portion of what is now Yugoslavia, including the Dalmation Coast, would have become Italian, as well as Albania. This Treaty was to cause much trouble at the Peace Conference.

Another country which established claims upon the Allies which were to prove embarrassing was Japan. In 1915 she had bullied China under threat of war into granting her extensive privileges in China and in particular agreement to her taking over the German rights and concessions in the Chinese province of Shantung.[19] In 1917, in return for increased naval activity in the Pacific, which the British badly needed, the Japanese obtained a secret agreement from Britain and France to support their position and aspirations in Shantung.[20] In another part of the Orient, the British and the French negotiated an agreement in 1916 concerning the division of their influence over the Arab territories of the Middle East, an area which had been a bone of contention between them since at least the British occupation of Egypt in the 1880s. The most important feature of this agreement from the point of view of the Peace Conference was the allocation of Syria to France as her sphere of influence in the event of the collapse of the Ottoman Empire. This agreement, known as the Sykes–Picot agreement, was also to cause much trouble.

Finally, there were the French efforts to assure herself an Eastern frontier on the Rhine, which was to be one of her chief demands at the Peace Conference. Early in 1917, France began to seek a definite commitment by her Allies to support her in this demand, which Frenchmen regarded as essential if they were to be safe from a further German invasion. On 12 January 1917, Briand wrote to Cambon that

> To our eyes it is evident that Germany must no longer be allowed to have a footing on both banks of the Rhine. The future organisation of the territory west of the Rhine, its neutrality and its

* Later the Allied and Associated Powers when America entered the war.

> temporary occupation must be raised in exchange of views between us and our Allies, but France, whose interest in the status of this region is the most direct, must have the preponderant voice in finding a solution to this vital question.[21]

The French were soon able to obtain support from the Russians in seeking to ensure that the Germans were not allowed to control the area west of the Rhine. This is apparent from a series of documents published by the Bolshevik Government and printed in the *Manchester Guardian* on 12 December 1917.[22] The most important of these documents was an account by the Russian Foreign Minister for the benefit of his Ambassador in Paris of an interview given by the Tsar to the French Ambassador in Petrograd.

> At an audience with the Most High, M. Doumergue submitted to the Emperor the desire of France to secure for herself at the end of the present war the restoration of Alsace-Lorraine and a special position in the valley of the River Saar, as well as to attain the political separation from Germany of her trans-Rhenish districts, and their organisation on a separate basis, in order that in future the River Rhine might form a permanent strategical frontier against a German invasion.[23]

This agreement was confirmed in a Note from the Russian Foreign Minister to the French Ambassador in Petrograd, setting out the terms agreed between Russia and France, which included

> 3. The rest of the territories situated on the left bank of the Rhine which now form part of the German Empire are to be entirely separated from Germany and freed from all political and economic dependence upon her.[24]

France thus gained assurance of this aim from one of her major allies, although it was to be rendered useless by the advent of the Russian Revolution.

France's other major ally, Britain, was from the first opposed to this proposal to create a Rhenish buffer state between France and Germany. On 2 July 1917 A. J. Balfour, then Foreign Secretary, wrote to Lord Bertie, the British Ambassador in Paris, that the French 'do . . . desire to see the territory to the west of the Rhine separated from the German Empire and created into something in the nature of a buffer state. . . . I said nothing to encourage this rather wild project, and I do not think that M. Cambon* himself had much belief in it';[25] and after the Franco–Russian pact had been exposed by the Bolsheviks, Balfour told the House of Commons that

> Never did we desire, and never did we encourage the idea that a bit of Germany should be cut off from the parent state and erected into some kind of independent Republic or independent government of some sort on the left bank of the Rhine so as to make a new buffer state between France and Germany.[26]

Thus the British Government firmly resisted French attempts to persuade them to promise acquiescence in the creation of a Rhenish buffer state after the war, though they were clearly trying to obtain support for this scheme in 1917.

Treaties made between the Allies, or those entered into by them to secure new adherents to their cause or greater efforts from one of their number, were not the only wartime commitments which were to limit the freedom of manoeuvre at the Peace Conference. Another limitation resulted from the use in the First World War of propaganda methods to produce the demoralisation of enemy populations, the collapse of hostile governments, or even the disintegration of polyglot Empires. The most famous example was the German *Revolutionierungspolitik* in Russia, culminating in their granting of a safe conduct for Lenin through Germany to Russia, and the October Revolution which brought success for the German policy by taking Russia out of the war and bringing about the Brest–Litovsk peace treaty between Germany and Russia.[27] The Allies also engaged in such activities, however, especially in encouraging nationalist revolts among the peoples of the Austro-Hungarian Empire. The French were particularly active in this regard, although the increasing restiveness of the nationalities of Austria–Hungary was also encouraged by the Americans. Clemenceau was to recall, rather smugly, in his memoirs that

> Our programme when we entered the war was not one of liberation. We had started as allies of the Russian oppressors of Poland, with the Polish soldiers of Silesia and Galicia fighting against us. By the collapse of military Russia, Poland found herself set free and re-created, and then all over Europe oppressed peoples

* Paul Cambon, then French Ambassador in London.

raised their heads, and our war of national defence was transformed by force of events into a war of liberation.[28]

After the Russian defection, the need to recreate an active Eastern front against the Germans emerged as the real, and less idealistic, reason to encourage the Poles, who had not known national independence since the partitions of the eighteenth century. On 4 June 1917, after Kerensky's Provisional Government in Russia had proclaimed the liberation and future independence of Poland, Poincaré proclaimed a Polish army on French soil, followed on 15 August by the establishment of a Polish National Committee at Lausanne. The subsequent events in Russia increased the urgency of building up Poland as a Power able to oppose Germany on her Eastern frontier and so ensure that pressure on two fronts could be maintained. Cambon's comment that the peace of Brest–Litovsk 'would cure France forever of an alliance with Russia' is indicative of the motive for French support of Poland, and on 3 June 1918 the French recognised the creation of an independent Poland as a war aim.[29] Later Poland was to assume great importance for the French, as a Quai d'Orsay memorandum of 20 December 1918 makes clear; it urged a strong Poland because 'Germany would not be really defeated unless she loses her Polish provinces'. What was more, as much German territory as possible should be given to Poland, since 'The more we aggrandize Poland at Germany's expense, the more certain shall we be that she will remain her enemy.' Finally, a strong Poland would prevent German collusion with Russia; she would form 'the necessary barrier between Russian Bolshevism and a German revolution'.[30] The extent of the French commitment to Poland was to cause serious problems at the Peace Conference.

The feelings and ambitions of other nationalities were also exploited for similar purposes. Thus a Czechoslovak National Council was set up in Paris under Masaryk in 1916, and after the signature of the Treaty of Brest–Litovsk,* France recognised this body as 'a supreme organ representing all interests of the nation and as a foundation of the future Czechoslovak Government', adding a promise that France would seek 'to realise at the proper moment

* The Treaty of Brest-Litovsk was imposed by Germany on the Soviet Government of Russia in March 1918. Under it, Germany made extensive territorial gains at the expense of Russia and Poland. See J. W. Wheeler-Bennett, *The Treaty of Brest-Litovsk* (London, 1939).

your aspirations towards independence within the historical borders of your premises'.[31] The Americans also recognised the Czecho-slovak National Council in September 1918 as a Government in a state of belligerency with the German and Austro-Hungarian Empires.[32] The British followed suit, but it is significant that it was the French who took the lead.

Clearly, then, the encouragement of the nationalities of Austria-Hungary, which was to lead to the break-up of that Empire and produce many problems when peace was made, was consciously pursued in order to strengthen the Allied position during the war. One other example of this policy in operation was the Pact of London, made in 1917, by which it was agreed that the Allies should support the creation of a unified State of Serbs, Croats and Slovenes. This pact was the result of negotiations between representatives of these three peoples under Allied auspices. The Serbs, Croats and Slovenes declared their intention to set up a free and democratic constitutional monarchy under the Karageorgevich dynasty, and said that

> Our nation demands nothing that belongs to others. It demands only what is its own. It desires to free itself and to achieve its unity. In accordance with the right of self-determination of peoples, no part of this territorial totality may without infringement of justice be detached and incorporated with some other state without the consent of the nation itself.[33]

Despite attempts to reach agreement between Italy and the new Yugoslav state,[34] the desire for the unity and independence of all the Serbs, Croats and Slovenes was to result in the bitter row between President Wilson and the Italians which has become one of the most famous incidents at the Conference.

Another wartime event which had an influence on the Conference is now regarded as the most momentous consequence of the Great War: the Russian Revolution. While recent students of the period have perhaps overrated its significance for the peacemakers, it had crucial effects. One of them – the universal importance for the Allies of wooing and strengthening the peoples of Eastern Europe in their bids for independence – has already been discussed, and this arose out of the loss of the Russian army fighting on Germany's Eastern borders. Two other effects were: first, the uncertainty among the Allies as to what ought to be done about Russia itself. The White leaders, Kolchak, Denikin and others, offered assurances that in the event of their overthrowing the Bolsheviks they would bring Russia back into the war, and in the meantime they did defend the territories they held against the Germans and in particular denied them access to the oilfields of the Caucasus. The Allies therefore supported them with forces and supplies. On 20 October 1918, for example, Lord Robert Cecil submitted a memorandum to the War Cabinet in which he stated that the two objectives of Allied intervention in Russia were to deny Russia to the enemy and, if possible, to reconstitute the Russian front, and supported further assistance for the 'Whites', saying that the Allies must seek to maintain 'good and stable government' in Russia.[35] Soon, however, doubts were to increase, as the prospects of overturning Lenin's Government declined, and once the war was over a major reason for intervention disappeared. Secondly, however, there was the fear engendered by Bolshevism in the minds of many politicians in Western Europe. Bolshevism was believed to be aggressive; Lenin, after all, had declared himself to be dedicated to world revolution, and the Allies were keeping a careful watch on Left-wing movements in their countries. In Britain, in 1918, the Home Secretary was keeping a watch on revolutionary organisations both at home and abroad, and was circulating fortnightly reports to the Cabinet. Early in November 1918, for example, he circulated such a paper, describing the setting up of Soviets in Britain in 1917 and a Socialist Convention held in Leeds in 1918. At this convention were present, among others, F. W. Jowett, Ramsay MacDonald, George Lansbury, Philip Snowden and R. Smellie, all of whom were described by the Home Secretary as 'declared pacifists of revolutionary tendencies'. He also described the activities of Maxim Litvinov, who was reported as calling for revolution in England,[36] and who was shortly afterwards deported for engaging in subversive activities. Colonel Sir J. Norton Griffiths, MP, wrote to Austen Chamberlain, the Home Secretary, on 1 November 1918, about the spread of 'revolutionary ideas' in Britain, urging that 'One of the best methods of counteracting this, in my opinion, is that every brass band in the country should be let loose as often as possible, and to encourage flag waving – one form of letting "steam" off.'[37] With a revolution bringing Germany to her knees, and unrest in most European countries, the danger of Bolshevism spreading was bound to be a major preoccupation of the statesmen of Europe in 1919.

These, then, were the chief influences created or brought about by the circumstances of war. In addition to these, and perhaps arising out of one of them – the institution of democratic government in all the major Allied Powers – must be considered wartime efforts to define peace aims. In face of demands from peoples and Parliaments to be told what their countries were fighting for, and in the face of demands from Allies, friendly Powers and Governments in exile, for reassurances as to post-war intentions, statesmen issued pronouncements on their aims after the war was won. Preparatory work was done, particularly on the idea of a League of Nations.

It is often imagined that the idea of a League of Nations sprang, fully clothed as it were, from President Wilson's head when he made his famous 'Fourteen Points' speech.* However, in January 1917 Lloyd George appointed a committee under the chairmanship of Sir John Philimore to consider the possibility of setting up an international organisation to preserve peace. This committee issued an interim report on 20 March 1917 recommending the creation of an organisation to arbitrate in international disputes, and breach of whose rules would result in a declaration of war upon the offender by all other members.[38] In that same year the French set up a committee under M. Léon Bourgeois which came to much the same conclusions. At this time it seems that President Wilson was discouraging discussion of a League of Nations in America, possibly to avoid antagonising the Senate, always touchy about international agreements which might limit the Congressional power under the Constitution to declare war and make peace. Lloyd George records that during 1917 Colonel House† told the British Ambassador in Washington that

> The President thought it better that the Government of the United States should not in any way be committed to a cut-and-dried plan for the establishment of a League of Nations. . . . Colonel House added that the President and he were discouraging in the United States discussions as to the League of Nations.[39]

However, during 1917 Americans became increasingly anxious about the need to prepare detailed plans for the future peace settlement; on 27 July, for example, Senator La Follette moved a resolution in the Senate by which

* See p. 18 below.
† See p. 28 below.

> Congress declares that there should be a public restatement of the Allied peace terms based on a disavowal of any advantages either in the way of indemnities, territorial acquisitions, commercial privileges or economic prerogatives, by means of which one nation shall strengthen its power abroad at the expense of another nation, as wholly incompatible with the establishment of a durable peace.[40]

Various enquiries were carried out by members of the Administration into aspects of the future settlement, which culminated in the creation of a special agency under Colonel House to prepare detailed proposals for peace, resulting in some friction between the new agency and the State Department.[41] This body, which became known as 'The Inquiry', issued a memorandum on 22 December 1917 recommending the creation of a League of Nations

> for common protection, for the peaceful settlement of international disputes, for the attainment of a joint economic prosperity. . . . Whether this League is to remain armed and exclusive or whether there is to be a reduction of armaments and a cordial inclusion of Germany, will depend upon whether the German Government is in fact representative of the German democracy.[42]

This passage reveals considerable uncertainty among the members of the Inquiry as to whether the future League would have to be an anti-German combination or a League of Nations in which all nations could be trusted to refrain from war and aggression and use their forces only to restrain the aggression of others. Concrete proposals for a League were being prepared in Britain and France before such an enterprise was begun in America.

One final point must be made about the various conceptions of a League of Nations which were prepared in 1917. The Bourgeois Committee conceived of the League as a means of gaining security against aggression, and included a proposal for an international force to keep the peace and laid down specific sanctions beginning with breaches of diplomatic relations, escalating to economic sanctions and finally the use of the international force against the aggressor.[43] France saw the League as a new alliance against Germany, who was bound always to remain an enemy of France. The British viewed the League primarily as a body to arbitrate in disputes, while the Americans were unsure which conception they favoured, the Inquiry evidently believing that this could not be decided until Germany's future character had emerged. These differences in the conception of the League's function were to become apparent at the Conference. Meanwhile, from January 1918 onwards, the creation of a League of Nations was to figure prominently in statements of war aims by the Governments of the Allied and Associated* Powers.

The first such declaration of war aims was made by Lloyd George at a meeting with a delegation from the Trades Union Congress on 5 January 1918. He began by asserting that after the war there must be a new basis for international relations, believing that the growth of democracy must be recognised:

> The days of the Treaty of Vienna are long past. We can no longer submit the future of European civilisation to the arbitrary decisions of a few negotiators striving to secure by chicanery or persuasion the interests of this or that dynasty or nation. The settlement of the new Europe must be based on such grounds of reason and justice as will give some promise of stability. Therefore it is that we feel that government with the consent of the governed must be the basis of any territorial settlement in this war.[44]

He then went on to say that 'We mean to stand by the French democracy to the death in the demand they make for a reconsideration of the great wrong of 1871, when, without any regard to the wishes of the population, two French provinces were torn from the side of France and incorporated in the German Empire.'[45] This pronouncement was followed by a statement of Lloyd George's attitude towards the territorial settlement which was to remain constant throughout the rest of the war and the negotiations at Paris. Speaking of the German seizure of Alsace and Lorraine in 1871, he said that

> This sore has poisoned the peace of Europe for half a century, and until it is cured healthy conditions will not have been restored. There can be no better illustration of the folly and wickedness of using a transient military success to violate national right.[46]

When, at the Peace Conference, Lloyd George was to declare that the British people were haunted by the fear of creating new Alsace-

* The United States of America was never formally in alliance with the European Powers fighting against Germany, and this category of association was added to the official description of the coalition of Powers which won the war to cover America's position.

Lorraines, he was echoing this statement that the peace must do justice to all nations in order that it might endure.

Lloyd George also promised an independent Poland, 'comprising all those genuinely Polish elements who desire to form part of it'[47] – a pledge which was to cause him much trouble later – and spoke of the need for a League of Nations: 'an alternative to war as a means of settling international disputes'.[48] This first statement of Allied war aims was followed three days later by the most famous of all, President Wilson's speech of 8 January 1918, in which he announced his famous Fourteen Points.

In dealing with this speech, and the further declarations of American war aims which followed it, it is necessary to examine their content closely to see what the President's declared aims were. These speeches were to raise hopes among the idealistic, and the dashing of these hopes resulted in the bitterness which has since distorted the record of the peacemaking. The atmosphere of hope engendered by Wilson's peace aims speeches can be recaptured in such remarks as Nicolson's that

> We were journeying to Paris, not merely to liquidate the war, but to found a new order in Europe. We were preparing not peace only, but Eternal peace. There was about us the halo of some divine mission. . . .[49]

or Keynes':

> What a place the President held in the hearts and hopes of the world when he sailed to us in the *George Washington*! What a great man came to Europe in those early days of our victory.[50]

The disillusion which followed the Conference was recaptured by Keynes:

> The disillusionment was so complete, that some of those who had trusted most hardly dared speak of it. Could it be true? they asked of those who returned from Paris. Was the Treaty really as bad as it seemed? What had happened to the President? What weakness, or what misfortune, had led to so extraordinary, so unlooked for a betrayal?[51]

If, however, Keynes, Nicolson and others like them had read the President's speeches, and even the Fourteen Points themselves, more carefully, they might have been less over-optimistic before the event, and less disappointed after. In his speech of 8 January Wilson declared that

> What we want in this war . . . is nothing peculiar to ourselves. It is that the world be made a fit and safe place to live in and particularly that it be made safe for any peace-loving nation. . . .[52]

and many of the Points themselves reflect this idealism, such as the hopelessly impracticable demand of Point 1, 'Open covenants openly arrived at', and the demand for 'a free, open-minded and absolutely impartial adjustment of colonial claims' in Point 5. Nonetheless, the Points from time to time make it clear that Wilson regarded Germany as being to blame for the state of affairs which had led to the war. In Point 8, echoing Lloyd George's words of three days earlier, Wilson declared that

> All French territory shall be freed, and the invaded portions restored, and the wrong done to France by Prussia in 1871 in the matter of Alsace-Lorraine, which has unsettled the peace of the world for nearly fifty years, should be righted in order that peace may once more be made secure in the interest of all.

Point 13 guarantees 'an independent Polish state . . . which should be assured a free and secure access to the sea, and whose political and economic independence and territorial integrity should be guaranteed by international covenant.' This need for security and the redress of wrongs done by Germany showed that the Fourteen Points were not entirely directed towards reconciliation, but were also concerned with ensuring that Germany would behave properly after the war. Wilson concluded his Points with the recommendation that a general association of nations should be set up 'for the purpose of affording mutual guarantees of political independence and territorial integrity to great and small alike'. Thus the League would guarantee peace; Point 14 carries a hint of the need to restrain and watch over certain members of the world community.

Certainly, in this speech and in the programme it contains lay a suspicion of Germany's character and doubts about her willingness to behave properly in the future. After promulgating the Fourteen Points, Wilson declared that

> We have no jealousy of German greatness and there is nothing in this programme that impairs it. . . . We wish her only to accept a

> place of equality among the peoples of the world ... instead of a place of mastery.

Germany must play her part and accept the New Order. On 11 February, Wilson reaffirmed his belief in a peace of justice and moderation, declaring that 'There shall be no annexations, no contributions, no punitive damages', and affirming that

> ... peoples and provinces are not to be bartered about from sovereignty to sovereignty as if they were chattels or pawns in a game, even the great game, now forever discredited, of the Balance of Power.

President Wilson's hopes were soon to suffer a severe setback, however. German statesmen spoke approvingly of the Fourteen Points, but on 3 March the Germans imposed the Treaty of Brest–Litovsk upon Bolshevik Russia, wresting territory from Russia which she had won two hundred years before.[53] Woodrow Wilson's reaction was vehement in the extreme. On 6 April he said of Germany that

> At Brest–Litovsk her civilian delegates spoke in similar terms [to Wilson's own]; professed their desire to conclude a fair peace and accord to the peoples with whose fortunes they were dealing the right to choose their own allegiances.

While, at the same time,

> Their military masters, the men who act for Germany and exhibit her purpose in execution ... are enjoying in Russia a cheap triumph in which no brave or gallant nation can long take pride. A great people, helpless by their own act, lies for the time at their mercy. Their fair professions are forgotten. They nowhere set up justice, but everywhere impose their power and exploit everything for their own use and aggrandisement.... The thing is preposterous and impossible; and yet is not that what the whole course of action of German armies have meant wherever they have moved? ... I judge only what German arms have accomplished with unpitying thoroughness throughout every fair region they have touched.[54]

The ambiguities of the Fourteen Points speech had now been followed by a massive revulsion against Germany for her imposition of the Treaty of Brest–Litovsk, and this mood of condemnation and hatred continued to be a main theme of President Wilson's peace aims speeches. On 4 July, he described the Central Powers as 'an isolated and friendless group of governments who speak no common purpose, but only selfish ambitions of their own',[55] while on 27 September, in a speech which included what came to be known as the 'Five Particulars' of peace, Wilson declared that the Germans

> have convinced us that they are without honour and do not intend justice. They observe no covenents, accept no principle but force and their own interest. We cannot 'come to terms' with them. They have made it impossible. . . . We do not think the same thoughts or speak the same language of agreement.[56]

Clearly, Woodrow Wilson was now bitterly hostile to the Germans, and the whole tenor of this his last speech setting out his policy for peace before the Conference opened is one of bitter hostility to the Germans and a demand that they be punished and held in check in the future.

Even the League of Nations, regarded by many as the very corner-stone of the New Order in international relations, was now seen as a guarantee of future safety from German greed and cruelty: in the 'Five Particulars' speech Wilson said of the League that

> without such an instrumentality by which the peace of the world can be guaranteed, peace will rest in part upon the word of outlaws, and only upon that word. For Germany will have to redeem her character not by what happens at the peace table, but by what follows.[57]

The League could keep the outlaw in check until he could be trusted to behave as a law-abiding member of society ready to respect the existence of his fellows. Such a conception of the League is far from idealistic brotherhood of man often regarded as Wilson's object in proposing its creation. The Five Particulars themselves appear to restore the mood of the Fourteen Points, but there are hints of another current of thought running through President Wilson's mind; thus the first of these particulars laid it down that 'Impartial justice . . . must involve no discrimination between those to whom we wish to be just and those to whom we do not wish to be just.'[58] To be just to Germany would be difficult, but it must be done.

By the end of the war Woodrow Wilson's idealism had been tempered by a violent hatred of the Germans and a deep distrust of them for the future. This hatred and distrust was to have a great deal of influence upon the negotiations for an Armistice, and afterwards upon the Peace Conference, and the conflicts between idealism and hatred, hope and fear, contained in the speeches makes Wilson's subsequent conduct far more easily comprehensible. It is to the end of the war and the Armistice negotiations that we must now turn.

# 2 The Armistice: *September - November 1918*

After the failure of the Ludendorff offensives in the Spring and Summer of 1918, it became clear that an Allied victory was only a matter of time. In September, expectations that the Central Powers would soon be asking for an armistice gave rise to increasing pressures to prepare detailed peace terms, and the problem of how to react to a request for an armistice when it came also became more urgent.

In the middle of September, Austria–Hungary made a preliminary approach to the Allies for an armistice, and immediately there was dissension about how to respond. Lloyd George, at least publicly, took the view that the request for an armistice was a trick to gain time for the Central Powers to re-form their lines, and he declared that 'there was no word of reparation, restoration or indemnity . . . and there was no breath of "peccavi" '.[1] Lloyd George was here commenting not only on the Austro–Hungarian peace feelers, but also on a German attempt to get a separate peace with Belgium. The following day, however, Lord Robert Cecil wrote to A. J. Balfour that

> I suppose the French and the Americans and G.N.C. [Curzon] will be for a flat rejection of the Austrian Note. But I am doubtful. . . .[2]

while on 17 September Sir Eric Geddes argued that if Austria–Hungary could be got out of the war, Bulgaria and Turkey would probably follow her, and thus 'we have never had so good an opportunity of isolating Germany as we have today'. Geddes then went on to make a prophetic remark: 'For post-war purposes I suggest that we want a strong united Austria and not a disintegrated collection of German vassal states.'[3] Geddes realised that to keep the Austro-Hungarian Empire together would give a better assurance of stability in Central Europe than to give the nationalities their heads and create a chain of weak states which could easily be dominated by one of the adjacent Great Powers, probably Germany.

On 27 September the British War Cabinet had a discussion on whether it would be expedient to grant an armistice to Bulgaria, who was then putting out feelers. Lloyd George, who was not at this meeting, had expressed opposition to granting an armistice since it would 'mean stopping our victory', but Bonar Law argued that they ought not to 'throw away an opportunity of getting her out on our terms', and was anxious lest the French 'send a *flamboyant* "You be d—d" answer without consulting us'.[4] One of the problems of the next few months was here apparent: distrust between Britain and France.

Preparations for peace also became more urgent. On 28 September, Barnes, the Minister of Labour, circulated a Cabinet Paper urging that attention be given to preparing a detailed proposal for a League of Nations, lest

> when peace comes it will be lost sight of altogether, and the nations will begin again their old bad way of preparing against one another for other wars.[5]

The French were more concerned about a different matter – how the damage done in French territory by the retreating German armies was to be repaired – and at the end of September the French Ambassador in London delivered a Note to the British Government asking for support in obtaining the fullest compensation.[6] It seemed that the end of the war was approaching; on 6 October Clemenceau sent a note to Lloyd George informing him that the German armies were withdrawing because of a lack of materials and demoralisation of the troops, and that the Kaiser was speaking 'more and more of abandoning power in the hope that his abdication will render less severe the conditions imposed on Germany by the Allies'.[7] In the meantime, the British were already resolving to reject their promise to France that Syria should become a French sphere of influence after the war as part of the Sykes-Picot Agreement.* On 3 October, Lloyd George told the Cabinet that this agreement 'was quite inapplicable to present circumstances, and was altogether a most undesirable agreement

* See p. 8 above.

from the British point of view'.[8] British troops were occupying Syria, and British troops had won the war in the Middle East, so there was no reason why we should hand Syria over to the French. This decision was to lead to a bitter row at the Peace Conference.

The expectation that Germany would soon sue for peace was confirmed on 4 October, when the Germans transmitted a Note to President Wilson asking him to arrange a settlement on the basis of the Fourteen Points.[9] Austria–Hungary followed suit on 7 October,[10] and both were clearly hoping that the President would compel the European Allies to restrict their demands to the President's Points instead of imposing a more severe peace. Wilson's initial response was a Note asking whether the German Chancellor accepted the Fourteen Points and agreeing that the German Government's 'object in entering into discussions would be only to agree upon the practical details of their application', and also whether the Chancellor could speak for the people of Germany.[11]

This approach to Wilson rather than to the European Allies delighted Americans and caused irritation in Europe. Colonel Repington wrote in his diary that in Paris all were anxious to make peace, and waited upon Wilson's reply – 'All await their master's voice'[12] – while Sir Maurice Hankey, the British Cabinet Secretary, recorded that

> Lloyd George is irritated with Wilson for replying [to the German Note] without consulting us. Not only because, in asking if the Germans accept his fourteen points, he almost seems to assume that we do accept them (although as a matter of fact we totally reject the doctrine of freedom of the seas), but still more owing to the statement that withdrawal from the occupied territories is an indispensable condition of an armistice. Lloyd George agrees that it is an indispensable condition, but, of course, many other conditions are indispensable and he fears that the Huns will try to assume that it is the only condition, and when we insist on other conditions, will say that we intervened and upset a promising negotiation for peace.[13]

Lloyd George feared that Wilson had closed too many options by the terms of his Note, and that any attempt to alter those terms now must inevitably make the European Allies appear unduly rapacious in their demands. Three days later, the Political Intelligence Department of the Foreign Office supported the Prime Minister's view in a memorandum in which they urged that the peace terms must include the restoration as well as the evacuation of the territories the Germans had invaded, and the restriction of Point 5, which demanded 'a free, open-minded and absolutely impartial adjustment of colonial claims', to the German colonies, otherwise the Germans might attempt to argue that, under the Wilsonian terms, all colonies, including the British Empire, must be redistributed. There was also no reference to reparations or to punishment of war criminals. In short, the Fourteen Points would not do as a basis for peace.[14] That same day, however, the Germans sent a second Note to Wilson reaffirming their acceptance of the Points and claiming that the Government could and was speaking in the name of the people.[15] It looked as though Wilson had stolen the show.

None of this, however, allayed anxiety in Britain and France. On 13 October, Lloyd George called a top-level meeting of Ministers and military and naval experts at Danny, in Sussex, to discuss the problems raised by Wilson's activities. They were faced with two particular questions: the need to decide what action to take, and the need to make some public comment on Wilson's Notes. Lloyd George said that it must be made clear that Wilson was 'alone responsible' for the negotiations so far, and that the Fourteen Points as they stood were inadequate. He was afraid also that an armistice which proved to be only temporary would be a bad thing;

> The Germans . . . were now in a panic. If they could not obtain a respite they might suffer disaster. On the contrary, if they could gain some respite they might obtain time to re-organise and recover.

Balfour felt that the Armistice terms must 'prevent any renewal of hostility' and must not confine the future peace terms to the Fourteen Points. Lloyd George was even doubtful whether peace was desirable at all; he

> raised for consideration the question as to whether the actual military defeat of Germany and the giving to the German people of a real taste of war was not more important, from the point of view of the peace of the world, than a surrender at the present time when the German armies were still on foreign territory.

The Germans must be taught a lesson, and Lloyd George doubted whether the punishment had really hurt the German people yet. All were agreed that Germany must not be allowed to reorganise so that she could fight a prolonged defensive war on her own frontiers.

The other major problem centred upon Point 2, the guarantee of 'Absolute freedom of navigation upon the seas'. For the British, dependent upon sea power, such a commitment was unthinkable. The point was raised by Admiral Wemyss, the First Sea Lord, and after some discussion it was agreed that this could not be accepted, and many of those present felt grave doubts about whether the British could accept the Fourteen Points as a basis of peace at all. Balfour 'said we could not possibly assent to them', while Winston Churchill said that 'he would accept the Fourteen Points provided we could place our own interpretation on them'; to this Wilson would obviously object strongly. In the end, it was agreed to send telegrams to Wilson explaining the British reservations and pointing out that the Allies had never discussed the Fourteen Points or accepted them as a basis for peace.[16]

At this point, however, Wilson's dislike and fear of the Germans became apparent. The First Lord of the Admiralty, Sir Eric Geddes, was at this time in America, and on 13 October he reported to Lloyd George that he had had a meeting with President Wilson at which it appeared that the President's attitude towards the Germans 'appears to be hardening towards caution'. One reason for this was his anger at the sinking by a German submarine of an Irish ferry, the *Leinster*, the day before, with the loss of 450 lives. Geddes, for his part, stressed that Britain could not accept the Wilsonian doctrine of the Freedom of the Seas and found the President conciliatory on this matter. It is interesting that Geddes reported that Wilson was determined to break up the Austro-Hungarian Empire 'owing to commitments to oppressed nationalities'. Many people, both at the time and later, have questioned the wisdom of this course of action, but the President was adamant.[17] Geddes' impressions of Wilson's attitudes were confirmed by the tone of Wilson's next Note to the Germans, dated 14 October. It was far more severe than the earlier Note, declaring that the terms of the Armistice must be such that Allied military supremacy would be maintained during the period between the cease-fire and the final signing of the peace settlement. Neither he nor his Allies would consider an Armistice 'so long as the armed forces of Germany continue the illegal and inhumane practices which they persist in'. Wilson goes on to refer to submarine warfare, and this phrase was in part a reference to the sinking of the *Leinster*. This

Note also points to a statement by Wilson in his speech of 4 July that arbitrary government must be destroyed.[18] Four days later Austria–Hungary was told that the Czecho-Slovaks must decide 'what action on behalf of the Austro–Hungarian Government will satisfy their aspirations and their conception of their rights and destiny as members of the family of nations'.[19] Wilson now seemed bent on the complete humiliation of the Central Powers. This stern reply was greeted with acclaim in France.[20]

In the meantime, Anglo–French relations were deteriorating. On 4 October, Lord Robert Cecil had a conversation with Paul Cambon, the French ambassador in London, at which they agreed that for the time being Syria should be occupied by British troops.[21] Three days later, Lloyd George and Clemenceau had a meeting at which they agreed not to inform Wilson about the terms they would offer to Turkey for an armistice: America had not declared war on Turkey and by this means the Allies could avoid trouble with Wilson and his principles in an area which they both particularly wanted to carve up between themselves.[22] Thieves soon fall out, however, and Lloyd George and Clemenceau had a violent quarrel over the Middle East, vividly described by Lord Robert Cecil in a letter to Balfour: Lloyd George was 'in a very *exalte* frame of mind', was determined to get Palestine for Britain, and declared openly that the British promise to give Syria to the French was 'unfortunate'. Lloyd George's attitude aroused Cecil's disquiet; he wrote to Balfour that although in the end it had been agreed to discuss only armistice terms at the present time,

> the incident disquiets me. He [Lloyd George] was really at his very worst yesterday – a tricky attorney negotiating about an unsavoury court case could scarcely have been worse. . . .

and then Lloyd George

> Went off to see Clem and had a great row with him and when the Conference met the two spat at one another like angry cats. . . .

after which 'they made common cause in sneering at Wilson'.[23] Relations between Britain and France were turning increasingly sour, but Lloyd George and Clemenceau seemed agreed on one thing – they must make common cause against Wilson, a fact which caused anxiety among Wilson's followers in the British Government: Cecil wrote to Balfour that at the Conference described above the American representative

> has been waiting outside the doors of the Conference to pick up crumbs of information, which are not given to him. Meanwhile, at the Conference itself Lloyd George and Clemenceau vie with one another in scoffing at the President.

He goes on to urge the need for America to have a strong representative in Europe: either Wilson must come himself or he should send Colonel House.[24]

This, then, was the state of relations in mid-October: the British and French suspicious of each other's intentions but united by a common suspicion of President Wilson; the Americans on the sidelines with no effective voice in the decisions of the Alliance. This situation was to be influenced by two other events in the next few days. First, Lloyd George wrote to Clemenceau saying that he refused to put the British fleet in the Aegean under a French admiral: it was a theatre of war where the British Empire had done most of the fighting, and he pleaded that he could not justify this step to British public opinion, since the Allied Armies on the Western front and in the Balkans were already under French command.[25] On 18 October, Lord Derby reported that Clemenceau's reception of this letter had been 'decidedly unfavourable'.[26] Relations between Britain and France were being continually soured by their suspicion of each other's motives in the Middle East.

The other, and more important, event was an American decision to leave the sidelines of the inter-Allied debate and enter the game. President Wilson decided to send Colonel House to Europe as his Special Representative; on 14 October Wilson gave House his credentials as

> my personal representative, and I have asked him to take part as such in the conferences of the Supreme War Council and in any other conference in which it may be serviceable for him to represent me.[27]

House wrote in his diary that

> I am going on one of the most important missions anyone ever undertook, and yet there is no word of direction, advice or discussion between us. He knows that our minds are generally parallel, and he also knows that where they diverge I will follow his bent rather than my own.[28]

From this point on, Colonel House was to play a most important role in the evolution of first the Armistice, and later the Peace Treaty. Far from sticking faithfully to Wilson's views, he was to play a prominent part in modifying them to render them more acceptable to the European statesmen, and his activities were at times to be questionable in the extreme, at least from a Wilsonian standpoint.

Colonel House arrived at a time when Allied attitudes towards Wilson's Fourteen Points were hardening. Scorn had been expressed by Lloyd George and Clemenceau at their meeting of 6 and 7 October;* now, within the British Cabinet, certain conditions were being laid down which seemed to run contrary to Wilson's policy. On 15 October, Lord Robert Cecil, normally moderate in his views on the severity of the terms which must be won from Germany, wrote to Lloyd George urging that one condition of an armistice must be the occupation of strategic points to ensure that Germany could not resume the war, and also enquiring what was to be done about the German colonies,[29] while two days later the Admiralty circulated a Cabinet Paper making it plain that Britain could not accept the Wilsonian doctrine of the Freedom of the Seas, and in particular the unrestricted right to blockade an enemy country must be preserved. Admiral Wemyss declared that

> (i) Acceptance of the proposal would result in making sea-power of little value to a nation *dependent upon it* for existence whilst providing a military Power with free lines of communication.
> (ii) The right to decide for ourselves questions which concern such vital interests, could not be surrendered to any League. . . . On this basis the British Empire has been founded, and on no other can it be upheld.[30]

Thus the British could not for a moment accept Point 2, and there was also anxiety in the Cabinet about the German colonies.

At this point, Wilson pronounced his view on armistice terms for Austria–Hungary, declaring that he

> is obliged to insist that [the Czecho-Slovaks], and not he, shall be the judges of what action on the part of the Austro–Hungarian Government will satisfy their aspirations and their conception of their rights and destiny as members of the family of nations.[31]

* See pp. 27–8 above.

Thus Wilson in effect decreed the break-up of Austria–Hungary, which many Europeans were reluctant to see,* and again Geddes' view of Wilson's attitude to the Central Powers was confirmed. The question now was how would the Central Powers respond to Wilson's severe demands, and whether the Allies, irritated at Wilson's failure to consult them and determined not to accept the Fourteen Points as they stood, would cooperate in securing an armistice at this time, with the German armies still on foreign soil. On 20 October the Allies' dilemma was rendered more acute by a German Note in reply to Wilson's Note of 14 October, reaffirming Germany's acceptance of the Fourteen Points and conceding that the extent of German withdrawal must be left to the Allies' military advisers. Solf, the German Foreign Minister, went on to say that the German Government 'trusts that the President of the U.S. will approve of no demand which would be irreconcilable with the honour of the German people and with opening the way to a peace of justice', and asserting that the new German Government was firmly founded on the will of the people and the Reichstag.[32] Three days later Wilson replied that he now felt that he 'cannot decline to take up with the Governments with which the Government of the United States is associated the question of an armistice', but renewal of hostilities by Germany must be made impossible. The correspondence between President Wilson and the German Government was now to be passed to the Allies for their consideration. However, Wilson then demanded the head of the Kaiser on a charger:

> The President deems it his duty to say, without any attempt to soften what may seem harsh words, that the nations of the world do not and cannot trust the word of those who have hitherto been the masters of German policy. . . . If it must deal with the military masters and the monarchical autocrats of Germany now, or if it is likely to have to deal with them later in regard to the international obligations of the German Empire, it must demand not peace negotiations, but surrender.[33]

This was the Note which was to play a part in finally persuading the Kaiser to abdicate.

Within the following week, two significant events were to occur. The first was a British formulation of the armistice terms to be

* See pp. 22–3 above, 31–2 below.

imposed upon the Turks. On 21 October a Cabinet Paper was circulated defining these terms and listing them in order of importance for the British Empire. The first three concerned the clearance of the Dardanelles and Bosphorus and free passage through them.[34] That same day General Sir Henry Wilson, the Chief of the Imperial General Staff, circulated a memorandum urging the importance of getting the Turks out of the war quickly, so that Austria–Hungary could be broken by an attack up the Danube. 'If we can get Turkey out of the war in the near future I see no reason why we should not inflict a final crushing defeat on German Armies on German soil.'[35] The War Cabinet met that day, and Lloyd George felt that immediate action was necessary. 'Moreover, the action should, if possible, be taken by the British rather than the French.' Once more, Lloyd George was seeking to strengthen his hand in the Middle East at Clemenceau's expense. It was agreed that free and clear passage through the Straits was the vital point to be obtained, even if this meant not obtaining all the terms previously agreed with the French and the Italians. Some members of the War Cabinet felt that Lloyd George's proposal was altogether too underhand and the French must be told; Lord Curzon, for example, said that 'we were dealing with a badly beaten enemy, we should not sweep away the conditions of an armistice concerted with our Allies in Paris', while A. J. Balfour wished to tell France and Italy of our perfidy if the British decided not to insist on the full agreed terms in order to secure the speedy opening of the Straits. This was the course of action finally adopted, and an armistice was offered to Turkey.[36] Not surprisingly, the French protested at this unilateral action, but were persuaded to accept that the most important issue was the clearance of the Straits, and the British agreed to a joint Anglo–French occupation of the Bosphorus forts.[37]

At the same time, of course, the Allies were having to decide how they should react to the Fourteen Points. The British War Cabinet was reluctant to be bound by the Points; on 22 October they agreed that the doctrine of the Freedom of the Seas was unacceptable, that Lloyd George had defined Britain's war aims three days before Wilson's speech, and that Wilson was weakening Allied morale by prolonging the negotiations on inessential matters.[38] The French, for their part, were furious at Wilson's high-handed pronouncements, especially his response to the Austro–Hungarian request for an armistice; Lord Derby reported from Paris that the French Press objected to the break-up of Austria–Hungary 'because it would add a number of Germans in Austria to the German Empire'.[39] On 25 October Derby reported that Clemenceau was 'much annoyed' at Wilson's activities and his failure to consult with the Allies,[40] and the Cabinet reaffirmed that the Points as they stood were unacceptable to Britain.[41] On 27 October both Germany and Austria–Hungary accepted Wilson's demands upon them, and once more pleaded their new-found democratic governments.[42]

It was at this time, with Allied opinion hardening against the Fourteen Points and with irritation at Wilson's failure to consult with the Allies growing, that Lloyd George and Clemenceau had a meeting with Colonel House at which he did much to allay their suspicions and fears, at the cost of weakening the President's principles. They met on 29 October, and House submitted to the Prime Ministers a 'Commentary' on the Fourteen Points which did much to reassure them. This document was never shown to the Germans, who did not request any clarification of the meaning of the Fourteen Points during the armistice negotiations. Thus, for example, Point 1, 'Open covenants openly arrived at', was interpreted by saying that it was not

> meant to exclude confidential diplomatic negotiations involving delicate matters. The intention is that nothing which occurs in the course of such confidential negotiations shall be binding unless it appears in the final covenant made public to the world.[43]

Secret treaties were thus excluded, but otherwise the old style of diplomacy could continue as before. Point 5, demanding an impartial distribution of colonies, would be applied only to claims arising from the war: the British Empire would not be called in question, and Italy was to be guaranteed a strong frontier. Again, France was offered reassurance on Point 10, relating to German Austria:

> This territory should of right be permitted to join Germany, but there is strong objection in France because of the increase in population involved. . . .[44]

and this was fully recognised by Wilson. The Allies were thus reassured at Wilson's expense, and it is ironic that on the very day that House produced his Commentary, Wilson should tell him in a cable that

> It is the Fourteen Points that Germany has accepted. . . . If it is the purpose of Allied statesmen to nullify my influence, force the purpose boldly to the surface and let me speak of it to all the world as I shall.[45]

Little did he know what was happening in Paris. It was about this time that Clemenceau made his famous gibe about the Fourteen Points:

> He exasperates me with his fourteen Commandments when the good God had only ten![46]

The Allies were at once suspicious, even with the reassurance of the Commentary: Professor Seymour gives the following account of the Prime Ministers' initial reaction to Colonel House's statement:

> Clemenceau at once stated that he was not inclined to commit himself and France blindly. 'Have you ever been asked by President Wilson,' he said to Lloyd George, 'whether you accept the Fourteen Points? I have never been asked.' 'I have not been asked either,' replied the British Prime Minister; and, turning to Colonel House, 'What is your view? Do you think that if we agree to an armistice we accept the President's peace terms?' 'That is my view,' replied Colonel House.[47]

In addition, as far as the British were concerned, there was a specific sticking-point: the Freedom of the Seas. Strengthened by the knowledge that Sir Eric Geddes had found that Wilson 'was very vague on the subject and his views uninformed',[48] Lloyd George stated bluntly that 'This point we cannot accept under any conditions',[49] as it would remove the power of blockade, essential to a country largely dependent in war upon her navy. After some argument, House made a veiled threat that unless agreement could be reached on armistice terms, America might make a separate peace; he told Wilson that 'my statement had a very exciting effect upon those present'.[50] Afterwards he suggested that the Allied Prime Ministers should agree on their reservations before they met House again. The Prime Ministers agreed that they had two major reservations: one was the Freedom of the Seas, and the other was that better provision must be made for the restoration of invaded territories and damage done by the aggression of Germany.[51] These points were agreed with House on 3 November, when House declared that

President Wilson 'freely and sympathetically recognises the necessities of the British',[52] and agreed to a reservation on Freedom of the Seas. Agreement was reached, and on 5 November Wilson despatched his final offer to Germany, now agreed with the Allies. In the meantime, armistices with Turkey and Austria–Hungary were being signed.

The Notes setting out the agreed terms for a German armistice must be considered in some detail, as they were to assume great importance at the Peace Conference. The Allied Note of 4 November accepted a peace on the basis of the Fourteen Points subject to qualifications. The first of these was on the Freedom of the Seas: the Allies declared that

> They must point out . . . that Clause 2, relating to what is usually described as the 'freedom of the seas', is open to various interpretations, some of which they could not accept. They must therefore reserve to themselves complete freedom on this subject when they enter the Peace Conference.

The other qualification was even more important, and was to cause a great deal of trouble at the Conference:

> . . . in the conditions of peace laid down in his Address to Congress of the 8 January 1918, the President declared that the invaded territories must be restored as well as evacuated and freed. The Allied Governments feel that no doubt ought to be allowed to exist as to what this provision implies. By it they understand that compensation must be made by Germany for all damage caused to the civilian population of the Allies and their property by the aggression of Germany by land, by sea and from the air.[53]

It is of interest that the word 'aggression' in the last sentence was substituted for 'invasion' in order to ensure that Britain got a share of the reparations to be extracted from Germany; she had not, after all, been invaded.[54]

The Note to Germany despatched by Robert Lansing, the American Secretary of State, on 5 November, stated these qualifications exactly as they appeared in the Allies' Note, and after the statement on reparations the President was declared to be 'in agreement' with this interpretation of his speeches. Marshal Foch was authorised to meet accredited representatives of the German Government and communicate the detailed terms of the Armistice.[55]

By this time, it was clear that Germany was crumbling fast. At the end of October sailors in the High Seas fleet, which had lain idle at Kiel practically since Jutland, had mutinied and taken over the town.[56] Her armies were in retreat. On 5 November, Colonel Repington noted in his diary that the Germans

> had lost the war, and the people know it at last. They are cowed by the severity and harshness of President Wilson's language, and recognise themselves to be the pariahs of the world.[57]

On 6 November, the Political Intelligence Department of the Foreign Office circulated to members of the War Cabinet a report entitled 'Memorandum on the Predicament of the Emperor William', informing them that the Social Democrats were threatening to resign from the Government and bring about the collapse of the Armistice negotiations if the Kaiser did not abdicate, although there were counter-pressures urging him to remain as a Constitutional monarch.[58] The day after, Erzberger asked by wireless for a meeting with Marshal Foch in order to arrange an armistice,[59] and by 8 November it became clear that the Kaiser's abdication was now inevitable; the Political Intelligence Department of the Foreign Office reported that the pressures for this were now 'too insistent to be evaded', and that authority in Germany was fast disintegrating. Indeed, this report questions whether the Armistice terms could be enforced by the German Government:

> It remains to be seen what authority will survive with sufficient strength to enforce the armistice terms, when, in obedience to the all but universal demand for immediate peace, these have to be accepted by the Government and the naval and military authorities.[60]

The war seemed over except for the actual signing of the Armistice.

Preparations for peace negotiations were gaining momentum as the end of the war approached. On 9 November Lord Stamfordham, the King's private secretary, wrote to the Foreign Secretary, A. J. Balfour, to inform him that the King was anxious that Germany and Austria should not be allowed to unite.[61] That same day, the British and French papered over the cracks in their relations which had opened as a result of developments in the Middle East, and issued a joint declaration to the Arabs which was widely broadcast in Syria and Mesopotamia. Britain and France declared that their aim in this area had been 'the complete and final liberation of the peoples so long oppressed by the Turks' and the establishment of democratic national governments, which they would 'encourage and assist'. The Allies denied any desire to interfere unduly with the governments in these new nations, but

> The foundation which the Allied Governments claim for themselves in the liberated territories is to ensure impartial and equal justice for all; to facilitate the economic development of the country by encouraging local initiative; to promote the diffusion of education; and to put an end to the division too long exploited by Turkish policy.[62]

The interpretation of this agreement was to cause much trouble later on.

In the meantime, Germany had still not accepted the terms of the Armistice, and on 10 November the War Cabinet became a little anxious at the line the French were taking in their dealings with the Germans. Germany was on the verge of revolution, and Foch and Clemenceau were both doubtful whether a signature by the present Government would be of any value: 'the signature of representatives who had not power to carry out the conditions would, in M. Clemenceau's opinion, be valueless'. Foch, for his part, was being firm, refusing to extend the seventy-two-hour deadline he had set, and refusing any cessation of hostilities before the Armistice was signed. Lloyd George was anxious; he 'feared that M. Clemenceau had it in mind not to sign the armistice, on the ground that Prince Max's four delegates might be repudiated by the replacing Government', and he did not want Germany to succumb to Bolshevism: 'it would seem that events were taking a similar course in Germany to that which had taken place in Russia'. It might even spread to the British troops; Lloyd George said that 'It would be most undesirable to march British troops into Westphalia, if Westphalia was controlled by a Bolshevist organisation'; the British troops might catch the virus. The French, however, did not seem to care about the danger of German Bolshevism – they 'were treating the situation as a revenge for the War of 1870'. The Cabinet agreed to urge Lord Curzon, then in Paris, to attempt to keep the French in hand until Lloyd George himself could go there.[63]

The following day, however, the Armistice was signed, and at 11 o'clock that morning the war came to an end. The military terms were designed to ensure that Germany could not renew the war: she was to surrender large quantities of war materials, and retreat east of the Rhine. The blockade of her ports was to continue, but the Allies would 'contemplate the provisioning of Germany during the Armistice as shall be found necessary'.[64] The acceptance by Germany of terms so severe shows in what desperate straits she now found herself.

The excitement at the signing of the Armistice was, of course, enormous. 'No more soldiering for me.' President Wilson proclaimed, arrogantly, that

> Everything for which America fought has been accomplished. It will now be our fortunate duty to assist by example, by sober, friendly counsel, and by material aid in the establishment of just democracy throughout the world. . . .[65]

and Colonel House flattered his master in a telegram with 'Autocracy is dead – long live democracy and its immortal leader. In this great hour my heart goes out to you in pride, admiration, and love.'[66] Rejoicing was universal, and Americans believed that they would now lead the world into a new and peaceful Nirvana.

Others were not so sanguine, however. The day after the Armistice was signed, the defeated Germans sought to reinsure their position by sending a Note to the Allied and Associated Powers reaffirming that

> The German Government has accepted the terms laid down by President Wilson in his address of January 8th and in his subsequent addresses on the foundation of a permanent peace of justice. Consequently, its object in entering into discussions would only be to agree upon practical details of the application of these terms.[67]

The Germans wanted to ensure that they could use the Fourteen Points as a shield against French vindictiveness.

Allied activities are well summed up in a letter from Lord Curzon, in Paris, to Lloyd George, also dated 12 November, in which he reported that the French were attempting to push Britain's part in the victory into the background, but that Clemenceau wanted to get down to immediate discussions on peace terms, whereas Colonel House wished to wait until the President arrived in Europe in mid-December. House had also been 'very reassuring' about the Freedom of the Seas and the German colonies; in regard to the latter House said that 'he had never heard Wilson talk about a Condominium or International Board and the idea had not been mentioned to him by others'.[68] So manoeuvrings on the final peace terms had already begun, and at this point it looked as though the British and the Americans would be able to concert their actions against the French.

The negotiations and proceedings which led up to the end of the war show that relations between the Allied and Associated Powers were rather fragile. Between Britain and France the Middle East was a divisive factor, and British policy in that area was arousing increasing distrust among the French, a distrust justified when we see that the British were becoming increasingly determined not to honour the Sykes–Picot Agreement. On the other hand, both Britain and France were agreed in disliking President Wilson's rather high-handed attempts to impose his views upon his Allies, and his failure to consult them on Armistice terms until a fairly late stage in the Armistice negotiations.

Some light is also shed upon the principal statesmen and their relations with each other. Clemenceau clearly distrusted Lloyd George, and relations between these two were edgy. On the other hand, neither of them liked Wilson. Colonel House emerges as the go-between, reinterpreting Wilson's views and personality in ways which made them more acceptable to the European Allies, but at a cost of making compromises which would appear to many to be a betrayal of Wilson's ideals. Colonel House, as the President's Special Representative in Europe, had great freedom of action, and his use of this freedom was questionable. In the months to come, as preparations were made for the Conference, his role was to become increasingly equivocal.

# 3 Preparations for the Conference:

## *Uncertainties and Disagreements, November-December 1918*

With the war over, preparations for the Peace Conference continued. Apart from the matters which would have to be decided in the course of preparing a Peace Treaty, the Allies faced other problems, perhaps the most important of which was Bolshevism, both in Russia and elsewhere. In the last days of the war Lloyd George was becoming increasingly anxious lest Germany should succumb to a Bolshevik revolution, both because this would probably mean that there would be no authority in Germany capable of executing the Armistice Terms, and because the contagion of revolutionary Socialism might spread to other countries, including Britain.

A measure of concern about the possibility of the spread of Bolshevik ideas to Britain is the fact that, throughout this period, the Home Secretary circulated fortnightly to members of the War Cabinet his reports on the activities of revolutionary organisations and maintained an extensive espionage network among the working class, in order to detect any spread of subversive ideas. One such report was made in early November 1918.* On 12 November, Sir Alfred Mond, the First Commissioner of Works, urged the War Cabinet to reduce discontent among the working and lower-middle classes by increasing food and fuel rations and curbing profiteering by retailers to bring prices down, coupled with quick demobilisation of the troops, since a man who had been fighting would have no sympathy with

> those who struck work while he was fighting, or those who enriched themselves during the period of his suffering. If generously treated he would make an element of order and stability.[1]

* See p. 13 above.

Earlier the Home Secretary had warned of danger after the war, when 'the public mind is occupied with peace terms, and there are real grievances upon which [the revolutionary agitators] can work'.[2] There was real fear of a British uprising unless care was taken to avert it.

Coupled with anxiety about Bolshevism at home was uncertainty as to what should be done about Russia. The civil war was raging, and after Lenin had made peace with the Germans at Brest–Litovsk, the Allies had assisted anti-Bolshevik forces in various parts of Russia who were also prepared to resist the Germans; thus valuable resources in Russia had been denied to the Central Powers. In any case, both the British and French Governments believed Bolshevism to be both dangerous and hostile to them, and wished to see it destroyed if possible.

At the end of the war, there were three concentrations of anti-Bolshevik 'White' forces in being: Admiral Kolchak's forces in Siberia, with a provisional capital at Omsk; a force under General Denikin in South Russia; and a toe-hold at Archangel and Murmansk, where a Provisional Government survived precariously with the assistance of a British Expeditionary Force. While the war was still going on, no-one thought much about what should be done about the Russian Civil War once peace was made with Germany. In October, Lord Robert Cecil had pointed out that once the war was over, the reasons for the presence of Allied troops in Russia would cease to exist, since they went there to deny Russia to the enemy, and, if possible, to reconstitute a Russian front against Germany. He felt that the Allies could not desert their Russian friends, and should seek to restore 'good and stable government' to Russia, although he was opposed to launching a 'crusade against Bolshevism'.[3] On 13 November, the Chief of the Imperial General Staff, Sir Henry Wilson, warned the War Cabinet that a decision must be taken on future policy in Russia. He said that Bolshevism was dangerous – 'a cult if not a religion' – and laid down a number of possible courses of action, including the establishment of a ring of hostile states around Bolshevik Russia to isolate it, an attempt to crush Bolshevism, and using German war material to strengthen the Border States and assist them to 'do the best they can'. A decision must be made soon.[4] Two days later the Director of Military Operations warned that a decision must be made as to what should be done about the force in Archangel and Murmansk.[5] The Cabinet did not actively consider the matter at this time, however, and the generals were left without guidance as to the policy they were supposed to be implementing.

Inaction and indecision in Britain was one thing; the Americans for their part had to try to meddle. President Wilson was concerned about who was to represent Russia at the Peace Conference, and on 20 November he forwarded to his Secretary of State, Robert Lansing, a letter from an American organisation called the Inter-Party League for the Restoration of Free Russia, which urged that Russia must 'get a full representation' at the Conference. Wilson had read this document 'with interest' and asked whether it would be possible to recognise Admiral Kolchak's Government in Omsk and ask them to send delegates.[6] Six days later Lansing replied, rejecting this proposal and saying that a coherent policy must be evolved:

> We resisted extraordinary pressure to sanction a purely military intervention; we have steadily declined to recognise separate movements or governments. We have said we wish to serve Russia, not to use her. . . . To my mind, we have defined conditions which we should not chance obscuring in the later discussion of intricate problems of peace.

His main suggestion is that Russian delegates must come with the authority of a clearly democratic Government or Constitutional Assembly.[7] But no action was forthcoming from America, either, for the time being at least.

In the meantime, other controversies were raising their heads. One was whether President Wilson should himself attend the Conference, a point which was to arouse considerable controversy in November and December 1918. On 14 November, Colonel House wrote to Wilson to inform him that many people in Europe hoped that he would not come personally. Americans in Paris had told House that 'They fear that it would involve a loss of dignity and your commanding position', while Clemenceau 'has just told me that he hopes you will not sit in the Congress because no head of a State should sit there'.[8] Two days later, however, Wilson replied making it clear that European resistance to his coming made him the more determined to do so:

> I infer that French and English leaders desire to exclude me from the Conference for fear I might there lead the weaker nations against them. If I were to come to the seat of the Conference and

## THE WORLD'S DESIRE.

PEACE (*outside the Allied Conference Chamber*). "I KNOW I SHALL HAVE TO WAIT FOR A WHILE; BUT I DO HOPE THEY WON'T TALK TOO MUCH."

From *Punch*, Vol. 156, p. 43.

> remain outside I would be merely the centre of a sort of sublimated lobby. . . . No point of disunity must prevent our obtaining the results we have set our hearts on. . . .[9]

and House's response was to declare that 'As far as I can see all the Powers are trying to work with us rather than with one another. Their disagreements are sharp and constant.'[10] This might reassure Wilson but he seemed determined to attend the Conference.

The possibility, indeed the likelihood, of the President's attending caused Clemenceau to approach Lloyd George with a view to obtaining a common Allied front. He sent a telegram to the British Prime Minister on 15 November suggesting that 'we draw up some preparatory memoranda. . . . If we should proceed thus, the President on arriving could make his observations without any delay and the task would find itself advanced.'[11] A common front with Britain would be useful in facing the President. In another direction, though, French collaboration with an ally seemed to be breaking down. In a letter to Balfour, Lord Derby reported that anti-Italian feeling was mounting in France; 'they all say that the signal for an armistice was the signal for Italy to begin to fight'.[12] Italy's Foreign Minister, Baron Sonnino, found support for his country in an unexpected quarter, as Colonel House's diary reveals; he says that he suggested to Sonnino that the Italian representatives at the Peace Conference should not press their territorial claims at an early stage in the Conference, but should wait until Britain had secured her domination over the seas of the world, and France had gained a safe eastern frontier. House went on:

> Sonnino was delighted with the suggestion and saw the point at once. I did this in a spirit of sheer devilry. I shall enjoy being present when Sonnino and Orlando make their argument based upon the British and French claims. I did not undertake to tell Sonnino that if they would listen to our plan for a League of Nations, Italy would be amply protected, for I did not wish to start an argument.[13]

One might ask where the trust that Wilson placed in House, and House's declared identity of ideas with the President, were now.

President Wilson was not the only person who would have been perturbed had he known about Colonel House's encouragement of the Italians. The British, bound by the Treaty of London to grant

Italy considerable areas of territory in the Adriatic, at the expense of the new Serbo–Croat–Slovene state which was to become Yugoslavia, were becoming increasingly anxious about Italy's attitude towards her new neighbour. On 17 October, the British Ambassador in Rome, Sir Rennell Rodd, had written to Balfour about an Italian refusal to release Yugoslav prisoners of war. Writing of Sonnino, Rodd said that

> Apparently he will not see, as many others now do, that a Yugo-Slav State is practically an accomplished fact now and that it is bad policy . . . that it should start with a feeling of resentment against Italy for having hindered instead of having helped.[14]

The Italians were to prove very obstinate in asserting their territorial claims, and House's encouragement was hardly a contribution to an amicable settlement.

More thought was now being given to the shape of the future territorial settlement. In mid-November Marshal Foch sent out plans for the occupation of the Left Bank of the Rhine,[15] a prelude to his insistent pleading for the creation of a Rhenish buffer state. A. J. Balfour circulated to members of the War Cabinet detailed proposals for European frontiers based on the principle of the self-determination of peoples, which principle should, however, 'be applied with caution'. His proposals included some kind of access for Poland to the sea, although this 'presents considerable difficulties', as the only good port, Danzig, had a predominantly German population. He concluded that the most Poland could expect was control over traffic on the Vistula and a guarantee of a free port at Danzig. He did not want the Bohemian Germans in the north of Czechoslovakia left in that state, but he could see no alternative. 'It seems, and perhaps is, absurd to redraw the Bohemia frontier so as to leave in German hands the whole mountain chain which guards the country from German invasion.' Even in the territory whose fate seemed most clear, Alsace–Lorraine, Balfour cast doubt on the ethnic justice in returning the territory to France, for since 1871 many Germans had settled there. However, it must be restored, to rectify the wrong of 1871, a 'violent interruption of a beneficient process of development'.[16] Balfour pointed out in these memoranda several of the territorial problems which were to exercise the delegates at the Conference. Another issue on which feeling was running high was the future treatment of the ex-Kaiser, and on 20 November the British

Imperial War Cabinet set up a Commission under the Law Officers of the Crown to consider what charges should be brought and what procedure adopted at the trial.[17]

Colonel House was becoming more and more anxious about the information that was reaching him about European plans for the Peace Conference. On 19 November he urged Wilson to have an estimate of the extent of the damage done in France and Belgium by German troops prepared by American experts in order to counter excessive claims for reparation,[18] and on 21 November he warned Lansing that the French were asking for the inclusion in the Treaty of

> stipulations of a moral nature, recognition by Germany of the responsibility and preferences of its rulers, which would emphasise the ideas of justice and of responsibility, and would legitimise the measures of punishment and precaution taken against her.[19]

It was becoming apparent to House that the French were proposing to seek a severe Treaty, and if this intention were to be successfully countered, preparations to do so must be made. From the other side of the world came news of another embarrassment for President Wilson, for the American Ambassador in Tokyo informed Lansing that the Japanese intended to ask for the inclusion of a guarantee of racial equality in the Covenant of the League of Nations,[20] a proposition which the Senate would not for a moment entertain. America must prepare carefully for the coming negotiations if she was to resist these various claims and proposals.

Further preparatory material became available as November drew to a close, and it gives more indication of what each of the Allied Great Powers regarded as their priorities for the negotiations. On 26 November the French Ambassador in London handed a Note to the Foreign Office which stated that three 'essential problems' must be solved 'in order to reconcile the necessary strategic guarantees with the principle of rights of peoples'. These were neutralisation of the Left Bank of the Rhine, and French annexation of Alsace-Lorraine and the Saar Valley. On the Left Bank, a 'special military regime' must be established.[21] The British, for their part, were preoccupied with how to deal with the ex-Kaiser; by this time the inflammatory election campaign was well under way. The Attorney-General, F. E. Smith, made a statement to the Imperial War Cabinet recommending that the ex-Kaiser be held personally responsible for the war and all its consequences. 'These things are very easy to understand, and ordinary people all over the world understand them very well.' He went on to say that

> It is necessary for all time to teach the lesson that failure is not the only risk which a man possessing at the moment in any country, despotic powers, and taking the awful decision between Peace and War, has to fear. If ever again that decision should be suspended in nicely balanced equipoise, at the disposition of an individual, let the ruler who decides upon war know that he is gambling, among other hazards, with his own personal safety.

So Wilhelm II should be charged with the invasion of Belgium and the crime of unrestricted submarine warfare, the easiest charges to bring, in the Attorney-General's opinion. When Lord Reading warned that making a public statement to this effect might cause difficulty with America, the Prime Minister retorted that

> America must paddle her own canoe. We have responsibilities in this matter greater than hers. Our sufferings have been very much greater.[22]

The extent to which Lloyd George was prepared to humour President Wilson was definitely limited.

The French were even more concerned to limit the American role at the Conference as far as possible. On 28 November, Balfour had a conversation with Paul Cambon, the French Ambassador in London, at which the Frenchman

> stated, quite categorically, that in his view England and France should settle all the questions in which they are in any way interested, before the Conference began; so that when the President came over he would find himself face to face with a united opposition and an accomplished fact.

Balfour goes on to express his complete disagreement with Cambon's view:

> I offered no opinion on this new apocalyptic revelation but I am convinced that, from the point of view of immediate diplomacy, Cambon's policy is little short of insanity. But diplomacy apart, the French seem to me so greedy that even if Germany and Italy did not exist we might find some difficulty in swallowing their terms whole.

Britain must therefore resist France's attempts to squeeze the Americans out of the effective decisions on peace terms, especially as Colonel House 'is undoubtedly anxious to work with us as closely as he can and it would be fatal to give him the impression that we were settling, or had the least desire to settle, great questions behind his back'.[23] It would thus be better for Britain to cooperate with America to curb French ambitions, in Balfour's view.

Nonetheless, on 1 December, Lloyd George, Clemenceau and Orlando met in London to discuss the coming Conference, and the attitudes of the Allies became clear. The only contemporary records of this meeting which appear to have survived are contained in the American documents. The first is a letter from D. H. Miller* to Colonel House informing him of developments in London during the inter-Allied Conference. He begins by discussing the French attitude to the League, as revealed in conversation between American and French advisers:

> Davis has talked freely with Monnet who Davis says is very close to Clemenceau and reports his views and Monnet says the French idea regarding a League of Nations has as basis the idea that the security of France against any attack should be guaranteed by Great Britain and the United States.

After this warning as to the French interpretation of the idea of a League of Nations, Miller goes on to summarise what occurred at the conference of European leaders:

> At Premiers' conference yesterday . . . it was resolved that Kaiser should be proceeded against, and this was cabled to you; also he says decided in favour of large indemnities as that question has become politically here of great importance. . . . Wiseman . . . in talking of conference between the British, French and Italians . . . said in a half-laughing way in answer to my enquiry as to what was going on 'Yesterday they hanged the Kaiser and got big indemnities agreed upon, and today I suppose they are arranging to present a united front to President Wilson'.[24]

However, it appears from a later telegram from Miller to House that Balfour forced a resolution through the Conference of Premiers making the decisions of that Conference subject to discussions with

* Chief Legal Adviser to the American Commission to Negotiate Peace.

President Wilson.[25] Later, the Secretary of State received a text of the resolutions which shows that these reports were accurate.[26] It appears that the British, and especially Balfour, who had forced through the resolution requiring discussions with Wilson before final decisions were taken, 'in face of considerable opposition and annoyance on the part of others',[27] were reluctant to exclude America from playing an effective part in the peace-making.

At this point, the Germans attempted to intervene in the peace preparations by making a request to the American Government that the origins of the war should be examined by a Commission of neutral experts with a view to determining where the responsibility for starting the war lay:

> In a correct appreciation of the course taken by friend and foe lies the augury for the future reconciliation of the peoples, the one possible foundation for lasting peace and a League of peoples.[28]

In view of the German acceptance of the 'Lansing Note' of 5 November as a basis for the Armistice, which talks of 'the aggression of Germany by land, by sea and from the air',* they were arguing from a position of weakness. Certainly, the British and French Governments gave the proposal short shrift, as Lansing recorded on 6 January 1919:

> His Majesty's Government and the French Government are informing the Swiss Ministers† in London and Paris respectively that they do not consider that the German proposal requires any reply as the responsibility of Germany for the war has been long ago incontestably proved.[29]

Significantly, the American reply was no less unequivocal in its affirmation of German war-guilt: the Acting Secretary of State wrote to the Swiss Minister in Washington on 8 January that

> I beg to inform you that the Government of the United States does not consider that the German Note requires a reply as the responsibility of Germany for the war has already been established.[30]

The Allied and Associated Powers were agreed at least that their task was simply to bring a guilty criminal into the dock for sentence: the verdict was beyond question.

* See p. 34 above.

† The Swiss were acting as intermediaries between the Germans and the Allies, since they were still at war and had no diplomatic relations.

Meanwhile, the question of how the Americans should react to the Conference of Premiers at the beginning of December 1918, and to the agreements and differences between the European Allies which it had revealed, was being considered. The British, or at least some members of His Majesty's Government, were keen to work with the Americans, and American advisers urged that this enthusiasm should receive a friendly American response. D. H. Miller, then in London, wrote to Colonel House on 4 December that, after conversation with British officials, he believed that British and American policy aims had much in common: in their desire not to claim a large indemnity, 'Britain and America were more alike . . . than any other two Powers', and he suggested cooperation between British and American officials in preparing detailed proposals for the Peace Conference. The following day, Walter Lippman prepared a list of the most pressing territorial questions, including the Rhineland, the Saar and Danzig. These questions were regarded by various European Powers as important, and would be pressed hard at the Conference. The Americans must therefore prepare their own proposals and policy on these matters,[31] and on 6 December, Miller reported to House a discussion between himself, two American economists, and J. M. Keynes of the British Treasury, on the subject of reparations. Two days before, British feelings about the French attitude to reparations seemed to be summed up by Harold Nicolson* of the Foreign Office, who informed Miller that 'French memorandum on indemnities had been presented which Nicolson described as fantastic'.[32] At the meeting on 6 December, Keynes expressed the view that 'French demand for huge indemnity was to be the basis for continued occupation and ultimate acquisition of the Rhine provinces', and Cravath, one of the American representatives, wrote a memorandum after this meeting urging that reparation claims must be based upon 'sound principles so that the Allies may share in proper proportions in the distribution of the aggregate amount of the indemnities which it is finally deemed wise to extract'. Cravath went on to consider the meaning of the Fourteen Points and the Lansing Note, and then warned that

> There is every indication that the French Government will be disposed to claim indemnities upon a much more liberal scale than is here advocated. Indeed, in the conference of French officials on

* Later Sir Harold Nicolson.

> this subject, no attention seems to have been paid to France's acceptance of President Wilson's Fourteen Points as modified by his Note to Germany of November 5th.[33]

On the subject of reparations, therefore, it would seem that Britain and America could and should present a united front against the French, who were preparing to demand that 'all damage resulting from the war' must be restored 'at the expense of the German Government',[34] so allowing a claim without any limitation whatever.

One issue which seems to have caused dissension at the Conference of Premiers at the beginning of December was Russia. Both Balfour and Curzon were against allowing Russia to be represented at the Peace Conference, since she had made a separate peace with Germany, and Clemenceau, perhaps understandably furious at Russia's desertion of the Allied cause, agreed with them:

> He would resist with the greatest energy any representation of Russia, which had betrayed the Allied cause during the war. The peace which was to be considered did not concern her.[35]

Lloyd George did not agree, however; Russia had probably lost more soldiers in the war than anyone else, and in any case,

> Russia, after all, represented something like two-thirds of Europe and a large part of Asia. It was a problem that must be faced. Could it be faced without giving the Russian people a right to present their case? The affairs of nearly two hundred million people could not be settled without hearing them. . . . The Bolsheviks, whatever might be thought of them, appeared to have a hold over the majority of the population. This was a fact, a sinister one, no doubt, but facts could not be neglected because they were unpalatable.[36]

There was a complete divergence of attitudes between the two men. Clemenceau was prepared neither to forgive Russia for her treachery nor to talk to the infamous Bolsheviks, whereas Lloyd George felt that no lasting peace could be made in Europe without Russian, and if necessary Bolshevik, participation. No agreement was possible, and it was agreed to wait until the American attitude became known.

In the middle of December, the Armistice was renewed, with an additional provision allowing the Allies to occupy the Right Bank of the Rhine at six days' notice,[37] thus weakening Germany's position, in the event of a renewal of hostilities, still further, since at the first sign of German war preparations, or of a refusal to sign the Peace Treaty, this provision could be brought into effect and Germany be deprived of the only natural obstacle to an Allied advance into her heartlands.

Meanwhile, President Wilson was on his way to Europe on board the *George Washington.* She sailed on 4 December and arrived at Brest on the 14th. On the way over, many members of the Commission to Negotiate Peace had become very discontented at the lack of consultation between the President and his advisers in preparation for the Conference; one of them, William C. Bullitt, told Wilson as they waited for a movie to start, that the experts on board felt that they were being treated 'like immigrants . . . [who] felt entirely left out of the game'.[38] As a result of this declaration of discontent, Wilson held the meeting recorded by another member of the Delegation, at which he made some of his most arrogant, and often quoted, statements. He told his advisers that they, the Americans, 'would be the only disinterested people at the Peace Conference', and that 'the men with whom we were about to deal did not represent their own people'. Considering that Wilson had just been decisively rejected by the American people in the mid-term Congressional elections of 1918, whereas Lloyd George had won a massive election victory and Clemenceau had achieved a large majority in a vote of confidence in the Chamber of Deputies, this was a remarkable statement indeed. He was, of course, obsessed with the League, although he had no detailed ideas as to how such an organisation would operate. All he could say was that 'the world would be intolerable if only arrangement ensues; that this is a peace conference in which arrangements cannot be made in the old style'.[39] Two particular defects of President Wilson's character were to cause trouble in the months to come: one was his hatred of the Germans, the other, so much in evidence here, was his essential arrogance. If Keynes was right to call Wilson a Presbyterian Minister because of his blindness to the tricks wrought by others, this was the result not so much of his own naïveté, nor the subtlety of others, as of his arrogance which was so much in evidence at this meeting.

Wilson's address nonetheless put heart into his own delegation,[40] and his arrival at Brest was greeted with acclaim throughout Europe: 'What a great man came to Europe in those early days of our victory!'[41] Wilson's arrival caused the Allies to hasten their own Conference preparations, while watching the President's every move and utterance with wary eyes. Two particular problems were worrying the British Government at this stage. One was the Treaty of London,* by which Britain had promised to support extensive Italian territorial claims in the Adriatic and Middle East areas, and on 11 December the Foreign Office circulated to the War Cabinet a memorandum pointing out that many of Italy's claims, including that to the port of Fiume† which was not included in the Treaty of London, would not be justified under the Fourteen Points, and could cause great bitterness among the peoples and politicians of the new states of South-Eastern Europe if imposed by the Peace Conference. An Anglo-Italian agreement of 1917 could be deemed to have lapsed as Russia had never signed it, while in the case of the Treaty of London, 'the agitation, which the Italian Government have taken no measures to discourage, for the annexation of Fiume to Italy would be, if it came to anything, a flagrant violation both of the letter and spirit of the Treaty'. In any case, the transfer of populations without their consent was against Wilson's principles, and also all belligerents, Italy included, had encouraged Yugo-Slav union and independence in order to weaken Austria-Hungary. By such means did the Foreign Office propose that Britain should wriggle out of a commitment which was now extremely embarrassing.

The second problem which was likely to become acute for Britain was what should be done with the former German colonies. The Dominions were anxious for their share of the spoils of war. Australia was anxious to annex New Guinea, and South Africa wanted the former German South-West African territory, for example, while India was hoping to be allowed to colonise East Africa,[42] though some members of the War Cabinet were strongly opposed to this last claim.[43] Another problem was the Japanese ambitions in Shantung,‡ where the American attitude would be very important.[44] So Britain was waiting anxiously to see what Wilson's attitude on these and other points would be. However, Lord Derby, in Paris, was able to offer reassurances on the problem of the Freedom of the Seas; after discussing the matter with Colonel House and others he told Balfour that

* See p. 8 above.
† Now Rijeka.
‡ See p. 8 above.

> The President is obsessed with the idea that the League of Nations is a panacea for all ills and if we can only get that settled all other matters, such as Freedom of the Seas, will at the same time be solved.[45]

Let the President have his way over the creation of a League of Nations, which few in England would oppose, and one of Britain's most important interests would not be questioned by him, despite the inclusion of this doctrine in the Fourteen Points. The following day, however, in a telegram, Derby warned Balfour, at Colonel House's insistence, that America would in no circumstances be bound by the Treaty of London when Italy's claims were discussed.[46]

As the Europeans prepared to meet the President, some Americans were becoming anxious about the lack of detailed preparations for the Peace Conference by the American delegation. One such was General Tasker H. Bliss, a member of the American delegation then in Paris, who wrote to Lansing on 16 December attempting to clarify the means by which the President's principles were to be applied to the territorial settlement. He began by specifying two possible reasons for modifying a frontier:

> 1. It is *right*, from the point of view of the peoples immediately concerned, to do so.
> 2. It is *expedient*, from the point of view of the interests of the world at large, to do so.

He then considered examples, including the problem of the Bohemian Germans, warning that Czechoslovakia would ask for their inclusion in their new State in order to give herself a good strategic frontier on her German flank. This kind of reasoning must be rejected by the Americans, as, 'if we have to consider strategic frontiers as such, we are committed to a mere revision of the Marquis of Queensbury rules for the European prize-ring. And our work will be futile in our own lifetime.' Later he declared, with almost Wilsonian arrogance, that

> The first object, and naturally so, of our European associates, is to secure certain territorial adjustments. Our first and only object is to secure certain principles.

Hence, if territorial claims were made which 'do not conform to our sense of justice', the American delegation must oppose them; in any case, the League of Nations must be 'the strategic frontier of every nation that has no other'.[47] Woodrow Wilson was not the only American who saw the League as the cure for all international ills. Robert Lansing's reply was almost worthy of Wilson himself:

> We are face to face with jealousies and selfishness which have drawn the map of Europe in the past. It will be attempted again unless I am greatly mistaken, and it will be a struggle to prevent the victor's desires from being the guiding influences.
>
> I am convinced that the two principal governments with which we are to deal have come to a working understanding and will endeavour to frustrate any plan which will defeat their ambitions.[48]

This combination of naïveté, arrogance and ignorance of the European situation was the source of the greatest weakness of the American delegates their lack of preparation for the months of hard negotiation to come. Keynes clearly perceived the weakness during the negotiations:

> As the President had thought nothing out, the Council was generally working on the basis of a French or British draft. He had to take up, therefore, a persistent attitude of obstruction, criticism and negation if the draft was to become at all in line with his own ideas and purpose.[49]

The source of this fatal weakness is apparent in the correspondence discussed above; not only Wilson himself, but most of his senior colleagues, believed that their goodness and objectivity rendered the issues so clear that preparation was unnecessary.

On 16 December, Wilson met Clemenceau for the first time, and the French Premier was impressed enough to renounce the common front which he had previously made with Britain, to oppose the idea that Wilson should attend the Conference.* Before his meeting with Clemenceau, Wilson had talked to Colonel House, who had persuaded him not to attend for the reasons discussed earlier, but then, at the meeting, Lord Derby told Balfour, 'Judge of [House's] surprise when Clemenceau admitted that he had turned completely round and begged the President to attend'.[50] In another telegram Lord Derby speculated 'quite between ourselves' as to whether the reasons for Clemenceau's *volte-face* was that 'having discovered, as

*See p. 42 above.

he has discovered, that the President has got a violent dislike for Lloyd George, he thinks that having him at the Conference would give him an ally against the "little man" '.[51] Clemenceau, suspicious of British intentions in the Middle East and elsewhere, might be trying to secure himself against British perfidy. Clemenceau's official explanation was that Wilson 'strongly pressed that he should be permitted to be present', and Clemenceau felt that 'if it became known that the President had expressed a wish to be present and had been refused the effect would be very bad, especially in France'.[52] That the real reason was that Clemenceau had revised his opinion of the President becomes clear from Lord Derby's account in a letter to Balfour on 20 December of a discussion Derby had had with Clemenceau and Poincaré, the French President, of their conversations with Wilson. 'They said that he was very amiable but shockingly ignorant of the European situation. They however thought on the whole he will not give much trouble.' This verdict borders on contempt. Derby urged that Wilson's 'one desire is to work with England,' since 'he is somewhat aghast at the demands for territorial aggrandisement of France and more especially of Italy and he feels that in resisting these demands he must have England's backing'.[53] Already Wilson was beginning to feel isolated in the midst of rapacious Europeans, and this might provide Britain with a chance to win him over to close cooperation with her. On 22 December, Lord Derby gave a dinner in honour of President Wilson at the British Embassy in Paris, and did his best to ensure that the problem of the German colonies should not come between the President and the British Empire: when Wilson suggested that they should be administered for the League by small Powers, 'I pointed out to him that past experience had not shown that small nations make the best colonists' and went on to suggest that it would therefore be better if the colonies were administered by the British Empire.[54] Colonel House was even more reassuring two days later when Derby discussed this conversation with him: he 'says that I need not be alarmed and that he [House] can talk him [Wilson] out of his views with regard to the colonies whenever it is necessary to do so'.[55] Colonel House seemed near to asserting that the real power was his at this point, and that he was prepared to use it to bend Wilson's principles and actions to suit British tastes.

While President Wilson was acclimatising himself to the atmosphere of European politics and meeting men with whom he would have to deal at the Conference, a variety of other preliminaries were going on. General Smuts produced a memorandum on the establishment of a League of Nations, urging that nations should adopt a new attitude to one another:

> My broad contention is that the smaller, embryonic, unsuccessful leagues of nations have been swept away, not to leave an empty house for national individualism or anarchy, but for a larger and better League of Nations. Europe is being liquidated and the League of Nations must be the heir to this great estate.[56]

The Peace Conference itself could not solve all the problems which would face Europe after the war, and the League must therefore continue the mediation between nations that the Conference would begin. At another level, the War Cabinet received a report from the Committee of the Imperial War Cabinet on Breaches of the Laws of War, proposing the setting up of an international tribunal to try the ex-Kaiser and other German leaders for war crimes.[57] The Foreign Office advised the War Cabinet that the French must be kept out of Syria, the Sykes–Picot Agreement notwithstanding, and that this should be done under the cloak of Wilson's principles:

> The falling out of Russia, the intervention of America, and the general development of the international situation have made the principles of nationality and democracy and the right of self-determination, in which these principles are translated into action, not merely one element among others in the aims of the Allies, but the essential aim and expression of their cause.

The Arabs must, therefore, be given the Government of their own desire, and they were definitely anti-French.[58] A few days later, the Imperial War Cabinet resolved that the Sykes–Picot Agreement must be cancelled by negotiation with the French.[59]

A problem which continued to worry both British and French statesmen and diplomats was the continuing chaos in Russia. Frenchmen regarded an Eastern ally against Germany as essential to their future security, but were no longer prepared to trust Russia; when the Treaty of Brest–Litovsk was signed, Jules Cambon remarked that 'this would cure France forever of an alliance with Russia'.[60] France's substitute was to build up the new states to Germany's east and cultivate close relations with them. France had done much to encourage the emergence of these states, and while the war was still going on most of the Governments in exile had their headquarters in Paris. France recognised the creation of an independent Polish State as a war aim in June 1918.[61] In their objective of creating a new Eastern partnership against Germany, the French regarded Poland as especially important, as the Quai d'Orsay Memorandum of 20 December 1918 makes clear,* and this was to lead to much trouble at the Conference.

The British, for their part, were becoming more and more anxious about their continuing involvement in the Russian Civil War. G. N. Barnes, who was under strong pressure from the Labour movement to procure an end to British involvement with the anti-Bolshevik forces, circulated a paper to the War Cabinet during December 1918, informing his colleagues that the British working classes were becoming increasingly uneasy about the Russian war, fearing that a capitalist Government was sending men out to fight 'what they regard as a Socialist Government', and urging a speedy decision by the Peace Conference on future policy in Russia. Barnes raised the matter in the Imperial War Cabinet on 31 December, urging once more that the Allies must have a definite policy.

> We could not leave the Peace Conference with Russia still a scene of warfare. It was equally clear that we could not fight Bolshevism in Russia except on a large scale. It was no use merely poking sticks into the kennel to infuriate the dog.

He therefore wanted an attempt to be made to secure a meeting between the various factions at war in Russia. Winston Churchill, the Secretary of State for War, was in no doubt that intervention against the Bolsheviks was the right course of action to take, but Lloyd George was doubtful: effective intervention would be both difficult and costly, and might in any case cause dissension in the armed forces: 'Our citizens' army were prepared to go anywhere for liberty, but they could not be convinced that the suppression of Bolshevism was a war for liberty.' In any case, foreign intervention might well cause Russians to rally to Lenin's Government in order to keep the invaders out: 'The one sure method of establishing the power of Bolshevism in Russia was to attempt to suppress it by foreign troops.' The Cabinet agreed only to fight the Bolsheviks if they attacked the other Russian Governments, and that otherwise

* See p. 11 above.

Allied help to the 'White' forces should be limited to such an amount as was necessary to contain the Bolsheviks.[62]

As the old year drew to a close, the Americans began to panic at the magnitude and difficulty of the task of peacemaking before them, and at their own lack of preparation for it. On 23 December, Robert Lansing wrote to Wilson expressing grave doubts as to the practicability of the League of Nations: Congress would never agree to a renunciation of the Monroe Doctrine or to a restriction on the power of Congress to declare war and make peace. The effectiveness of any military sanctions proposed for the League must therefore be strictly limited in order to reduce the likelihood of the Senate rejecting the Treaty.[63] General Bliss was worried about the general lack among the American delegates of detailed plans or knowledge; on 26 December he wrote to Lansing that

> The Allies . . . know exactly what they are going to ask in the way of territorial cessions. Their demands will be immediately accompanied by their reasons and arguments. Are we agreed that the Alsace–Lorraine of 1871 shall be ceded? Or the Alsace–Lorraine of 1814? Or Alsace–Lorraine extended by an economic boundary? Or Alsace–Lorraine with the boundaries of Marshal Foch? Are we agreed on a principle with which we will meet a demand for the cession of the entire left bank [of the Rhine]? How are we going to get the President's views or instructions on such questions?[64]

The lack of preparations, and the lack of effective means of communication within the American delegation, were causing General Bliss acute anxiety, which cannot have been allayed by the appearance of the draft Treaty of Peace prepared by the Technical Advisers to the Commission to Negotiate Peace, four days after he wrote to Lansing. This document was merely a list of the problems the Conference would have to deal with, and of the solutions proposed by various statesmen and Governments. One of the most contentious problems, for example, was clearly going to be the future status of the German territory west of the Rhine, but all that the American experts could say was that

> These provinces, with the bridgeheads on the Rhine, being in occupation of the United States and the Allies, provision for their future will be necessary in the Treaty of Peace.[65]

The Americans were poorly prepared for the battle to come.

In the first days of January 1919, European countries prepared to take their stands at the negotiations, and the Americans went on trying to evolve a policy. Friction was developing between some of the Allies: Lord Derby warned Balfour on 6 January that the French and the Belgians were likely to quarrel over Luxemburg. The Grand Duchy of Luxemburg was an enemy country, since she had been so closely tied to Germany that she had been obliged to join the war on the side of the Central Powers; she had been a member of the *Zollverein* and the Grand Duchess was related to the Hohenzollern dynasty. Her fate had now to be decided, and the Belgians were anxious to be allowed to annex her. The French were reluctant to do so, and the King of the Belgians was pressing for Lloyd George to meet the Belgian Foreign Minister, Paul Hymans. Lord Derby wrote:

> I think it is obvious that the French and the Belgians are not getting on very well together and I should think it arises from the fact that the Belgians are most anxious to get Luxemburg.[66]

Another likely source of trouble was Italy, who was arousing antagonism on all sides. Lord Robert Cecil told the British Ambassador in Rome, Sir Rennell Rodd, early in January that

> I do not deny that the French are not always tactful in their dealings with the Italians, and that they also have an exaggerated appetite, nor am I prepared to maintain that the Yugo Slavs have never claimed more than is their just due, but Sonnino's stubbornness and the extravagant nature of Italy's claims have had as a result that it is now literally true that Italy has not a friend in Europe except ourselves, and she is doing her best to make her isolation complete.[67]

Americans were alarmed by Italy's attitude too; on 11 January D. H. Miller told Colonel House that the acceptance by the Allies of the Fourteen Points and the Lansing Note rendered the Treaty of London invalid and the American delegation must be firm in its opposition to the Italian claims to Fiume and part of Dalmatia.[68]

The French, for their part, were busy staking their claim to a Rhine frontier. Lord Robert Cecil had a conversation in Paris with Marshal Foch on 8 January during which Foch spoke of 'the necessity for France to hold the Rhine', as the Germans would have a population of seventy-five million, as compared with France's forty-eight million, and Russia was now useless. The Rhine was the only natural strategic frontier against a German invasion. Cecil had tried to discourage him. Foch 'was very earnest and persuasive on the subject but I did not conceal from him that I thought his proposal involved very great difficulties'.[69] That same day, Warrington Dawes, a member of the American delegation, discussed the same subject with Marshal Foch, who insisted that 'only the Rhine as a frontier can offer to France absolute security against future aggressions'. Dawes goes on to remark that 'we cannot and must not violate the principles of the freedom of peoples'.[70] Two days later, Foch sent a memorandum to the Allied Governments repeating that the Rhine frontier was essential to France; the League of Nations was a good idea, but

> until this embryo League acquires sufficient authority to become, by itself, a sufficient guarantee of peace, it is necessary that it should be supported by adequate forces to ensure its development into a strong body.

If this were to be done, Germany must be watched carefully, and must not be given the chance to wage another war of aggression. The Hohenzollern dynasty had gone, probably for ever, but

> a republic built upon the same centralisation of power, and upon the same basis of militarism, including at least the whole of Germany, will present dangers just as grave and just as dangerous a threat to peace. It is easy to realise . . . that in a country imbued with the Prussian spirit and methods and militarism, and where authoritarianism will still rule over the people, as in the past . . . Germany will, in brief, until she has achieved transformation in politics and philosophy, remain a great danger to civilisation.

Prudence therefore demanded strong measures of defence, and if France was not to be invaded before British and American help could arrive, Germany must be deprived of her territory west of the Rhine:

> To stop German military enterprises in the West . . . we must appeal first to all the means provided by Nature. There is only one natural barrier across the invasion route; the Rhine. . . . Unless the Rhine is taken from German control, the peaceful, industrial

> countries of the North-West of Europe will be submerged at once beneath the devastating flood of a barbaric war which no effort will be able to resist.[71]

For Foch, only a sure defence would guarantee the future safety of France. He recognised, however, that in view of the Allies' acceptance of the Fourteen Points, the French could not demand to annex outright the German provinces west of the Rhine, so he proposed the creation of an independent State under Allied military occupation, including the occupation of the Rhine bridgeheads. No other basis for peace could satisfy France. At the same time, Foch urged Allied occupation of territory formerly belonging to Austria–Hungary, so that Germany could immediately be threatened from the east as well as from the west if she refused to sign the Peace Treaty or showed signs of wishing to reopen the war.[72]

The Peace Conference was now about to open. The French and the British had done a great deal of preparatory work, the Americans remarkably little. Since Wilson's arrival in Europe in mid-December, the leaders of the Allied and Associated Powers had been circling continuously round one another, talking, sounding each other out, getting to know one another. Clemenceau realised that Wilson would be easier to deal with than originally supposed. The British were apprehensive about French obstinacy and were determined not to honour the Anglo–French agreement on the Middle East. The Italians were irritating everyone by their arrogant demands. No-one really knew what to do about Russia. This was the position in which Governments and politicians found themselves on the eve of the negotiations.

# 4 The Conference Opens: *First Problems, January 1919*

Although the Paris Peace Conference was officially opened with much trumpeting abroad on 18 January 1919, it had gradually gained momentum during the fortnight before the official opening, so that the opening marked the engagement of top gear, as it were, rather than the start of the journey. Indeed, preparatory discussions had been going on ever since President Wilson's arrival in the middle of December 1918. Early in January, a series of meetings of the Supreme War Council were held to prepare the ground, and this body became, by a simple metamorphosis, the Supreme Council of the Peace Conference, which came to be called the Council of Ten, since it consisted basically of the Prime Ministers and Foreign Ministers of the five principal Allied and Associated Powers: the United States, Britain, France, Italy and Japan. It is often forgotten, however, that these men were usually accompanied by specialist advisers, depending on what topics were on the agenda for a particular meeting, and on one occasion there were no fewer than fifty-three people present at a session of the Council of Ten. In this, the Council was merely continuing the Supreme War Council's practice.

The problem which was chiefly exercising members of Allied Governments was that of Russia and Eastern Europe. Early in January, the Poles had appealed for help in fighting the Bolsheviks, a request which the British War Cabinet discussed on 10 January. The Polish request was supported by Marshal Foch, who was urging that the Allies should occupy the railway from Danzig to Warsaw via Thorn in order to ensure that supplies could be sent easily to the Poles; if this were not done, the Germans might attempt to obstruct the delivery of military supplies which the Poles might later use against them. Lord Curzon feared that Poland might 'cease to exist in a few weeks', and it was agreed to send supplies and volunteer troops if any were forthcoming, though of this most members of the Cabinet were doubtful. Churchill hoped that some British soldiers would volunteer. It was also agreed that the subject should be raised at the Peace Conference.[1]

Two days later, the Supreme War Council met and at once became preoccupied with the Russian and Central European problem. Marshal Foch raised the urgent need to send assistance to the Poles, and submitted a Note urging that the Danzig–Thorn railway be occupied to facilitate the sending of aid. Both President Wilson and Lloyd George were dubious about this idea; Wilson felt that it would be foolish to commit Allied troops for this purpose 'until we had agreed on a general policy as to how to meet the social danger of Bolshevism', while Lloyd George declared that he had 'serious doubts about Marshal Foch's propositions'.[2] No drastic actions could be taken until a general policy had been agreed. Later that afternoon another problem relating to policy in Russia was discussed: who, if anyone, was to be allowed to represent her at the Peace Conference. There were in Paris a number of émigré Russians, including a number of former Ministers and some Socialists, and Baron Sonnino, the Italian Foreign Minister, urged that these people should be allowed to speak for Russia before the Supreme Council. Lloyd George was strongly opposed to this idea. The Allies must decide on their policy in Russia, and depending on this decision, their forces in Russia must be either reinforced or withdrawn; at present 'they were no use whatever'. He then went on to oppose Sonnino's suggestion:

> He had nothing to say against these people, Prince Lvov etc. We were told they represented every shade of opinion. As a matter of fact, they represented every opinion, except the prevalent opinion in Russia.[3]

At this, President Wilson demurred, saying that Bolshevism was only prevalent 'in some respects', but Lloyd George could not accept this; he

> feared the fact that it was prevalent must be accepted. The peasants accepted Bolshevism for the same reason as the peasants

> had accepted the French Revolution, namely, that it gave them land. The Bolsheviks were the *de facto* Government. . . . To say that we ourselves should pick the representatives of a great people was contrary to every principle for which we had fought.[4]

He was supported by Pichon on behalf of France, and it was agreed to do no more than invite the Russian émigrés to submit memoranda or be interviewed.

Not all of Lloyd George's Government would have supported him in his reluctant toleration of the Bolshevik regime. On 13 January, Lord Curzon urged that the Bolsheviks must be crushed; they were formenting revolution in Germany, and Poland could not stop them. 'The Bolsheviks are not only destroying Russia but may, if left alone, destroy other parts of Europe.'[5] It would seem that the French took a similar view, for at a meeting of the British Empire Delegation in Paris Lloyd George told his colleagues that 'the French had adopted a very strong line, they wished to fight Bolshevism. This was certainly not President Wilson's point of view', and they also wanted to recognise the émigrés in Paris as Russia's representatives at the Conference. The British were in agreement with the Americans in opposing this, and the Delegation resolved not to agree to interference in the Bolshevik area of Russia and that other countries should only be assisted to defend themselves against a Bolshevik attack: no support should be given to an anti-Bolshevik offensive.[6] Lloyd George was not prepared to engage in a crusade against Bolshevism, however wicked Lenin's régime might be. That afternoon, the Supreme War Council agreed that a decision as to who should represent Russia at the Conference must be deferred until Allied policy in Russia had been decided.[7] Lloyd George, however, could not be sure that his Cabinet colleagues in London would support his moderate line, and he became especially suspicious of Churchill's intentions when he learned that Churchill had submitted to the Cabinet a plan for a post-war conscript army of 1,700,000 men. Lloyd George sent his War Minister an angry telegram from Paris:

> I am surprised that you should think it right to submit such a scheme to my colleagues before talking it over or at least before submitting it in the first instance to me. It is hardly treating the head of the Government fairly.[8]

Lloyd George was fearful of what some of his colleagues might do in his absence.

An issue to which the British Government had paid a good deal of attention was the trial of war criminals, and on 13 January, the Attorney-General presented the Interim Reports of his Committee of Enquiry into Breaches of the Laws of War, which recommended that the Kaiser should be prosecuted:

> While there is no exact precedent for punishment, there is also no exact precedent in modern times for a series of crimes brought about by a group of men of whom the ex-Kaiser was one. To suffer him . . . to go free and unpunished, while minor offenders acting under his orders, or with his sanction, were tried and punished, would be inequitable.

The details of the charges and the nature of the tribunal were then discussed. The verdict was already assumed, of course: the Kaiser had been personally responsible for the war and all the suffering that had resulted from it; he 'was in truth War-Lord'.[9] Fortified by this document, Lloyd George proposed at the Supreme War Council on 17 January that the Peace Conference should set up an expert Commission to consider 'punishment of those guilty of offences against the Law of Nations', a proposal which was accepted by the other members without demur.[10]

Meanwhile, the Russian headache continued to plague the Council. On the morning of 16 January, Lloyd George introduced a proposal that the Peace Conference should urge a truce upon the warring Russian factions, after the acceptance of which their representatives should be invited to Paris to explain their position so that the Allies could attempt to reconcile them. He reviewed the possibilities open to the Allies. No-one was prepared to fight another major war to crush Bolshevism, and the policy of isolating the Bolshevik area, the policy of the '*cordon sanitaire*', must lead to enormous suffering and many deaths among the ordinary people of Russia – 'Our blockade of Russia would lead to the killing, not of the ruffians enlisted by the Bolsheviks, but of the ordinary population, with whom we wish to be friends.' In any case, the people feared that the 'White' leaders, and especially the strongest of them, Admiral Kolchak, wished to restore the old régime, and the people would therefore not support them. So the only alternative was to attempt to mediate between the factions.[11] Pichon, however, still hankered after hearing the émigrés, and especially Noulens, who had recently arrived from Archangel.[12]

President Wilson supported Lloyd George because he believed that Bolshevism had won a good deal of support throughout the world. In retrospect it is odd to find an American President saying that

> there was throughout the world a feeling of revolt against the large vested interests which influenced the world both in the economic and in the political sphere. The way to cure this domination was, in his opinion, constant discussion and a slow process of reform; but the world had grown impatient of delay. . . . The vast majority who worked and produced were convinced that the privileged minority would never yield them their rights. . . . Bolshevism was therefore vital because of these genuine grievances.[13]

From this it followed that Allied troops would probably refuse to fight the Bolsheviks and hence 'the British proposal contained the only suggestion that led anywhere'.[14] However, at French insistence, it was agreed that Noulens and Scavenius, the former Danish Minister in Petrograd, should be heard.

While these discussions were going on, the Supreme War Council had spent some time discussing arrangements for the Conference. Such matters as the order of precedence of delegates had had to be settled, and there had been some argument as to what should be the official language of the Conference, as a result of which English and French were both adopted, after three debates in the Supreme Council.[15] It was also agreed that expert Commissions should be set up to consider the various subjects with which the Conference would have to deal.[16] The normal procedure was to be that each issue coming before the Conference would be referred to such a Commission after preliminary consideration by the Supreme Council, and the final terms would be decided by the Council on the basis of the Commission's report. Some of the most contentious issues were to remain in the hands of the Supreme Council throughout, however. At these meetings, secretarial arrangements were also made and agreed.

All was now ready for the official opening, which took place on 18 January. As President of the host country, Poincaré welcomed the delegates and at once set what the French hoped would be the tone of the Conference:

> This very day, forty-eight years ago, on 18th January, 1871, the German Empire was proclaimed by an army of invasion in the Château at Versailles. It was consecrated by the theft of two French provinces. It was thus vitiated from its origin and by the fault of its founders. It contained at its birth the germ of decay and of death.
>
> Born in injustice, it has ended in opprobrium. You are assembled in order to repair the evil that it has done and to prevent a recurrence of it. You hold in your hands the future of the world.[17]

When Poincaré sat down, Wilson proposed the election of Clemenceau to the Chair of the Conference. This was seconded by Lloyd George and carried unanimously. The old Frenchman was to preside over Germany's humiliation – a life-long ambition was to be fulfilled.

The problem of Russia was still unsolved, and no policy decision had yet been taken. Despite President Wilson's support, the British proposal that the Conference, or rather the Supreme Council, should attempt to mediate between the factions, was still not acceptable to the French. One difficulty was their adamant refusal to invite Bolshevik representatives to Paris, for fear that they might attempt to stir up a revolution in France. On 19 January, Balfour wrote to Lloyd George telling him that Clemenceau was 'quite unmoved and immoveable' on the subject of inviting the Bolsheviks to Paris. Not only did he fear riots, he also feared the effect upon the bourgeois parties in France of a decision by the Conference to enter into 'relations with Lenin and his gang', indeed, the hostility which such an invitation would arouse both in the Chamber of Deputies and from Poincaré might well result in Clemenceau being compelled to resign. Balfour concluded that

> Unless I am very greatly mistaken, you will not get him to modify these views, and you will therefore have to consider very carefully how far it is worth pressing him.[18]

Some other way would have to be found round this obstacle.

On 20 January, the Supreme Council gave a hearing to Noulens, the French Ambassador to Russia, who was violently anti-Bolshevik. Since he had left Petrograd in February 1918 he was able to contribute nothing to the Supreme Council's knowledge of conditions in Russia, and his tales of Bolshevik atrocities evoked little comment from the members of the Council.[19] Afterwards, Lloyd George told a meeting of the British Empire Delegation that Noulens had been able to contribute nothing of value, but the French were still determined to crush Bolshevism, despite British and American opposition to any such attempt. However, something must be done soon, as the working class in Britain was becoming restive at British involvement in the fighting against the Bolsheviks, and the British delegation decided to press on with their proposal for mediation, suggesting that the meeting between the factions could take place on neutral territory instead of in Paris, so meeting Clemenceau's objection to allowing Bolshevik representatives into France.[20] The following day the Council of Ten heard Scavenius, who also urged that the 'White' forces were worth supporting,[21] after which the Council met to decide its policy.

The Allies were still divided in their attitude towards the Bolsheviks. Sonnino urged that representatives of the Russian factions should be heard in Paris. When Balfour pointed out that Clemenceau refused to allow Bolshevik representatives to come to Paris, Sonnino 'explained that all the Russian parties had some representatives here, except the Soviets, whom they did not wish to hear', to which Lloyd George retorted that 'the Bolsheviks were the very people some of them wished to hear'.[22] Lloyd George and Wilson put forward the plan agreed by the British delegation for a meeting on neutral ground. No-one wanted to talk to the Bolsheviks: Wilson said that they 'were all repelled by Bolshevism', but that

> The Allies were making it possible for Bolsheviks to argue that Imperialistic and Capitalistic Governments were endeavouring to exploit the country and to give the land back to the landlords, and so bring about a reaction. If it could be shown that this was not true, and that the Allies were prepared to deal with the rulers of Russia, much of the moral force of this argument would disappear.[23]

Clemenceau was even more reluctant to hold talks with the Soviet Government:

> Had he been acting by himself, he would temporise and erect barriers to prevent Bolshevism from spreading. But he was not

> alone, and in the presence of his colleagues he felt compelled to make some concessions, as it was essential that there should not be even the appearance of disagreement among them.[24]

He was also willing, therefore, to accept the proposal. Only the Italians were obstinate in their opposition to meeting the Bolsheviks, Orlando declaring that Italy 'could make no further contribution'. President Wilson was therefore asked to draft a proclamation to be broadcast to the parties in Russia. The following day he had his draft ready. It declared the Allies' desire 'to help the Russian people not to hinder them, nor to interfere in any manner with their right to settle their own affairs in their own way', and offered mediation if 'every organised group that is now exercising, or attempting to exercise, political authority or military control' in Russia would send up to three representatives to meet the Allies on Princes Island in the Sea of Marmora, and call a truce in the civil war.[25] These representatives would be expected by 15 February.

President Wilson's draft was accepted, and was broadcast by radio to the various Russian Governments. The nature of this invitation was such that the Russian problem must be deferred until the middle of February at least, and the Conference could turn its attention to other tasks. One other event was to occur a few days later which seemed to confirm the fears of many delegates at the Conference that Lenin's Government intended to subvert the peoples of all non-Soviet countries and to bring about Bolshevik revolutions throughout the world: the formation, on 24 January, of the Communist International, and the issue of an invitation to Socialist parties to send delegates to its first Congress, to be held in Moscow in March:

> . . . it is necessary to form a bloc with those elements in the revolutionary workers' movement who . . . now stand by and large for the proletarian dictatorship in the form of Soviet power.[26]

It therefore seemed that Bolshevism had aggressive intentions, and despite Lloyd George's warning during the discussion of the Prinkipo initiative that Bolshevism 'could not be crushed by speeches', but only by troops, which were not available, many people in the Allied delegations and Governments believed that, sooner or later, the Bolsheviks would have to be fought, beaten and destroyed.

Another country which was causing anxiety to the Supreme Council at this time was Poland. Situated between Germany and

Russia, her position was precarious. On her western frontier there were reports of German aggression and persecution, coupled with obstruction to the sending of supplies to her, while on the east she was threatened by the Bolsheviks, and the Allies were anxious that Poland should play her part in containing, and perhaps eventually defeating the Soviet Government in Russia. If these problems were not enough, however, Poland was herself busy picking a quarrel with the Ukraine over Eastern Galicia. After the collapse of Russia, the Ukraine had declared itself an independent State under a Directory until a properly constituted Government should be established. This Directory laid claim to the province of Eastern Galicia, the majority of whose population was Little Russian, although there were sizeable Polish settlements as well, with the result that the Poles were also claiming the territory, and were fighting the Ukrainians for possession of it. On 21 January, this conflict was brought to the attention of the Council of Ten by President Wilson, who read out a letter from the Polish Prime Minister, the concert pianist Paderewski, requesting the Allies to send a collective Note to the Ukrainian Directory ordering them 'to withdraw from Galicia and to cease interfering in Polish territory', and asking for supplies and assistance to defeat the Ukrainians. Wilson seemed on the whole to be inclined to accede to the Polish request, but Lloyd George was doubtful: he

> questioned whether it was safe to admit that Galicia was Polish territory. Any summons to Kiev should be accompanied by a similar summons to the Poles to abstain from entering disputed territory such as Eastern Galicia.[27]

Lloyd George did not wish to prejudge the issue, and in any case he was suspicious of Polish intentions.

The French, however, were anxious to bolster Poland up so that she would fight both the Bolsheviks and, if necessary, the Germans. On the morning of 22 January, at Clemenceau's request, Marshal Foch was allowed to address the Council of Ten on the subject of Poland. He began by urging once more that allied troops should occupy the Danzig–Thorn railway in order to ensure that Allied help could be got through to the Poles,* though he was prepared to ask Poland to assure the Germans that troops and supplies sent by this route would only be used in Russian Poland.[28] Balfour, however,

* See p. 63 above.

was very doubtful whether the Poles would voluntarily accept such a restriction:

> The Poles were using the interval between the cessation of war and the decisions of the Peace Congress to make good their claims to districts outside Russian Poland, to which in many cases they had little right. . . . He suggested that the Polish representatives should be gathered here and told that they must limit their actions to the protection of indisputable Polish territory against invasion from without. The ultimate frontiers of Poland should be left to the Peace Congress.[29]

The Poles must be kept firmly in order. President Wilson was also dubious about Marshal Foch's proposal: 'Danzig must remain an open question, yet its occupation was suggested. With the object of sending troops into Poland we were going to prejudge the whole Polish question,'[30] while Lloyd George was opposed to the whole idea of sending troops to Poland, and especially to sending all the Polish troops still in France under the command of General Haller to Poland:

> We could not expect the Germans to allow arms to go through if they were to equip a Polish army to attack them. This would be asking more than was laid down in the Armistice. Fairness was due even to the enemy. He was not prepared at the present moment to make any declaration concerning the rights to Posen, which the Poles were attempting to conquer by force and thereby to prejudge what the Conference was assembled to do.[31]

The difference between the attitudes of Lloyd George and Wilson towards the Poles emerged clearly in the discussions which followed this remark by the British Prime Minister:

> PRESIDENT WILSON observed that Mr Paderewski asked for this help specifically for defence against the Bolsheviks.
>
> MR LLOYD GEORGE replied that he had no doubt of the honourable character of Mr Paderewski. But the Poles were not all united and Mr Paderewski was unlikely to maintain complete control of the situation. The arms might pass into other hands. . . .
>
> PRESIDENT WILSON pointed out that in sending Polish troops to Poland we should not only be sending armed men, but strong

> partisans on Polish questions. These were burning questions and great caution should be exercised in dealing with them.[32]

Wilson was unsure of himself, wavering between his concern not to allow the Poles to present the Conference with a *fait accompli* by conquering territory to which the Conference might well say they were not entitled, and his fear that if help were not sent Poland might herself be overrun by the Bolsheviks. Lloyd George and Balfour were more distrustful of the Poles than Wilson and were determined not to give them the means to carry on an expansionist policy without firm assurance that such a policy would not be pursued, while Marshal Foch still felt that the most urgent task was to ensure Poland's survival, despite her folly and greed – the rights and wrongs of the situation must wait until later. He

> said that he wished again to draw attention to the danger that Poland might be suffocated before its birth. It had no bases, no outlets, no communications, no supplies, no army. The Poles were fighting the Bolsheviks who might be attacking them, the Ukrainians whom they chose to attack and the Germans from whom they wished to wrest Posen. From a military point of view, the policy they were pursuing was likely to be fatal to them.[33]

The Supreme Council therefore decided to send an inter-Allied Commission to Poland to investigate and recommend what action should be taken. Its members were nominated a few days later. The following day Lloyd George reported this decision to his delegation, outlining his suspicion of Polish motives:

> The real difficulty was that the Poles were giving the appearance of an attempt to forestall the decisions of the Peace Conference by seizing territory whose rightful possession could fairly be said to be a disputed question.[34]

The Poles' activities in Posen and in Eastern Galicia were already giving rise to suspicion, especially in British minds, that they cared little for moderation or for the principle of the self-determination of peoples.

At this meeting an issue which was to cause a bitter row between Wilson and the British early in the Conference was raised: the fate of the German colonies. The Delegation was informed that the following day the Dominions representatives were to be invited to attend a meeting of the Council of Ten to discuss the matter.[35] Lloyd George and others had already been putting out feelers and seeking to discover what the President's attitude on this question would be,* as the British Dominions were determined to obtain their share of the spoils of war. On 19 December, Lord Robert Cecil and General Jan C. Smuts had a long talk with Wilson which proved satisfactory except on the colonial question. The following day Smuts told Lloyd George in a letter that

> I hope you will speak strongly to him [Wilson] on the subject [of the German colonies]. . . . I need not point out the trouble you are going to have with these Dominions on this matter. You are helping Wilson in getting the League established, but he *must* be made to realise your difficulties and assist you to overcome them.[36]

South Africa was determined to annex South-West Africa, and however strongly Smuts might support Wilsonian ideals in other contexts, in this one he was determined to pursue his country's ambitions, the President notwithstanding.

The matter was first discussed in the Council of Ten on 24 January, when the Prime Ministers of the Dominions were invited to be present. All were agreed that the colonies could not be returned to Germany, but then Lloyd George posed the problem. Either the colonies could be administered internationally by the League or by a Power acting on the League's behalf, under conditions designed to ensure that the territory was administered 'not in the interest of the mandatory, but in the interest of all the nations in the League', or other countries would be allowed to annex them outright. If this were the chosen course, South Africa would annex South-West Africa, Australia would annex New Guinea, and New Zealand Samoa.[37] The Dominion Prime Ministers were then invited to speak, and all pressed their claim to be allowed to annex the colonies near to them. William Hughes of Australia began, saying that

> If there were at the very door of Australia a potential or actual enemy Australia could not feel safe. The islands were as necessary to Australia as water to a city. If they were in the hands of a superior power there could be no peace for Australia . . . he was

* See p. 55 above.

> prepared to say that in the mandatory Power established in New Guinea under international control, Australia would see a potential enemy.[38]

Australia's case was thus based on strategic necessity.

General Smuts then spoke on the subject of South-West Africa. His case was economic – only the Union of South Africa could develop the territory. 'South-West Africa was a desert country without any product of great value and only suitable for pastoralists. It could, therefore, only be developed from within the Union itself.' He went on to urge that South Africa was, in any case, entitled to some reward:

> In conclusion, he would like to add that the Union had made great sacrifices. . . . He believed that the effort made by South Africa, sometimes with a divided heart, would prove on examination to be second to none among the small states which had partaken in the war.[39]

He was followed by the New Zealand Prime Minister, W. F. Massey, whose case, like Hughes' case for Australia, was based on strategic needs: Samoa was 'the key to the Pacific', and

> on behalf of his fellow-citizens, and on behalf of the people in the Islands of the South Pacific, for the sake of the native races, and for the sake of humanity, he most strongly urged that the claim he was making in regard to Samoa should be granted by the Congress.[40]

These, then, were the first major claims of self-interest to come before the Conference. For the present, Clemenceau, in the Chair, thanked the Dominion Prime Ministers for their attendance and statements, and closed the meeting.

The issue was not taken up again until after the second Plenary Session of the Conference,* but on 27 January the Supreme Council considered it again, after first hearing another statement of claim, this by the Japanese delegation in respect of the Chinese province of Shantung and some islands in the North Pacific. Wilson said that the application of the mandatory principle must be considered, and the

* See pp. 79–80 below.

Council agreed not to take the matter further until both the Japanese and Chinese delegations could be present.[41] The Council then returned to the problem of the German colonies, and President Wilson stated his case. He spoke of 'the feeling which had sprung up all over the world against further annexation' and explained that from his view of the feelings of the world arose the proposal that territories not capable of independent self-government whose fate had to be decided should be administered by another country on behalf of the League. This administering Power, or mandatory, would be chosen by the League itself. Pompously, he explained that

> The fundamental idea would be that the world was acting as trustee through a mandatory, and would be in charge of the whole administration until the day when the true wishes of the inhabitants could be ascertained.[42]

He thus ruled out the granting of the Dominion claims:

> If any nation could annex territory which was previously a German Colony, it would be challenging the whole idea of the League of Nations. Under the League of Nations they were seeking to lay down a law which would rally the whole world against an outlaw, as it had rallied against Germany during the last war. . . . Therefore, all danger of bad neighbours was past, and the only question remaining was whether administration by a mandatory would not be as useful as direct Australian administration [as in the case of New Guinea].[43]

Not surprisingly, this rejection of their claims caused consternation among the Dominion representatives. Louis Botha launched into a long argument as to why South Africa should get South-West Africa, while William Hughes was openly impatient at President Wilson's whole argument:

> Why have a mandatory? The President replied: Because the world was against annexation. To that he would reply: Was it proposed then, to adopt that principle to all questions to be dealt with by the Peace Conference? Was it proposed to appoint mandatories to the New States to be created in Europe? . . . It was for those who wished to apply the principle to prove their case.[44]

No mandatory would be appointed over Poland, Czechoslovakia, or, for that matter, Alsace–Lorraine, and Hughes was not prepared to see the principle applied to his disadvantage. The following morning, Lloyd George added his support for the Dominions' claims, appealing to Wilson to regard them as 'a special case', while Massey pleaded once more to be given Samoa.[45]

It was beginning to look as if President Wilson and the British Empire were fast approaching a head-on collision. Wilson was determined that the League should be the heir to the German colonial estate: the Dominions were equally determined that they themselves should. Some British statesmen were becoming anxious about the effect of such a collision on future Anglo–American relations. On 27 January, Lord Robert Cecil wrote to Balfour that

> I am disturbed at what I am told about the German Colony question and am asking L.G. to let us be heard on its League of Nations aspect before a decision is come to. Please don't think me very pompous if I say that an immense responsibility rests on you. I saw House yesterday. He is now as much disillusioned about the British as he was a week or two ago about the French.[46]

There was a risk of giving grave offence to the Americans if the Dominion claims were pressed. On 27 January, the British Empire Delegation agreed to Lloyd George's suggestion that 'it was now desirable to clear up the position as to the significance of the mandatory system', after he had congratulated the Dominions on their 'powerful statements of the case for annexation'.[47] After the stormy meeting of the Council of Ten on the morning of the 28th, the British Empire Delegation met again to consider its position. Lloyd George reported that Wilson was opposed to the naming of mandatory Powers by the Peace Conference: this should be left to the League. The two men had then had an argument. Lloyd George had

> pointed out to President Wilson that if this principle were adopted, then none of the European Powers would sign the Treaty of Peace. President Wilson had replied that he could not return to America with the world parcelled out by the Great Powers.

He was, however, prepared to vary the terms of the mandate in various cases.

The British delegates then began arguing among themselves. Hughes was strongly opposed to the whole idea of mandates, while

Lord Robert Cecil felt that the British delegation should accept the principle:

> To insist on annexation was to weaken the British argument against the extensive claims which France and Italy were about to make. Claims for annexation represented the spirit of the Congress of Vienna, which was opposed to the spirit upon which the hope of a new system for the world was based.

He also assured Hughes that giving a mandate for New Guinea would give Australia 'absolute security'. Hughes, Massey, and Botha, however, decided to draft their own resolution on the subject.[48]

After the meeting of the British delegation adjourned, the Council of Ten debated the issue further. President Wilson still insisted that the principles he had laid down must be adhered to. He told the members of the Council that

> they must consider how this treaty would look to the world, for as it looked to the world it would be, since the world would not wait for explanations. The world would say that the Great Powers first portioned out the helpless parts of the world, and then formed a League of Nations. The crude fact would be that each of these parts of the world had been assigned to one of the Great Powers.[49]

This would inevitably mean a return to old national rivalries and jealousies, which he could not accept. It looked as though there was a complete deadlock between President Wilson and the British Dominions. Colonel House wrote in his diary that Wilson was

> much disturbed at the turn of things this afternoon. The French and British are demanding that if the mandatory is used by the League of Nations as to the German colonies, it shall be used immediately and the different Powers designated now rather than later. . . .[50]

and it was at one of these meetings that President Wilson asked Hughes, 'Am I to understand that if the whole civilised world asks Australia to agree to a mandate in respect of these islands, Australia is prepared to defy the appeal of the whole civilised world?' to receive the reply, 'That's about the size of it, President Wilson', with Massey of New Zealand nodding his agreement.[51] The deadlock seemed complete and bitter.

The British delegates met again on 29 January to consider the position. Haste was essential as the matter had to be settled before Wilson returned to America to close Congress in February. Lloyd George proposed a resolution by which three classes of mandate would be established, 'according to the stage of development of the people, the geographical situation of the territory, its economic conditions, and other similar circumstances'. Thus the states of the former Turkish Empire would become independent States receiving only administrative advice and assistance from a mandatory. Lloyd George was to explain this to the Council of Ten as a situation in which the people were 'civilised, but not yet organised'.[52] Other areas, especially in Central Africa, would need careful administration by a mandatory, while the third class consisted of territories such as South-West Africa and the Pacific Islands – the subjects of the dispute with Wilson – which were so close in geographical terms to a particular Power that that Power must inevitably receive the mandate, and this could be recognised at once. This proposal was accepted by the British delegation, and Lloyd George put it to the Council of Ten the following morning. The proposal was accepted by the Dominions' representatives, though somewhat reluctantly in Hughes' case.

> Australia fully recognised that grave interests involving the fate of humanity were at stake, and therefore he did not feel justified in opposing the views of President Wilson and those of Mr Lloyd George, beyond the point which would reasonably safeguard the interests of Australia.[53]

Wilson hesitated to accept the proposal, however, even though he felt that it was 'a very gratifying paper'.[54] He was reluctant to commit himself on the allocation of mandates to the Dominions until other issues, such as the way mandates would operate and other territorial issues, had been settled. Lloyd George said that this approach 'filled him with despair', as 'should that attitude be taken about each question, no agreement would ever be reached', since no issue would be decided until all the others had been decided – an impossible position for the Council to take up. Furthermore, the Dominions had only agreed to this document with great reluctance, and could not be expected to make further concessions. Wilson was still dubious, and so were Hughes and Massey, but in the afternoon General Botha of South Africa, 'one of those who would give up everything to reach the highest ideal', urged the Council not to 'stop at small things'[55] and to accept Lloyd George's proposal. Sir Robert Borden proposed the adoption of a resolution imposing conditions on mandatory Powers, including the abolition of the slave trade and an undertaking not to use mandated territories for military purposes, which Wilson said 'made it clearer'.[56] After further discussion Lloyd George's proposal was accepted as a basis for the settlement, although President Wilson still felt doubts, and Belgian and Portuguese representatives were allowed to enter and demand a share in the spoils also, and their position was reserved for further consideration.[57] A solution had been found, however, to the dispute between President Wilson and the British Dominions, and the Council had survived its first major controversy. The matter would now be referred to the Commission set up to draft the Covenant of the League of Nations.

While this dispute had been raging, the Council had agreed on the creation of this Commission which was to include representatives of the five Great Powers and a number of representatives of the smaller Powers,[58] as well as Commissions to discuss Reparations and the trial of war criminals. It is interesting that Wilson obtained the deletion of the words 'and indemnity' from the title of the Reparations Commission,[59] and that the War Guilt Commission was to consider, among other things, 'the responsibility of the authors of the war'.[60] These proposals by the Supreme Council came up for approval at the second Plenary Session of the Conference, most of which was devoted to the proposed League of Nations.

This second Plenary Session was convened at three o'clock on 25 January. On the Agenda was the proposal to set up these various Commissions, but the proceedings were devoted entirely to the League. President Wilson moved the setting up of the Commission whose task would be to draft the Covenant, and of which he was to take the Chair, saying that

> In coming into this war the United States never thought for a moment that she was intervening in the politics of Europe, or the politics of Asia, or the politics of any part of the world. Her thought was that all the world had now become conscious that there was a single cause which turned upon the issue of this war. That was the cause of justice and liberty for men of every kind and place. Therefore, the United States would feel that her part in this war had been played in vain if there ensued upon it merely a body of

> European settlements. She would feel that she could not take part in guaranteeing those European settlements unless that guarantee involved the continuous superintendence of the peace of the world by the Associated Nations of the world.[61]

Lloyd George seconded the resolution, speaking of the devastation he had seen in France and saying that

> these were the results of the only method . . . that civilised nations have ever attempted or established to settle disputes amongst each other. And my feeling was: surely it is time . . . that a saner plan for settling disputes between peoples should be established than this organised savagery.[62]

The French interest in setting up a League of Nations was rather different, as Leon Bourgeois made clear:

> You who have fought for Right are about to set up an organisation to impose penalties and to ensure their enforcement. Having established compulsory arbitration, having fixed . . . the penalties to be imposed for disobedience to the common will of civilised nations you will be able to make your work solid and lasting and enter with confidence and tranquillity the Temple of Peace.[63]

The League was to be used primarily to restrain Germany and ensure France's future safety. The Commission was set up, and its task would be to reconcile these various conceptions of the League of Nations. With it were established the other Commissions, and the Conference was now ready to get down to the detailed work of preparing a Treaty. The Germans were not, of course, present: this was the Preliminary Peace Conference, and the terms it prepared would be presented to the Germans at the final Peace Congress. First, however, the Allied and Associated Powers had to reach agreement on what they were going to demand.

# 5 Detailed Work: *February 1919*

With the setting up of the Commissions on the various subjects of the Treaty, the delegates at the Conference began consideration of the many detailed problems which had to be solved. Between the second Plenary Session on 25 January and the beginning of March when the Commissions produced their first Reports, the detailed work was done. The problems were many, and some of the more important work that was done during this period must be discussed.

First, however, it will be useful to consider the conditions under which the Conference was working. Delegates were conscious of the pressure of events; the continuing civil war in Russia, starvation in Germany and Austria, disputes, wars and dissension among and within the new states of Central Europe. The pressure of work was enormous, and many of those who were at Paris have written of the confusion that often seemed to reign supreme, of the anxiety, the quarrels, the difficulties, which were occurring all the time. When Lloyd George defended his conduct at Paris in the House of Commons on 16 April, he painted a vivid picture of the difficulties of the peacemaking:

> The Congress of Vienna was the nearest approach to it. You had then to settle the affairs of Europe. It took eleven months. But the problems at the Congress of Vienna, great as they were, sink into insignificance compared with those which we have had to attempt to settle at the Paris Conference. It is not one continent that is engaged – every continent is affected.[1]

He went on to say that

> We had to shorten our labours and work crowded hours, long and

late, because whilst we were trying to build, we saw in many lands the foundations of society crumbling into dust, and we had to make haste. I venture to say that no body of men have ever worked in better harmony. I am doubtful whether any body of men with a difficult task have worked under greater difficulties – stones clattering on the roof, and crashing through the windows, and sometimes wild men screaming through the key-holes.[2]

The work of the Conference was done in hotels and Government buildings hastily made available by the French authorities, and it is clear that working conditions were far from ideal. Urgency, coupled with the huge range of issues which had to be discussed and decided, gave the proceedings an air of bewildering complexity well captured by Sir Harold Nicolson. Sketching a scenario of the Conference, he wrote of the appearance of the principal delegates and went on:

Such portraits would be interspersed with files, agenda papers, resolutions, *procès verbaux*, and communiqués. These would succeed each other with extreme rapidity, and from time to time would have to be synchronised and superimposed. The Plenipotentiaries of the United States of America, of the British Empire, of France, of Italy and of Japan as the one part. . . . It is resolved subject to the approval of the Houses of Congress the President of the United States of America accepts on behalf of the United States. . . . Si cette frontière était prise en considération, il serait nécessaire de faire la correction indiquée en bleu. Autrement le chemin de fer vers Kaschaun serait coupé. . . . These coupons will be accepted in settlement of the table d'hote meals of the hotel, the whole ticket is to be given up at dinner. . . . M. Venizelos told me last night that he had concluded his agreement with Italy in the following terms. . . .[3]

And so on. Over all hung the need for haste; the feeling of 'Better a bad Treaty today than a good Treaty four months hence';[4] the constant pressure from the Statesmen for a speedy settlement; Clemenceau's oft-repeated plea: '*Mais voyez-vous, jeune homme, que voulez-vous qu'on fasse, il faut aboutir*.'[5] Only from such accounts can one glean any impression of what it was like at the Conference in these months when the detailed work was being done.

The Conference was also hindered by organisational problems, which often gave rise to friction between delegates. Leaks to the Press were one problem: one early example of this is a letter from Sir

Eric Geddes to Philip Kerr, Lloyd George's private secretary, enclosing a draft of a letter to be sent by the Prime Minister to President Wilson relating to an article which had appeared in the *Daily Mail* which purported to give Wilson's views on the territorial settlement in the Adriatic. The prevailing idea was that the article had been based on 'some unintended indiscretion on the part of those who discussed this subject with you [Wilson] at the Hotel Murat'. Since only Wilson and three British Cabinet Ministers had been present, Lloyd George was 'a good deal perturbed', though in fact the article was based on an earlier meeting between Wilson and Orlando whose results 'had not been satisfactory to the Italian Minister'.[6] This might have been a false alarm, but leaks to the Press were to cause much trouble and annoyance.

It was partly concern about security which led Sir Maurice Hankey, the Secretary of the British delegation, to write to the Secretary General of the Conference, Dutasta, on 19 January, asking him to try to keep down the number of advisers and secretaries attending meetings of the Council of Ten. Each Power's delegates should confine themselves to two assistants in order to ensure 'secrecy and entire freedom of discussion', and the British delegation would at once apply this self-denying ordinance to themselves.[7] Two days later the Canadian Prime Minister, Sir Robert Borden, wrote to Lloyd George expressing anxiety, even at this early stage, at the delay involved in the Conference's work and also at the possibility that the Council of Ten might settle major issues which ought to be decided by the Conference as a whole.[8] The confused and vast organisation of the Conference, in which even an important delegate could soon lose any sense of effectiveness, gave rise to personal tensions and squabbles.

Everyone wanted to be in on the act. Nicolson describes Colonel T. E. Lawrence, Lawrence of Arabia, who had no official position at the Conference but was concerned about the decisions the Conference might make about the Arab world, who 'the while would glide along the corridors of the Majestic,* the lines of resentment hardening around his lips: an undergraduate with a chin'.[9] Memoranda were received from all sorts of bodies, ranging from the Federation of British Industries, urging that the whole cost of the war should be claimed from the enemy,[10] to the Order of the Golden

* The hotel which served as the headquarters of the British Delegation.

Fleece, which wished the Conference to compel the Austrians to return its treasures, which had been taken to Vienna (a request the Order made wherever the frontiers of Europe were re-drawn).[11] The attempts of outsiders to influence the Conference were to be important, especially in the case of Reparations.

At this point it will be necessary to depart from a strictly chronological account of the Conference, and consider in turn negotiations relating to particular subjects. In what follows, we shall consider the chief preoccupations of the Conference between late January and the end of February, and the progress made in resolving disputes and solving problems between the second and third Plenary sessions.

### THE LEAGUE OF NATIONS

The Commission set up under the Chairmanship of President Wilson to prepare the Covenant of the League of Nations met for the first time on 3 February, and at this meeting, President Wilson, Leoén Bourgeois and Vittorio Orlando each laid a draft Covenant before the meeting. The American draft, prepared by members of the Commission to Negotiate Peace, was the most complete; at last the Americans were getting down to detailed preparations and studies. The drafts reflect differences in attitude between the major Allied Powers. Wilson's draft began by simply defining the organisation of the League: an Assembly of all member nations; an elected Council to serve as the supreme executive body when the Assembly was not sitting; and a permanent secretariat. Bourgeois' draft began by setting out the purpose of the new organisation: to protect the world from aggression and to 'establish the reign of justice on sure foundations throughout the world'. The French went on to say that while the League should not become a new international State, 'it shall . . . aim at the maintenance of peace by substituting Right for Might as the arbiter of disputes'. Such an objective was important to the French, fearful as they were of neighbouring Germany, with a larger population and certain, so Frenchmen believed, to develop fresh designs of conquest sooner or later. The Italian draft opened in much the same vein.

When it came to the method of guaranteeing mutual protection the Americans urged disarmament 'to the lowest point consistent with domestic safety and the enforcement by common action of international obligations', and an agreement to apply to transgressors sanctions, beginning with withdrawal of recognition and escalating to economic and ultimately military sanctions. The French, of course, wished to go further. Either the League should have at its disposal an international military force, or one Power should be given a mandate to enforce sanctions when these were demanded by the League – 'The International Body shall have at its disposal a military force supplied by the various member States', of sufficient strength to overcome any transgressor's forces. The Italians did not go so far. The American draft was more complete, covering as it did mandates, freedom of trade, supervision of the arms trade, and other subjects, and it was agreed that the Commission should take this draft as a basis for discussion.[12] The following day the Commission began considering it article by article.

The first dispute arose over the composition of the Council, the supreme body under the authority of the Assembly. The proposal in the draft was that this should consist only of the Great Powers, that it should, in effect, be a continuation of the Supreme War Council and the Council of Ten, and that representatives of other states should be invited to attend when matters concerning them were discussed. A Brazilian delegate said that if the permanent governing body of the League were to consist only of representatives of the Great Powers, 'the Council would be . . . not an organ of the League of Nations, but an organ of Five Nations, a kind of tribunal to which everyone would be subject'. He was supported by other representatives of small states – Hymans of Belgium, Vesnitch of Serbia, Wellington Koo of China, and Reis of Portugal. He was also supported by Orlando and Bourgeois, for the French and the Italians believed that their interest lay in supporting the small states against the Anglo-Saxon Great Powers, since the small states were more determined to take a harsh line with Germany than Britain and America, and would be valuable allies in the Council. Lord Robert Cecil opposed their proposal that all nations should have permanent representation on the Council, but he undertook to prepare a new draft clause on membership of the Council.[13] This was presented next day, proposing that the Council should include a number of representatives of the smaller Powers, to be chosen by election. They could not agree, however, on how many such representatives there should be, so the Commission accepted the idea in principle, while holding over until a later meeting a decision on the number of representatives.[14]

At this meeting, another major problem was raised for the first time, namely the method by which new members should be admitted, and the criteria which they would be required to satisfy. This was seen by many delegates as a crucial matter, as it involved the question of whether, and if so when, Germany was to be admitted to the League. The American draft Article on admission, Article 6, proposed that States desiring membership but who were not admitted at the beginning, should be admitted if the Assembly voted in favour of this by a two-thirds majority. Applicants must conform with the disarmament requirements imposed by the League.[15] At once, amendments were proposed. Wilson wanted to restrict admission to democratic states, while Bourgeois wanted admission to be by unanimous vote of the Assembly:

> There should be no doubt left as to the character of the new member. That member should be without reproach. However important it may be to introduce the condition of self-government,* the moral test is the true and final test, and unanimity should be the measure.[16]

Wilson was unhappy about the problem of defining democratic self-government, referring particularly to Germany: 'Regardless of how it appeared on paper, no one would have looked at the German government before the war and said that the nation was self-governing. We know that in point of fact the Reichstag was appointed by the Chancellor, that it was an absolute monarchy.'[17] Wilson did not want to admit Germany until he was sure she had reformed. Bourgeois also wanted to use admission to the League as a means of guaranteeing the payment of reparations and of future peaceful intentions on Germany's part:

> I am strongly in favour of including a reference to 'those who have reparations to make'. And those violators of law who have acted like Germany ought also to be specifically provided for. They cannot be admitted on a par, or under a blanket provision covering all states.[18]

All were agreed that for a time, and on certain terms, the League should be an anti-German combination, particularly concerned to ensure that Germany would not misbehave once more. The diverg-

* By this term delegates meant democratic government rather than national independence.

ence was on the length of Germany's exclusion and the terms of her admission. Lord Robert Cecil proposed an addition to the clause saying that the Assembly might also, by two-thirds majority, 'impose on any State seeking admission such conditions as it may think fit'.[19] That President Wilson was fully in agreement with the general feeling that Germany should be excluded for the time being was apparent when, at a later meeting of the Commission, he declared of the period of reconstruction after the war that 'Germany will not be a member of the League during this period'.[20] Wilson disliked the Germans as much as everyone else.

At its next meeting, the Commission began to consider the role the League should play in the settlement of international disputes. The parties to the Covenant were to be bound to 'respect and preserve against all aggression the States members of the League'. At President Wilson's instigation, an amendment was accepted giving the Council of the League power to control plans to resist any such aggression. They then considered disarmament, and Bourgeois objected to a clause aimed at abolishing conscription in member States, for compulsory military service was, he claimed, 'a corollary of universal suffrage', and so this clause was deleted. It was also agreed at this meeting that if arbitration in an international dispute failed, the parties should be obliged to wait three months before taking further action.[21]

At the Commission's fifth meeting, on the evening of 7 February, there was further discussion on methods of arbitration, at which Bourgeois urged that decisions in such cases should be by majority vote. This was opposed by Wilson and Cecil, and a sub-committee was set up to consider the matter.[22] At this stage, the Commission's work was proceeding smoothly, and there had been no major disagreements. A Covenant seemed to be evolving without serious difficulty. Lord Robert Cecil wrote to Lloyd George on 7 February telling him that the Commission was making 'continuous and excellent' progress and that the result of its labours should be 'a real and commonsense scheme' for a League of Nations.[23]

The next day, however, the Commission had to consider the vexed question of mandates. Not only had the problem of the disagreement between Wilson and the Dominions to be faced – this had been resolved in principle but there was much doubt about the details* –

* See pp. 72-9 above.

but other countries, notably France, Italy and Japan, were hoping for a share in the colonial spoils of their victory. General Smuts presented a draft listing the areas in which the League would give mandates over the former German and Turkish empires. Orlando and Bourgeois did not want the application of the principle too closely defined and Bourgeois urged that it would be better 'to lay down principles without entering into too great detail'. The French and Italians did not want to lose the chance of bargaining over mandates too early in the Conference.[24] Two days later, they discussed freedom of trade and agreed that Germany must not be allowed to take advantage of the bad industrial condition of France and Belgium by dumping her goods on their markets.[25] The following day the question of the enforcement of sanctions was raised. For the French this was perhaps the most vital matter of all, apart, possibly, from securing the exclusion of Germany from the League, and Bourgeois proposed the creation of an international force under the Council, to be used for this purpose. He appealed especially to Wilson, and asked in addition that demands for a nation's disarmament should be related to the danger in which she found herself:

> President Wilson clearly recognised this necessity when, speaking from the platform of the Chamber of Deputies, he pronounced those splendid words, for which I here thank him: 'The frontier of France is the frontier of the world's liberty'.[26]

President Wilson admitted the justice of this demand, but said that he could not agree to the establishment of an international force under the League, despite his sympathy for France:

> I know how France has suffered, and I know that she wishes to obtain the best guarantees possible before she enters the League, and everything that we can do in this direction we shall do, but we cannot accept proposals which are in direct contradiction to our Constitution.[27]

The United States Constitution places the power of declaring war and making peace with Congress, and if the Covenant contained any provision which might limit their freedom of action in these matters, the Senate would never ratify the Treaty. Americans would not risk having their armies sent to fight in far-away places at the behest of the League. If France was to be safe, they must make certain that Germany was effectively disarmed, and this would be done elsewhere in the Treaty. Above all, if France were attacked, help would be forthcoming: Wilson said that

> It must not be supposed that any of the members of the League will remain isolated if it is attacked, that is the direct contrary of the thought of all of us. We are ready to fly to the assistance of those who are attacked, but we cannot offer more than the condition of the world enables us to give.[28]

Wilson was facing up to the realities of American politics, and was trying to get his colleagues on the Commission to do the same, but Bourgeois would not be satisfied. He asked for the inclusion in the Covenant of 'something that will give to public opinion the feeling of safety which it demands'.[29] The clause was referred to the Drafting Committee of experts which was preparing the Covenant for further consideration. At this point, the Commission had worked through the entire draft once, and at the next two meetings it went through it again, before it was presented to a plenary session for debate.

At the Commission's ninth meeting, on 13 February, a French representative, Larnaude, tried to get an affirmation of German war guilt written into the Covenant, but this was rejected as inappropriate in 'a work of union and concord between peoples', as Reis, the Portuguese representative, put it.[30] Membership of the Council was defined as the five Great Powers and four representatives of the smaller Powers, after which there was another discussion of the problem of Germany's position. Bourgeois reiterated France's determination to keep her out: 'There is no question of opening the doors of the League of Nations to those who are not worthy to come in', though states which had been neutral in the war would be invited to join. This view was generally accepted.[31] Next day, the problem of disarmament was raised again; Wilson was absent from this meeting, and Lord Robert Cecil was in the Chair. Larnaude urged that the Covenant should contain a clause obliging members to open their arms establishments to international inspection. He was supported by Bourgeois, and by Kramarsch, the Czechoslovak representative, who said that 'although the Allies trusted one another it was important to establish guarantees against Germany and to create a special control for her'.[32] The French also tried once more to have the League set up a permanent military Commission, but Cecil opposed him, as the League must not be seen as an alliance against Germany: 'nothing would more quickly imperil peace'.[33] Both these proposals were rejected. Baron Makino of Japan wanted a guarantee of racial equality written into the Covenant, but Colonel House, present in Wilson's place, said that he could not accept such a proposal in Wilson's absence, and the question was reserved for future discussion. The remaining articles of the Covenant were read without discussion and the document was now to be put to a plenary session for discussion, although no vote was to be taken.

The plenary session was held on 14 February, and President Wilson introduced the Commission's Report and the draft Covenant, saying that it was 'a definite guarantee of peace . . . a definite guarantee by word against aggression . . . a definite guarantee against the things which have just come near bringing the whole structure of civilisation into ruin'.[34] In his peroration, he made plain his view of the war and the moral which must be drawn from it:

> Many terrible things have come out of this war, Gentlemen, but some very beautiful things have come out of it. Wrong has been defeated, but the rest of the world has become more conscious than it ever was of the majesty of Right.[35]

Bourgeois warned that as far as France was concerned the task was not yet finished:

> Special dangers exist for certain countries, for France, for Belgium, for Serbia, and for the States which have just been created or reconstituted in Central Europe.[36]

The Commission had recognised this fact and would look again at means of providing these countries with effective protection. This, perhaps, summarises the nature of the work of the League of Nations Commission up to the time of the third plenary session of the Conference. The Commission had reached unanimous agreement on a draft Covenant, but only by avoiding the most contentious issues, either by deferring a decision until later, or by referring them to the Drafting Committee, which amounted to the same thing. No immediate final decisions were necessary yet on these matters, and when the time came, some of them would prove to be so difficult that only the Supreme Council would be able to solve them. However, the Covenant of the League of Nations had been conceived, even if it was by no means completely formed.

RUSSIA

The issue of the invitation to the warring parties in Russia to call a truce and meet the Allies at Prinkipo to discuss a settlement had to some extent shelved the problem so far as the Peace Conference was concerned. It continued to worry many people, both in Paris and elsewhere. In Britain, Winston Churchill, the Secretary of State for War, continued to press for decision and action, and on 27 January he wrote two letters to Lloyd George which indicate his attitude to the continuing Civil War. In the first, he expressed alarm at the situation of British forces operating in Russia, in view of the lack of a firm policy decision as to our ultimate course of action; British troops had great influence, especially in Siberia because

> they are thought to be the vanguard of Britain. They are nothing of the sort. Individual officers and soldiers are keeping large towns and districts up to duty against the Bolshevists by giving the impression that 'Britain is behind them'; whereas long ago Britain has quitted the field.
>
> We are at the moment heavily and indefinitely committed in all sorts of directions, and we have, as far as I can see, not the least intention of making good in any of them.[37]

Churchill would have liked to crush the Bolsheviks, but he realised that to embark upon a major war in Russia was a political impossibility, for the British people, and especially the working class and the Labour Party, would not for a moment accept this. He did not wish to evacuate all British troops from Russia, however. This 'is a policy; it is not a very pleasant one from the point of view of history',[38] so he urged that limited assistance, including volunteers, be given to the 'White' forces. The second letter was a reply to Lloyd George's letter of 15 January expressing alarm at Churchill's desire to maintain a large conscript army after the war,* pointing out that post-war commitments would necessitate the continuation of conscription: 'I hope you will not allow the vague fears expressed in the note you have just sent me to paralyse necessary action', and he goes on:

> The question raised by Bonar Law is whether we should boldly and frankly face this situation, proclaim it to the nation and ask

* See p. 64 above.

> Parliament to support us from the outset; or whether we should live from hand to mouth and from month to month as if we were nursing a guilty secret in the hopes of something turning up to save us the exposure.[39]

Churchill, the man of action, wanted quick decisions and the chance to exercise firm leadership. Lloyd George, however, did not trust him, for he feared that if Churchill were given his head he might embark on a crusade against Bolshevism, with in all probability disastrous results, in both political and military terms.

On 1 February the Council of Ten met to discuss a new development. Chicherin, the Soviet Commissar for Foreign Affairs, had requested that his Government should be sent an official invitation to the Prinkipo meeting. President Wilson was dubious about acceding to this request, since to do so might imply Allied recognition of the Soviet Government, which he did not wish to grant. Lloyd George agreed, and 'expressed the view that M. Chicherin had received his notice like everyone else'.[40] The matter was left undecided and no official invitation was sent.

Back in London, Churchill was becoming restive. In mid-February Lloyd George returned to London to attend to essential Government business, and on 13 February he presided at a meeting of his Cabinet at which the Russian problem was discussed. After Lord Curzon had pointed out that, although we had not actually recognised Admiral Kolchak's Government in Siberia, we had sent 'very friendly messages', Churchill urged that the only way to defeat Bolshevism was to use the 'White' forces, and if they were to be effective, they must be helped by the transport of General Haller's Polish army in France to Poland, which the Germans were still obstructing, and by aid to the 'Whites'. 'He was unable to vouch for their troops or plans, but unless a definite policy were materialized there was no use going on.' If help were not sent, 'we should have a succession of disasters, followed by wholesale massacres and the extermination one way or another of the whole of the people who had been supporting us'. So either withdraw now and tell these people to make the best peace they could with the Bolsheviks, or resolve to support them. Lloyd George wanted a clear military assessment before a decision was taken, and Churchill agreed that this should be done, but he pointed out that once the limit of assistance to the 'Whites' was decided, there must be a 'wholehearted effort within the limits described'. But he would ask the General Staff to assess the chances of success. For himself, however, his view was clear:

> Unless we were able to go to the support of the Russians there was a possibility of a great combination from Yokohama to Cologne in hostility to France, Britain and America. He regarded a friendly government in Russia and a strong Poland as the two essentials.[41]

Either a Bolshevik Germany, or a German Government nursing its humiliation and seeking revenge for Germany's defeat, might join hands with the Bolsheviks to overrun Europe. Russia's friendship with the Allies must, therefore, be guaranteed, and this could be done only if the Bolsheviks were defeated. The following day Churchill circulated a memorandum to the Cabinet in which he asked the Chief of the Imperial General Staff whether success might be possible by the Summer or Autumn of 1919.[42] Churchill's statements at the Cabinet meeting aroused anxiety among other Ministers. E. S. Montagu, the Secretary of State for India, warned his colleagues that 'the War Office really do not intend merely to send munitions and money. The Secretary of State for War yesterday made that quite clear'; volunteers would be sent as well. This must involve the use of scarce money and manpower, and also there was a risk of Bolshevism at home if we try to fight it in Russia – 'If we fight the Russian Bolshevists we are allies of our own Bolshevists.'[43] Churchill's views were causing alarm and dissension among his Cabinet colleagues.

Meanwhile, Churchill had been sent to Paris to explain the Cabinet's view to the Council of Ten. On 14 February, he told the Council that the Cabinet were anxious to have a decision: 'Great Britain had soldiers in Russia who were being killed in action. Their families wished to know what purpose these men were serving.'[44] Clemenceau tried to resist a quick decision, but Wilson felt that the Bolsheviks were equivocating over Prinkipo, since their initial answer 'was not only uncalled for, but might be thought insulting'.[45] Churchill then stated his opposition to ending intervention:

> There would be no further armed resistance to the Bolsheviks in Russia, and an interminable vista of violence and misery was all that remained for the whole of Russia.[46]

He was supported by Baron Sonnino, but the general feeling of the

Council was that no decision could be taken until the result of the Prinkipo initiative became apparent.

The following day the Council met again. This time Wilson, as well as Lloyd George, was absent, and Churchill was invited to attend once more. Military sources reported Red Army advances on nearly all fronts, and Churchill once more intervened to urge the Allies into speedy action. He said that

> everyone present knew the reason which had led the Conference to adopt the policy of Prinkipo. Since then a month had passed and no decision which made any effect on the forces of the Allies had yet been reached. On the other hand . . . very disastrous events had been taking place in Russia during that period. In his opinion it was essential to try and bring the faction war in Russia to an end, and Great Britain adhered entirely to the position previously taken up. But if Prinkipo was not going to come to anything, the sooner it was got out of the way, the better. At the present moment all military action was paralysed by suspense, and there was a very grave danger that as a result, the Allied and friendly armies would gradually melt away.[47]

He therefore proposed that the Bolsheviks be given ten days to call a truce and agree to the meeting, and to reply in these terms within five, and also that the Allies and 'White' forces in Russia should establish a unified military command. It was necessary to be ready for war and decide on a policy.

The American representative, the Secretary of State, Robert Lansing, accepted Churchill's proposed message to the Bolsheviks but was opposed to his proposal for a united command. Clemenceau pointed out that he had opposed the Prinkipo policy, and had only accepted it 'to avoid the introduction of elements of discord into the Conference'. The policy 'had not been a great success either in Europe or elsewhere. . . . He thought that [the Conference] should get out of its troubles as discreetly and as simply as possible.'[48] An immediate decision should therefore be taken on military policy in Russia, whether or not Churchill's message was sent. Balfour supported sending the message, while Clemenceau and Orlando both urged that the Prinkipo initiative should be dropped at once. Churchill, however, said that the Cabinet could not accept this unless one further attempt were made; in this he was probably reflecting the Cabinet's collective view rather than following his own inclinations. The matter was adjourned for two days, and there is no trace in subsequent minutes of any decision being taken. Such was the perplexity of the Conference when faced with the question of what to do about Russia.

Back in London, information lending support to the policy of supporting the 'White' forces became available to Ministers at this time. The Chief of the Imperial General Staff circulated a memorandum recommending such support.[49] and the Political Intelligence Department of the Foreign Office issued a report that the Bolshevik Government was split and most Russians would turn against them if they were given the chance.[50] After his discussions with the Council of Ten in Paris, Churchill sent a telegram to Lloyd George reporting that Wilson was ready to assist in doing whatever the Allies considered 'necessary and practicable' to support the 'Whites' and urging the sending of his proposed message to the Bolsheviks and the creation of an Allied Command on Russian Affairs to permit unified political and military direction. As to Prinkipo, 'it was evident that everyone felt very strongly that a perfectly fair and reasonable breaking-off point had been reached', as the Bolsheviks were attacking on all fronts and 15 February had originally been named as the day when the Russian delegations should arrive at Prinkipo. Finally, he attempted to allay Lloyd George's suspicions of him by saying, 'Note please that I have made it perfectly clear throughout that we can in no circumstances send men by compulsion to Russia'.[51] Churchill had been careful not to stray too far from his Cabinet brief.

The following day, however, Lloyd George in his reply made it clear both that he distrusted Churchill and that he was opposed to his policy. 'Am very alarmed at your second telegram about planning war against the Bolshevists. The Cabinet have never authorised such a proposal.' The future destiny of Russia was a matter for Russians, not the Allies:

> If Russia is really anti-Bolshevik, then a supply of equipment would enable it to redeem itself. If Russia is pro-Bolshevik, not merely is it none of our business to interfere with its internal affairs; it would be positively mischievous: it would strengthen and consolidate Bolshevik opinion.

There was also the risk of Bolshevism at home: 'if we are committed to a war against a continent like Russia it is the direct road to bankruptcy and Bolshevism in these islands'. After a warning that 'The French are not safe guides in this matter. . . . There is nothing they would like better than to see us pull the chestnuts out of the fire for them', Lloyd George returned to this point:

> Were it known that you had gone over to Paris to prepare a plan of war against the Bolsheviks it would do more to increase organised labour than anything I can think of; and what is still worse it would throw into the arms of the extremists a very large number of thinking people who now abhor their methods.[52]

Lloyd George was still anxious about the possibility of a Bolshevik uprising in Britain. That same day Balfour advised Churchill that he would be reluctant to see Britain take the lead in bringing the Prinkipo initiative to an end.[53] Faced with this strong stand by Lloyd George, Churchill felt that it would be politic to moderate his demands, and on 17 February wrote reassuring him that all he was asking for was that the Allied military authorities should assess the possibilities for intervention. 'When military authorities have sifted and weighed all the available information we shall have their recommendation as to whether there is or is not a reason of military hope.'[54] There was no point in pressing for all-out war if the Prime Minister were adamantly opposed to this policy. When the British Empire Delegation met to discuss policy in Russia on 17 February, under Balfour's chairmanship, it agreed only to press for such an investigation as Churchill suggested in this last letter.[55]

The problem of what was to be done about Prinkipo was soon to solve itself. The Bolsheviks had made some gesture towards accepting it on 4 February, but President Wilson had described the terms of their reply as 'an insult'.* On 20 February, a message was received by the Foreign Office from Admiral Kolchak rejecting the proposal. The Omsk Government

> entertained no doubt as to the entire unacceptability of this proposal. The Government immediately rejected any possibility of an agreement with the Bolsheviks, as well as any negotiations with them. . . .[56]

while Zinoviev made a speech to the Petrograd Soviet attacking both the Peace Conference in general and the Prinkipo initiative in parti-

* See p. 93 above.

cular as a bourgeois fraud, and urging the Red Army to fight on.[57] Neither side was prepared to accept the proposal, and at the end of all the argument about Prinkipo and intervention, the Allies were left with neither peace nor a policy, as far as Russia was concerned. Churchill's mind remained made up. On 25 February Colonel Repington noted in his diary that 'I have met Winston twice at dinner lately. . . . He is very anti-Bolshevik and is for strong measure against them.'[58] But Lloyd George was equally strongly opposed to such measures.

EASTERN EUROPE

During late January and February, much of the Council of Ten's time was occupied with hearing territorial claims by the smaller States. Among the most difficult and contentious issues of this kind were the frontiers of the new States of Eastern Europe, especially Poland, Czechoslovakia, and Yugoslavia. The procedure adopted by the Council was first to hear the delegates of each country present their case, to discuss its broad outlines, and then to refer to it a committee of experts for detailed examination and the preparation of a proposal for a frontier. The first delegation to be heard by the Council of Ten were the Poles. The activities of the Poles were arousing anxiety among the Allies,* for they were attacking the Germans and the Ukrainians in order to seize territory which was not rightfully theirs and whose fate ought to be decided by the Peace Conference and not by armed force. At their meeting of 29 January, at which the Polish case was to be presented, the Council decided to instruct Allied delegates in Poland to warn the Polish Government against 'adopting a policy of an aggressive character. Any appearance of attempting to prejudice the decisions of the Conference will have the worst possible effect.' They warned further that 'the invasion by the Poles of German territory tends to restore the German military spirit and to delay the break-up of the German army', and asked that the Poles should confine their military activity to preserving internal order and protecting their existing territory from attack.[59]

After this point had been settled, the Polish Foreign Minister, Dmowski, was invited to enter the room and present his case. He began by talking about the danger Poland faced from Germany. She

* See pp. 69–72 above.

needed supplies which could only be brought in along the Danzig–Thorn railway, which should be occupied. In German Poland there were perhaps five million Poles, 'some of the most educated and highly cultured of the nation, with a strong sense of nationality and men of progressive ideas', who had set up an independent Polish Government despite German attempts to crush them.[60] The danger from Germany was great:

> He compared Germany to the god Janus. Germany had one face towards the West, where she had made peace, and the other face towards the East, where she was organising for war. . . . She might have given up the West, but she had not given up her plan for extending her empire to the East.[61]

Firm action and a secure frontier were therefore necessary for Poland's safety. Turning to Russian Poland, he spoke of danger from the Bolsheviks and from 'Ukrainian bands'.[62] Poland was in great danger, and needed help.

Dmowski then turned to the question of territorial claims, asking that Poland should be restored to her position before the first Partition in 1772, with, in addition, the whole of Silesia, part of which had not been Polish since the fourteenth century. His justification for this was that

> the whole territory of Eastern Germany was not naturally German but was Germanised and quoted von Bülow as saying that what Germany had lost in the West as a result of the break-up of the Empire of Charlemagne, she had gained in the East. He quoted Danzig as an illustration. . . . As the Poles [in Danzig] were mostly employees, they would be afraid of stating that their nationality was Polish for fear of being dismissed.[63]

Vast tracts of naturally Polish territory had suffered from German colonisation and domination, with the result that its Polish allegiance had been suppressed. There was much more in this vein, and indeed the Council of Ten spent all day listening to Dmowski and his colleagues rehearsing the greedy and evil actions of Germans down the centuries. Towards the end, he touched on the subject of Eastern Galicia, acknowledging that its attribution was a disputed point, but pointing out, somewhat strangely, that in the intellectual professions, excluding small farmers and clergy, there were 400,000 Poles and only 16,000 Ruthenes.

From this he drew the conclusion that the Ruthenes were too ignorant and unorganised to form a Government. 'They might be entitled to Home Rule, but they were unable to create a separate State.'[64] At the end of this marathon speech, there was no time for discussion, except for Balfour to remark that the problems of help to Poland to resist German and Bolshevik aggression, and of her future delineation, were separate, and must be dealt with separately.

The next new nation to be heard was Czechoslovakia, on 5 February. Her case was presented by Beneš. The atmosphere he sought to create was very different from that of fear, anxiety, and desire for extensive territory established a week earlier by Dmowski. He began by stressing Czechoslovakia's close ties with the Allies, and her support of their ideals. 'The Nation had plunged into the struggle without asking for any guarantees or weighing the probabilities of success. All the Nation wanted was to control its own destinies. The Nation felt itself to be a European Nation and a member of the Society of the Western States', and she accepted the Allies' principles.[65] Notwithstanding all this, however, she must protect herself against the Germans:

> The Germanic mass, now numbering some 80 millions, could not push westwards as its road was blocked on that side by highly developed nations. It was, therefore, always seeking outlets to the South and to the East. In this movement it found the Poles and the Czechs in its path. Hence the special importance of the Czecho-Slovak frontiers in Central Europe. It might be hoped that the Germans would not again attempt forcible invasions, but they had done so in the past so often that the Czechs had always felt that they had a special mission to resist the Teutonic flood.[66]

For this reason, Czechoslovakia must have a secure frontier between herself and Germany, and the only way to achieve this was to draw the frontier through the Bohemian mountain chain, enclosing within the new state an area with a majority of German inhabitants.

This problem had arisen because this fringe area had contained most of the industrial areas of the Austro-Hungarian Empire, and this industry had, of course, been controlled by Germans. Beneš claimed that the German population had been deliberately exaggerated by the Austrian authorities, and in any case the industry was vital to Czechoslovakia's survival, for 'without the peripheral areas, Bohemia could not live'.[67] In any case, the Bohemian Germans would, he believed, accept incorporation in Czechoslovakia.

> The Bohemian Germans fully understood their position. Whether they were bourgeois, worksmen or peasants, they all realised that they must remain in Bohemia. They said freely in their Chambers of Commerce that they would be ruined if they were enclosed in Germany. The competition of the great German industries was such that they could not possibly survive.[68]

There were good economic justifications for including the peripheral area, known to Germans as the Sudetenland, in Czechoslovakia, despite the German race of the majority of inhabitants.

Beneš' statement was very different from Dmowski's. He did not stress the strategic argument for Czechoslovakia's claim, realising that such arguments would be countered by reference to the Fourteen Points, the right of the self-determination of peoples and the promise that frontiers would be drawn according to the nationality of the population contained in President Wilson's speeches. He founded his case on economic arguments, some of which would, he argued, induce the people of the area in question voluntarily to accept inclusion in Czechoslovakia. Nonetheless, Lloyd George was doubtful as to whether the claim should be admitted, as can be seen from an exchange between Beneš and the British Prime Minister which occurred after Beneš had finished his statement:

> MR LLOYD GEORGE asked whether the area in question had been represented in the Reichsrat* by German deputies.
> M. BENEŠ replied in the affirmative, and explained that the voting areas were so contrived as to give the Germans a majority. Nevertheless, in two such districts, the Czechs had put up candidates of their own who obtained substantial majorities in their favour.
> MR LLOYD GEORGE enquired whether the inhabitants of these districts, if offered the choice, would vote for exclusion from the Czechoslovakian State or for inclusion.
> M. BENEŠ replied that they would vote for exclusion, chiefly through the influence of the Social-Democratic Party, which thought the Germans would henceforth have a Social-Democratic

* The Parliament of the Austro-Hungarian Empire.

> regime. . . . It would be for reasons of this kind, and for nationalistic reasons, rather than for economic reasons, that the German Bohemians would be likely to adhere to their fellow-countrymen outside Bohemia.[69]

Beneš thought reason should prevail over nationalism or socialism, but Lloyd George was doubtful. After a discussion of other matters, notably a dispute between Czechoslovakia and Poland over the Teschen area, which lay between them – a dispute which had brought the two countries close to war – the Council of Ten agreed to refer the claims Beneš had made to a Committee consisting of two representatives each from the American, British, French and Italian delegations.[70] This problem was thus shelved for the time being.

Poland, however, was a continuing worry for the Supreme Council. On 7 February Clemenceau raised the question of German activities in Poland, where they were pursuing an aggressive policy contrary to the terms of the Armistice:

> He knew the German people well. They became ferocious when anyone retires before them. Was it forgotten that they were still at war; that the Armistice was a status of war? The Germans had not forgotten it.[71]

This outburst was typical of Clemenceau's attitude to the Germans: fear them, never trust them, insure oneself against their aggression and their perfidy. Foch had reported in a Note to the Council that the Germans had refused to cease fighting the Poles:

> The President of the German Commission immediately asserted the absolute right of the German Government to ensure the protection of their subjects within their own territory. He added that present events necessitated a rapid intervention so as to re-establish order in view of the assassination of German subjects and of pogroms against the Jews.[72]

Such arguments could not, in Clemenceau's view, be allowed to prevail:

> The Allies were exposed to great dangers unless they menaced the Germans now. There was need of a strong Poland. Furthermore, President Wilson had, as one of his Fourteen Points, assumed the obligation of reconstituting Poland. The League of Nations was a very fine conception, but it could not be constituted without

> nations. As one of the nations concerned, Poland was most necessary as a buffer on the East, just as France formed a buffer on the West.[73]

It must always be possible to threaten Germany with a war on two fronts, and in order to stop the German attacks in Poland, the Allies should threaten to renew the war in the West. 'A state of war still existed, and any appearance of yielding would be construed as an evidence of weakness.'[74] Firmness was essential, and only force would compel the Germans to behave.

No decision was reached at this meeting, but the next day Clemenceau raised the matter again, urging that as one of the terms for the renewal of the Armistice which was due to expire on 16 February, Germany should be ordered to stop fighting the Poles. President Wilson agreed, and in the absence of Lloyd George, no British delegate opposed Clemenceau's suggestion, which was adopted.[75] The Allies' resolve to enforce this condition was strengthened by reports that the Germans had signed an anti-Polish agreement with the Ukrainian Directory,[76] and was being obstinate in her insistence on being allowed to defend her citizens.[77] When the Armistice was renewed, however, the Germans accepted an obligation to cease all hostilities against the Poles.[78] Meanwhile, a Committee of experts from the chief Allied Powers was appointed to consider the Polish territorial claims which had been put to the Supreme Council by Dmowski.*[79] The frontier problem was now shelved for the moment.

This did not bring agitation in this area to an end, or allay anxiety about the progress of the negotiations, however. On 16 February the Political Intelligence Department of the British Foreign Office reported increasing irritation in France at Clemenceau's apparent subservience to Britain and America. Clemenceau regarded the continuance of the wartime Alliance as of paramount importance,[80] and had therefore accepted the League from Wilson and the British view on mandates in order to ensure lasting unity and friendship. The Political Intelligence Department's report goes on:

> Perhaps . . . he has still further irritated the impatience of Frenchmen less well-informed and less clear-sighted than himself . . . they wonder why M. Clemenceau, who is President of the Con-

* See pp. 98-9 above.

> ference, whom they know to be a strong man, and whom they expected somehow to make France lead the Conference, has allowed himself to be so much overshadowed by President Wilson and Mr Lloyd George.[81]

Clemenceau was facing political difficulties, and with the experts settling down to their labours he was unlikely to be able to offer his countrymen any reassurances for some time, although he had been firm in insisting on checking German activities in Poland.

Meanwhile, both the Germans and the Poles complained of aggression by the other. On 15 February Paderewski complained of German aggression,[82] and two days later the Council of Ten considered a memorandum submitted by Erzberger, a member of the German Government, which asserted that

> It is not we who are the aggressors, but the Poles who, in Posen, have everywhere assumed the offensive militarily. . . . The objection [to the German actions against the Poles] is rendered untenable by the fact that Polish agitation, especially in Upper Silesia, but also in the provinces of the North, is working in close communion with Bolshevism. The Bolshevist agitators are, almost without exception, Poles. The Poles seem to have the intention of creating a state of general insecurity to have the pretext of intervention for the sake of re-establishing order.[83]

Amid these accusations and counter-accusations, the Council decided that it was impossible to determine who was at fault, and it was decided to order the Poles as well as the Germans to stop fighting at once.[84]

The French, however, were still determined to strengthen Poland as much as possible in order to enable her to act as a check on Germany's assumed Eastern ambitions. On 24 February Marshal Foch appeared before the Council of Ten in order once more to press for an Allied occupation of the Danzig–Thorn railway. Balfour resisted this demand by saying that the Germans had given an assurance of free Allied use of this railway in the Armistice, and that all that was necessary was thus to give effect to this clause. Foch insisted that the only way in which this could be done was to occupy the railway.[85] The following day, Pichon urged the fixing of at least a temporary frontier between Germany and Poland in order to ensure the safety of the Polish troops then in France when they were transported to Poland, and Marshal Foch extended this demand to a request for a quick preliminary peace fixing the German frontier, a solution which would be less troublesome and expensive than occupying the Danzig–Thorn railway. Balfour took strong exception to this attempt to hustle the Conference into making hasty and ill-considered decisions, saying that

> everybody must admit that Marshal Foch had made a speech covering a wide field and of far-reaching importance. On the other hand, the proposition which he (Balfour) had moved yesterday was that the Polish divisions now in France should be sent to Poland: a small and modest suggestion involving no particular question of principle at all. On that narrow foundation Marshal Foch had started out to build a great plan stretching from the Rhine to Vladivostock, which involved the immediate conclusion of the preliminary terms with Germany.[86]

French hastiness was firmly held in check. The German–Polish frontier was referred to a Commission, and all parties, the French and the Poles in particular, would have to possess themselves in patience until it reported, which it was asked to do by 8 March.[87] French pressure for a hasty settlement had been successfully resisted.

## THE RHINELAND

Another issue on which the French were constantly bringing pressure to bear on their colleagues during this period was that of the future status of the German provinces west of the Rhine. In January, Marshal Foch and other French Generals had devoted themselves assiduously to urging that these provinces must be separated from the rest of Germany, and that France, or the Allies, must control the west bank of the Rhine and the bridgeheads, since the river constituted the only natural obstacle to a fresh German invasion of France.* On 19 February, Colonel House reported these views to Wilson, then in America,† saying that Foch was

> strongly in favour of saying to the Germans in the preliminary peace treaty that, whatever may be the fate of the Rhenish provinces and whatever form of government for these provinces the

* See pp. 59–61 above.
† He had returned to America to close Congress.

> Allies may decide in favour of, under no circumstances will the German Empire extend beyond the Rhine. That in his opinion is essential for the security of France, and makes the settlement of the frontier a simple matter.[88]

Such simplicity was not for President Wilson, however. He replied that the French proposal must be resisted 'immoveably' in order to allow for the free self-determination of the people involved.[89] However, House then had a meeting with Clemenceau, at which the French Premier insisted on the creation of a Rhenish republic independent of Germany. He was prepared to excuse the inhabitants any responsibility for reparations or indemnity, and in general he said that 'everything should be done to make them prosperous and contented so that they will not want to join the German Federation and if they have such a desire they will not be permitted to do so'.[90] The French and President Wilson held firm and opposed views on the fate of the Rhenish provinces. Colonel House, although basically in agreement with Wilson, felt some sympathy with the French point of view, for there were, after all, 'practically two Germans to one Frenchman',[91] and he persuaded Tardieu and Balfour to agree to consider the setting up of a temporary Rhenish buffer state, whose inhabitants would be given the chance to decide their fate by a plebiscite after five or ten years,[92] since this way both the French desire for security and Wilson's determination to protect the right of peoples to decide their own fate would be satisfied. Balfour included this proposal for a temporary buffer state in his 'Brief Notes on the Present Conference Situation' prepared on 25 February.[93]

That same day, the French Government sent a Note to Britain asking for support in making their claim to the Rhine frontier. The war of 1914 had only been possible, they said, because of the strength of Germany's position:

> Because of her control of the Rhine bridges and of the offensive positions she had prepared on the left bank of the river, Germany believed herself capable of crushing the Western democracies before help could come from the maritime democracies, Great Britain and the United States.[94]

Once again, the argument that only by controlling the Rhine could France ensure her safety was rehearsed. Germany could not be trusted, despite her new democratic constitution:

THE FOCH-TERRIER.

"I KNOW ALL ABOUT THAT SILLY DOG IN ÆSOP. I'M NOT TAKING ANY CHANCES."

From *Punch*, Vol. 156, p. 203.

> Can we . . . count upon a faithful execution of their engagements when the so-called German democracy . . . has put at its head the men who were the most active agents of imperialism and militarism: Ebert, Scheidemann, David, Erzberger, Brockdorff – Rantzau, not forgetting Hindenburg?[95]

In view of this, Germany could not be trusted sincerely to support the League of Nations, and hence France must have 'a physical guarantee', which could only be an Allied occupation of the Rhine bridgeheads, especially as Germany's population was larger than that of France, and was also growing more rapidly.[96] So the Rhenish provinces must be an independent buffer state under Allied occupation. The French saw this as the equivalent for them in terms of security of the destruction of the German navy for Britain and America.[97] They too had a right to complete security.

This document was discussed by the War Cabinet on 28 February, when Churchill expressed surprise at the French demand for permanent control of the bridgeheads. He felt that while we should show ourselves to be 'as sympathetic as possible' to France, one should seek to moderate their demands 'with a view to the adoption of a merciful policy towards Germany', and he suggested that the French might feel more secure if the Channel Tunnel were built, so enabling British troops to be sent more easily and more quickly to France if she were invaded.

The Prime Minister agreed. He could not commit Britain to sending large numbers of troops to Europe in perpetuity, and in any case, there was the question of what would be most likely to secure the future peace of the world:

> At present he inclined to the view of the Secretary of State for War [Churchill] that we should give France all possible support in respect of her claims and desires in the West, so long as these claims did not leave a legacy of injustice which would rankle as Alsace–Lorraine had rankled.

Here Lloyd George was returning to one of his main themes in his peace aims speech to the Trades Union Congress*, the need above all to ensure that the seeds of future antagonism and war were not sown by the Peace Conference. Lord Curzon wanted the issue settled as part of 'an all-round composition of our outstanding diffi-

* See p. 16 above.

culties with the French', notably Syria. In the main, however, the Cabinet supported the view taken by Lloyd George and Churchill, that the French demand must be treated with caution, and the Foreign Office was to prepare a complete assessment of the French Note for the Prime Minister before he returned to Paris. It was also resolved that it was highly desirable to 'compose all outstanding differences between this country and the French, with a view to securing the complete and harmonious cooperation of their representatives at the Congress'.[98] The Rhineland issue should not be settled between the two Allies in isolation. The one important Minister not at this meeting was Balfour, who was deputising for Lloyd George in Paris. On 2 March he informed Curzon that the French 'strenuously deny that they have any territorial aims in Europe at all' apart from the Rhineland and the Saar. Balfour adds: 'I am inclined to believe this.'[99] Nonetheless, these aims were going to be enough to cause much difficulty. He also referred the Rhenish buffer state proposal to the Foreign Office, saying that the scheme was 'certainly more defensible than the one originally proposed'. French fears were based on doubts about the efficiency of the League or the disarmament of Germany, and the inevitable delay before British and American help could reach France in the event of a German attack. 'Their terrors may be ill-founded, but they are intelligible.'[100] At this point, the British position in relation to the buffer state proposal was uncertain, with Lloyd George tending towards opposition, supported by Churchill, but with other Ministers, such as Balfour and Austen Chamberlain, more inclined to feel that the French fears were reasonable and they had a right to safeguards. The Americans were also divided, with Wilson hostile, House more ready to compromise. At this stage, therefore, the chances of the French getting what they wanted seemed fairly good.

### BELGIUM

Belgium had a special emotional significance for the Conference, and especially for the British. It had been the invasion of Belgium by Germany, in defiance of the Treaty of 1839 whereby all the European Powers had guaranteed Belgian neutrality, that had brought Britain into the war in 1914, and her resistance to the Germans had earned her the famous epithet, 'plucky little Belgium'. Now the problem of her international status would have to be settled afresh.

Of this the Belgians themselves were, of course, conscious, and the question of whether they should remain neutral or join the Western Alliance was arousing controversy among them.[101] On the one hand, a guarantee of neutrality would enable Belgium to resist economic and military pressures from her neighbours and the re-admission of Germany as a guarantor might help her to recover her self-respect and encourage her to forget the wounds of her defeat and the peace. On the other hand, if Germany was likely to remain hostile, Belgium would be safer within the Western Alliance.

That German domination or hostility was not the only possibility which was giving Belgians cause for concern became apparent when Balfour met the Belgian Foreign Minister, Paul Hymans, on 6 February, when the Belgian stressed that although his country wished to develop close relations with France in the future, she did not wish to come under French domination. His chief concern was with the future status of the Grand Duchy of Luxemburg, whose fate was to be decided by the Conference as she was technically an enemy country.* French statesmen had declared that they did not intend to annex Luxemburg, but Hymans claimed that the behaviour of the French troops occupying the Grand Duchy was not consonant with that expressed intention. They were encouraging pro-French sentiments among the people, and therefore hoping to render it more difficult for Belgium to press her claim to the territory.[102] There had previously been tension between France and Belgium over this question, and it would sooner or later have to be resolved at the Conference.

Like the other small Powers, Belgium was allowed to present her statement of claims to the Council of Ten. Her *audition*, as these hearings were officially described, took place on 11 February. Like everyone else who made a statement on behalf of his country to the Council, Hymans began with a rehearsal of the history of his country, and the wrongs she had suffered at German hands. He asked for Belgian control of the Scheld, which belonged to Holland, a neutral country in the war: 'History showed that the naval policy of Holland had always aimed throughout the centuries at the ruin of the port of Antwerp.'[103] He also wanted some territory around Limburg to allow Belgium access to the Rhine, and finally, Belgium should be allowed to annex Luxemburg:

* See p. 59 above.

> Detached from the *Zollverein*, Luxemburg was too small to survive alone, and must lean on one of its neighbours. He would therefore say to the Powers that it was the Belgian solution that was the just one, as it corresponded with past history and rested on national affinities and sympathies.[104]

In reply to a question from Robert Lansing, Hymans said that a plebiscite should not be held in Luxemburg because opinion there was 'uncertain', and

> the present Grand Ducal Government might organise a referendum in favour of the maintenance of a political constitution dangerous to European public order, but a people could not be permitted to neglect its international obligations.[105]

The Belgians could not be sure that a plebiscite, if held, would go their way, so they sought to avoid the holding of one by arguing that annexation by Belgium was in the general interest, especially as France professed not to want Luxemburg. He also claimed the area around Malmédy and Moresnet, saying that 'pro-Belgian manifestations of an undoubted character had recently taken place'.[106] The Belgian claims were small in area, but controversial. During the next few days a Commission was established to examine the Belgian claims, with the exception of Luxemburg.[107]

Luxemburg was clearly going to be a bone of contention between Belgium and France. The Belgians were already suspicious of French intentions. In his 'Brief Notes on the present Conference situation' of 25 February, Balfour warned that the Belgians 'are very sore about this, and are getting more sore', and were 'constantly appealing to me to do something', urging that he should suggest that the Allies favour the link with Belgium. Balfour went on:

> I have not seen my way to doing anything of the kind. A hint from one Power without the full knowledge and assent of the other Powers would do more harm than good.

However, he was inclined to favour Belgium in this matter,[108] but was not prepared to act in a way which would give an unnecessary appearance of treachery to the French.

Balfour's refusal to support Belgium behind France's back did not solve the problem. The Council of Ten felt that as Luxemburg was an enemy country it would not grant her a hearing,[109] thus preventing the Luxemburgers themselves putting their case. On 8 March, Balfour had discussions with Clemenceau, Hymans and others on the subject. Hymans was grateful for British support, and Balfour discussed his complaints with Colonel House. The problem was the activities of French troops and the French propaganda authorities in Luxemburg – 'the consequence was that the Luxemburgois, who quite recognised that the war must inevitably produce some change in their status, were now looking more in the direction of Paris than in the direction of Brussels'. Colonel House agreed to support the Belgians, so they went to see Clemenceau, whom they found to be 'not unsympathetic' to their arguments in favour of Belgium, while asserting that if the Luxemburgers wished to join France, he could not refuse to receive them. He did, however, agree to have the offending troops withdrawn, saying that their commanders were acting without authority in conducting pro-French propaganda, and that Marshal Foch had occupied Luxemburg without orders from above. He also suggested holding a plebiscite, which provoked a strong reaction from Hymans, who

> observed that France had never admitted that it was possible to use a plebiscite to determine the feelings of Alsace–Lorraine, and it was hard to see in what respect Luxemburg stood in a different position.[110]

The Belgians could not be sure of winning, and were determined to obtain their share of the spoils of victory. Clemenceau's promise to have the French troops withdrawn from Luxemburg gave some reassurance, but others were also to be told in the future that French soldiers were acting without authority when they were attempting to further French claims. The rift between France and Belgium was thus somewhat thinly papered over, but the problem was not resolved.

### THE MIDDLE EAST

Since the late nineteenth century, the Middle East and North Africa had been a bone of contention between Britain and France. Their colonial rivalries in this area culminated in the Fashoda incident in 1898, when British and French forces met face to face in the upper reaches of the White Nile, and the French withdrew, after which

British and French spheres of influence were defined.[111] The composition of differences over the Middle East was one of the main achievements of the negotiations which led to the *Entente* of 1904,[112] but the collapse of the Turkish Empire as a result of her defeat in the First World War meant that many vexed questions would have to be reopened, and the problem was made worse by the existence of the Sykes–Picot Agreement,* about which the British became very dubious in 1918 and 1919,† especially because the Allies, and especially the British, had encouraged Arab nationalism in order to weaken Turkey, and the British and French had made a joint declaration in November 1918 promising the Arabs liberation and national self-determination, with only limited influences from the Great Powers.‡ The French still expected this influence to be allotted in accordance with the Sykes–Picot Agreement.

Members of the British Government continued to express doubts about the implementation of this agreement. On 6 February 1919, Lord Robert Cecil wrote to Lloyd George urging that the Conference had no right to impose upon the Arabs a Government they did not want, and that in particular the French should be kept out of Syria and the British should control Palestine.[113] That day the Council of Ten began its consideration of the Middle-Eastern questions by giving a hearing to the Emir Feisal, whom both the British and the French recognised as head of the Arab Government in Damascus.[114] The Emir was heard on 6 February. He requested Arab independence and unity in accordance with Wilson's affirmation of the principle of the self-determination of peoples, and in recognition of the many Arab lives lost during the war. Turning to Britain and France, he said that the Arabs 'were most grateful to England and France for the help given them to free their country. The Arabs now asked them to fulfill their promises of November, 1918.'§[115] The independent Arab state must include Syria, although Palestine could be left aside for the moment. Feisal reaffirmed the Arabs' desire for close links with the West, but they wanted to be free to tell the advanced countries which would be given mandates over them what assistance was required and in answer to a question from Wilson, said that the Arabs should be allowed to say whether there should be one mandatory Power or several. Lloyd George confined himself to questions about the extent of the Arab war effort.

* See p. 8 above.
† See pp. 27 and 57 above.
‡ See pp. 35–6 above.
§ See p. 36 above.

A week later, however, the Council heard a conflicting Arab view, when they gave a hearing to an American resident in the Lebanon, Dr H. S. Bliss. He called the essential unity of the Arabs into question, and asked that an Allied or neutral Commission should be sent out to the Middle East to determine what the opinion of the people was; the people 'are easily frightened and intimidated, even if there is nothing to fear from any source'[116] and hence only an investigation on the spot would be likely to discover their real views. A Syrian delegation was then called in, one of whose members denied that the Arabs wanted unity under Feisal: 'What affinities exist between the native of the Hedjaz and the Syrian, the nomad and the settler on the soil?'[117] An independent Syrian state should be established with the support and help of a foreign power. Any 'sincere and educated Syrian' would accept the need for such help, in order to secure economic development,[118] and the delegation expressed a preference for France. To hold a plebiscite at that time would be impracticable, in view of the chaos and confusion in the country. Thus the Council had heard the view of Feisal, who was hostile to the fulfilment of French ambitions in Syria, and a contrary view from other Syrian representatives. Two days after this, the Council heard Daoud Bey Mammon speak on behalf of the Lebanon, who urged Lebanese autonomy under French protection, adding that Syria would also need French help, while yet another Syrian, Negil Bey Abdel Malek, asked for an integrated Syrian state, including the Lebanon, under French protection.[119] The impression given to the Council was that most Syrians would welcome French supervision, and were hostile to the Emir Feisal, to whom the British, and especially Colonel Lawrence, were committed.

In the meantime, events in Syria were causing Anglo-French relations to deteriorate. In particular the French objected to the activities of the British forces there. Between 23 January and 21 February, the French delivered a series of Notes on this matter to British diplomats and Ministers, complaining that French activity in Syria was being impeded: that 'the object of all the British intrigues, no less than their obvious result, has been to present France with a *fait accompli*',[120] and that British officers there 'were encouraging a local campaign against the French and a future French Syria'.[121] Lord Curzon did not reply until 19 March, when he handed a Note to the French Ambassador in London asserting that the Sykes-Picot agreement was obsolete, and rejecting the French complaints about the activities of British officers and officials in Syria as the product of French officials, who 'find an outlet for their activities in telegraphing home voluminous complaints as to incidents, many of which appear to be quite undeserving of serious consideration, and which in the large majority of cases ought to admit of a local solution'.[122] This was not a background likely to produce trust or amity in the discussion at Paris.

Lord Curzon was finding that the division of British foreign policy decision-making between London and Paris* added to his difficulties in dealing with Cambon. He wrote to Lord Harding in late February that it appeared that a new draft agreement between Britain and France on the Middle East had been drawn up without his knowledge,

> in accordance with an informal arrangement which was believed to have been arrived at between Clemenceau and Lloyd George. The latter had apparently said that Mosul and Palestine were all he wanted. Clemenceau had jumped at this and Pichon had thereupon drawn up another Sykes–Picot agreement conceding this point, but in most other aspects almost as bad as the first. It was only by accident that I first heard of this draft, and only because Montagu† happened to have brought over to England a copy of it in his own pocket. . . . Meanwhile old Cambon and I were talking about the matter in complete ignorance of what was passing at the other end.[123]

No other trace appears to have survived of this informal agreement, and it is not mentioned by Nevakivi,‡ but this letter of Curzon's is indicative of the lack of coordination of policy within the British Government at this time, the result partly of the division of staff and responsibility between London and Paris, but partly also of Lloyd George's habit of carrying on personal negotiations and discussions without informing his colleagues.[124]

On 27 February, the Council of Ten gave a hearing to yet another

* During the negotiations leading up to the signing of the Treaty of Versailles, Lord Curzon, the Lord President of the Council, was left in charge of the Foreign Office in London while Balfour, as Foreign Secretary, was in Paris as a British plenipotentiary and Lloyd George's deputy in the Supreme Council. This state of affairs led to much tension and confusion.

† E. S. Montagu, Secretary of State for India.

‡ See p. 112, n. 114.

party to the problem of the Middle East: the Zionists. They came, said the head of their delegation, Sokolow, to 'claim their historic rights to Palestine, the land of Israel, where, in ancient times, the Jewish people had created a civilisation which had since exercised an enormous influence on humanity'.[125] They requested the creation of a Jewish National Home there, but in answer to a question from Lansing, Dr Chaim Weizmann said that the Jews did not want an autonomous Government, only an administration under a mandatory Power. There were Jews, especially in Russia, who were suffering persecution and needed help, which could only be given by providing them with somewhere to go and live in peace. The problem was possible objections from the Arab inhabitants of Palestine. The Council of Ten was confronted with a rift between Britain and France which threatened at any time to cause an open breach within the Conference, and a number of conflicting pressures from the inhabitants of the area. The Council did nothing for some time, and when a member of the Foreign Office Staff, Robert Vansittart,* suggested in March that the continuance of subsidies being paid to France under wartime arrangements should be traded for concessions in the Middle East, the Prime Minister minuted curtly that he thought 'it would be undesirable to mix up these two questions'.[126] No-one could see a solution, and to make matters worse, the Americans were unwilling to intervene by accepting a mandate in the area.[127] The problem seemed insoluble.

## ITALY AND THE YUGOSLAVS

Italy had aroused much antagonism over her territorial demands before the Conference opened,† and trouble was to be expected from her delegates when the Conference came to consider these demands. The Italian Foreign Minister, Baron Sonnino, was particularly obstinate in his determination to obtain all the territorial cessions promised in the Treaty of London, with the addition of the port of Fiume. Sonnino's obstinacy had provoked a Cabinet crisis in Italy at the end of 1918 when he had clashed with a Cabinet colleague who wished to abandon Italy's claims in Dalmatia in exchange for the cession of Fiume and Istria. A report to the British Cabinet from the

* Later Lord Vansittart.

† See p. 59 above, for example.

Foreign Office described what had occurred: the other Minister, Signor Bissolati,

> had . . . warned Sonnino both against the burden to Italy involved in her presence on the Dalmatian mainland and of the probability of a diplomatic defeat at the Conference, where he would have to encounter the opposition of Wilson and the unwilling support of France and England.[128]

Sonnino had refused to listen, and Bissolati had resigned, provoking a Cabinet crisis and weakening the authority of the Government.

The Italian claims first came before the Council of Ten when they heard a statement from representatives of the new Serbo-Croat-Slovene State, which was to become Yugoslavia, on 18 February. Stressing the principle of the self-determination of peoples, and the sacrifices of the peoples in this area during the war, Vesnitch asked for fair treatment, especially in relation to Italy. He and his colleagues pressed for Fiume and Dalmatia, including the islands in the Adriatic Sea, to be given to the new state.[129] After the Yugoslavs had withdrawn, the Council discussed what procedure should be adopted in dealing with them, A. J. Balfour suggesting the usual reference of the statement to an expert Commission.[130] Sonnino objected at once to this proposal:

> He wished to be quite frank. Italy could not take part in any Commission or in any discussion outside the Conference, or allow any Committee to make recommendations regarding questions outstanding between Italy and the Yugoslavs.[131]

The delegations could consult their experts, but the decisions must be taken at the highest level. He refused to yield on this, and the other members of the Council were obliged to agree that the Italo-Yugoslav frontier must be negotiated at the Supreme Council itself.

On 22 February, anxious about increasing impatience about the slowness of the proceedings of the Conference, Balfour moved a resolution in the Council of Ten designed to speed up the work of the Conference by concentrating on the major questions relating to Germany.[132] This proposal evoked an immediate protest from Sonnino:

> Should the military, economic and financial conditions to be imposed on Germany first be settled, what would happen to the

> other questions requiring settlement? He felt compelled to ask that question in the interests of his own country. Germany was an enemy of Italy, and the Italians had fought against her. But Italy also had another enemy, Austria, and in fighting her she had borne the full consequences of the war. . . . What guarantees, what pledges would Italy have that all these other questions would be dealt with? It seemed to him that Mr Balfour's proposal would have the effect of adjourning all these other questions indefinitely.[133]

If, as Balfour had proposed, the Allied armies were rapidly demobilised once the German treaty was signed, there would be no means available whereby the Austrian treaty could be enforced.

The other members of the Council attempted to persuade Sonnino to accept Balfour's proposal, but he persistently refused, sometimes clashing angrily with his colleagues, as when Pichon said that he 'thought the Conference should consider first of all the German question, because it was . . . the principal and essential question', whereupon Sonnino interjected 'for you'.[134] In the end Balfour made a further proposal, which, in addition to requiring settlement of the major questions relating to Germany, would require all the Commissions to report by 8 March and would include among the items on the Conference agenda to be given priority all frontier questions relating to enemy countries.[135] Sonnino still wanted more certain guarantees of an early settlement of Italy's claims, but in the end, faced with the opposition of all other members of the Council, he accepted a modified version of Balfour's proposal. By his obstinacy, Sonnino had isolated himself from all his colleagues, had aroused their united hostility, and was obliged to give way to quite a large extent. The German settlement was to receive first priority, in order that armies might be demobilised and normal international trade and relations be resumed as soon as possible.

The attitude of the Italians, and especially of Sonnino, gave rise to anxiety among the other delegates. The American delegation discussed the matter on 24 February, when Lansing pointed out that the Yugoslavs were very anti-Italian and that this hostility, coupled with Italian obstinacy in asserting their territorial claims, was likely to cause serious trouble at some stage,[136] and on 26 February, Herbert Hoover, in charge of relief operations in Central Europe, reported that his agencies were having difficulty in shipping food through Trieste as a result of the Italo–Yugoslav hostility, and suggested that he be allowed to threaten to cease sending relief to Italy unless these obstacles were removed, thus making it plain where he thought the obstacles to his shipments originated. This proposal received general assent from the members of the delegation.[137] On 12 March, the delegation passed a resolution relating to the policy to be followed in relation to the case of Fiume, where the city had an Italian population, but all the suburbs and hinterland were Slav, which laid down that 'the disposition of territory should be considered from the point of view of the ethnic condition of the hinterland and not of the littoral or of individual ports on the coast'.[138] The Americans thus adopted a policy line which would result in adamant opposition to the Italian claims in Dalmatia.

The Italian attitude posed a difficult problem for the British, bound as they were by the Treaty of London. The Americans did not consider this treaty binding, although Colonel House had given Sonnino encouragement in pressing his claims,* but the British and the French had signed the Treaty and Italy was clearly going to demand her pound of flesh. On 2 March the Ambassador in Rome, Sir Rennell Rodd, reported to Lord Curzon that Orlando had told the Italian Parliament that Italy 'could not turn a deaf ear to Fiume, to preserve for her that national character and political independence which had been upheld through centuries',[139] while another British diplomat, Sir C. Cochrane, informed Lord Curzon that during a discussion with a Frenchman familiar with Yugoslav affairs he had been warned that

> unless Fiume were given to the Yugoslavs no-one could say what might not happen. He said that the Serbian or Yugoslav representatives would scarcely dare to return to their country if they were not given Fiume.[140]

Britain looked like becoming embroiled in a singularly nasty quarrel. In his memoirs of the Peace Conference, Lloyd George quoted some lines by the poet Clough which illustrated the depth of the hatred which existed between the Italians and the Southern Slavs:

> I see the Croat soldier stand
> Upon the grass of your redoubts;
> The eagle with his black wings flouts
> The breadth and beauty of your land. . . .[141]

* See p. 43 above.

and recalled that Britain was bound to assist Italy in reducing and weakening the new Yugoslav state; the War Cabinet had decided that

> While every effort should be made to persuade Italy to take up a reasonable attitude on these questions, the British Government was undoubtedly bound to give Italy its genuine support if Italy insisted on the fulfilment of the terms of the Pact of London.[142]

With America likely to oppose Italy's claims, Sonnino obstinate, and the Yugoslavs hotly contesting them, Britain and France would be caught between two fires and put in a most unpleasant dilemma.

The matter came up again in the Council of Ten on 11 March, when its Chairman, Clemenceau, read out a letter from the Yugoslav delegation asking for a further hearing on their dispute with Italy, saying that the Adriatic frontier must be fixed

> between two Governments whose peoples had been friends in the past, who desire to remain friends in the future and, what is even more important, between two countries which have fought for the selfsame cause of right and justice and have substantially contributed, in proportion to their strength and their resources, to the common victory.[143]

The Yugoslavs were appealing to President Wilson, to whom they had offered to submit the dispute for arbitration.

When Lloyd George proposed that the Yugoslav delegates should take a full part in the discussion and decision of the Italo–Yugoslav frontier, Sonnino at once objected, saying that the small Powers had no right to a voice in the Council's decisions – an extraordinarily arrogant stand to take.[144] Orlando expressed reluctance to see the new State even recognised by the Conference. 'Certainly, the recognition of the new State would not constitute an amiable act towards Italy',[145] and he opposed allowing Yugoslav representatives to take part in the deliberations of the Conference on the ground that although the Serbs had fought with the Allies during the war, the Croats and Slovenes had fought on the side of the Central Powers as part of the Austro–Hungarian Empire and were thus enemy peoples who should not be heard. Notwithstanding all this, Lloyd George felt that the Yugoslavs should be heard, and was supported both by the French members of the Council, and by Lansing, who thought that the creation of the new State must be considered

> just in the same way as England had acquired or annexed Scotland and called herself Great Britain. It was all a mere technicality, and in his opinion, it was important to uphold the decisions already reached. When questions affecting Roumania and Serbia had been considered by the Conference, both parties affected had been heard. Consequently, he favoured the conclusion that either both parties should be included or both parties should be excluded. In any case one of the contending parties should not be allowed to sit as a judge of its own case.[146]

In view of the Italians' obstinacy, however, agreement was impossible and the Council was compelled to adjourn the question of whether to hear the Yugoslavs for consideration later. The obstinacy of the Italian delegates, and especially Sonnino, meant that this dispute would be very difficult, if not impossible, to resolve amicably.

## CHINA AND JAPAN

The only member of the Council of Ten whose position we have not yet considered is Japan. She had compelled China to sign two agreements which provided that the German sphere of influence in the Chinese province of Shantung should revert to her, and had obtained an Allied guarantee of support in return for increased naval effort in the Pacific.* On 27 January, the Council of Ten discussed the procedure for dealing with this matter, and it was agreed to hear the Japanese in the presence of Chinese delegates, despite the insistence of Baron Makino, one of the Japanese plenipotentiaries and a former Foreign Minister of Japan, that the Japanese submission was concerned only with Germany, and not with China.[147] That afternoon, Makino was allowed to read his statement claiming Shantung and the islands in the Pacific Ocean north of the Equator, his reason being to ensure that Germany was permanently excluded from any position of influence in the Far East. A Chinese representative then asked for the matter to be held over until the Chinese had been heard, and this was agreed.[148] There followed the dispute between President Wilson and the British Dominions over the application of the mandate principle to the former German colonies,† and during the discussion of this vexed issue Clemenceau pointed out that the

* See p. 8 above.
† See pp. 72–9 above.

application of mandates concerned Japan as well. Clemenceau was anxious, lest in reaching a decision on the Dominion claims, the Council should prejudge the Shantung issue as well. Makino tried to reassure, saying that the Japanese were only seeking to take over the territory in order to return it to China in return for limited economic concessions in the area, including use of the port of Kiao-Chow, use of railways, and trading rights. 'Before disposing of it to a third party it was necessary that Japan should obtain the right of free disposal from Germany.'[149] Wellington Koo of China then requested the return of this territory to China, since it was an integral part of China and its people were of Chinese race. The German lease had been 'extorted by force'[150] and 'on the principles of nationality and of territorial integrity, principles accepted by this Conference, China had a right to the restoration of these territories'.[151] It was true that the Germans had been driven out of China by the Japanese and the British, and for this his people were grateful. But,

> grateful as they were, the Chinese Delegation felt that they would be false to their duty to China and to the world if they did not object to paying their debt of gratitude by selling the birthright of their countrymen, and thereby sowing the seeds of discord for the future.[152]

Baron Makino would not accept restoration of Shantung to China, however, unless it were first given to Japan to restore. Yet another conflict was developing.

While all these discussions were being carried on, the Great Powers were also wrangling about German war guilt and the basis upon which reparations should be claimed. It is clear so far that the delegates were expounding their positions, and points of dispute were becoming clear, while much detailed work was being done. The Conference could not decide controversial points, however, and these were almost invariably postponed for resolution later. A Treaty had to be made. Sooner or later these Gordian knots would have to be cut, but for the present the delegates shied away from them. The Conference lacked an effective final court of appeal, a place where minds could be made up once and for all, and the great issues resolved. Perhaps, like Lady Macbeth's cat, they 'let "I dare not" wait upon "I would" '. At any rate, they were not prepared to tackle these problems at that time.

# 6 The Guilt of Germany: *Reparations, Disarmament and War Guilt, February 1919*

Historians have long debated the question of who, if anyone, was responsible for starting the First World War. No-one at Paris in 1919 had any doubt that Germany had been entirely to blame. The principle of guilt and restitution had been incorporated in the Armistice.* A German request for an impartial investigation of the origins of the war had been turned down by America and the Allies as not worthy even of consideration.† Germany's guilt was self-evident, and she must make good the damage she had caused, and steps must be taken to ensure that she should never think of attempting to overrun Europe again. On this all the statesmen at Paris were agreed, but when it came to the way these ends were to be achieved, there proved to be almost unlimited scope for disagreement. Thus, when, on 10 February, the question of whether the Allies should demand the surrender by Germany of *prima facie* war criminals was raised in the Supreme Council, Balfour opposed the idea since

> The clause would merely state that the Germans should give up a number of people whose names would be communicated at a later date. The Germans would already know who these people were, and they would resent these men being taken away to be tried before a foreign tribunal. . . . But by what other means could these people be brought to justice? It would obviously be very lamentable, after all the expectations raised in the public mind, if when the time came, after the tribunal had been established, none of the criminals could really be brought to trial.[1]

* See p. 34 above.
† See p. 48 above.

The guilty must be punished, but it was necessary to find the best means by which this might be done. President Wilson agreed with Balfour: 'When the terms of peace were made it would be possible to know the names of the guilty people, and a demand could then be made for their surrender.'[2] Wilson as much as anyone at Paris believed the Germans to be guilty of a terrible crime, and for this their leaders must be punished. The only point at issue was how best to proceed. The Council agreed to wait until the Commission established by the second Plenary Session of the Conference to prepare the clauses of the Treaty relating to the punishment of war criminals* had reported, before taking any action.

By far the most complex issue connected with Germany's responsibility for the war was that of reparations. The French were dependent upon the extraction of funds from Germany to avoid national bankruptcy as a result of debts incurred to finance her war effort, while one of the slogans on which Lloyd George's coalition Government had been returned to power in December 1918 had been 'Make Germany Pay', even if Lloyd George himself had been somewhat cautious in adopting it.† President Wilson had proclaimed that in the peace settlement there should be 'No annexations, no contributions, no punitive damages', thus sowing a seed which could grow into a massive conflict of principle over the basis upon which compensation should be extracted from Germany. That such compensation was payable had been laid down in the Armistice.

In Britain, reparations were a major preoccupation for Ministers. Thus, for example, on 11 February 1919, a Minister without Portfolio, Sir L. Worthington Evans, warned the Cabinet that unless steps were taken to prevent it, Germany would use her poor economic condition as an excuse to allow the mark to depreciate, thus at once gaining a trade advantage and reducing the real value of the indemnity it was decided to extract from her,[3] and a week later the Federation of British Industries requested the Cabinet to be firm in demanding payment of the total cost of the war from the enemy countries, even if a discretion were allowed to waive some of the debt at a later time. 'The Federation believes, however, that the paying power of the enemy countries will prove to be far greater than is anticipated.'[4] There were thus plenty of pressures for a large demand for reparations.

* See p. 79 above.
† See p. 6 above.

The Commission set up at the second Plenary Session to consider the reparations problem* had been at work since mid-January, and on 20 February Lord Sumner, one of its British members, reported on progress to Balfour's personal secretary, Ian Malcolm. It had been agreed in principle to claim the 'costs of the war', but on the one hand the French were uncertain how large their claims would be, while the Americans wished to restrict the scope of the claims on the strength of the Fourteen Points and the Lansing Note. The British and the French were resisting this. The Americans had said, 'Let us ask the four men who signed them [the Armistice terms] what it was that they intended by them', but the British representatives had rejected this proposal, since it would mean undue delay, with Wilson, Lloyd George and Orlando all at home attending to their Parliaments, and Clemenceau in bed after being injured in an assassination attempt. The Commission therefore faced deadlock.[5] Sir Maurice Hankey had a similar story to tell Lloyd George a few days later. The committee preparing the total bill, chaired by Lord Sumner, was making little progress since only the British had their demand ready for presentation, while the others had no figures available as yet, and American opposition to the inclusion of war costs in the reparation claim was 'absolutely obdurate'. This difference of opinion was clearly a serious worry to Hankey, who said that the British and American representatives 'do not work together at all, and are unsympathetic to one another. My personal belief is that before very long, you yourself will have to take this matter up with Colonel House, with a view to some agreement on broad lines.'[6] Hankey realised that this kind of disagreement could only be resolved by the Heads of Delegations, who would have to accept the responsibility of making final decisions if any Treaty were to be drawn up at all.

The degree of friction within the Reparations Commission can be illustrated from the memoirs of those who were at the Conference. André Tardieu recalled two opposing interpretations of the Lansing Note, one put forward by Hughes, the Australian Prime Minister, who declared that 'the right to reparation rests upon the principle of justice pure and simple, in this sense, that where damage or harm has been done, the doer should make it good to the extreme limit of his resources'. This view was supported by Lord Sumner, who declared

* See pp. 79–80 above.

that 'the reimbursement of war costs is the constant practice of international law. . . . No particular clause, either in the Fourteen Points or in the Armistice, excludes this reimbursement.'[7] Opposing this view for the Americans, John Foster Dulles said that

> The American delegation associates itself absolutely and without reserve with all that has been said concerning the enormity of the crime committed by Germany. . . . Why is it that we propose only a limited reparation? It is because we are not facing a blank page, but a page covered with a document at the foot of which are the signatures of Mr Wilson, M. Clemenceau, M. Orlando and Mr Lloyd George.[8]

There was complete disagreement on the question of whether, under the terms of the Armistice, the Allies were entitled to charge up to Germany all the costs of the war. The Lansing Note had provided for reparation for all damage caused to the civilian population of the Allies, and while the Americans were as eager as anyone else to punish Germany, they believed that the terms of the Lansing Note must lead to the exclusion of military costs from the reparation claim against Germany. The deadlock was complete. On 21 February, Colonel House wrote in his diary that

> Thomas Lamont and Vance McCormick came to report on the progress of the Committee on Reparations. . . . The British now put in a tentative total demand on Germany of one hundred and twenty billions of dollars, and the French think Germany should pay a total of two hundred billions of dollars. In other words, the French want Germany to pay two hundred times as much as the French paid the Germans in '71, and which the French then claimed to be excessive. . . . Our people think that the maximum cannot be over twenty-two billion of dollars and are inclined to believe that it should be under that amount.[9]

The gap between American and European assessments of Germany's obligations and capacity to pay was huge, and the Reparations Commission seemed headed directly for deadlock.

The problem was discussed by the American plenipotentiaries on 24 February, when Colonel House proposed that

> If in the Committee of Ten the French still insisted on carrying out a project which was contrary to the wishes of the President and

> contrary to the pledge which had been given to Germany before the signing of the Armistice we should then state that we wash our hands of the whole business, and that for our part we absolutely refuse to ask for any indemnity from Germany.[10]

His reasons for this proposal are of interest. If Germany repudiated the Reparations Chapter of the Treaty a few years hence, saying that it was contrary to the Armistice agreement, 'all of the world would sympathise with her and there would undoubtedly be a new war with a different line-up'.[11] To comply with the pre-Armistice agreement and make only a moderate claim would increase the chances of a long period of peace. Colonel House's colleagues did not demur from his view, and that same day he sent a cable to Wilson in America proposing that

> In the event . . . that this principle [the Lansing Note] is seriously threatened with repudiation by the Allies, it may be wise for us to intimate that, as we do not wish to impair in any respect the agreement between the Associated Governments and Germany at the time of the Armistice, we would prefer to withdraw from any recovery from Germany except to the extent of our own claims for reparation which we can satisfy out of the funds in the hands of the Alien Property Custodian. If this intimation is given it may be that the Allies will reconsider their position.[12]

If this threat were put into effect, no American help would be available in enforcing the Reparations Chapter, which would impose a heavy burden on the European Powers. Those among them who desired continuing American involvement in Europe after the Treaty was signed would be influenced by this danger. President Wilson took some time to consider this proposal, and in the meantime the deadlock in the Commission seemed more and more complete; on 27 February Colonel House recorded in his diary a meeting with two of the American representatives on the Commission, when he

> advised them to agree to the sum of forty billions of dollars, but to hedge it around with safeguards as far as the United States was concerned, so that in no event would we be either legally or morally bound to help enforce its collection. That amount seems perfectly absurd.[13]

America should not be compelled to assist in enforcing a settlement which her representatives could not accept as reasonable. The prospect for agreement was gloomy, and on 3 March Colonel House wrote in his diary that 'all our Commissioners, experts and economists tell of the same impasse and come almost hourly for consultations'.[14] The Conference seemed to be in danger of breaking up altogether over the Reparation question.

Members of the British Government and Delegation were also becoming anxious about the lack of progress being made. On 24 February, E. S. Montagu wrote to Lloyd George to question the wisdom of including war costs in the bill to be presented to Germany and thus causing friction with the Americans. Germany would not be able to pay such a bill, and it was more important to ensure that Britain got a fair deal after the war:

> If France gets first cut, there will not be enough for us, but if France does not get first cut, it is held that she will not be in a position to pay us the large sums which she owes to us and that therefore we shall get something indirectly from Germany through France.

The problem of what to include in the total demand was thus irrelevant, and Britain should concern herself with her own interests. The Conference should abandon its present concern with war costs, which Montagu described as 'this work of supererogation . . . likely to lead to no practical results', and turn its attention first to determining the extent of Germany's capacity to pay, and then to deciding the principles to be applied in dividing the spoils among the Allied Powers.[15] On 1 March J. M. Keynes circulated a paper setting out the conflicting estimates of Germany's capacity to pay, ranging from the American estimates of between £200 million and £310 million annually to a reduced French estimate submitted by their Minister of Industrial Reconstruction, of £400 million per year. Keynes himself had suggested that the total could not exceed between £6,000 million and £9,000 million, but 'I understand that Lord Cunliffe suggested a much higher figure to the Committee'.[16] There were thus divisions both within and between delegations on their estimates of Germany's capacity to pay. Lord Sumner was becoming resentful at the American attitude. When the American representatives on the Reparations Commission informed their colleagues that they could not accept present estimates of Germany's capacity to pay and had threatened to declare this openly, Sumner complained that this constituted 'an unpardonable bêtise', and went on to say that he could 'only hope that there was more bluff than anything else about this, calculated rudeness'.[17] Both the American and the British members of the Commission were becoming exasperated at the others' attitude.

The problem now was how to break the deadlock. On 7 March Colonel House reported to Wilson that Lloyd George had proposed that three parts of whatever sums were extracted from Germany should be devoted to the repair of damage in the devastated areas for every two parts allotted to war costs. House's comment was that he 'thought this proposal of George fair, but there must be no demands on Germany inconsistent with our terms of armistice with Germany and the Fourteen Points'.[18] The issue of principle still remained unsolved. British opinion was, on the whole, stern on the need to extort large sums of Germany. A. J. Balfour, for example, who was not by temperament a vindictive man, commented on reports of starvation in Germany that they 'do confirm what we all know or suspect, namely, that the Germans are distributing their food in the manner most likely to influence the Allies on their behalf'.[19] Such attitudes were unlikely to lead to a compromise on the British side. On 11 March, however, Keynes proposed that the demand for reparation should be left undetermined, since no accurate estimate of the extent of the bill or of Germany's capacity to pay could possibly be made at that time, and it should therefore be left to an inter-Allied Commission to fix a sum which could be extracted over thirty years without damaging the economic interests of the world as a whole.[20] This offered a possible way of escape from the deadlock. The next day, Montagu urged Lloyd George to realise that the question could be settled only by 'the very greatest men among us'.[21] The deadlock was discussed at a meeting of the British Empire Delegation on 13 March, but no-one had any new suggestions for resolving the dispute.[22]

Before leaving this subject, we ought to consider the French view, although at this stage the most acrimonious wrangling was going on between the British and the Americans. The French were unwilling to compromise, and Clemenceau was particularly firm. Montagu told Lloyd George that Loucheur had been to see Clemenceau on 13 March to discuss ways of breaking the deadlock over reparations, and 'said . . . that he had seen Clemenceau who was very fierce. I said his fierceness was distressing but would not *at any rate at third hand* offend my judgement as to the interests of my country.'[23] The British were falling out with the French as well. One reason for this was undoubtedly French indebtedness as a result of the war, and the tendency of the French Finance Minister, Klotz, to allay fears in the Chamber of Deputies about future rates of taxation arising from this indebtedness by asserting that the money would be obtained from the defeated foe. In his memoirs of the Conference Lloyd George recalled of Klotz that 'in the Chamber of Deputies, "*L'Allemagne paiera*" was his answer to every financial claim or complaint',[24] and when telling Lord Curzon about the French budget debate in March 1919, the British Ambassador in Paris, Lord Derby, wrote that Klotz had 'declared that he proposed to ascertain the amount of the sums to be paid by Germany before estimating what the French taxpayer could provide'.[25] When Lloyd George dined with Briand, an eminent French politician then out of office, and expressed the opinion that Germany would not be able to pay more than a third of the probable bill for reparations, Briand agreed and went on to say 'how criminal it was for Klotz to have said under these circumstances in the Chamber that Germany would pay'. Both Lloyd George and Briand feared that Germany would succumb to Bolshevism if the peace terms were too stiff.[26] Those in power in France, however, were tied to making an extreme demand for reparations from Germany.

To some extent, of course, the British were as well, in view of the climate in which the 'Coupon Election' of December 1918 had been fought, and the opinion of most Members of Parliament. The Americans recognised this, but felt that Lloyd George and his colleagues must face up to this problem and tell Parliament and the British public the truth. On 16 March Colonel House wrote in his diary that 'Davis* and I feel, and I so expressed myself to Balfour, that the wise thing to do would be to tell the British public that Germany was bankrupt and that the British financial experts and statesmen were mistaken in believing she could pay the enormous sums they and their public had at one time had in mind'.[27] Lloyd George and his colleagues dared not do this. The following day House learned that Lloyd George 'was worried about the question of Reparation, both as to amount and how he was to satisfy the British public'.[28] The British were constrained to maintain their demands by public and Parliamentary opinion, and Colonel House felt obliged to recognise this.

* Norman H. Davis, Financial Commissioner in the American delegation and thus the most senior American financial adviser.

By the middle of March, then, the discussions on reparations were completely bogged down. The Americans insisted on ruling out charging war costs to Germany as the Allies had bound themselves not to do this by accepting the Fourteen Points and the Lansing Note, and also felt that the claim should be moderate. The British were obliged by Parliamentary and public opinion to make a heavy demand, but while some members of the British delegation, most notably Lord Sumner, were determined to do this, others sought ways of escaping from the deadlock by proposals such as that of Montagu, which was adopted by Lloyd George at this time, of concentration on how the spoils were to be divided, while leaving the determination of their extent to a later date, and of Keynes, who had proposed an indeterminate settlement with only a time-limit of thirty years determining what was finally extracted. The French were bound to make a heavy demand, again by Parliamentary opinion encouraged by their Minister of Finance. There seemed to be no acceptable way of escape.

The third method by which Germany was to be punished for her aggression in the past, and constrained to be of good behaviour in the future, was by extensive disarmament. Under the terms of the Armistice she had been compelled to surrender most of her armaments, military supplies and warships, for the Allies were determined that in the future Germany should not have the opportunity again to build up massive military and naval forces as a prelude to making war upon her neighbours. In the minds of the idealistic, and in that of President Wilson, this was bound up with universal disarmament, which Point 4 demanded in the form of 'Adequate guarantees given and taken that national armaments will be reduced to the lowest point consistent with domestic safety'.[29] The subject first came up in mid-February, when the Armistice was about to be renewed, and on 10 February the Council of Ten established a committee to consider how the terms of the Armistice, which Germany was alleged to be evading, could be enforced.[30] The Committee reported the following day, submitting to the Council a list of German infringements of the Armistice conditions, and recommending that pressure be brought to bear on Germany to conform by withholding food supplies and strengthening the blockade, although this should be done only after careful consideration in view of conditions in Germany and the effect such action might have in producing disorder there.[31] The only satisfactory answer to German evasion of the Armistice was to prepare the final naval and military terms of peace as soon as possible and impose them, so securing a permanent settlement which could reasonably be enforced by all the means at the disposal of the Allies.[32]

The Council of Ten were doubtful whether this could be done, however. Clemenceau pointed out that these clauses of the Treaty would have to be prepared by an expert committee, and this could not be done before the Armistice, which was due to expire six days later, must be renewed. Foch urged the inclusion of more severe interim terms in the Armistice if the final terms could not be prepared in time, but Balfour, heading the British delegation in Lloyd George's absence, was opposed to this course of action:

> Doubts had been expressed as to the advisability of using the renewal of the armistice each month as a means of getting new terms out of the Germans. . . . No satisfactory end could . . . be put to that procedure until the conditions of the final peace terms had been decided, and he agreed that a decision could not be reached on that day. His proposal, therefore, was that only inevitable small changes, or no changes whatever, should be made in the Armistice until the Allies were prepared to say to Germany: These are the final military terms of peace.[33]

President Wilson supported this resistance by Balfour of French attempts to prejudice the decisions of the Conference by imposing extra disarmament terms on Germany when the Armistice was renewed. Clemenceau was anxious lest demobilisation proceed too far before the terms were imposed:

> . . . the final conditions of peace would be settled after . . . the Americans, the English and the Italians had gone. . . . The final military conditions to be imposed might be extremely difficult, and it might be that the enemies, having been left free to act on the other side of the frontier, a great deal of blood would have to be shed to conquer them a second time. . . . Ebert had said, 'We will not accept terms which are too hard'.[34]

France must feel safe from a renewed German attack. Without that, for Clemenceau all else was pointless: 'He was aware that President Wilson considered the Armistice to be a threat continually hanging over the heads of the Germans. But he knew the Germans better, and he would assure the Council that they would not take it thus.'[35]

All were agreed that firmness with Germany would be necessary in future – the issue at stake was whether it was necessary or reasonable to demand further concessions now, before the terms were prepared. The French thought it was necessary, whilst the British and the Americans thought it was unreasonable. In the end it was agreed to renew the Armistice indefinitely and prepare the final naval and military terms as soon as possible.[36]

When the discussion of the military and naval disarmament terms of the Treaty was resumed in the Council of Ten the following afternoon, President Wilson opened the proceedings with a speech which showed clearly what his attitude to Germany was. Having said that all that was necessary was to decide what forces Germany would require in order to maintain internal law and order, and resist Bolshevism, which could be fixed by the Allied military advisers, he went on to say that

> In general, he felt that until we knew what the German Government was going to be, and how the German people were going to behave, the world had a moral right to disarm Germany and to subject her to a generation of thoughtfulness.[37]

The problem was therefore simply one of deciding what forces Germany would need to maintain law and order and resist Bolshevism, and of restricting her to these. The military terms could, therefore, be prepared and imposed before the rest of the Treaty was ready, if this were considered necessary. This proposal was accepted by the Council. The tone of Wilson's remarks, and his readiness to disarm Germany at once to the lowest possible level, indicate the depth of Wilson's hatred and distrust of the Germans. But for his fear of Bolshevism, he would, perhaps, have gone even further. He also proposed that at the renewal of the Armistice, the Germans should not be informed, as Balfour had suggested they should, that once the preliminary peace terms were signed the Allies would feed Germany and help her restart her industries. Wilson was supported by Clemenceau, and no promise of succour was held out to the Germans.[38] It was also agreed to appoint an expert Commission to advise the Council on the disarmament provisions of the Treaty.[39]

The Commission took some time to prepare a draft for the Council of Ten's consideration, and this was a cause of some concern. On 24 February Lord Milner told the Council that this question was 'extremely urgent', to be told by Tardieu that the military terms would be ready 'in a few days'.[40] On 3 March Marshal Foch presented the results of the Commission's deliberations to the Council. Neither Lloyd George nor Wilson was present, so Balfour and Colonel House were deputies for their respective chiefs. The Commission proposed that Germany should be allowed an army of 200,000 plus an officer corps of 9,000, and no air force after 1 October 1919. The officers should be recruited on a basis of long-term service – twenty-five years for officers and fifteen years for non-commissioned officers – while the men should be conscripts for a maximum of one year. This provision was designed to restrict the effectiveness of the training the men would receive, for a soldier could not be taught much in a year. The Council wished to adjourn the matter for consideration, but Foch, in a hurry as ever, pointed out that a quick decision was necessary, since Allied demobilisation was proceeding at such a speed that after 1 April they would no longer be able to impose their will upon Germany by weight of numbers in arms. Balfour protested that in making their plans the generals had been jumping to conclusions, since they had assumed that the settlement would be ready by 1 April, although they had received no instructions to this effect: 'they wished to force the Council to settle peace by that date under pain of not being able to enforce their will upon the enemy. This was tantamount to holding a pistol at the head of the Council.'[41] The generals must not be allowed to usurp the rôle of the political leaders gathered at Paris.

Balfour did wish, however, to provide the generals with some guidelines. One problem was how long the disarmament clauses were to remain in force, since they could not draw up the military, naval and air terms on the basis of different assumptions about this:

> He thought it would not do to say to the Germans, 'Here are aerial terms to last a short time, naval terms to endure for perhaps a generation and military terms to last until the Day of Judgement.' He thought that the task of the experts would be made easier if they were told exactly what they were to provide for.[42]

Foch asked with seeming innocence whether the Council had not resolved that the terms to be settled were not to determine the 'final military condition of Germany',[43] and started a wrangle between the British and the French. Balfour did not agree with Marshal Foch's interpretation of the Council's previous decisions. The word 'final' he thought could not be held to convey the meaning of perpetuity,[44] and he proposed that the duration of the disarmament provisions should be determined by the League of Nations, but this Clemenceau was not prepared to allow, saying that

> President Wilson in that very room had declared that Germany must be disarmed. He did not say that Germany must be temporarily disarmed. Other countries might be content with transitory naval terms. He himself was not prepared to sign an invitation to Germany to prepare for another attack by land after an interval of three, ten, or even forty years. He would not be prepared to sign a peace of that character.[45]

There was no alternative, in the face of such stubbornness, but to adjourn consideration of the matter.

On 16 March, with Lloyd George back from England, a further draft submitted by Foch was discussed. Balfour said that agreement had only been reached on the Commission by omitting all reference to a period of time, and that would still have to be decided.[46] Lloyd George then raised another objection. He felt that to compel the Germans to base their army on short-term conscription was a serious mistake:

> Why should the Allies present Germany a scheme which would enable her to raise four or five million trained men in the next twenty years? . . . Under the proposed scheme, Germany would have an Army of three to four million trained men led not by donkeys, but by officers who had had considerable war experience. He himself would be very sorry to leave France after the signing of peace with that threat facing her across the Rhine.[47]

Lloyd George did not want to give Germany any chance to renew her aggressive plans, but Foch rejected this solicitude for France's safety, saying that once men had been demobilised for three or four years they would be virtually useless as soldiers. Lloyd George pointed out that for years to come the Germans would have at their disposal vast numbers of wartime officers and N.C.Os who could easily retrain the troops, and asked for time to prepare fresh proposals, which was granted.[48]

Having taken Marshal Foch to task on military matters, Balfour and Lloyd George were next obliged to resist an American demand, put by Lansing, that the Germans 'should not be required to dismantle all their coastal fortifications; in his opinion, Germany should be permitted to defend herself'.[49] Balfour said that coastal fortifications under modern conditions were built as 'jumping-off places for offensive operations' and was supported by Lloyd George.[50] This clause also had to be referred back to the experts. Procuring agreement, even when all members of the Council were agreed upon the objective they were trying to achieve – the weakening of the German armed forces to a point at which they could constitute a threat to no-one – was not easy. It was agreed at this meeting, however, that the area fifty kilometres east of the Rhine, and all German territory to the west of the river, must be demilitarised and all fortifications demolished.[51]

The following day, the controversy over the terms of service of German soldiers was resumed, with Lloyd George making a renewed plea for a long-service army on the grounds already discussed. He warned that Germany might obtain assistance in training soldiers or maintaining their training from another country, such as Russia, and also pointed out that a long-service army would be more expensive, and therefore a greater drain on Germany's resources, than a conscript army: 'If Germany had to maintain a voluntary army in addition to paying compensation to the Allies, there would be no money left for military adventures',[52] and Europe would be safe. The French generals still took the opposite view, but Lloyd George had never had much faith in the wisdom of generals, and this came out now:

> He would never agree to an army raised in Germany by short conscript service. No General's opinion would shake his decision. This was a matter for Governments to decide. . . . He declared for a long-service army as the only guarantee of a small army.[53]

Lloyd George's proposal for a German army of 200,000, in which all ranks would serve at least twelve years with the colours, was referred to the expert Commission for their opinion.

Marshal Foch reported back once more on 10 March, telling the Council that he would still prefer a short-service army, but would accept a long-service one provided its members were cut to 100,000.[54] This was accepted out of deference to France's feelings, although Balfour urged that general disarmament must follow:

> If the Germans were told that they were to have only 100,000 armed men, while France, Poland or Bohemia could have as many

as they wished, they would say that the Allied Powers were leaving them at the mercy of their small neighbours.[55]

Clemenceau deferred this to an indefinite future by saying that this was a matter for the League of Nations. A long-service army was adopted. In the light of this controversy it is perhaps of some interest to point out that after 1919, the restriction of the German army to 100,000 long-serving men resulted in the existence of thousands of unemployed former officers and soldiers, who formed the basis of the political armies – the Freikorps, the Rotfrontkämferbund, and later the Sturmabteilung – which were so fatally to undermine law and order in the Weimar Republic. If military employment could have been provided for more of them, German democracy might have had a better chance of survival, and, ironically, Europe might have been safer. No-one foresaw these developments in Paris in 1919.

One person who was becoming anxious about the evolution of the disarmament terms was Lord Robert Cecil, who was worried lest the League of Nations, for which he was an enthusiast, should become involved in the repression of Germany and thus acquire a tarnished image as an anti-German combination. He wrote to Lloyd George on 10 March to ask that the League should not be involved in the enforcement of the disarmament provisions – it 'must not be converted, as the French wish (I am told that the proposal comes really from Foch) into an alliance against Germany. This is not only wrong in itself, but will give colour to the charge brought against the Government that it is a mere perpetuation of the present coalition – or as it is put, a modern Holy Alliance.' The same objection applied equally to Klotz's proposal that the League should take charge of the exacting of Reparations. The League should only enforce general disarmament and only admit Germany when she has shown 'a genuine repentance' by disarming in accordance with the Treaty and by other means.[56] The League must not be jeopardised, even in the desirable cause of repressing and restricting Germany.

The story of the disarmament clauses of the Treaty can be completed by considering one more meeting of the Council of Ten, which took place after President Wilson's return, on 17 March. He approved of the Military, Naval and Air Clauses as they had been drawn up, except that he was anxious lest the Germans would not have enough forces, with an army of only 100,000, to resist Bolshevism within and on her frontiers. This was a consideration which stopped the Allied Powers disarming Germany to an even lower level than they did. Marshal Foch reassured them that 100,000 troops plus the police would suffice, and this was accepted.[57]

The other point which he disliked was the proposed establishment of military commissions to supervise German disarmament and inspect her military installations, since this would cause continual irritation and friction between Germany and the Allies. 'In his opinion, if the Allied armies were to be maintained for ever in order to control the carrying out of the Peace Terms, not peace but Allied armed domination would have been established.' In any case, such maintenance would be expensive and contrary to the American Constitution.[58] Lloyd George agreed, 'such a condition would constitute a constant source of insult, whilst, on the other hand, it did not really serve any useful purpose. Should the Germans mean to evade it, they would merely refrain from making the required notification.'[59] In view of this, Marshal Foch agreed provisionally to delete this condition.

Thus, in discussing the trial of war criminals, reparations, and disarmaments, all issues on which the Allies were agreed as to their basic objectives, there was much disagreement. In the case of the trial of war criminals and disarmament the disagreements were over the best means by which the agreed ends should be achieved, but in the case of reparations the disagreements went deeper. The items which could properly be charged against Germany, the extent to which her capacity to pay should be taken into account, as well as conflicting estimates of that capacity, these were all questions involving vital political and economic interests of the Allied and Associated Governments. Political interests, because on this issue more than any other those Governments would be judged by their Parliaments, to whom they were responsible and upon whose continued support they were dependent for survival; economic interests because reparations formed a vital plank in the economic strategy of the Allied Governments for post-war reconstruction and the resumption of normal economic activity. The dispute engendered by this issue was quite beyond the power of the decision-making structure evolved by the Conference up to March to resolve.

# 7 The Tensions Increase: *March 1919*

By the beginning of March, much had been achieved. A Covenant for the League of Nations had been prepared, and other sections of the Treaty had either been drafted or were in the process of preparation by Commissions of experts. The most controversial problems, however, were proving to be stubbornly insoluble. On reparations, the western frontier of Germany, Poland and other issues no agreement was forthcoming, and they were causing distrust and irritation. Italy worried about Fiume, Britain and France bickered about the Middle East, and small Powers fought wars with one another and quarrelled over their future frontiers. Paris at the beginning of March 1919, was not, in short, a very happy place, and over everyone hung the knowledge that decisions would have to be reached, problems would have to be solved, a Treaty covering all these points and more would have to be prepared and signed.

With the issues which were likely to have to be decided at the highest level becoming clearer, it was time for Governments to reassess their positions. The British Cabinet devoted its meetings on 28 February and 4 March to a discussion of the future frontiers of Germany, especially the western frontier. At the first of these meetings Churchill expressed anxiety at the privations of the Germans, and urged that if peace were not made soon and the Germans fed, their government might collapse. At the same time Britain and France must cooperate closely, but Lloyd George was reluctant to assume the obligation of maintaining British forces permanently on the Rhine.*[1] At this time France had won a con-

* See also pp. 107–8 above.

siderable measure of support in the Cabinet for her desire for a military frontier on the Rhine.

On 4 March the Cabinet began by discussing France's desire to be allowed to annex the Saar valley as well as Alsace–Lorraine, thus restoring the Franco–German frontier of 1814, instead of that of 1871, in that area. Lord Curzon posed the basic dilemma in which the Conference would find itself:

> This claim could not be defended either on grounds of nationality or self-determination. It could only be determined on grounds of strategy or because France was entitled to the Saar coalfields as compensation for damage done to, or loss of, other coal mines during the war.

The only justification for this claim, it was agreed, was that of compensation, in view of which Lloyd George said that, if France received the Saar, its value must form part of what France would receive as reparations.

On the proposal for a buffer state west of the Rhine and a permanent military occupation of the Rhenish provinces, Lloyd George felt that Marshal Foch's proposals for a permanent occupation would be 'intolerable'; the population 'was entirely German. . . . In the future, how would it be possible to prevent such a state moving in the direction dictated by its ethnological instincts?' However, the British 'should do our best for France and . . . support her claims with a view to directing the French from their colonial ambitions'. There was always the Middle East to consider. Nonetheless, he was definitely opposed to the buffer state proposal, but both he and the Chief of the Imperial General Staff had to admit that they had had very little success in their attempts to persuade Marshal Foch to drop or modify his proposal. Lloyd George also floated the idea of an Anglo–American Treaty of Guarantee to France, but doubted whether President Wilson would accept any such suggestion since he 'would not hear of any entangling alliances, as he put his faith in the League of Nations'. After further discussions of these and other issues, the Cabinet could arrive at no definite decisions and left the British representatives at Paris to pursue the policy outlined by Lloyd George.[2] Churchill also tried, without success, to get a decision on policy in Russia, for no-one wanted to make up their minds yet. Lord Curzon wrote to Lord Derby in Paris after the meeting to inform him of the Cabinet's refusal to support the

A HOME FROM HOME.

PRESIDENT WILSON (*quitting America in his Fourteen-League-of-Nations Boots*). "IT'S TIME I WAS GETTING BACK TO A HEMISPHERE WHERE I REALLY AM APPRECIATED."

From *Punch*, Vol. 156, p. 175.

Rhenish buffer state proposal, since it would be of no military value and it would be extremely difficult, he thought, to persuade President Wilson 'to agree to anything that will be an open violation of his Fourteen Points'.[3] The British were preparing to resist French pressure for the Rhine frontier, and it looked as though the Conference would become bogged down in yet another irreconcilable dispute.

This could not be allowed to happen. Against the background of a continual stream of reports that the Germans were starving, and that they were an easy prey for a Bolshevik revolution, haste in preparing the Treaty seemed essential. In his letter of 4 March to Lord Derby, a close friend, Lord Curzon expressed grave anxiety about the likelihood of a collapse of Government in Germany:

> Like you I regard the recent proceedings at Paris with some anxiety and the future almost with dismay. When the Peace Treaty is presented there will very likely ... be no German Government to sign, and if there is, I fully expect that its signature will be refused. What then?[4]

The prospect seemed to be either chaos or a renewal of the war. Such gloomy prognostications seemed confirmed when a report of a British agent, V.77, on a journey through Germany, was circulated to the Cabinet on 7 March. V.77 warned that conditions were very bad, and that this meant that Bolshevism was growing. 'The extent to which this kind of argument meets with success among the lower classes in Germany is in direct and immediate dependence on the conditions of food and labour prevailing at the time.' Poor families find it impossible to heat their homes as a result of a shortage of coal, and hence

> Any public meeting therefore combines the double attraction of excitement and warmth, and of these two the latter is undoubtedly the more potent. The middle classes who can afford it go to the theatres and public dances. The poor who cannot buy tickets for these entertainments fall back on political meetings when admittance is free.[5]

The middle classes kept warm at the opera, the working classes at political meetings, including those of the Spartacus League.* The

* The German Bolshevik movement.

danger that the combination of dreadful conditions of life and the inflamatory oratory of the Spartacists would lead to a breakdown of law and order, meant that peace must be made soon so that Germany could be helped back to a normal way of life.

The decision procedures of the Peace Conference had proved themselves inadequate to resolve the major disputes, and the formal bodies were from now on to be increasingly displaced by small, informal gatherings of leading members of delegations as the place where decisions were made. The most important series of such meetings was to become institutionalised as the Council of Four. The first instance of such a meeting is an interview between Clemenceau, Lloyd George and Colonel House which took place on 7 March, during which they discussed the major problems facing the Conference.[6] Lloyd George asked for the destruction of most of the German navy on the understanding that Britain and America would not begin a battleship construction race after the war – a pious hope, as it turned out, since at the Conference of Washington in 1920 America used the certainty that she would win such a race to bully her Allies into accepting her idea of naval limitation. When they came on to the question of reparations, Lloyd George made it clear that Britain was determined to get part of the spoils, the problem being that since Britain had suffered little damage to her civilian population or territory during the war she would get next to nothing from payments made by Germany for the repair of such damage, unless her merchant shipping losses were included.[7] Lloyd George was therefore determined to extend the purposes for which money was to be claimed from Germany to include a heading under which Britain could claim a share in the loot. He therefore insisted in talking about 'Reparations and Indemnity', despite President Wilson's insistence that under the terms of the Fourteen Points and the Lansing Note the Allies had ruled out any claim to an indemnity, and he told Clemenceau and House that

> He could not agree to any proposal that postponed payment in respect of indemnity until the reparation claims had been completely discharged; that it was more than possible that Germany might not be able to do more than pay the reparation claims, in which case Britain would be left out altogether.

He was not prepared to allow the French too big an advantage in the distribution of whatever it proved possible to extract from Germany.

He therefore proposed that the sums paid by Germany should be allocated in the proportion of three parts to reparations, in which Britain would have little share, and two parts to indemnity, where she could claim a higher proportion. Clemenceau, not surprisingly, demurred at this, but when he asked Colonel House what he thought of the proposal, House replied that 'he thought that it was a very fair plan and he afterwards repeated this observation. This seemed to make an impression on Clemenceau.' In view of the general American stand against a demand for an indemnity,* House's acquiescence in Lloyd George's proposal might be surprising, but in the light of his previous efforts to reconcile American and European points of view by making concessions on his own initiative, often of a kind of which President Wilson and other Americans could hardly have approved,† it is not so surprising to find Colonel House willing to concede that the principle of 'No Indemnity' should not be rigidly applied either.

They then moved on to discuss the western frontier of Germany, when Colonel House offered to accept the creation of a Rhenish buffer state provided that its people were allowed to determine their own fate once Germany had fulfilled the terms of the Peace Treaty. This would not do for Clemenceau, however, who

> said that he did not believe in the principle of self-determination, which allowed a man to clutch at your throat the first time it was convenient to him, and he would not consent to any limitation of time being placed upon the enforced separation of the Rhenish Republic from the rest of Germany.

Lloyd George expressed British unwillingness to take part in a permanent military occupation of the Rhine, and was supported by Colonel House. Lloyd George

> then said that Marshal Foch had not explained what his plan really meant. Clemenceau said there was a good reason why he had not explained it; it was because he did not understand it himself. He did not think he had thought it out and that as a matter of fact he was always changing his mind from day to day and that he never knew where he was.

* See p. 79 above, for example.
† See pp. 32–4 and 43 above, for examples of this.

There were tensions among the French as well as in the other delegations.

They next considered the Eastern frontier of Germany. Lloyd George expressed Britain's dislike of a French proposal to create a German–Polish frontier between Danzig and Thorn, which would mean the inclusion in Poland of large German areas: 'we did not want any more Alsace–Lorraines in Europe, whether in the East or in the West. Clemenceau answered neither did he, he had had enough of them.' Colonel House, however, supported the French proposal, saying that 'the American delegates had come to the conclusion that Danzig ought to be incorporated in Poland and he expected that ultimately the British delegates would also agree,' and also suggested that East Prussia should become a separate republic. Clemenceau welcomed this latter proposal with open arms. 'The more separate and independent republics were established in Germany, the better he would be pleased.' It was agreed to await the report of the Commission on Polish Affairs before discussing the matter further, but already it was apparent that the Americans were closer to the French position on this issue than they were to the British.

Turning to the Middle East, Lloyd George asked Colonel House whether America would accept mandates in this area, and he then said to Clemenceau, 'France, I suppose, will undertake Syria', and urged him to come to some agreement with the Emir Feisal. Clemenceau's response and the further discussions are indicative of the division between Britain and France over Syria. Of negotiations with Feisal, Clemenceau

> said that was a question for us. I said no, if we are trying to get at Feisal your newspapers say that we are stuffing him up. So, therefore, you had better deal with him. He said that he had failed and would not do this. 'I am afraid we shall have to fight him.' I said that that would be a disaster and we did not want another Ab-del-Kader.

It was agreed to seek further advice. Moving on to Italy, Clemenceau turned out to be fiercely hostile to her claims both to her rights under the Treaty of London and to Fiume, which was not included in the territory promised to Italy under that Treaty. The most he was prepared to concede was the internationalisation of Fiume, and in general he was bitterly hostile to the Italians. Lloyd George agreed with his point of view.

The question of whether supplies of food should be sent to Germany provoked another passage of arms between Lloyd George and Clemenceau. Lloyd George spoke of

> the deplorable condition of the German population and the danger of spreading Bolshevism unless Germany were fed. He [Clemenceau] treated that as purely a German story circulated with a view to intimidating the Allies into giving favourable terms to Germany. He was rather scornful of the idea.

Lloyd George commented that Clemenceau

> is not prepared to take the proposal on its merits. He is anxious to preserve the demeanour of the conqueror towards Germany. There will therefore be some difficulty, I fear, in inducing the French to assent to any reasonable plan for feeding Germany.

Clemenceau did not believe any report which came from a German source, and was determined to give them no aid or succour, while Lloyd George was more anxious to prevent her succumbing to Bolshevism. All agreed, however, that an invasion of Russia was not practicable. If Bolshevism could win there, it was too expensive for the Allies to do anything about it, and Lloyd George said that his General Staff's estimate of the cost of effective intervention in Russia 'staggered him'. The conversation ended with a discussion on inter-Allied indebtedness which was comparatively friendly.

On 7 March, therefore, the heads of the three principal delegations ranged over all the major issues then before the Conference. Sometimes they clashed, and this meeting was the first of many – Lloyd George's own copy bears the annotation, added by him later, that this was the first of 'almost daily interchanges of this informal kind'.[8] New decision procedures were being evolved, although disputes were still serious and at times acrimonious at this meeting. Most of the serious difficulties at this stage lay between Britain and France – the German–Polish frontier, the Rhine occupation, the Middle East. America seemed to have fewer points at issue with France than Britain, but to some extent this was the result of Colonel House's readiness to acquiesce in French positions, and the more extreme British demands, as in the case of reparations, and on the German–Polish frontier issue Colonel House and his delegation were clearly prepared to support the French demand for the expansion of Poland at Germany's expense against Britain's concern to avoid the creation of a new running sore in Eastern Europe. Much work remained to be done.

The question of the future status of the Rhenish provinces was one issue which was pursued further immediately after this meeting. It was discussed by the Council of Ten on 10 March, when a draft of the military terms was before them, which included the demilitarisation of these provinces, including a prohibition on the construction of fortifications, another against conscription being applied to the inhabitants of the area and on army military training on a voluntary basis, and a ban on any contribution by the area through taxation towards the cost of the German armed forces.[9] Clemenceau asked for this clause to be deleted as it was clearly intended as a substitute for the French buffer state proposal; he did so

> as the Governments had not yet decided on the fate of the area in question. He thought it would be of no use to ask the Germans to agree to any terms regarding it before its final allotment. They would have to sign another document concerning territorial adjustments.[10]

The matter was left open, and was considered during the next two days by a secret committee of three set up by the three Great Powers to discuss the frontiers of Germany. The members of this committee were Dr Sidney Mezes for America, Philip Kerr, Lloyd George's private secretary and his close *confidant* for Britain, and André Tardieu for France.[11]

This committee seems to have been set up privately and informally. Certainly it was not established as a result of a resolution by the Council of Ten, and there is no reference to it in the Council's minutes. Tardieu opened the discussion by proposing three possible solutions to the dispute over France's eastern frontier. A French frontier on the Rhine, an independent and neutral Rhenish republic, and an Allied occupation of the Rhine bridgeheads. All these proposals had appeared in the French Note to Britain of 25 February,* when the Cabinet had found them to be unacceptable.† Accordingly, Kerr now opposed all three proposals, on the grounds that the British Parliament and people would not wish permanently to maintain forces on the Continent, and that any of these arrangements

* See pp. 105–7 above.
† See pp. 107–8 above.

would lead to constant irritation between France and Germany, in which Britain would inevitably become involved. He said that in his judgement 'the real security of France lay in maintaining a complete understanding with Britain and America', and warned that French insistence upon the occupation of the Rhineland might lead to a breach between herself and Britain.

Dr Mezes did not entirely support Kerr. While joining him in opposing the future presence of Allied troops within Germany proper, he was prepared to agree to the occupation of the Rhineland, though not in perpetuity – 'he was at pains to make clear that America was anxious to do everything possible to give France the security she desired'. At this point, Kerr left the room to consult with Lloyd George, who felt that Mezes had gone too far to meet the French; he 'said he had just as strong objections to maintaining Allied troops in the Rhenish provinces as in Germany proper'. All that Tardieu would concede when Kerr returned, however, was that the permanent separation of the Rhenish provinces from the rest of Germany against the wishes of the population was impossible. No progress had been made.

The following day, 12 March, the discussion was resumed, with Kerr declaring that his colleagues in the British Empire Delegation 'were not going to leave a man in Europe or to bind themselves to interference in any way in purely European questions such as the future of the Rhenish provinces'. At this point Dr Mezes again proved that America was an unreliable ally when attempts were made to moderate French demands. He said that Colonel House 'wished him to say that President Wilson was very sympathetic to France and was deeply interested in the [French] proposal'. Considering that part of this proposal, the enforced separation of the Rhenish provinces, was a blatant violation of the principle of the self-determination of peoples, this was a remarkable statement. It should also be noted that it came from Colonel House, whose readiness to accept European proposals despite the Fourteen Points had already become evident both before and during the Conference. Tardieu, perhaps encouraged by Mezes' statement, then made a plea on behalf of France:

> It was extraordinarily difficult for any maritime Power to realise what the presence of 80 million Germans on their borders meant to the French, in view of the experience of the last 100 years.

Kerr remained firmly opposed both to the separation of the Rhenish provinces from Germany and to a permanent occupation of the Rhineland, and argued that the disarmament clauses of the Treaty would provide a sufficient guarantee of safety for France. Tardieu could not be convinced, however, that the perfidious Germans would not find some way to evade these provisions, and in the end all three agreed that they could make no further progress and that the committee's usefulness was at an end. Even hints of some kind of guarantee by Britain and America of the future safety of France could not wean Tardieu away from the established French policy. As the deadlock became apparent, Kerr wrote,

> We . . . agreed that there did not seem to be any point in prolonging the conversation. M. Tardieu said it was clear that there was a deep difference of opinion between the British and the French Governments. . . . He then suggested that the Prime Ministers and the President should meet, say on Sunday, and try to reach agreement on the fundamentals.

Only discussions at the highest level could offer any possible way out of the *impasse*.

Reporting to Balfour and Lloyd George on the work of this committee, Kerr described Tardieu's advocacy of the separation of the Rhenish provinces from Germany, calling it 'a shell-shock proposition',[12] and urged the offer of an Anglo-American guarantee to France coupled with a short occupation of the Rhineland, of not more than five years. Tardieu's proposals must be resisted in the interest of future peace. 'I would . . . urge them [the French] strongly in their own interest not to insist on incorporating 1,300,000 Germans in France merely for strategic reasons.'[13] It was a matter of conflicting judgements as to what was necessary to ensure the future safety of France.

In the middle of March President Wilson returned to Europe and the negotiations. He did not approve of everything that had happened in his absence. When he had received his first briefing on events at Paris, he is reported to have said to his wife that

> House has given away everything I had won before we left Paris. He has compromised on every side, and so I will have to start all over again and this time it will be harder, as he has given the impression that my delegates are not in sympathy with me.[14]

Wilson was not entirely blind to what was going on behind his back.
On 14 March, Clemenceau, Wilson and Lloyd George had a meeting at the Hotel Crillon, at which the Rhineland problem was discussed once more. Clemenceau still stood firm; in André Tardieu's words, he

> explains once more the French proposals. He tells our needs, our dangers of yesterday and of tomorrow. Alone against Germany, invaded and bleeding, we do not ask for territory, but for guarantees. Those offered us – disarmament, demilitarisation, League of Nations – are inadequate in their present form. Occupation is indispensable. It is essential that this occupation be inter-Allied. It is essential that the left bank be closed to the political and military schemes of Germany.[15]

It looked as though the old deadlock would develop once more, with Lloyd George and Wilson resisting Clemenceau's pleas. Then they made a new proposal – America and Britain would each sign a treaty of guarantee pledging their assistance if France were invaded, coupled with a short occupation of the Rhineland. Tardieu, who was close to Clemenceau at the time, described this as 'an entirely different and most capital proposal',[16] but Clemenceau, while welcoming the offer, asked for time to consult his experts. This was the second informal meeting of the leading figures at Paris, and it was becoming clear that this kind of intimate, informal meeting was the best way to discuss the most difficult problems before the Conference. Certainly only the leading members of the delegations of the Great Powers could now hope to make progress. At this time Lloyd George began to suggest that he ought to return to Britain to attend to domestic politics, but so essential had the presence of the Prime Ministers and President become that on 17 March, Wilson, Clemenceau and Orlando wrote a joint letter to Lloyd George urging him to stay on:

> It seems to us imperative, in order that the world may wait no longer for peace than is actually unavoidable, that you should remain in Paris until the chief questions connected with the peace are settled, and we earnestly beg that you will do so.

They expressed the hope, optimistically, that another fortnight would suffice.[17] Faced with such a demand, Lloyd George felt obliged to remain, and informed Bonar Law, who as Lord Privy Seal was in charge of minding the store in London, that he could not return, and could only discuss pressing industrial problems, especially in the mining and railway industries, by letter.[18]

On 17 March, the French made their next move in the negotiations over the Rhineland. Clemenceau sent a Note to the British and American delegations reasserting France's right to demand the permanent occupation of the Rhenish provinces and their separation from the rest of Germany. He was able to play on the fact that under the terms of the Armistice Britain and America had already secured complete freedom from the danger of a German attack: 'The complete elimination of the German fleet has not been a sufficient reason for the maritime powers to disarm their own navies. On land France also has a right to a physical guarantee,' and the Allies had recognised this by offering the Treaty of Guarantee to France, a valuable offer, but one which must be 'completed and rendered precise'. Then Clemenceau returned to a well-worn theme – British and American help could not arrive in time to prevent the Germans invading and devastating much of France and taking many French lives, as they had in 1914, and the occupation of the Rhine must therefore last for at least thirty years. He also asked for the cession of the Saar valley with its mines, as a compensation for damage done by the German armies to the coal mines of North-Eastern France.[19] The French had not yielded much.

This was not a view which the British were disposed to accept. The following day Balfour prepared a comment on the French Note in which he said that the French view was 'very forcible, but very one-sided', assuming as it did that France must live in perpetual fear of a new German invasion, and must above all have protection against that possibility. Balfour believed that this was not the real danger for the future, but that any new German attempt at expansion would concentrate on the East, with the replacement of the Russian and Austro-Hungarian Empires by a chain of small, weak states. Thus the Rhine frontier provided only a 'narrow and incomplete' protection which 'concentrates its whole attention upon bridge-heads and strategic frontiers, upon the Rhine and the Treaty of 1814, and draws all its inspiration from Generals and Statesmen absorbed in the military memoirs of 1870 and 1914'. He concluded with a general criticism of the French attitude at the Conference. The only real cure for the French predicament was

> a change in the international system of the world, a change which French statesmen are doing nothing to promote, and the very possibility of which many of them regard with ill-concealed derision. They may be right; but if they are, it is quite certain that no manipulation of the Rhine frontier is going to make France anything more than a second-rate Power, trembling at the nod of its great neighbours to the East, and depending from day to day on the changes and chances of a shifting diplomacy and uncertain alliances.[20]

Balfour wanted a better future for France and Europe than French policy promised to produce. Colonel House, for his part, was doubtful whether the American Senate would ratify the Treaty of Guarantee, but it seemed to be the only way of reducing the extent of French demands on the Rhine frontier.[21] At this time, agreement still seemed far away. On 20 March Clemenceau had another meeting with Lloyd George and Wilson, and afterwards saw House, who recorded in his diary that

> Perhaps the most interesting feature of the day was going with André Tardieu to call on Clemenceau at his request. He had had a meeting with Lloyd George and the President all afternoon. I asked him how they had gotten on. . . . 'Splendidly, we disagreed about everything.'[22]

Even the leading statesmen seemed unable to cut through the tangles of disagreement and dispute in which the Conference was enmeshed, and in particular the question of the future status of the Rhenish provinces remained unresolved.

Other problems were also pressing upon the Governments of Europe. The Russian civil war continued unabated, and European Governments lived in fear of the possible spread of Bolshevism. On 17 March the British Cabinet discussed Russia. Churchill declared that 'everything was going wrong', and the Bolsheviks were advancing on every front; 'he could only express the profound apprehension with which he awaited what was coming', while Austen Chamberlain, guarding the purse-strings as Chancellor of the Exchequer, said that only the Americans could afford to finance an effective resistance to Bolshevism, and they would not. The Cabinet could only agree to put pressure on the Conference to act,[23] especially as the Prime Minister was absent in Paris and they could take no unilateral action without his agreement; as we have already seen, there was a rift between Lloyd George and his Secretary of State for War over Russia.* In the Council of Ten, meanwhile, Marshal Foch was pressing for assistance to be given to the Poles to attack Russia and defend her territory against the Bolsheviks, especially in Eastern Galicia:

> The gravity of the situation was such that the very existence of this nation [Poland], which the Allied and Associated Governments had decided to recognise, to reconstitute and to assist, was in question. The most imminent danger related to the town of Lemberg,† which was infested by the Ukrainians, and whose fall would entail that of the Polish Government.[24]

Immediate action was necessary if Poland was to be saved.

Lloyd George, however, was determined not to be rushed into further intervention by the impetuous Marshal. First, he was not going to commit Britain to large-scale action against the Bolsheviks on the pretext of saving Poland. Secondly, he was profoundly suspicious of Polish activities and intentions in Galicia anyway:

> In regard to the question of Lemberg, he would enquire whether any decision had been reached that the town should belong to Poland. In his opinion no decision had been reached by the Committee appointed to enquire into the frontiers of Poland. Why, therefore, should the Conference decide the question in favour of the Poles and against the Ukrainians before the question had been properly examined? Had the Poles felt very strongly on this question he thought they would be able to defend themselves.[25]

Lloyd George, with President Wilson's support, refused to be rushed into determining the fate of Eastern Galicia before the nationality of its population, and hence its rightful allocation, had been determined.

Marshal Foch was not the only person who wished to get a quick decision in favour of Poland on this issue. On 19 March the chief American adviser on Polish affairs, Dr Robert H. Lord, formerly Assistant Professor of Modern European History at Harvard University and an expert on the Partitions of Poland, presented proposals

* See pp. 91–7 above.

† Otherwise Lvov, the chief town in Eastern Galicia.

for an armistice to be imposed by the Conference upon the Poles and the Ukrainians, under which Poland would be allowed to occupy most of the territory, including Lemberg, for the time being. This proposal immediately evoked a question from Lloyd George, who

> enquired what was the national character of the population in and around Lemberg.
>
> DR LORD replied that in the city itself 10–12 per cent were Ruthenians, 50 per cent Poles and the remainder Jews. The Polish character of the city population had been strikingly demonstrated by the events of the last four months. The town had been defended against the Ukrainians street by street and house by house.[26]

Lord's mind was made up – Eastern Galicia should be Polish – but Lloyd George was still not convinced:

> According to the maps he had the majority of the population in Eastern Galicia was Ukrainian. According to the principle of the Allied and Associated Powers the country should, therefore, be attributed to them, unless very cogent reasons to the contrary existed. . . . The Report of the Polish Committee* showed that the Poles were not incapable of claiming more for themselves than was theirs by right. They had done so in respect of their frontiers with Germany and Russia. They might be doing so in this region too. It was desirable that the Conference should be strictly impartial. It was not improbable that what the Poles chiefly wanted in Eastern Galicia was the oilfields.[27]

Thus Lloyd George was opposing both the Americans and the French in the name of the principle of the self-determination of peoples. The French wanted to strengthen Poland as much as possible so that she would be a firm check on both Germany and the Bolsheviks, while American expert opinion as it reached the Council of Ten was strongly pro-Polish. The Council finally decided to offer both the Poles and the Ukrainians a hearing, provided that they both accepted and observed a cease-fire in Eastern Galicia. It was agreed to notify both Governments of this offer.

This same balance of forces within the Council operated when the Commission on Polish Affairs' first report, on the German–Polish frontier, was discussed that same afternoon. The Report was intro-

* This was also considered at this meeting. See below.

duced by the French chairman of the Commission, Jules Cambon, who proceeded at once to explain why the Commission's recommendations did not conform with the nationality of the peoples of the area:

> Economic and strategic requirements had also been taken into account, in order that the new state should be so delimited as to be capable of life. At all points save one the frontier adopted by the Committee gave the Poles less than they asked for.[28]

President Wilson had promised the Poles free and secure access to the sea in his Fourteen Points, and to this end they were to be given the only good port in the area, Danzig, a city of largely German population, plus a strip of territory linking Danzig with the interior of Poland so delimited as to give the Poles control over both of the two railways that ran between Danzig and Warsaw, one via Thorn and the other via Mlawa, as well as control over the entire length of the Vistula. The total effect would be to include territory containing over two million Germans in Poland.

To this proposal Lloyd George at once objected. He believed that to include so many Germans in the new state 'might spell considerable trouble for Poland in the future', and also the Germans might refuse a treaty containing such a provision, and he enquired whether the number of Germans to be included in Poland could not be reduced.[29] Cambon replied that this was impossible without dangerously weakening Poland, whereupon Lloyd George reverted once again to his concern that no new sources of international friction should be created by the territorial settlement: he

> agreed that it was hardly possible to draw any line that would not have Germans on both sides of it, but he thought it was very dangerous to assign two million Germans to Poland. This was a considerable population, not less than that of Alsace–Lorraine in 1870. . . . To hand over millions of people to a distasteful allegiance merely because of a railway was, he thought, a mistake.[30]

Once again, Lloyd George was to find that American support for the principle of nationality was not forthcoming, and this time it was the President himself who let him down. Wilson pointed out that the Germans who lived in the area under discussion were only there because of German colonisation policies – the problem only arose because of the past wickedness of German Governments. When

BALTIC SEA
Memel
Königsberg
EAST PRUSSIA
Danzig
Marienburg
Bromberg
Mlawa
River Bug
Poznan
Warsaw
Lódz
Piotrkow
River Vistula
Lublin
SILESIA
River
R. San
Crakow
Przemysl
Lemberg
G A L I C I A
R. Dniester
R. Zbruch
POLAND
German inhabited areas
Mixed German-Polish
Little Russian inhabited areas
Mixed Polish-Little Russian
Frontiers after 1921
Pre-1914 frontiers
Railways

Cambon protested to Lloyd George that the Commission's decisions had been unanimous, Lloyd George replied that its British members had only accepted them reluctantly:

> They regarded them as a departure from the principles of the Fourteen Points which had been adopted by the Allies. . . . Because fifty years ago some capitalists had built a railway that was convenient to the Poles, the area surrounding it must be ascribed to Poland, in spite of the undoubted German nationality of the population.[31]

He agreed with Cambon that Poland must be given access to the sea, but this was the wrong way to achieve that end:

> A railway could be removed, but a long-settled population was not removed with the same ease. He thought that in accepting these proposals, the Council would be abandoning its principles and making trouble, not only for Poland, but for the world. . . . Should the populations of these areas rise against the Poles, and should their fellow-countrymen wish to go to their assistance, would France, Great Britain and the United States go to war to maintain Polish rule over them?[32]

Despite the force of this argument, based directly on the Fourteen Points, President Wilson did not support his British colleague. His immediate response was to point out that Germany had been warned that access to the sea for Poland would be demanded in the Treaty, and later he supported the Commission in its attitude towards the principle of nationality: he

> said that it must be realised the Allies were creating a new and weak state, weak not only because historically it had failed to govern itself, but because it was sure in future to be divided into factions. . . . It was therefore necessary to consider not only the economic but the strategic needs of this state, which would have to cope with Germany on both sides of it, the Eastern fragment of Germany being one of a most aggressive character.[33]

Wilson's hatred of the Germans, coupled with the determination of the American experts to preserve the new Poland, combined to drive Wilson to make common cause with the French against Lloyd George, who was arguing for the freedom of people to live under the government of their own kind, and for a peace which would not contain among its provisions the seeds of future wars. When Lloyd George sought at the end of the meeting to secure the reference back of the report for redrafting in accordance with the principle of nationality, Wilson opposed him and asked simply for reference back for further consideration in the light of the Council's discussion.[34] This weakened reference was agreed.

The Commission reported back three days later, rejecting Lloyd George's view; they remained of the opinion that 'the importance to Poland of retaining complete control over the Danzig–Mlawa–Warsaw railway overrides the historical and ethnographical arguments in favour of Germany', and also pointed out that the populations were so mixed that no ethnographical frontier could be drawn.[35] None of this made Lloyd George happier, and he expressed a particular fear about the effect the Commission's proposals would have in Germany:

> The Allies should not run the risk of driving the country [Germany] to such desperation that no Government would dare to sign the terms. At the present time the Government at Weimar was not very stable, and all the currents of German life went on their way without taking much notice of its existence. It was tolerated, however, as there was nothing to put in its place. The Conference must avoid presenting such a Treaty that no Government would dare to sign it, or such as would cause the immediate collapse of any Government that undertook the responsibility of accepting it.[36]

Lloyd George did not wish to see the German government disintegrate, with the probable result of a Bolshevik takeover. Germany must be able to establish and maintain law and order if this were to be avoided, and if the nascent German democracy was to be given a chance of survival. Also, Lloyd George did not wish to have to renew the war in order to impose the Treaty when it had finally been drawn up. Cambon, however, could not accept this point of view: the Commission's proposals were designed to give Poland 'some chance of survival', and must be carried out.[37] The difference between Lloyd George's attitude on the German–Polish frontier and that of his colleagues in the Council of Ten was complete.

The problem of Russia still rumbled on, and the Allies were still unable to deal effectively with it. On 20 March Lord Curzon handed a memorandum to the French Ambassador in London protesting at a failure of Anglo-French cooperation in giving assistance to the forces of General Denikin in South Russia. The French, it seemed, were on the point of making an agreement with the Ukrainian Directory which would seriously undermine Denikin's authority, and Lord Curzon added to this complaints of French military misconduct.[38] Clearly, Allied intervention was not working well. Anxieties were increased by the successful Bolshevik revolution in Hungary, led by Bela Kun, which took place on 20 March,[39] which caused Colonel House to record in his diary on 22 March that

> Bolshevism is gaining ground everywhere. Hungary has just succumbed. We are sitting upon a powder magazine and some day a spark may ignite it.[40]

Little effective action was being taken to stem the spread of Bolshevism, however, and with the Peace Conference deadlocked over most of the major issues before it, there seemed little chance of an early peace with the revival of prosperity that should follow it, so reducing the hardships of the European peoples which made them a prey for the Bolsheviks. Nor could the Allies agree on a policy in Russia. At one of the Council of Four's first meetings, on the afternoon of 25 March, assistance for Admiral Kolchak was suggested, but Lloyd George was unwilling to grant assistance unless he was sure that Kolchak had the support of the people in Siberia, where his Government operated.[41] The Conference was virtually helpless when it came to deciding what should be done to limit the spread of Bolshevism and if possible to destroy it.

Meanwhile on 12 March, Robert Lansing reported to the Council of Ten that the Committee on Breaches of the Laws of War had decided that no-one could be tried for starting the war, since their responsibility was a moral, not a legal, one.[42] On reparations, an informal subcommittee of three members reported on 20 March in favour of a relatively moderate total demand, since Germany could not be expected to make a large balance of payments surplus after the war and world opinion would more readily support the extraction, by force if need be, of a moderate total.[43] These and related matters were discussed by the Council of Four during its first few days of recorded meetings.[44] On 25 March they began by discussing the question of whether Germany should be admitted to the League of Nations, a matter which the League Commission had been unable to

THE PERIL WITHOUT.

From *Punch*, Vol. 156, p. 263.

decide.* President Wilson wished to have the Covenant of the League written into the Peace Treaty, but Clemenceau would only agree on condition that Germany's signature would not admit her to the League. Lloyd George said that he would prefer Germany to be admitted, as this would give the Allies more effective means of keeping an eye on her, but 'I understand the reason for M. Clemenceau's objection and the public feeling to which it is a response'.[45] All were agreed that Germany must not be admitted at once; she could not be trusted, and Lloyd George's only doubt was whether she could not be more effectively watched if she were in the League and hence bound by the provisions of the Covenant.

The Council then went on to discuss reparations. Wilson, nervous of what he expected to be enormous European demands, opened the discussion by urging that the settlement must not be so severe that no German Government would sign it. Lloyd George, who had long since realised that the extent of the funds which would become available would be determined by the German capacity to pay and not on how much it was finally decided to demand, was more concerned to see that Britain got her fair share of the spoils. He therefore raised the question of damage done to persons, rather than to the property, of the civilian population of the Allied states, and urged that the amounts that Allied Governments had paid out for pensions for men, or dependents of men, who had been killed or wounded in the war should be included. That way Britain would get a larger share of the spoils than she would if only damage to property were taken into account. He also alleged that French and Belgian estimates of the damage done in their countries were exaggerated, and he proposed that the spoils be distributed in the ratio of fifty per cent to France, thirty per cent for Britain, and the remaining twenty per cent for all the other nations.[46] Lloyd George always had an eye to the main chance, and was also conscious of the strength of public and Parliamentary feeling on this issue. In a further discussion the following morning, the Council of Four discussed the problem of Germany's capacity to pay, with the financial and economic advisers to the Great Power delegations present.

The French Minister for Reconstruction, Loucheur, argued strongly that France must be allowed to make a large claim, but Wilson warned him not to raise his expectations too high – 'Do you not think that you are being over-optimistic to think that after all we

* See pp. 86–7 above.

are going to take from her, Germany is going to be in a better position to export goods than she was before the war?'[47] He was supported in this by Lloyd George, who warned that the Germans might give themselves over to Bolshevism rather than to a lifetime of labour to pay reparations: 'if they prefer to risk some years' anarchy rather than submit to thirty-five years of slavery, where will we be then?'[48] It was a difficult problem in view of public opinion on the matter:

> It will be as difficult for me as for M. Clemenceau to disperse the illusions which reign in the public mind on the subject of reparations. Four hundred members of the British Parliament have sworn to extract the last farthing from Germany of what is owing to us; I will have to face up to them. But our duty is to act in the best interests of our countries.... I am convinced that the Germans will not sign the sort of terms some people are suggesting. I would not sign if I were them. Germany will succumb to Bolshevism, and Europe will remain mobilised, our industries stopped, our treasuries bankrupt.[49]

An excessive demand for reparation could only lead to Bolshevism in Germany and probably elsewhere, and for this reason it would be necessary to face up to publics and Parliaments and convince them that moderation was the best course. Wilson agreed; indeed he admired this speech of Lloyd George's, and remarked that 'We must not ask too often what we are owed because of our losses, but rather what it will be possible and wise to extract'.[50] For once, Wilson and Lloyd George were united. Clemenceau, however, remained firm in support of his colleague, Loucheur. He reminded the Council that the Allies had claimed freedom from the Fourteen Points in this matter and asked for all parties to be allowed to submit claims for arbitration, whereupon Lloyd George declared that the experts could not agree, so that discussion at any level below the highest would be useless.[51] That afternoon they discussed the ratio of distribution of reparation payments between the Allies, and again could not agree. Lloyd George wanted the fifty: thirty: twenty ratio he had already proposed, whereas the French wanted seventy-two per cent and eighteen per cent for Britain. At the end of the discussion, Loucheur declared that:

> In my heart and conscience I cannot recommend what is not just. I have made a big step towards you and I am sorry that it has not been better appreciated.[52]

The more the Council discussed the reparations issue, the more problems and disagreements seemed to appear between them.

Relations between Britain and France were not improved by the continued presence of the problem of Syria. The British were still determined to wriggle out of the Sykes–Picot agreement, and Lord Curzon had been annoyed at the tone of the French Notes of January and February complaining about the activities of British forces and officials in Syria, which he described in a letter to Lord Derby on 4 March as 'very insolent', and said that he would 'comment in somewhat severe language upon the unusual and almost offensive tone'. In his reply of 19 March he rejected the French complaints completely.* He found the French attitude exasperating.[53] On 20 March the matter was raised at a meeting between Clemenceau, Lloyd George, Orlando and Wilson, attended also by various advisers.[54] Pichon explained the terms of the Sykes–Picot Agreement whereby France and Britain were each to assume responsibility for a zone in the Arab territories and assist them to attain independence and democratic government, which had been reaffirmed by the Anglo–French declaration of November 1918. He therefore requested that France be given a mandate for Syria as the means of fulfilling the terms of the Sykes–Picot Agreement. Britain was trying to restrict France's role in Syria, but the French could not accept that.

Lloyd George attempted to be conciliatory. Britain did not wish to take the mandate for Syria, but she had done most of the fighting there and must keep her bargains with the Emir Feisal and King Hussein to support Arab independence and unity: 'There would have been no question of Syria but for England. Great Britain had put from 900,000 to 1,000,000 men in the field against Turkey, but Arab help had been essential.' He could not, therefore, agree to the imposition upon the Arabs of a mandatory to whom they might be hostile, while Pichon refused to allow France to be bound by agreements between Britain and Arab rulers which had been made unknown to her. President Wilson said that his only concern was that the mandatory should be someone the people of the area wanted, and he had been told that if France began occupying Syria, the Arabs would make 'instant war', an opinion supported by General Allenby, who said that the Arabs would resist a French occupation of Syria: 'Feisal had insisted that if put under French control, he would oppose

* See pp. 113-4 above for a discussion of these Notes.

to the uttermost.' In his opinion, the French and the Arabs did not get on well together, and there was a risk that any attempt to impose French domination upon Syria would result in a 'huge war'. Britain and France had opposite views on what was possible and desirable, and after an adjournment so that the statesmen could confer with other members of their delegations, Wilson proposed that an inter-Allied Commission should be sent out to the Middle East to determine the wishes of the population. After Clemenceau had asked, and Lloyd George had accepted, that the Commission should consider the British sphere of influence defined in the Sykes–Picot Agreement as well as the French, this proposal was accepted.

This proposal aroused some anxiety among members of the British Government. Balfour sent a memorandum to Lloyd George urging that the proposed inter-Allied Commission must give full weight to the interests and views of the Jews, when they considered the future of Palestine, as well as taking account of the feelings of the present Arab population.[55] Lord Curzon circulated to the War Cabinet a 'Note of warning about the Middle East' on 25 March expressing fears that if Britain and France were to quarrel over the area, the way would be open for German and Turkish intrigue there. There was the danger that if the Turks lost a great deal of territory, as they would, they would seize upon an Anglo–French dispute as a chance to 'strike another blow . . . for Islam and the few remaining vestiges of their freedom'. This must be avoided by care on the part of the military and naval authorities.[56] Be this as it may, the terms of reference of the inter-Allied Commission which was to investigate the opinion of the Arabs were prepared on 25 March. They were to determine who should act as mandatory for the various Arab states, bearing in mind that 'the Conference . . . feels obliged to acquaint itself as intimately as possible with the sentiments of the people of these regions with regard to the future administration of their affairs', and they were to decide what divisions of the territory 'will be most likely to promote the order, peace and development of those peoples and countries'.[57] The agreement to send a Commission would shelve the problem for the time being, but there was to be a further dispute between Britain and France before it was allowed to depart for the Middle East.

Another country which was tenaciously hanging on to her territorial ambitions was Italy. On 14 March Balfour wrote from Paris to Sir Rennell Rodd in Rome that Italy's determined hostility towards her Eastern neighbours, especially the Yugoslavs, 'appears to be perfectly insane'.[58] Rodd replied on 22 March that the Italians were 'in all the relations of life hesitating and reluctant to venture and yet are acquisitious and grasping'.[59] On 25 March, Sir C. des Graz, British Ambassador in Belgrade, informed the Foreign Secretary that if Italy was determined to wrest Fiume from the new Yugoslav state, the people were equally determined to keep it, and a rumour that the Conference had reached a decision in favour of Italy had sparked off widespread popular demonstrations and the authorities there had had to erect placards proclaiming that the reports were not official, in order to calm the people down.[60] Here was yet another problem for the Conference which involved deeply and obstinately held demands which conflicted and would have to be resolved, somehow.

The month of March, then, had seen attempts to create new and more effective methods of reaching decisions – informal secret committees of senior advisors or plenipotentiaries, and the informal meetings of the heads of the most important delegations which led up to the establishment of the Council of Four. As Commissions of experts reported or failed to agree, tensions rose, and they were further heightened by the knowledge that decisions would have to be taken soon.

# 8 Fontainebleau and After: *Territorial Questions, March-April 1919*

Lloyd George was the first of the statesmen at Paris to attempt to present to the Conference a set of conclusions based on the discussions of the first three months. In mid-March he received expressions of dissatisfaction about the way the Conference was going and the Treaty developing. Sir Maurice Hankey wrote to Lloyd George on 19 March to express his own concern and that of Philip Kerr, and in view of the fact that Hankey and Kerr were two of Lloyd George's closest friends and most intimate *confidants* at this time, and in the light of what was to happen afterwards, this letter is of considerable significance. Hankey began by saying that

> For some time past I have felt a vague and indefinite uneasiness as to whether the Peace Treaty was developing on sound lines of policy. Mr Philip Kerr has several times pointed out to you and to me that, while any exaction on Germany can be justified on its merits, the accumulation of these will put Germany in an utterly impossible position.

If this were done, peace could never become securely established, and Bolshevism would spread into Europe. It is interesting that Hankey says that the Chief of the Imperial General Staff, General Sir Henry Wilson, agreed with this view. The new States could not withstand Bolshevism, since they were weak and 'apparently incapable', and were already quarrelling among themselves – Poland and Czechoslovakia over Teschen, Italy and Yugoslavia over Fiume, and so forth. So the terms must be moderated to secure peace and stability: 'Our first object is not to secure the humiliation of Germany but the peace of the world.'[1] Such a letter, expressing the views of people whose judgement the Prime Minister trusted and valued, was bound to make an impression, especially since he had already been urging moderation on his colleagues in the Council of Four, above all in the matter of the frontiers of Germany, and the letter gave support to the views he had been expressing that no new causes of friction must be created and Germany must not be driven to desperation by the terms offered to her.

The effect of such protests as these, and the discussions he was having in the Council of Four, where agreement, it seemed, would never come, and if it did, only on terms which would produce the results which Lloyd George most feared, caused him to retire briefly to the château at Fontainebleau, some miles outside Paris, to confer with a small group of his closest friends, including Hankey, Kerr and General Wilson. Lord Hankey has left us an intriguing account of the discussions at Fontainebleau. It seems that each participant was given a rôle or series of rôles to play, imitating a device used by Wilson at staff conferences. Thus Wilson played both the German and French parts, and Hankey the English, while Kerr was to record the discussion and Lloyd George would sum up. After preparing their briefs, using the Conference records as a basis, the group met. Hankey recalls Wilson, speaking as a German, when 'he wore his military cap back to front (i.e. with the eye-shade at the back of his head) which gave him the appearance of a German officer!' He later spoke as a French woman, who had borne the grief of the huge French losses, and Hankey as an Englishman spoke of sea-power and the traditional British dislike, since Cromwell's time, of a large standing army and compulsory military service. Lloyd George summed up, and Kerr began drafting the document which would be sent to the other participants in the Conference.[2]

During the next two days, Kerr produced a number of drafts, on which Lloyd George and the other members of the group commented,[3] culminating in the final version sent to the other delegations on 25 March.[4] It began by eloquently setting out what Lloyd George and his colleagues believed to be the supreme task of a Peace Conference. The opening sentences are:

> When nations are exhausted by wars in which they have put forth all their strength and which leave them tired, bleeding and broken, it is not difficult to patch up a peace that may last until the generation which experienced the war has passed away. . . . What is

difficult, however, is to draw up a peace which will not provoke a fresh struggle when those who have had practical experience of what war means have passed away.

Peace must be stable, for once the terrible memories then so fresh had faded, any source of international friction might lead to a fresh outbreak. Then the document becomes more specific. Germany will always be a major European Power, and as such her future position and actions must be considered:

> You may strip Germany of her colonies, reduce her armaments to a mere police force and her navy to that of a fifth-rate Power; all the same, in the end, if she feels that she has been unjustly treated in the peace of 1919, she will find means of exacting retribution from her conquerors. . . . The maintenance of peace will then depend upon there being no causes of exasperation constantly stirring up the spirit of patriotism, of justice and of fair play. To achieve redress our terms may be severe, they may be stern and even ruthless, but at the same time they can be so just that the country on which they are imposed will feel in its heart that it has no right to complain. But injustice, arrogance displayed in the hour of triumph, will never be forgotten or forgiven.
>
> For these reasons I am, therefore, strongly averse to transferring more Germans from German rule to the rule of some other nation than can possibly be helped.

This last sentence is important, for he moved on to deal with the German–Polish frontier, on which the report of the Commission of experts appointed to consider it had particularly affrighted him. He had strongly opposed their recommendations,* which involved the transfer of more than two million Germans to Polish rule, in the Council of Ten, and in his memoirs of the Conference Lloyd George said that he was particularly suspicious of the members of the Commission of Polish affairs. The French, in this as in other matters, were 'bent on taking the fullest advantage of their opportunity to reduce the potential strength of Germany',[5] while the American experts were equally suspect, in Lloyd George's view:

> The American Polish experts were fanatical pro-Poles, and their judgement in any dispute in which Poland was concerned was

* See pp. 153–7 above.

> vitiated by an invincible partisanship. There was therefore no hope for redress in a reference back to the Commission.[6]

The Commission was useless as far as Lloyd George was concerned. The Franco–American alliance in the Council of Ten reflected a similar combination among the experts, and the only hope lay in an appeal to Governments and heads of delegations. Hence, after his appeal for moderation in order to secure lasting peace, Lloyd George turned to this problem first, asking for a corridor to Danzig drawn regardless of transport or strategic considerations in order to include as small a number of Germans as possible – to adopt the present recommendations 'must, in my judgement, lead sooner or later to a new war in the East of Europe'. His other major concerns were that Germany should be admitted to the League as soon as possible and that France should accept the Anglo–American guarantee as a substitute for a Rhine frontier, buffer state or permanent occupation. His other major concern was with Bolshevism. The Russian problem must be solved, but above all the peace terms must not be so severe that Germany would succumb to Bolshevism either to avoid signing them or because they reduced her population to such poverty that they rebelled. Lloyd George's fear of Bolshevism is well illustrated by the following passage from the Fontainebleau Memorandum:

> The revolution is still in its infancy. The supreme figures of the Terror are still in command in Russia. The whole of Russia is filled with the spirit of revolution. There is everywhere a deep sense not only of discontent, but of anger and revolt amongst the workmen, against pre-war conditions. The whole existing order, in its political, social and economic aspects, is questioned by the masses of the population from one end of Europe to the other. . . . The greatest danger that I see in the present situation is that Germany may throw in her lot with Bolshevism and place her resources, her brains, her vast organising power at the disposal of the revolutionary fanatics whose dream it is to conquer the world for Bolshevism by force of arms.

Bolshevism was the greatest of all dangers, and it could only be met by statesmanlike moderation. The Fontainebleau Memorandum is full of such pleas, stemming from Lloyd George's two cardinal beliefs: that the Treaty must not sow the seeds of future discord, and that it must allow all peoples, including the Germans, a chance of a reasonable life.

Attached to the memorandum was an outline of peace terms. Poland should be given a corridor to Danzig drawn on ethnographical lines, the Rhenish provinces must not be separated from Germany, though they should be demilitarised and France should be guaranteed safety from invasion by Britain and America. She should have the use of the Saar mines as compensation for damage to her other coal-fields, but should not be allowed to seize the territory. The Brest–Litovsk Treaty would be abrogated and Germany should accept the principle of making 'full reparation' for the damage she had caused. She would not be able to do this, however, so payments to the limit of her capacity should be exacted for an agreed number of years, to be distributed on the basis Lloyd George had proposed earlier: fifty per cent to France, thirty per cent to the British Empire, and twenty per cent for the rest. The Kaiser and other war criminals must be surrendered. Finally he urged that 'the Allied and Associated Powers [should] do all they can to put [Germany] on her legs once more'. The Germans must not be left to starve.

This eloquent plea for moderation, coupled with comprehensive proposals for the German Treaty, would, Lloyd George hoped, provide a way out of the series of deadlocks in which the Conference found itself, and would provide guidelines for a peace which would last and would prevent the spread of Bolshevism.

The Fontainebleau Memorandum having been prepared and circulated, the question was what reactions it would bring forth from the other delegations. It was soon apparent that the French were unlikely to accept Lloyd George's proposals. Although on 27 March agreement was quickly reached on the destruction of fortifications west of a line fifty kilometres east of the Rhine, and Lloyd George reassured Clemenceau that 'We are ready to give France a promise of immediate and unlimited assistance if she is invaded',[7] they soon became embroiled in another wrangle over the German–Polish frontier, when, at the morning session of the Council of Four,[8] Lloyd George asked Clemenceau whether he had received the Fontainebleau Memorandum. The Frenchman first rejected outright Lloyd George's plea for Germany's early admission to the League of Nations, saying that 'the Germans are a servile people who need force in order to support an argument', and went on to take Lloyd George to task, by way of example, over Danzig:

> Notice that no-one in Germany makes any distinction between the just and unjust demands of the Allies. Over no other issue is their resistance so strong as it is over the attribution of Danzig to Poland, yet in order to rectify the effect of the historic crime committed against Poland, we are bound, in order to restore this nation to life, to give her the means of life.

Poland had suffered terrible things at German hands: 'We recall to our minds the children butchered for having prayed to God in the Polish tongue, the peasants whose lands were expropriated, who were chased from their homes, in order to provide a place for occupants of the German race.' He went on to reject entirely the spirit which had animated the Fontainebleau Memorandum:

> I pay homage to the spirit of equity shown by Mr Lloyd George when he expresses his desire to give Poland as few German subjects as possible. But I cannot accept the phrase where he says that, in drawing the corridor to provide communication between Danzig and the interior, we must leave to one side all strategic considerations. If we follow this advice, we will leave a sorry inheritance to our successors.

Safety was more important to Clemenceau than the avoidance of putting Germans under a foreign yoke. The assurance of adequate protection in the event of a new war was more important than attempting to avoid creating issues which could be the *casus belli*. Clemenceau was not convinced by the arguments of the Fontainebleau Memorandum, as this discussion of the German–Polish frontier makes clear. Lloyd George, in reply, warned once more of the danger that Bolshevism might overrun Europe if the Allies did not proceed with care:

> I know something of the danger of Bolshevism in our countries: I have been fighting it myself for some weeks now. . . . I fight Bolshevism, not by force, but by seeking to satisfy the legitimate aspirations whose frustration gives it birth. The result has been that the Syndicalists like Smillie, the General Secretary of the miners' union, who could have been formidable opponents, ended up by helping us to avert a conflict. . . . But so far as the peace terms are concerned, what could provoke a Bolshevik explosion in England is not asking too little of the enemy, but asking too much.

He then went on to quote from a letter he had received from General Smuts,[9] in which Smuts had warned of the danger of Germany succumbing to Bolshevism and also of renewing warlike ambitions in future. Writing of the proposals made so far, Smuts said

> I am simply amazed at all this. Are we in our sober senses, or suffering from shell-shock? What has become of Wilson's 14 points, or of your repeated declarations against the humiliation and dismemberment of Germany?

The small states were not reliable. Moderation was the only salvation. Smuts was particularly aghast at the Danzig and Polish corridor proposals, and Lloyd George quoted his views with approbation to the Council of Four: 'I declare great fear on the subject of Danzig.' They were going to give over two million Germans to the Poles, which was bound to cause trouble. 'The Polish Germans might revolt, in which case they would be crushed: if Germany wanted to intervene, do you envisage sending troops to keep the Germans in Poland under the Polish yoke?' Yet again he evoked the spectre of Alsace–Lorraine, in the hope of appealing to Clemenceau not to do to the Germans what had been done to France in 1871: 'What struck me most on my first visit to Paris was the statue of Strasburg in mourning. We do not want to enable Germans to erect similar statues in their towns as a result of what we have done.' He therefore advocated making Danzig a free port, leaving the Poles in Poland and the Germans in Germany; he concluded:

> General Smuts wisely wrote to me that 'Poland cannot exist except with the good will of Germany and Russia'. When our forces have returned home, the Poles will be alone, isolated, surrounded on all sides by enemies.
> M. CLEMENCEAU: What is your conclusion?
> MR LLOYD GEORGE: My conclusion is that we must not create a Poland separated from her birth by an ineradicable quarrel from her most highly civilised neighbour.

No progress could be made and the Council shifted its attention for the time being to other problems.

On 27 March, also, Colonel House presented a draft of the Anglo–American Treaty of Guarantee to the Council of Four. It contained an affirmation of German war guilt.[10] In the Council of Four Clemenceau resisted a suggestion from President Wilson that the guarantee should be only temporary, as he felt there should be no permanent groupings of Powers within the League. In the end Wilson proposed that they should pledge themselves to take action in the case of unjustifiable aggression as determined by the Executive Council of the League, and Clemenceau accepted so long as in Germany's case unjustified aggression was defined as the entry of military forces into the demilitarised area whose boundary was to run fifty kilometres east of the Rhine.[11]

The following day, the Council of Four turned their attention again to the vexed question of reparations,[12] with the French Minister of Finance, Klotz, present – later, Wilson was to remark bitterly, 'we got Klotz on the brain'.[13] He opened the meeting by producing a list of the damage done to France by the Germans and declared, 'We want nothing that is not our rightful due'. He suggested that the total should be fixed by an inter-Allied Commission in a year or two years' time in order to allow for a more thorough determination of the extent of the damage. Wilson cut him short by saying that they need not discuss matters of detail now, but only the principles upon which a claim was to be based: if the total were not to be decided until later, this was even more important. Lloyd George reacted favourably to Klotz's proposal, saying that J. M. Keynes had already made such a suggestion to him;* they could tell the Germans that they had not decided how much they could pay. Wilson, however, felt that Klotz's proposal amounted to a demand for unlimited credit from Germany, but Lloyd George believed it offered a way out of their gravest difficulty – the effect of any announcement of a total demand for reparations on the peoples and Parliaments of the Allied countries:

> I see great advantages in not today declaring a figure representing the total Germany owes. Be persuaded that whatever figure we may decide upon, many people, in England as much as in France, will at once shout, 'It's too little'.

It would also enable the Council to avoid prolonged discussion of the subject, with the risk that at the end of it public resentment might result in their fall from power. 'If our Parliaments were to lose confidence in us because we had not demanded enough, what would happen to the governments who would follow us in trying to do the

* See p. 128 above.

impossible?' On this issue more than any other, a way to settle without further inflaming public opinion must be found. Wilson was still dubious, however, and reserved his judgement.

The following day, Lloyd George prepared a new proposal on reparations for consideration by the Council of Four. He began by recognising that the Allied claims were certain far to exceed Germany's capacity to pay and proposed that it should be established in principle that the Germans were under an obligation to make good all damage to the Allied populations, including the cost of pensions for those disabled by the war and for the dependents of those killed. Germany should make an initial payment in goods, securities and gold of £1,000 million after which her liability would be determined by an inter-Allied Commission before which the Germans would be given a hearing.[14] That afternoon, however, Wilson took exception to the inclusion of any military damage, which included pensions for the wounded and dependants of the dead, but Lloyd George argued that under the Lansing Note formula they could claim all this and more. Wilson did not agree.[15] In this Lloyd George received support over the next two days from Lord Sumner and General Smuts, who are often seen as representatives of extremes of opinion in the British Delegation – Sumner for a severe settlement, Smuts for moderation. Writing of the Lansing Note, Sumner asked, 'Will it really be contended that the authors of this document actually intended and had it in mind to stipulate for benefits for unenlisted men from which they consciously designed to exclude the uniformed soldier?',[16] while Smuts declared bluntly that war pensions 'are all items representing compensation to members of the civilian population for damage sustained by them, for which the German Government are liable'.[17] No-one saw fit to mention that the inclusion of war pensions would give Britain a larger share of reparations than she would be entitled to if they were omitted. The matter would have to be pressed further. At a meeting of the Council of Four on 31 March, Klotz welcomed Lloyd George's proposal, but Wilson was dubious, since he did not want a settlement which would lead to endless discussions with the Germans.[18] However, Lloyd George's proposal had led to more common ground being found between the 'Big Four' on this, one of the most controversial, if not the most controversial, of all the issues before the Conference, than had been possible to discover or create before. In particular, by means of it the gap between Britain and France was largely closed.

On other matters, however, the circulation of the Fontainebleau Memorandum had pushed them further apart. Lloyd George and Clemenceau had had an acrimonious discussion of the German–Polish frontier problem on 27 March.* On 31 March Clemenceau sent a Note to the British Prime Minister setting out his Government's considered reactions to the Memorandum. He began by pointing out that it was not only French demands that would irritate the Germans – the loss of her navy and her colonies, both of which would particularly benefit Britain, would also annoy them, probably more so:

> We are . . . dealing her the blow which she will fear most, and we imagine that we shall appease her by certain improvements in our territorial conditions. . . . It is not in Europe that we must endeavour to [satisfy Germany] . . . we must offer her colonial advantages, naval advantages, or advantages connected with commercial expansion.[19]

Thus did Clemenceau try to put the onus for the pacification of Germany and Europe back on Britain. The British said this could only be achieved by the sacrifice of French interests, but it could also be achieved by sacrificing Britain's.

Clemenceau also rejected Lloyd George's view of how best to combat the influence of Bolshevism. This could best be done by strengthening and encouraging the new States of Europe, for otherwise they might go Bolshevik:

> The Conference has decided to call into existence a number of new states. Can it, without committing an injustice, sacrifice them by imposing on them out of consideration for Germany unacceptable frontiers?
>
> If these peoples, especially Poland and Bohemia, have hitherto resisted Bolshevism, it is by national feeling. If we do violence to that feeling, Bolshevism will find in them a prey.[20]

Clemenceau thus took a completely different view from Lloyd George. For him the real danger of Bolshevism was that the new states might succumb and thus France would lose her potential allies to the east of Germany, not that Germany might succumb. He ended on a resentful note. By the suppression of the German Navy

* See pp. 169–71 above.

and the capture of her colonies, the maritime Powers had secured 'absolute and definite guarantees' against a German attack, but Lloyd George's proposals would mean that 'for the Continental countries . . . that is to say, for those who had suffered most by the war, would be reserved . . . partial and temporary solutions'.[21] Clemenceau suspected the British of ulterior motives, of seeking to secure their own interests and then to deny the same gratification to others. No doubt his suspicions were reinforced by the apparent British determination to break the Sykes–Picot Agreement, and the activities of their soldiers and officials in Syria, which appeared to Frenchmen to be designed to prevent them from obtaining what they had been promised.

That same day, Marshal Foch presented a memorandum to Wilson, Lloyd George and Orlando repeating his arguments for the necessity of France having a military frontier on the Rhine. If this were not done, 'the battle which we will have to face in the plains of Belgium will be one in which we shall suffer from a considerable numerical inferiority, and where we shall have no natural obstacle to help us'.[22] The Rhine frontier was thus indispensable. After all, British and American help was no use if Germany could capture the Channel ports, or even the whole of France, before it would arrive. Foch argued his case orally before the Council of Four that afternoon, but Lloyd George was determined not to give in. He did, however, suggest that if France would accept the Treaty of Guarantee as sufficient, Britain and France might quickly agree to build a Channel Tunnel in order to speed up the arrival of British help, but for Foch this was still no substitute for the Rhine frontier.[23] The following day, however, France did make a concession on the terms of the Treaty of Guarantee, in order to meet Wilson's objection to a permanent alliance – the Treaty would lapse when all parties to it accepted that the League of Nations was strong enough adequately to guarantee their safety.[24] This would give the French effective control over the duration of the Treaty of Guarantee, while enabling Wilson to preserve the Covenant unblemished by a prior and contrary alliance.

On 2 April, Lloyd George replied to Clemenceau's Note of 31 March. In it there is a distinct note of exasperation at French obstinacy in clinging to demands which were not in her own best interest, while apparently rejecting the alternatives she had been offered:

> Judging by the memorandum, France seems to attach no importance to the rich German African colonies which she is in possession of; she attaches no importance to Syria; she attaches no importance to indemnity and compensation, not even although an overwhelming priority in the matter of compensation is given her as I proposed in my memorandum. She attaches no importance to the fact that she has Alsace–Lorraine.[25]

After more in the same vein, Lloyd George, referring the traditional British dislike of Continental commitments, threatened to withdraw the offer of a Treaty of Guarantee if France were not more reasonable:

> Especially would it be welcome to a large section of opinion in England who dislike entangling alliances to know that M. Clemenceau attaches no importance to the pledge I offer on behalf of Britain to come to the support of France if the invader threatens.[26]

Lloyd George was suggesting that France might have to choose between insistence on the Rhine frontier and the Treaty of Guarantee, and Clemenceau badly wanted the latter, since the lynch-pin of his policy at the Conference was to maintain the alliance which had brought victory in the war.[27] The issue still remained unsolved for the present, despite Lloyd George's efforts to prod his colleagues into making a decision.

In the meantime another dispute had arisen, this time between Wilson and Lloyd George on the one hand, and the French on the other, over the attribution of the Saar valley, with its valuable coal mines. On the afternoon of 28 March, André Tardieu presented the French argument that they should be allowed to annex the Saar to the Council of Four. It had only been handed over to Germany in 1815, after Napolean's 'Hundred Days', whilst in 1814 it had been left to France. He claimed that the Saarois wished to return to French rule, and argued that Alsace–Lorraine, which all were agreed should be returned to France, was not economically viable without the supply of coal and coke from the Saar. Finally, this was the best way to compensate France for the damage done to her own coalfields.[28] This last argument was the only one which Lloyd George would accept and he suggested the creation of an autonomous province, with France being given the ownership of the mines. President

Wilson also agreed that France was entitled to the mines, but not necessarily to the territory. For once he stood firmly by his principles:

> We must not forget that my principles are binding on us in making our settlement with Germany, since in the Armistice convention we accepted certain definite engagements.[29]

Nonetheless, France should be given ownership and control of the coal mines.

Clemenceau was not prepared to relinquish without a struggle his hope of including the Saar in France:

> America did not experience the first three years of this war; in that time we lost a million and a half men. . . . Our experiences have created in this country a strong demand for the compensation which is due to us. . . . The doctrine which you have just invoked could, if strictly applied, be used to deprive us of Alsace–Lorraine as well. . . . It is a mistake to believe that the world is governed by abstract principles. These are accepted by some people and rejected by others.[30]

He also expressed his conviction that no-one would ever succeed in appeasing Germany. Inevitably she would wait for the opportunity to revenge herself upon the Allies.

President Wilson retorted to this that it was not only French interests and opinions that the Conference had to consider:

> The belief which had brought together peoples from all corners or the earth to fight in the war was the belief that they were fighting together for justice. . . . This enthusiastic hope for a peace of justice would turn to cynical scepticism if people get the impression that we are going back on the rules of justice that we ourselves have announced.[31]

Lloyd George agreed with Wilson's view that French annexation of the Saar would be unjust, and declared that 'the English people are haunted by the fear of creating new Alsace–Lorraines'.[32] Yet again Lloyd George pleaded with Clemenceau not to create new running sores in Europe, and pressed him to accept ownership of the mines and autonomy for the region. Orlando agreed, but Clemenceau was adamant – France must receive her due.

Three days later Wilson proposed that France should be given the ownership of the mines with a guarantee of full facilities to operate them freely and transport the coal, while refusing to impose an allegiance on the Saarois. Clemenceau said he would examine the document, but he was dubious about it if Germany was to retain any control over the valley. 'I want the ownership of the mines by France very much, but not under conditions which would result in perpetual disputes with the Germans in the future.'[33] He could not trust the Germans not to make trouble.

During the next few days, the problem was considered by a small committee consisting of André Tardieu for France, James Headlam-Morley[34] of the British Foreign Office, and Dr Charles H. Haskins for the Americans. This committee had ten meetings and Tardieu held out obstinately for the institution of a special régime for the area, despite the fact that the committee was able to devise means whereby the French could own and run the mines while the territory remained German. Finally, all three members signed a declaration that they

> are agreed in the opinion that if [the mines were transferred to France] which appear[s] to be necessary from the social and economic point of view . . . without the establishment of a special administrative and political regime, serious difficulties and conflicts would inevitably arise.[35]

This conclusion was communicated to the members of the Council of Four. On the morning of 8 April Lloyd George said that he felt that President Wilson's suggestion, made on 31 March, that France should take over the mines while leaving sovereign control over the territory to France, was impracticable. 'It will be a cause of continual incidents and will create a serious risk of war.'[36] He therefore proposed that a settlement be adopted on the lines of the position of Luxemburg – an independent state linked closely in economic terms with a neighbouring Power, in this case France. Such a proposal had been made by the three experts, and Colonel House, who was representing President Wilson on this occasion, said that this proposal seemed 'very reasonable' to him.[37] That afternoon, however, Wilson himself was present and said that his experts advised him that the creation of a semi-independent state was impracticable, and he thus rejected House's views and also those of Haskins, and urged that Germany should not be compelled to give up her rule over the territory, but rather that the Conference should set up a tribunal to arbitrate between Germany and France when disputes arose between them over the operation of the mines, to be followed after fifteen years by a plebiscite, after which, if the vote went in favour of continuing under German rule, the Germans would be allowed to repurchase the mines by payment in gold.[38] This proposal was at once rejected by Clemenceau, who felt that it would make the operation of the mines impossible. Wilson stuck to his scheme, which Lloyd George believed would not work, since it involved the virtual annexation of the territory by France, though Germany would retain the titular sovereignty and would probably disrupt French activity. Equally, Wilson still objected to creating an autonomous state, saying that to ask Germany to agree to autonomy for the Saar was like asking the United States to agree to autonomy for Pittsburg.[39] He was willing to see the Saar operate within the French customs union, but Clemenceau still thought that such a system would lead to 'interminable disputes' if the Germans retained any control.[40]

The following morning there was a further inconclusive discussion, Tardieu accepting the idea that there should be a plebiscite after fifteen years and asking Wilson to concede the need for a special régime for the Saar in the meantime.[41] In the afternoon the British presented three alternative suggestions for solving the problem, but all three involved a suspension of German sovereignty, to which Wilson would not agree, because he believed that to do this would prejudge the result of the plebiscite. He was prepared, however, to compel Germany to cede sovereignty during the fifteen years which would precede the plebiscite to a Commission appointed by the League of Nations.[42] Clemenceau then asked why France could not have a mandate for the area, whereupon Wilson's temper began to rise:

> I am trying with all my might to find a solution which will satisfy you and me, and I cannot see any acceptable solution which involves the abolition of German sovereignty. . . . I cannot return to the United States and say to the American people, 'We have found it convenient, after examining the problems, to go back on our word'. People will say that we are bound by the terms of the Armistice and by the declarations we made when we signed it. I ask you to help me to find a way in your direction. I have taken many steps towards you; do not make it impossible for me to help you as much as it lies in my power to do so.[43]

Wilson was not unsympathetic to French fears and demands, but on this occasion he felt that he must stand firm, at least to the extent of not imposing upon the people of the Saar a sovereignty which might well be alien and unwelcome to them. One is entitled to ask why he did not do the same in the case of the Polish corridor.

When Lloyd George pointed out to Wilson that what the French really wanted was control over the mines, Clemenceau replied that that was not really so – the industrialists wanted the mines, but the rest of the people wanted the territory.[44] Lloyd George reiterated that future causes of conflict must not be created, and no French proposal so far made met this condition, although Wilson's new proposal did. Clemenceau then said that he had no fundamental objection to this proposal – the fifteen-year-League régime followed by a plebiscite – and it was submitted to the three experts for consideration. The verdict of Dr Haskins, James Headlam-Morley and André Tardieu was sought, and it was agreed to wait until they reported. Meanwhile, Clemenceau wrote a letter to Lloyd George in which he criticised the idea of a special régime because it was likely, in his opinion, to lead to disputes between Germany and France. He tried to persuade Lloyd George once more that France should be allowed to annex the territory. Even the plebiscite was still suspect, since Clemenceau alleged that the people of the Saar would not feel free to vote for inclusion in France after a century of oppression by the Prussian civil service.[45] On 10 April there was a further discussion in the Council of Four during which Tardieu also expressed doubts about the plebiscite, for France would still need Saar coal fifteen years hence and he was not prepared to risk her being deprived of it if the plebiscite went in Germany's favour.[46]

The next day, however, a solution was agreed. After a discussion of methods by which France's supply of Saar coal could be guaranteed, it was agreed that a set of clauses along the lines proposed by Wilson should be prepared. For fifteen years the League was to administer the Saar, at the end of which time a plebiscite would determine its final destiny. Whatever happened, France would be guaranteed a fixed supply of coal at a fair price. Furthermore, only people resident in the Saar at the time of the signing of the Treaty would be eligible to vote in the plebiscite, in order to allay French fears that otherwise the Germans could move in settlers who would vote for annexation by Germany.[47] The experts were to draft the clauses in this sense, and they were presented and accepted by the Council of Four on 24 April, except for a few details of the price to be charged for Saar coal supplied to France.[48] The attribution of the Saar valley had aroused considerable acrimony during the discussion in the Council of Four, but finally a compromise was reached. German sovereignty was not abolished, which satisfied Wilson and Lloyd George, whilst France got a supply of coal to make up for losses of production in her own coalfields resulting from sabotage by the retreating German armies. It might well be that many Frenchmen would resent Clemenceau's failure to secure the territory for France, but he recognised that if a settlement were to be made at all, compromises would have to be reached and he could not hold out for demands which his colleagues in the Council of Four regarded as unreasonable or dangerous. The settlement of the question of the Saar might satisfy no party to it completely, but it went some way to meeting the wishes and interests of each of them.

Another problem with which the Council of Four began to deal at the end of March was the Belgian territorial claims. Relations between Belgium and France had been soured by Belgian suspicion that France had designs upon the Grand Duchy of Luxemburg which the Belgians wished to annex.* The British had tried to mediate, with some success, but the time had now come for the Belgians formally to present their claims, which their Foreign Minister, Paul Hymans, did at a hearing before the Council of Four on 31 March. Hymans made an unfortunate impression. He had presented his country's claims on 11 February, and was now becoming impatient at the long delay by the Conference in replying to his statement:

> I came to the Conference and explained the Belgian viewpoint. You listened to me; but I have had no word from you. I do not know your opinion. We need to know what you are thinking; we need your counsel. Such silence and the way we are treated are creating an unfortunate impression in Belgium, which may turn against the Allies.

This complaint brought a curt rejoinder from Lloyd George: 'You have no right to speak of France and Great Britain in this manner. English soldiers have died in their hundreds of thousands for the liberation of Belgium.'[49] Hymans got no satisfaction, and when news of his reception reached Brussels it caused considerable anger. The

* See pp. 109–11 above.

British Ambassador there reported to Curzon that Lloyd George's attitude in particular had caused great anger, especially as he was reported in Belgium as having alleged that the Belgian contribution to the war effort had been greatly exaggerated. As a result, the King of the Belgians had deemed it necessary to go to Paris to intervene personally in the discussions of the Belgian claims.[50]

The King was invited to attend the Council of Four's meeting on 4 April, when Hymans again argued his country's claim to Malmédy, and control of the railway between Malmédy and Eupen. He asked for a French blessing upon negotiations with Luxemburg for a voluntary union of the two countries. Clemenceau, objecting to this, invoked the principle of self-determination, for once:

> You cannot ask me to say to the Luxemburgers, 'I want you to become Belgians'. We must leave them free to decide. You know quite well that I am not claiming Luxemburg for France. . . . I only ask one thing; the disappearance of the German dynasty.[51]

When the King of the Belgians referred to promises by French statesmen during the war, Clemenceau retorted, 'Do not ask me to throw the Luxemburgers into the arms of the Belgians: I do not know their feelings',[52] and he later said that 'the only thing I do not wish, is that the union of Luxemburg and Belgium be accomplished in such a way as to appear a defeat for France'.[53] The Belgians refused a plebiscite, as they had in the earlier negotiations on this issue, and despite Lloyd George's plea that the issue 'must be settled',[54] the meeting ended without any conclusion being reached. Relations between Clemenceau and the Belgians were now poor indeed, and the tone of this meeting was acrimonious, the presence of Royalty notwithstanding. The King of the Belgians refused at this meeting to support one of Clemenceau's most cherished schemes – the occupation of the Rhine. On 7 April, Hymans went to see Lord Derby, the British Ambassador in Paris, in an attempt to get British support for his country's ambitions in Luxemburg. He got no encouragement.[55]

The Council of Four considered the problem again on 13 April, when Clemenceau reaffirmed his attitude to the Belgian claim: 'I am ready to do everything to help them, except to appear to make them a gift of Luxemburg',[56] and on the 15th, when A. J. Balfour attempted to persuade Clemenceau to yield to the Belgian demand. Lloyd

George was in London facing Parliamentary critics on his handling of reparations. Balfour argued that

> if France, having recovered Alsace and Lorraine and obtained the collieries of the Saar, and Belgium, after events which gained her the sympathy of the entire world, obtained no part of her demands, the impression created would be deplorable, especially if Luxemburg became French.[57]

Clemenceau said that he accepted 'every word you have just spoken',[58] but still refused to give his blessing to negotiations between Belgium and Luxemburg. He did agree, however, that Belgium should be told that the Allies were sympathetic to her cause so long as no violence were done to the feelings of the Luxemburgers. They should wait until the wishes of the Luxemburgers became clearer.[59]

Other questions in which Belgium was concerned – her neutrality and her other territorial claims – had been referred either to committees of experts or to the Council of Foreign Ministers, otherwise known as the Council of Five, which had been set up to deal with questions not needing the attention of the 'Big Four'. On 16 April, Belgium's territorial claims other than Luxemburg were discussed by the Council of Four in the presence of Hymans, Haskins and Tardieu. The only controversial point was the railway between Malmédy and Eupen, where it was proposed to cede an area populated by Germans to Belgium in order that the entire course of the railway might be under her control. Hymans said that only four thousand Germans would be affected, but, true to Lloyd George's policy line on the Polish corridor, Balfour, still deputising for him, objected to this breach of the principle of drawing frontiers according to the nationality of the population. Hymans was prepared to accept a plebiscite in part of the territory, but on the railway route he held firm, whereupon Wilson intervened to argue in favour of the principle of nationality which he had so completely rejected in the case of Poland:

> Does it not seem to you that, despite the small number of people interested, 4,000, we would be running the risk of departing, in this case, from the principle we are striving to apply to greater problems? Ought we not to have just as many scruples, whether it be a matter of 4,000 Germans or of 4 million?[60]

Later he referred directly to the case of the Danzig–Mlawa–Warsaw railway, employing against Hymans the very argument which Lloyd George had used against Wilson in the Polish case:

> We do not believe that the fate of a population can be bound up with that of a railway, but rather that the problem of the railway must be solved so as not to violate the rights of the people.[61]

To explain such inconsistency is almost impossible. When the issue of the German–Polish frontier came before the Council again, Wilson stuck to his previous pro-Polish line, so he had not been persuaded by Lloyd George's appeal to the principle of nationality in that case. One possible explanation has already been mentioned: that Wilson's judgement on the Polish issue was warped by the advice he received from his experts. This and other contradictions in Wilson's actions at Paris show that he was incapable of following through a consistent policy line and applying it to all the details of the settlement. Instead he acted in accordance with his feelings and the advice he was receiving at the time. In the end, it was agreed to allow Belgium to annex the territory in the first instance, but to allow the inhabitants a plebiscite after six months to determine the territory's final allocation. Since the vote would cover the whole of Malmédy and Moresnet, the Germans of the disputed area would be swamped by the Walloon majority in the rest of the territory. The Council of Four saved its face but gave away the substance of the principle so firmly enunciated by Balfour and Wilson.

Meanwhile, the British were more definitely trying to help Belgium secure Luxemburg. On 15 April Balfour wrote to Hymans to tell him that he had seen President Wilson about this matter, and Wilson had said that he was 'most desirous of doing all he could for Belgium', and suggested deferring a decision and a plebiscite until later. He also remarked that Clemenceau was sympathetic to Belgian aspirations, 'provided no violence was done to the wishes of the Luxemburgers themselves'.[62] After further discussions by an expert committee, to which the matter was referred by the Council of Four on 25 April,[63] the Four adopted a rather indefinite provision for the German Treaty relating to Luxemburg. Germany was to renounce all her rights and was to agree to accept any agreement which might be reached by the Allies in the future about the final destiny of the country. The issue was thus deferred beyond the concern of the Peace Conference, and could be left until after peace was signed. The Council of Four and the Belgians all accepted this provision without demur, and a nasty little problem, which had caused considerable friction, was thus avoided, though not solved.[64] Franco–Belgian relations, however, were still shaky, quite apart from the Luxemburg issue. The French were pressing Belgium to agree to the creation of a customs union between their two countries, but the Belgians feared that the French intended to subordinate Belgium and were anxious to resist this pressure. To this end they sought British help, and a Belgian Minister consulted Lord Derby about this in late April.[65] Franco–Belgian relations remained poor, but they ceased, after 29 April, to concern or embroil the Peace Conference.

The most thorny of all the issues relating to the western frontier of Germany was still, of course, the question of the Rhine and the Rhenish provinces. The British were still strongly opposed to the French suggestion of a Rhenish buffer state, as Lord Curzon made clear to Jules Cambon in London when they met on 2 April. He told Balfour, in Paris, that he had asked Cambon 'to consider whether France was not a little too much affected by bygone memories', for Germany had been beaten and now recognised her inferiority, and she would not try to conquer France again.[66]

Despite the fact that Belgium, like France, had been invaded by the Germans in 1914, the French proposal for a permanent occupation of the Rhine got no support from the King of the Belgians when Clemenceau appealed to him for support on 4 April: 'If we are invaded, Frenchmen and Belgians will have to fight a great battle before help from Britain and America has had time to arrive.'[67] Germany must therefore be kept so closely under surveillance in future that she would not have the chance to deliver a surprise attack – the Rhine must be occupied by Allied forces and an inter-Allied Commission must be able to examine activity within Germany which might be a breach of the disarmament clauses of the Treaty. The King of the Belgians did not agree. Germany could not be a threat to peace again for at least twenty years, and Belgian opinion was against a prolonged occupation. Lloyd George said the same about British opinion. Clemenceau's response was to urge that if the buffer state were set up the French would see it as in their interest to treat its inhabitants well. Also, the people were Roman Catholic, and this could be used to encourage them to accept separation from the rest of Germany. He was alone in this, however.[68]

On the question of whether a commission should supervise Germany, however, Clemenceau found an unexpected ally. This proposal had been rejected by President Wilson some time before,* but he was absent from this meeting, and Colonel House had taken his place. He now openly betrayed his leader:

> I feel bound to say that I do not support President Wilson's views on the subject of the commission of inspection. In my opinion, if a country does only what she has a right to do, she can have no reason to take offence at any form of inspection.[69]

Lloyd George was left to oppose the idea, saying that he would only accept this argument if it were applied universally – 'to carry on an inspection by foreigners in one single country, perhaps for fifty years, could give rise to difficulties'.[70] Colonel House was ready to adopt French positions even when they had been opposed by Wilson himself.

The question of what to do about the western frontier and France's fears of another German invasion was still acute. On 12 April, President Wilson sent a note to Clemenceau saying that, like Lloyd George, he was totally opposed to a prolonged occupation of the Rhineland. The Treaty of Guarantee, disarmament and possibly a short occupation 'represent the maximum of what I myself deam necessary for the safety of France, or possible on the part of the United States'.[71] Within the next few days, however, the issue was settled behind Lloyd George's back while he was in England to defend himself against attacks in the House of Commons,† and settled on terms of which he did not approve. In this the crucial man was Colonel House, who acted as a go-between. On 14 April he saw Clemenceau, who suggested a possible means of settling the dispute. In addition to the Treaty of Guarantee, which both Lloyd George and Wilson had always seen as an alternative to the buffer state or occupation proposals for the Rhineland, the Rhenish provinces would be occupied by Allied forces for fifteen years as a security for the faithful execution of the peace terms by Germany. If she observed the terms, part of the area would be evacuated after five years, a further part after ten years, and the rest after fifteen.[72] The next day Colonel House took the proposal to President Wilson, who accepted it. He then returned to Clemenceau, who 'was perfectly delighted with what I was able to tell him concerning . . . the length of occupation'.[73] This settlement was not, as we shall see, at all to

* See p. 137 above.
† See pp. 207–8 below.

Lloyd George's liking, and he was sufficiently resentful of it to suggest in his memoirs of the Conference that Wilson and House traded the fifteen-year occupation for the cessation of attacks on the President which had been appearing in the Paris Press.[74] In fact, this suggestion is quite erroneous: as House recorded in his letter to Wilson, quoted above, he only mentioned the Press attacks to Clemenceau for the first time after he had told him of Wilson's agreement to the Rhineland proposals. Wilson's agreement undoubtedly created a friendly climate which made Clemenceau more disposed to put a stop to the Press attacks, but this is as much as we can say, and certainly the documents give no support to Lloyd George's allegation that a deliberate trade was made, the fifteen-year occupation for a friendly French Press.

Be that as it may, Lloyd George was not at all pleased at the way events had turned out. On 22 April, Clemenceau presented the draft clauses relating to the left bank of the Rhine to the Council of Four, to which Lloyd George had now returned. He at once expressed concern at the length of the occupation, and Clemenceau appealed to him not to oppose the recommendation: 'I could not consider reducing the period of occupation. We are already having difficulty getting it accepted in France.'[75] Lloyd George then said he could not consider committing British troops to remain on the Rhine for so long, which provoked an impassioned plea from Clemenceau: 'All I ask of you, in truth, is to leave me a battallion and a flag,' and he went on: 'If I do not have your flag beside mine on the left bank of the Rhine, I will not be able to appear before our Parliament.'[76] In face of this, and Wilson's prior agreement, Lloyd George felt he could do nothing other than accept the clauses, but he did so reluctantly. That day, the Council also set up a committee to draft clauses relating to Alsace-Lorraine.[77] All were agreed that these provinces should be restored to France and this was agreed without argument on 30 April.[78]

There was still to be a little more trouble over the Rhineland. On 28 April the President of France, Raymond Poincaré, wrote to Clemenceau insisting that the fifteen-year occupation was not a sufficient guarantee of safety for France, and that he must reopen the negotiations and secure the permanent attribution of the territory to France:

> Let us take ourselves in our minds sixteen or seventeen years from now. Germany has regularly paid reparations for fifteen years. We

> have evacuated all the left bank of the Rhine, and have withdrawn behind our frontiers, political frontiers which give us no solid line of military defence. Suppose Germany once more takes up imperialism. Suppose only bad faith on her part. She suspends her payments. We are obliged to reoccupy the Rhine. We give the necessary orders, but who will ensure that they can be carried out without difficulty?[79]

The Treaty of Guarantee was very valuable, but it was not enough, for help could not arrive at once. The occupation was therefore indispensable. Clemenceau passed this letter to Lloyd George, who rejected its arguments:

> To compel Germany to accept Allied occupation of the Rhine and the Rhenish provinces for an indefinite period, which almost certainly could not be less than thirty years, would probably be a serious provocation to fresh tension and even war in Europe.

He therefore thought it essential that it should be

> made clear to the German people that provided they did not again embark upon the path of militarist ambition the term of occupation of German territory was limited and would come to an end within a reasonable time.[80]

This was the way to peace and eventually to harmony. The Council of Four did agree, however, that if at the end of the fifteen-year period the guarantees against a new German attack appeared to be insufficient, the occupation could be prolonged.[81] This issue was settled, even if not to everyone's liking.

The other major problems relating to German frontiers concerned Eastern Europe. As March drew to a close, one such issue which came to be decided was the frontier between Germany and Czechoslovakia. The Czechoslovaks had claimed the strip of Bohemia known as the Sudetenland, which was largely inhabited by Germans, a claim about which the British had already expressed doubts on ethnic grounds.* These doubts were strengthened on 26 March, when the British Chargé d'Affaires in Prague reported to Lord Curzon and the British delegation in Paris that the Czechs had been treating the Bohemian Germans badly and had succeeded in an-

* See pp. 100–1 above.

tagonising them and other racial minorities. He had made representations about this to President Masaryk, after which things had improved, but he feared that there would be further trouble between the Czechs and the Bohemian Germans.[82] On 5 April, Balfour replied from Paris saying that he 'entirely approved' of the Chargé's action and urging him to put pressure on Masaryk to ensure better treatment for the Bohemian Germans.[83]

Meanwhile, the expert Commission which had been appointed by the Council of Ten in February to consider the Czechoslovak claims delivered its report to the Council of Foreign Ministers. The report was introduced by Jules Cambon, who had taken the chair of the Commission, who said that he and his colleagues

> had attempted to do justice to ethnic claims but economic and strategic considerations had also to be given weight as a purely racial frontier had left Czechoslovakia defenceless and economically crippled.[84]

These were familiar problems: the Bohemian German strip contained the only good strategic barrier, the Bohemian mountains, and most of the country's industry. Balfour had that day circulated to members of the British delegation a warning that their policy in relation to the Bohemian Germans must be consistent with that adopted in the case of the Polish Corridor. Knowing what would be in the Commission's Report he advised that the Bohemian Germans must not be left within Czechoslovakia for economic or strategic reasons.[85] He opposed the Commission's proposals in the Council of Five, and was joined by the American Secretary of State, Lansing, who declared that 'the American delegates objected to the whole method of drawing lines on strategic principles',[86] and later he declared roundly that

> the fixing of frontier lines with a view to their military strength and in contemplation of war was directly contrary to the whole spirit of the League of Nations, of international disarmament, and of the policy of the United States as set forth in the declaration of President Wilson.[87]

Cambon retorted that if the ethnological criterion were strictly applied they would end up with 'a country as discontinuous as the spots on a panther's skin. Such, he presumed, was not the result the

Conference desired the Commission to recommend.'[88] The discussion became more and more heated, ending with an open quarrel between Lansing and the Frenchmen present:

> M. CAMBON said that it was for the defence of Bohemia that the commission had decided to keep the railway lines alluded to by Mr Lansing within Czechoslovakia.
>
> MR LANSING said that he made reservations on this point.
>
> M. PICHON said that on behalf of France, he also had reservations to make. He could not allow Germany to be fortified by populations taken from what had been Austrian dominions, taken, moreover, from Bohemia, which he trusted would remain an ally of France, and handed over to Germany, which as far as he was concerned still remained a country to be feared. If America refused to take into account considerations of national defence, France was not in a position to neglect them.[89]

Further discussion was useless, and the matter was referred to the Council of Four for decision.

The Council of Four took up the matter on the afternoon of 4 April, and President Wilson was not present, his place being taken, as usual, by Colonel House. Clemenceau introduced the subject, saying that the Commission's proposals for the Czech–German frontier were very complicated, and it seemed to him that it would be simpler to leave the frontier as it had been in 1914, and leave Bohemia and Germany to negotiate a change later if they wished. When he had said this, both Lloyd George and House accepted the suggestion without demur,[90] Colonel House thus betrayed Lansing outright, for this meant that the Bohemian Germans went to Czechoslovakia, since their homeland had formerly been part of the Austro–Hungarian province of Bohemia. Lloyd George also failed to conform to the line taken by Balfour in the Council of Five, although Balfour had not been nearly as emphatic in the matter as Lansing had been. Once again, House betrayed the Wilsonian declaration that frontiers should be decided on the basis of nationality. Why Lloyd George did not resist Clemenceau's proposal is not clear. In his memoirs of the Conference he says that the Foreign Office advised that the Bohemian Germans would enjoy more economic prosperity in Czechoslovakia than they would in Germany. It has also been suggested that Lloyd George believed that the issue was not important, since the Germans would not unduly resent not being given a territory which had never been part of the Reich, even though it was inhabited by Germans.[91] At any rate, Colonel House had betrayed a colleague, Lloyd George had not stood firm, and the French got their way. Europe was to hear more of the Bohemian Germans.

At this time, the Council also resumed consideration of the German–Polish frontier, which had given rise to heated arguments in the Council of Ten.* On 1 April President Wilson suggested that the best course of action would be to place Danzig temporarily under the supervision of the League of Nations with the proviso that when it was ceded to Poland it could still have some measure of autonomy.[92] Lloyd George then declared that he would prefer to revive the mediaeval idea of a Free City. Danzig should become autonomous within the Polish customs union; eventually the city's German inhabitants might opt voluntarily for a union with Poland:

> The inhabitants of Danzig would know that their future prosperity was linked to Poland, since from this quarter would come the port's commerce. By giving them both independence and an interest in the prosperity of the Polish state, they would gradually become attached to Poland as a result of the economic link.[93]

Having made this suggestion, he returned to the problem of the route of the Danzig–Mlawa railway, which passed through the German province of Marienwerder, which the Commission on Polish Affairs had recommended should be ceded to the Poles in order to give them control of the railway. Lloyd George now repeated his opposition to this idea:

> My greatest preoccupation is to avoid putting too many Germans into Poland. If we follow the Commission's report, the province of Marienwerder, which contains 420,000 Germans on its own, would become Polish. I would leave this province in East Prussia, while giving Poland an absolute right to use the railway.[94]

He said that he would accept a plebiscite, in reply to a question from Wilson, but Wilson was doubtful whether the Poles would accept this: 'When I earlier mentioned the idea of making Danzig a free city to M. Dmowski, he nearly jumped through the roof.'[95] A little later an exchange occurred between Clemenceau, Lloyd George and Wilson which well illustrates their respective attitudes towards the Poles:

* See pp. 153–7 above.

M. CLEMENCEAU: We cannot take a definite decision on this subject except with the Poles present.
PRESIDENT WILSON: No, but we can agree among ourselves to start with.
MR LLOYD GEORGE: I think it would be vain to imagine that anything we decide can hope to satisfy the Poles.
PRESIDENT WILSON: They must accept what we consider reasonable.
M. CLEMENCEAU: They will not accept without difficulty.
MR LLOYD GEORGE: If they do not accept, let them try and do better by themselves. My advice is to prepare a proposal and then invite the Poles to discuss it with us.[96]

Clemenceau was anxious to secure as much for the Poles as he could, regarding them as he did as a future ally against Germany. Wilson's feelings were fairly neutral, while Lloyd George was definitely hostile – the Poles were greedy and must be compelled to accept what the Council decided was a reasonable settlement. Lloyd George proposed the Free City solution for Danzig, and Wilson suggested a plebiscite in Marienwerder. These proposals would be drafted by the experts and discussed with the Poles. Before the meeting closed, Lloyd George gave a final word of warning to his colleagues:

> What I ask is that we should not write into the Treaty articles in defence of which we will not be willing to go to war in the future. France would fight tomorrow for Alsace, if it were taken from her, but would we make war for Danzig?[97]

It was useless to put in the Treaty provisions which would not be considered worth defending if ever it became necessary.

Just over a week later, on 9 April, the Council resumed its discussion of Danzig and Marienwerder, and invited the Polish Prime Minister, Paderewski, to attend. Before inviting Paderewski to come in, the Council accepted a draft by their experts of clauses which would make Danzig a Free City. Wilson accepted: 'this text would give the Poles the necessary guarantee of free access to the sea',[98] and thus satisfied Wilson's thirteenth Point. The city would be governed by the League of Nations and would be within the Polish customs union. The Poles would be given full facilities in the port and on the railways. The text also provided for a plebiscite in Marienwerder, and this was also accepted by the Council.

Paderewski was then invited to join the Four and give his reactions, after Wilson had explained what was proposed and why: 'Our concern has been to avoid the danger which would be caused to her by the existence of a *Germania Irredenta* within her borders.'[99] Paderewski's reaction was immediate, and hostile. Speaking on behalf of his Parliament, the Polish Diet, he declared that the Diet

> wanted above all the closest alliance and agreement with the *Entente* Powers, but it also wanted the territorial guarantees essential for our very existence. We know the Germans better than you, we have been their neighbours and their victims for seven hundred years. Be persuaded that however little you take from Germany, that will always be a *Germania Irredenta*.[100]

Poland, he said, could not live without Danzig, and the number of Germans in Marienwerder had been exaggerated. When Lloyd George asked whether that was not all the more reason for having a plebiscite, Paderewski said that he thought the people would be too frightened to vote for Poland because of what would happen to them if they lost and Marienwerder remained German. As for Danzig, that was a question of life and death for Poland. Lloyd George's reply was that the Free City proposal was 'a sort of Home Rule for Danzig. Her foreign relations will be in your hands, and Danzig will be less independent of you than Canada is from Britain,'[101] but Paderewski could not put any faith in any such guarantee:

> We are too well acquainted with the Germans to put any faith in any guarantee they have accepted. . . . We have long known about their scraps of paper. I could tell you of a Grand Master of the Order of Teutonic Knights who, having signed a treaty with several Pomeranian and Polish princes from the areas surrounding his domain, invited them all to a banquet during which he had them all murdered. That is the sort of treaty we have had from the Germans in the past.[102]

Paderewski could not be reconciled to the compromises proposed by the Council of Four.

Strengthened by Paderewski's opposition, Clemenceau decided to reopen the issue of Danzig four days later, and suggested that if the Poles were given Marienwerder, they might be persuaded to accept the Free City proposal for Danzig. Lloyd George was adamant: 'That would be against our principles, to leave within the Polish State a territory so obviously German in character which has always been a part of Prussia.' Clemenceau replied that Paderewski was very upset about it – 'he almost burst into tears' – whereupon President Wilson remarked, rather sarcastically, 'Yes, but remember, he is very sensitive'. Lloyd George was impatient at what he considered to be the immoderation of the Poles:

> After all, the Poles are assured of independence at last, after a century and a half of slavery. Surely they cannot claim that they cannot live if we refuse them a little piece of territory which contains 150,000 Germans![103]

Lloyd George was not going to be bullied by either a tearful Paderewski or a stubborn Clemenceau into changing his mind. On 15 April, while Lloyd George was away, Clemenceau attempted to raise the question of Marienwerder again, but Wilson refused to let him, revealing as he did so his own lack of concern with the German–Polish frontier: 'I think we will have to wait to discuss this question until Mr Lloyd George comes back, as it is he who is most interested in this issue.'[104] Wilson was not interested in a dispute which, one would have thought, deeply involved his principles and his declared views. On Lloyd George's return, however, the proposals for a Free City in Danzig and a plebiscite in Marienwerder were accepted without much trouble.[105] The dispute was over, and another section of the Treaty was complete.

Lloyd George's irritation with the Poles was undoubtedly increased by their continuing attempts to take Eastern Galicia from the Ukrainians by force.* On 2 April the Council of Four agreed to send a telegram to the Polish Government urging them once more to conclude an armistice with the Ukrainians.[106] On this occasion even Wilson spoke of 'our awkward Polish friends', and a telegram was therefore sent both to Warsaw and Kiev asking for an armistice after which the Conference would send out a Commission to help negotiate a settlement.[107] On 15 April the Council of Four were informed that Polish troops were behaving badly in Lemberg, and agreed to make further representations to the Polish Government,[108] and on 21 April they learned that the Poles were planning to send General Haller's army, which had been sent from France with Allied help for

* See pp. 152–3 above.

the purpose of defending Poland against the Bolsheviks,* to Lemberg. This annoyed Wilson:

> That is contrary to our intentions. Should we not inform M. Paderewski that having agreed in principle to conclude an armistice he must cease hostilities and not allow General Haller's troops to be sent to Lemberg, or be used to relieve other troops which could then be sent to the same destination? If our representations go unheeded, we could threaten to stop sending supplies.

Lloyd George was fearful lest such a move drive the Poles into the arms of the Bolsheviks, but he agreed.[109] Thus Poland's western frontier had been discussed by the Council of Four against the background of Polish behaviour in Eastern Galicia which caused much irritation and cannot have helped their case or their general standing with the 'Big Four'. What was more, on 26 April the Council were told that on ethnic grounds Eastern Galicia must go to Ukraine. Poland was definitely not entitled to it.[110]

Another German frontier issue was the future status of the German part of the Austro–Hungarian Empire, known as German Austria. The basic French demand was that Austria should not be allowed to unite with Germany and thus add to her population and military strength, and this was presented to the Council of Four by Clemenceau on 22 April.[111] On 2 May President Wilson took exception to the proposed enforced separation of Austria from Germany because he saw in it a breach of the principle of the self-determination of peoples – 'It is not the interests of Germany that concern me, but those of Austria. We can forbid annexation, but we cannot stop a country joining another if her people wish to.' Lloyd George said they could if it were essential to the future security of Europe, but Wilson would not accept this, though he would accept a temporary prohibition. Lloyd George said that a text proposed by the experts would forbid Germany from taking any action designed to procure a union of Austria with Germany, but Clemenceau regarded such a proposal as useless: 'Germany would sign an article like that today, do the opposite tomorrow and render it inoperative.' In the end, Wilson proposed to hand the problem over to the League of Nations, while giving in to the French in the meantime. Germany would be obliged to 'recognise and respect the independence of Austria', which

* See pp. 103–4 above.

would remain inalienable except by approval of the League. This solution was accepted,[112] and four days later Austria was defined by its 1914 boundaries.[113] The problem was solved, and Austria and Germany compelled to remain separate.

This, then, was the way in which the frontiers of Germany were finally drawn up. After Lloyd George's attempt to break the deadlock, solutions had been reached, after much argument, acrimony, and the burning of midnight oil. When the members of the Council of Four began from standpoints far distant from one another's, as they did on all these issues, compromise was inevitable, and the nature of the compromise depended on the conduct of the three chief negotiators and their immediate henchmen. Clemenceau was perhaps the most consistent – safety, defence against Germany and, as far as possible, her dismemberment, were his objectives, and he pursued them at every opportunity, either on his own account or on that of the new States of Eastern Europe. The only occasion on which he appealed to considerations of nationality and the self-determination of peoples was in the negotiations on Luxemburg, where he used them simply to protect French interests and prestige against Belgian ambitions there. Lloyd George was also consistent, for he wanted a lasting peace and the creation of no more running sores, no new Alsace–Lorraines in Europe; and only on issues which he believed were not important in the light of this objective, or where the French case was too strong, did he yield without a stubborn fight. He got his way on the German–Polish frontier, and was tricked over the occupation of the Rhineland when he was compelled to return home at the vital moment. It was Wilson who was completely unpredictable. Personally emotional and unstable, hating the Germans more than he loved his principles, he reacted differently to each issue which came before him, reacting as he felt on each occasion. Even if he had not been unstable and ill-prepared, the activities of Colonel House further weakened American stands on behalf of the Fourteen Points, and prejudices among the American experts further diluted Wilson's supposed principles. Little wonder that those in the American delegation who believed in the Fourteen Points became increasingly unhappy about what was happening. Robert Lansing, who fought a stubborn defensive stand for the principle of the self-determination of peoples in the case of the Bohemian Germans, became deeply anxious about the course of events. On 30 March he wrote two memoranda to the President, which were distributed to other members of the American delegation. The first was to warn him against undue haste:

> I am sure now that there will be no preliminary treaty of peace, but that the treaty will be complete and definitive. This is a serious mistake. Time should be given for passions to cool. . . . The President's obsession as to a League of Nations blinds him to everything else. An immediate peace is nothing to him compared to the adoption of the Covenant. The whole world wants peace. The President wants his League. I think that the world will have to wait.[114]

Here may be a further reason for Wilson's inconsistency. He believed that if wrong was done in the Treaty it would not be irrevocable, it could be set to right by the League.

Lansing's second memorandum was a warning against the methods adopted for reaching decisions, especially the secret meetings of the Council of Four. Extreme secrecy had been adopted to avoid leaks to the Press. Colonel Repington recorded in his diary on 31 March that 'owing to some indiscretion, L.G.'s hostile views about the Polish corridor have become known, and also his fury thereat, the result being that he, Clemenceau, President Wilson and Orlando now meet in secret and little comes out'.[115] Lansing believed that this method of procedure was dangerous:

> I am convinced that the method of personal interviews and private conclaves is a failure. It has given every opportunity for intrigue, plotting, bargaining and combining. The President, as I now see it, should have insisted on everything being brought before the Plenary Conference. He would then have had the confidence and support of the smaller nations because they would have looked to him as their champion and guide. . . . A grievous mistake has been made.[116]

Such a move could hardly have been practicable unless considerable delay in making the settlement had been acceptable. In any case, in the light of their behaviour over German frontier questions it is hard to believe that the small Powers would have behaved in any such magnanimous way. They were all out for what they could get.

Members of the British delegation had become anxious about the Council of Four's procedure for another reason. A. J. Sylvester*

* Lloyd George's private secretary.

recalls that at first, in order to ensure as far as they could that secrecy was preserved, the 'Big Four' refused to have a secretary present to take minutes – they met with only their interpreter, Professor Paul Mantoux, present, so,

> At one period, the Council of Four met daily for nearly a fortnight, being without a secretary and having no proper records of their discussions and decisions, they got themselves in a glorious muddle. . . . It was not always possible for the members of the Council of Four to remember what had transpired, or what decisions had been reached. And since they could not remember, how were the unfortunate officials whose duty it was to carry out the decisions to know what they had to do?[117]

At the very beginning of the new Council's deliberations, Sir Henry Wilson expressed concern about this same point. According to Lord Riddell, General Wilson told Lloyd George on 24 March that

> he ought to have Hanky-Panky [Hankey!] with him. The trouble is that the four of them meet together and think they have decided things, but there is no-one to record what they have done. The consequence is that misunderstandings often arise and there is no definite account of their proceedings and nothing happens.[118]

Some little time later Hankey himself, 'a very pertinacious fellow', in Sylvester's words,[119] wrote to Lloyd George pointing out that the Council of Four was suffering from all the defects of Asquith's war-time coalition Cabinet, which Lloyd George had put right when he had taken over.[120] He wrote on 13 April that

> the main criticism that can be directed against the system [the Council of Four] is that it is open to all the defects of the old Cabinet system which no-one has exposed more ruthlessly than yourself. . . . It might be said that decisions affecting the whole fate of the world for centuries to come are being taken without record of the reasons for them.[121]

As a result, Lloyd George persuaded the Council to have Hankey present at all its meetings, instead of only some, and the decision-making machinery of the Conference was thus made more efficient. In any case, in April decisions were at last being taken and the Treaty was emerging.

# 9 War Guilt, Reparations and Other Issues:

## *March-April 1919*

By March the Supreme Council had been edging towards a solution of the dispute over reparations which would in effect postpone the assessment of what Germany owed, and what she could pay, until a future date. They had also touched on the problem of warguilt, and had discussed who should be arraigned and what charges should be brought.* Although Lloyd George had been one of the prime movers towards an indefinite settlement as a way out of the deadlock on reparations and in particular to avoid the public outcry which any reasonable demand would be bound to produce, some of his colleagues were doubtful as to whether he would succeed in this second objective. On 31 March Bonar Law warned that such a proposal 'would cause a wild storm here' and urged Lloyd George to try to get a fixed figure. 'The indemnity cry so far has not diminished' and must be satisfied.[1] Bonar Law's fears were to prove fully justified before very long. There were other pressures to be considered, however, especially the need for haste. Colonel House wrote in his diary on 3 April that 'it was more important to bring about peace quickly than to haggle over details; and I would rather see an immediate peace and the world brought to order than I would see a better peace and delay'.[2] Maybe this was the reason for Colonel House's willingness to compromise and even yield on territorial questions.† Further evidence of the need for haste was contained in a report, received by Lloyd George on 4 April, on conditions in Berlin, which gave clear indication that unless some measure of prosperity was restored to Germany soon, a Bolshevik revolution would probably occur:

* See Chapter 6.
† See Chapter 8.

> Spartacus is a marvel of energy and organisation. But the masses are still undecided, though pretty nearly desperate. Food is the only medicine....

and the following day a similar report was received indicating that within the next few days a Soviet Government of Bavaria would be set up in Munich.[3] This report proved to be accurate – such a Soviet Republic was declared on 7 April, bringing the threat of Bolshevism vividly to the attention of the Allies once more.[4]

The first of these issues which the Council of Four discussed was war guilt. On the afternoon of 1 April, they began to consider the report of the Commission set up in January to consider this matter. President Wilson expressed doubts about the wisdom of trying the Kaiser, but not for any motive of compassion. He was concerned that if the Kaiser were tried and punished he might become a martyr in the eyes of history:

> Charles 1st was an evil person and the biggest liar in history, but he had been surrounded with poetry and revered as a martyr as a result of his execution. The same applied to Mary, Queen of Scots, whose career had nothing to recommend it.

To this Lloyd George retorted that 'there was another explanation: she was a very seductive female'.[5] Wilson shifted his ground and said that the imprisonment of Napoleon on St Helena had made a hero and martyr out of him too, but Lloyd George rejected all these arguments – 'I want to see the man responsible for the biggest crime in History pay the penalty.' Wilson's reply was to ask whether universal condemnation was not punishment enough.[6] At this meeting Wilson accepted the indefinite reparation proposal in principle, but said that it must be made clear to the Germans exactly what they would be required to pay compensation for, under the terms of the Lansing Note, and his experts were therefore preparing a list of items to be included in the demand.

The following afternoon the 'Big Four' had another argument about war guilt. Lloyd George did not like the suggestion that no-one should be tried for starting the war,* but was prepared reluctantly to accept it since the Commission had recommended that the breach of the Treaty of 1839 by which Belgian neutrality had been protected was a triable offence:

* See p. 158 above.

> They have accepted that those responsible for the breach of treaties which has caused the death of millions of men should be avenged. Similarly, punishment must be levied for acts against individuals, atrocities of all sorts committed under orders, the taking of young girls who were forced into prostitution, the sinking of ships on the high seas by submarines, leaving the crews in their lifeboats thousands of miles from land; we must demand that in the treaty the enemy recognises our right to judge those responsible for these crimes and must undertake to deliver them to us.[7]

Wilson said that some accounts suggested that the Kaiser himself had been reluctant to declare war, and Lloyd George added that he only wanted to punish those responsible, whoever they were. They went on to argue about the propriety of prosecuting the guilty men before a tribunal nominated by the victor Powers. Wilson doubted the propriety of this, but Lloyd George did not regard Britain and America as injured parties, as were France and Belgium. Britain and America had fought only in the interest of justice.[8] Wilson also thought it would create a dangerous precedent for the future. If one nation conquered another which had attacked it contrary to international law, it could by itself try to punish the leaders of its defeated attacker. Lloyd George retorted that in future the League of Nations would do this. Wilson then made it clear that his motives for resisting the trial of the Kaiser did not stem from any desire to be merciful:

> What I want to avoid is leaving historians any chance to be sympathetic to Germany. I want to condemn Germany to the execration of History, and not to do anything which might cause someone to say that we went beyond our rights in a just cause. We must not allow History to condemn us for judging our enemies before we have determined clearly our right to do so.[9]

Lloyd George felt that History might also condemn them if they were too feeble. The argument went on. At one point towards the end Clemenceau intervened to say that surely a judgement in anger was morally justified on certain occasions – 'Was not Jesus Christ swept away by anger the day he chased the vendors from the Temple?'[10] – and supported Lloyd George in demanding a trial. Wilson's line was still that 'I feel as you do about the crimes which have been committed, but I want us to act in a way which will satisfy our consciences'.[11] Although all were agreed that terrible punishment was merited, they could not agree on the proper means of bringing those responsible to justice.

They took up the matter once more on 8 April. Wilson was now prepared to accept trial by an Allied tribunal but feared that there might not be enough evidence properly to secure a conviction. Lloyd George had no doubts as to this, and the only question in his mind was that of an appropriate punishment:

> The man who broke his treaty commitment and by doing so brought all this criminal suffering upon the whole world is the worst of criminals. We can treat him in two ways: either we can intern him by a political decision, as the Allies did with Napoleon in 1815, or we can make him stand in judgement. The method matters little to me as long as the Kaiser is punished and put out of harm's way; we must at once ensure that there can be no intrigue around him which could make him dangerous again, and make an example of him. Whether we send him to the Falkland Islands or the island of Hell, or whatever we wish, does not matter to me.[12]

Clemenceau had a definite preference for 'a solemn judgement', while President Wilson was dubious about holding a trial unless the Kaiser could be tried for starting the war. He wanted to destroy the Kaiser utterly, and if he were not tried for starting the war, he could only be tried for the methods by which it had been conducted, for which there were plenty of precedents in earlier wars. The argument went on for some time, Wilson saying later that 'what I want is the most severe lesson. . . . The worst punishment is public execration', but Clemenceau was sceptical – 'Do not count on that'[13] – and was supported by Lloyd George, who urged a trial on a charge of breaking the 1839 treaty before the highest judges of the Allied countries. This seems to have been broadly accepted by them all.

They then had an argument about whether the verdict should be by unanimous or majority vote. Lloyd George was fearful of the possible consequences of an obligation to secure a unanimous verdict:

> Think of the effect if the Kaiser were acquitted by one vote against four, and I would not entirely trust our Japanese friends. If we left it for one voice, that of Japan, to pronounce the Kaiser innocent, that would have a very bad effect on European opinion.[14]

Even Orlando had doubts about whether they had the right to punish a sovereign Emperor for an act of his as a sovereign, but despite this opinion, on behalf of his country he would support the trial. Clemenceau once more demanded a trial, and finally the proposal that the Kaiser should be tried for breaking the Treaty of 1839 was accepted. All wanted to punish the Kaiser. It was only a question of the best way to go about it.

On 5 April, the Council of Four returned to the reparations muddle. Britain and America had proposed schemes for an indefinite settlement, but at the morning meeting Klotz criticised a reference in Article I of the draft terms to limits on Germany's capacity to pay all that was due. Lloyd George said that complete reparations would be quite impossible and Clemenceau agreed – 'Without a doubt, Germany could not pay all that she owed' – but he wished to strengthen the clause to force Germany to recognise that she owed the Allies compensation for all damage done to their civilian population, and that the Allies were only taking account of her limited capacity out of the goodness of their hearts.[15] Colonel House, sitting in for Wilson, said that they could not even state that Germany owed the whole cost of the war, under the Lansing formula, but he agreed with Clemenceau's view for the rest.

Moving on to Articles 2 and 3, Klotz objected to a proposal to restrict the payments to be made by Germany, and therefore her capacity to pay, to a period of thirty years. There was some confusion as to what the clause meant and Davies, the chief American financial expert, explained it:

> Two years from now, the Reparations Commission* must declare the total sum which is owed to us. If it finds that this sum is more than Germany can pay in thirty years, it will fix a sum which appears to them to be what Germany can pay in that time, and this last sum must be paid in full, even if subsequently it turns out to be necessary to prolong the period of payment.[16]

To the clauses thus interpreted, the French at once offered resistance. They did not want to restrict the total which could be extracted in thirty years – Klotz said that 'I recognise that it is highly desirable that Germany should be able to get herself out of debt in thirty years, but if this is impossible, we should not be the victims'.[17] The French

* Not, of course, the Commission of the Conference, but a new inter-Allied body whose task would be to assess reparations.

were supported in this by Orlando, who felt that any restriction of Germany's indebtedness to her estimated capacity to pay would place a premium on German honesty and goodwill. By idleness and ill-will Germany could prevent money being taken, because it would not be there to take. Lloyd George supported the Americans, and proposed the preparation of a new text. The Commission would estimate Germany's capacity to pay and would, at the same time, prepare a scheme for annual payments by which this sum would be paid in thirty years. In other words, the estimate of the total would be made before the plan of payments within thirty years was drawn up.[18] The Council adjourned to allow Lloyd George time to prepare his new text.

The discussion was resumed that afternoon, when Clemenceau demanded that the total payment should be based on what Germany owed in respect of the damage she had done, and not on her capacity to pay. On that basis the scheme of annual payments should be prepared. 'Mr Lloyd George's text seems to allow the Commission the right to fix a lower figure than that which is owing to us; that I cannot accept.'[19] When Colonel House, standing in for President Wilson, said that the French position seemed close to his own, Klotz thought it necessary to disillusion him:

> This is what M. Clemenceau has said: that which is due is due, and the Commission shall not have the right to decide that Germany shall pay less. Later, Governments may take the right to reduce the sum they seek to extract. The Commission shall be confined to varying the size and number of annual payments.[20]

All was now clear to the Americans. Varne McCormick said that 'in other words, this meant that Germany would pay all that she owed, however long it took', and Davis protested that the French were proposing completely to abandon their earlier decision that Allied demands should be related to Germany's capacity to pay.

This stubbornness on the part of the French severely discouraged the Americans, and indeed there seemed little point in going on. On 6 April Colonel House recorded in his diary a conversation he had had over lunch with the President on the subject. They had decided that 'if nothing happened within the next few days, the President would say to the Prime Ministers that unless peace were made according to their promises, which were to conform to the principles of the Fourteen Points, he would either have to go home or he would insist on having the Conference in the open',[21] and early on 7 April Wilson sent his famous telegram to Admiral Benson ordering the *George Washington* back to Brest so that he could leave quickly if he decided to walk out of the Conference.[22] He was 'thoroughly discouraged when we talked the matter over, and wondered what the outcome would be,' House wrote in his diary.[23]

That afternoon, the Council of Four took up the matter again. The meeting opened badly, with Klotz in characteristic form, attacking the draft before the Council because 'the formula, "Whatever may be the financial consequences of paying reparation for the enemy", has been replaced by "Up to the extreme limit of Germany's capacity to pay". I propose that we should return to the original text; it conveys a note which we should like to keep.'[24] Lloyd George insisted that the Commission must be allowed to take Germany's capacity to pay into account, and was supported by the Americans. In the end the French gave in. Germany, according to the agreed text, must recognise that she owed reparation for all the damage caused to the Allied peoples by her aggression, but the Allies would fix what she would actually be called upon to pay in the light of her capacity, taking into account reductions in that capacity arising from other clauses in the Treaty, such as territorial cessions, and her depressed state. Agreement was thus reached on the principle by which assessment for reparation would be carried out, though House refused a European plea that the Commission should reach its decisions by unanimous vote, for one country ought not to be allowed to hold up its decisions. The basic nature of the reparations settlement was now agreed – an indeterminate settlement, with the future assessment to be based on Germany's capacity to pay.

It was now Lloyd George's turn to run into trouble. Advised by Keynes, he had played a prominent role in securing the inclusion in the Reparations Chapter of recognition that Germany would be unable to pay all she owed. Rumours of the Prime Minister's activities had leaked out to the Press, and were prominently featured in the *Daily Mail*, owned by Lord Northcliffe, a bitter opponent of Lloyd George. Northcliffe had always urged heavy reparations, and in December 1918 Lloyd George had admonished him: 'Don't be always making mischief.'[25] Lloyd George himself attributes Northcliffe's spleen against him to his refusal to give Northcliffe a seat in the British Delegation at Paris.[26] The reports in the *Daily Mail* aroused great concern in Parliament, and on 8 April 233 Conservative Members of Parliament signed a telegram to Lloyd George saying that

> The greatest anxiety exists throughout the country at the persistent reports from Paris that the British delegates instead of formulating the complete financial claims of the Empire are merely considering what amount can be exacted from the enemy.

Lloyd George replied that 'I mean to stand faithfully by all the pledges we gave',[27] but decided that he would have to return to London to defend himself before the House of Commons.

Meanwhile, the finishing touches were being put to the Reparations Chapter. On 10 April the Council of Four reopened the question of how the Commission was to reach its decisions. Klotz said that France wanted any cancellation or reduction of the German debt to be subject to a unanimous vote, whereas Wilson preferred a majority vote except for cancellation. Then there was the question of an immediate payment in kind. Lloyd George felt that to fix a figure now would be unwise – 'A figure of £150 million has been suggested. Our Members of Parliament will at once cry out, "Is that all you are going to demand from Germany?".'[28] In the end Clemenceau reluctantly accepted that no figure at all could be fixed:

> I could accept that, but I do not understand the difficulty in fixing a figure. Someone has stolen my watch, my pictures, my furniture. The thief has been caught; it is not difficult to fix a figure before a detailed estimate is available; that is the constant practice of the courts of law. But in a spirit of conciliation I shall accept the proposal made by President Wilson and Mr Lloyd George.[29]

Finally, provisional agreement was reached on most of the outstanding points.

Meanwhile, Lloyd George was getting into more trouble over reparations. On 11 April he told his colleagues in the Council of Four that he would have to return to England to face his Parliamentary critics on the reparations issue. He apologised and promised that if he left on the following Wednesday, he would return by Friday, 'unless the House of Commons refuses me its confidence, in which case it will be with Lord Northcliffe or Horatio Bottomley that you will be resuming these talks'.[30] Lloyd George knew that his fall would mean a far more extreme and intransigent line from his successors. Earlier, arguing for an indefinite settlement, he had warned that to name a figure might bring their Governments crashing down, 'and what would happen to our successors who would have to try and do the impossible?'[31] He also faced tensions within the Delegation at Paris. On 11 April the Australian Prime Minister, William Hughes, wrote to him to say that he disagreed totally with the proposals agreed in the Council of Four and did not see why he should sign the Reparations Chapter. Lloyd George retorted on 14 April, 'I quite understand your attitude. It is a very well-known one. It is generally called "Heads I win, tails you lose".'[32]

Lloyd George was becoming bitter at the blast of criticism he was meeting. When the British Empire Delegation discussed the matter, Lloyd George refused a request from Hughes to reopen the question of reparations: 'if he was going to wreck the Conference by asking for something he knew he could not obtain, it would necessitate one million five hundred thousand men being maintained for an indefinite period under arms. Would the Dominions be willing,' he asked, 'to supply their quota?' Sir Robert Borden warned that if they did not accept the scheme, America might leave them in the lurch and make a separate peace, and without American help they could not hope to impose terms upon the enemy. Even Lord Cunliffe, always an extremist on reparations, said that he 'would stake his reputation that these were the best terms that could be got'. Hughes was not to be appeased, and the Delegation could not agree on their attitude to the proposed clauses.[33] The Americans were not entirely content either. On 12 April Davis once more urged the Council of Four to fix a figure, but Lloyd George refused, since it would be too dangerous politically.[34]

Lloyd George then returned to England to defend himself before the House of Commons. It was during this absence that Wilson and Clemenceau made their deal over the occupation of the Rhineland behind his back.* He appeared before the House on 16 April, and began by describing the difficulties of the Conference to its members.† He then ranged over the work of the Conference, explaining the reason for the Anglo-American Treaty of Guarantee, the need not to draft such a treaty that it would provoke the Germans to prepare for vengeance: he expounded his belief in the need to avoid peace terms 'which would create a legitimate sense of wrong, which

* See pp. 186-7 above.

† See pp. 81-2 above.

would excite national pride needlessly to seek opportunities for redress'.[35] He spoke of the need for a speedy peace to avert starvation and Bolshevism. He then turned upon Lord Northcliffe, identifying his Parliamentary critics with him. Speaking of the 'reliable' rumours which had given rise to the Parliamentary revolt, he said of Northcliffe, 'Reliable? That is the last adjective I would use. It is here today, jumping there tomorrow, and there the next day. I would as soon rely on a grass hopper.'[36] The combination of Lloyd George's *tour de force* in explaining events at the Conference and his brilliant attack on Lord Northcliffe won the day, and he received his vote of confidence and returned to Paris. He was rapturously congratulated by Lord Robert Cecil, who wrote, 'I expect N. will burst'.[37] His position was safe from effective attack at home.

The Reparations Chapter was now ready for presentation to the Germans, but the problem of how to get European industry restarted and commerce moving again was exercising the economists at Paris, especially Keynes. In April, he sent Lloyd George, through the Chancellor of the Exchequer, Austen Chamberlain, details of a scheme for restoring European credit and trade. Chamberlain supported the scheme, while pointing out that American help would be essential. Keynes' idea was that the Central European Government should issue bonds to be taken up by the Allied and Associated Governments in order that they might obtain sufficient credit to restart trading and investment. Keynes commented that, at present, 'the economic mechanism of Europe is jammed'. He also urged an early end to the blockade of Germany, and that reparations should be part of the security the Allies should accept as backing for the bonds.[38] Lloyd George communicated this proposal to President Wilson on 23 April, saying that he believed some such measure was essential if tolerable conditions were to be restored in Europe. The enemy countries were 'at an almost complete economic standstill', and conditions in the new states were 'hardly better', while the Allies themselves were weak. The task was too great for private enterprise: 'The more prostrate a country is and the nearer to Bolshevism the more presumably it requires assistance. But the less likely is private enterprise to do it.' Only Governments, therefore, could act to forestall Bolshevism by helping to restore the economic life of Europe.[39]

Despite these pleas, President Wilson rejected the scheme. On 3 May he replied to Lloyd George saying that his advisers said the scheme was unsound. Moreover, Congress would not consent to

America guaranteeing bonds of European origin, and he felt that it would be better for America to give such assistance as she saw fit independently of other Governments. He then expressed resentment that such a suggestion should be made after the way the discussions on reparations had gone. The Reparations clauses

> demand that Germany shall deliver over at once all her working capital, that is, practically the whole of her liquid assets. . . . Throughout the reparation discussions the American delegation has steadily pointed out to the other delegations that the plans proposed would surely deprive Germany of the means of making any appreciable reparations payments. I myself, as you know, have frequently made the same observation. But when any of us was urgent on this point, he was accused of being pro-German. . . . How can your experts or ours be expected to work out a new plan for furnishing working capital to Germany when we deliberately start out by taking away all Germany's present capital?[40]

President Wilson allowed his own irritation and disgust at the attitude towards reparations taken during the negotiations which led to the indeterminate settlement to influence his judgement on the Keynes scheme. Keynes himself was horrified by this reaction to his 'grand scheme for the rehabilitation of Europe',[41] and wrote to Philip Kerr on 14 May that the President's reply

> indicates a spirit far too harsh for the human situation facing us. In particular, it is surely impossible for the Americans to disclaim responsibility for the Peace Treaty to which, wisely or not, they have put their name equally with the other governments.*[42]

The Americans refused to back the scheme, and this undoubtedly helped to build up in Keynes' mind the bitterness which was to lead him to resign from the British Delegation in early June. In mid-May he told a close friend that the Americans had turned down his scheme 'as a most immoral proposal which might cost them something and which senators from Illinois would not look at. They had a chance of taking a large, or at least humane, view of the world, but unhesitatingly refused it. Wilson, of whom I have seen a good deal more lately, is the greatest fraud on earth.'[43] Reading Keynes' reaction to the

* The Treaty was accepted by the Peace Conference on 6 May, and presented to the Germans the following day. See pp. 239–42 below.

rejection of his scheme, it is easy to see whence came the bitter brilliance of the polemic contained in the early part of *The Economic Consequences of the Peace*. Generosity failed to triumph, and Europe would have to drag herself to her feet by her own efforts once peace was made.

The only other major section of the draft Treaty was the Covenant of the League of Nations. After its acceptance in principle by the Plenary Session of the Conference on 14 February,* the League Commission went through the Covenant a third time to take up certain outstanding problems. They began on 22 March, when there was a dispute as to whether the seat of the League should be at Geneva or Brussels, and Wilson resisted the idea of compulsory inspection to ensure compliance with the Covenant's agreement to disarm, since this would 'seriously offend the susceptibilities of sovereign states'.[44] On 24 March, Bourgeois tried to persuade the Commission to approve of a permanent military occupation of the Rhineland. This was refused.[45] Two days later, the question arose of whether states should be allowed to withdraw from the League, and, if so, on what terms. Wilson hoped that such a provision would prove unnecessary, for he 'did not entertain the smallest fear that any state would take advantage of the proposed clause. Any state which did so would become an outlaw,' but he felt obliged to insist on such a provision being included in the Covenant in order to reassure Congress: 'Americans would have to be assured that they were not giving up the sovereignty of their state.'[46] It was agreed to allow withdrawal after the giving of two years' notice, but this was only a legal right – it was not a moral right, the Commission decided. Any nation which withdrew would arouse strong disapproval.

A problem which was arousing increasing concern in relation to the League Covenant was the Monroe Doctrine. If he were to have a chance of getting the Covenant through the American Senate, Wilson would have to ensure that the Monroe Doctrine was preserved despite provisions of the Covenant relating to the abrogation of old treaties and arrangements inconsistent with its provisions. It seems that Lloyd George was unwilling to countenance this. On 27 March, Lord Robert Cecil wrote to Balfour saying that the Prime Minister was 'very obstinate' on this issue, even though Wilson was sure he would need a concession on this matter if he were to get the

* See p. 90 above.

Treaty accepted by the Senate. Admittedly the situation had been made worse by 'the intolerable habit of the Americans of chattering so that all their papers are filled with talk about the expected concession', but Colonel House had complained 'rather bitterly' to Cecil that he had conceded most of what the British wanted, especially on mandates and the separate representation of the Dominions at the League of Nations, and when Wilson 'asked one thing we could not give it him. This was roughly true,' so Cecil asked Balfour 'to do your best to help me with the little man.'* He enclosed a draft amendment which would permit regional understandings like the Monroe Doctrine to exist side by side with the Covenant.[47] One possible reason for Lloyd George's obstinacy may have been advice from the Admiralty that Britain should not sign the Covenant unless America undertook not to build a fleet to rival Britain's. Cecil felt that such an ultimatum 'would be very unwise if true', and asked Lloyd George whether this meant that 'your policy is no longer favourable to the League?'[48] The Monroe Doctrine would raise problems when it was discussed at the League Commission.

The matter came up at the Commission on 10 April, after an unseemly wrangle over the seat of the League. The draft Covenant laid down that it would be in Geneva, whereupon Hymans, grasping as ever, demanded to know why Belgium 'should . . . be set on one side? Is it because she took part in the war? The fact of having been unjustly attacked, brutally invaded and oppressed in defiance of treaties is thus made a reason for exclusion.'[49] Lord Robert Cecil tried to smooth him over. Geneva had been chosen 'because impartiality and not the preservation of the glorious memories of the war, was the object of the League',[50] and was supported by Wilson: 'the present question was not one of awarding honour but of finding the best surroundings for international deliberation'.[51] Hymans reluctantly accepted defeat.

Wilson then raised the subject of the Monroe Doctrine. The French were at first suspicious, fearing that this might allow America to opt out of European disputes, and were reassured by Wilson: 'if the United States signed this document they would be solemnly obliged to render aid in European affairs, when the territorial integrity of any European State was threatened by external aggression'.[52] Finally, the French reluctantly accepted Lord Robert Cecil's

* Lloyd George.

proposal that the Monroe Doctrine should be allowed to stand, after he had pointed out that 'the Monroe Doctrine had never in a single instance been applied to American policy with regard to American participation in Europe'.[53] The Monroe Doctrine was then accepted, and one hurdle as far as the American Senate was concerned had been avoided.

The next day the Commission held its fifteenth and final meeting. The Monroe Doctrine was discussed further and a French amendment providing that this and other such arrangements 'do not in any way prevent the signatory states from executing their obligations under this Covenant'[54] was accepted. The final topic was racial equality, which was raised by the Japanese Prime Minister, Baron Makino, who wanted an obligation to recognise racial equality written into the Preamble of the Covenant. Lord Robert Cecil opposed it, since the Commonwealth would object, and President Wilson also opposed him, fearing controversies in various countries in which it would not be desirable to involve the League. Nonetheless, a majority of the members of the Commission voted for Makino's proposal. Wilson as Chairman then ruled that the Japanese proposal was not accepted as the vote had not been unanimous and there had been 'strong opposition', whereupon Makino reserved his right to raise the matter at the Plenary Session which would approve the Covenant.[55] It is probable that Wilson's opposition stemmed from a fear of the reaction of the members of the American Senate who represented the Southern States. Feeling in California against Japanese immigrants had been running high for some time and in 1907 Congress had passed a Bill restricting immigration, under which almost all Japanese immigrants had been refused admission to the United States. Still more restrictive measures were to be imposed in 1922. This was a highly sensitive issue in the United States, on which Wilson had good reason to be cautious, and the Japanese to be bitter.

Once the Commission had completed its work there remained some loose ends to be tied up by the Council of Four. On 25 April the League was given the task of determining when special economic provisions relating to Germany should lapse, after a French plea that if Germany were not controlled French industries might suffer from unfair German competition.[56] Three days later the League Council was empowered to investigate any default by Germany on her obligations. At Clemenceau's request this was to be done by majority vote.[57] Thus the League was to play a role in ensuring that Germany behaved herself and fulfilled the obligations to be laid upon her by the Treaty.

That afternoon, the League Commission presented its second and final report to a Plenary Session of the Peace Conference. The report was introduced by Wilson, but the chief feature of the debate was the raising of three proposals which had not been accepted by the Commission. First, Baron Makino raised afresh his demand that the Covenant should include a recognition of racial equality; secondly, Hymans made another appeal for the selection of Brussels as the seat of the League; and finally Bourgeois made another plea on behalf of France for compulsory inspection of armaments. France did not want the League to be 'powerless and ineffective'.[58] In the end, the Covenant was adopted after all had had their say, and the new institution was now ready to be established when the Treaty was signed.

One problem to which the Council of Four failed to find any solution during this period was that of Russia. They discussed it on a number of occasions and from several viewpoints. On 27 March President Wilson told his colleagues that Odessa was in danger of falling to the Bolsheviks. When Marshal Foch had been asked what would be necessary for the Allies successfully to relieve the town, his reply had involved the capture of a line of territory extending from the Baltic to the Black Sea, and he had also spoken of 'restoring Hungary to sanity; that is to say crushing Hungarian Bolshevism'.[59] The only problem which concerned them really, Wilson felt, was whether they should help Roumania to resist the Red Army. Orlando pointed out that in his view there were only two alternatives. Either the Allies should march to Moscow and crush Bolshevism or they could recognise Lenin's Government as the legitimate Government of Russia and establish relations with it:

> We have done neither one thing or the other, and as a result we have suffered the most adverse consequences of both policies at once. Without declaring war we are in a state of war with Russia. At the moment, in any case, the Russian and Ukrainian Bolsheviks were only defending their rightful territory.[60]

The Council did not feel like making up its mind that day, but did consider giving assistance to Roumania.

It was not only the Council of Four which was perplexed by everyone's reluctance to commit themselves to a definite policy in relation to Bolshevik Russia. On 28 March Lord Curzon, in London, wrote to Balfour in Paris informing him that the Esthonian Government had submitted a request to the British Government for a loan. Esthonia, as one of the small Baltic states bordering on Russia, would form an essential link in any chain of border states which the Allies might decide to create in order to restrain the Bolsheviks, and with the French demanding an attack on Soviet Russia, the British Treasury felt that no loans should be made to such countries until a definite Russian policy had been decided. He therefore requested a decision on the Allied attitude to the Baltic States. Were they to be bolstered in order to present a hostile barrier to Bolshevism, or encouraged to seek agreement with Lenin's Government in order to ensure their continued existence. Britain could not act until 'authoritative statements on these points were forthcoming – and the Paris Conference is alone competent to pronounce them'.[61] Only the Council of Four could resolve the uncertainty, but for the time being it made no attempt to do so. On 31 March, however, the British Cabinet agreed to prepare to evacuate British forces from Russia, in view of reports that the French were doing likewise.[62]

At this time it appeared that the Bolsheviks were becoming both more successful and more aggressive. Zinoviev declared late in March that revolution was coming in Europe, especially in France – 'Another reason why the French bourgeoisie cannot come to the help of their Russian comrades is that the ground is already burning under their own feet'[63] – and such beliefs were strengthened by the declaration of the Soviet Government in Bavaria, which Chicherin hailed as follows:

> We may rest assured that the day is not far off when revolutionary socialist allies will join forces with us and will give support to the Bavarian Soviet Republic against attack. Every blow aimed against you is aimed at us. In absolute unity we carry on our revolutionary struggle for the well-being of all workers and exploited peoples.[64]

Despite these brave words the Bavarian Soviet Republic collapsed within a week, but in general the Bolsheviks were increasingly victorious in the Russian civil war at this time. As a result, pressures, especially in Britain, grew for both increased intervention and peace with the Bolsheviks. Churchill, ever anxious to get his Cabinet colleagues firmly committed to war against Bolshevism, circulated to them a memorandum, dated 15 April, urging the recognition of Admiral Kolchak's government in Siberia, as he alone was having some degree of military success and he should therefore receive the boost which recognition would give,[65] and at this same time the Foreign Office warned that the Bolshevik Government was both ruthless and unscrupulous.[66] Optimistic reports about Kolchak's military successes caused Lord Curzon to write to Balfour to urge that the Allies should agree to recognise Kolchak: 'Admiral Kolchak and his troops require some external stimulus to ensure their final success, and this is now in the power of the Allied Governments to bestow.'[67] Even among the Americans, as William Bullitt was to recall, pressure built up for recognition of Kolchak. He told the Senate Foreign Relations Committee that in April 1919

> Kolchak made a 100-mile advance, and immediately, the entire Press of Paris was roaring and screaming on the subject, announcing that Kolchak would be in Moscow within two weeks; and therefore everyone in Paris, including I regret to say members of the American Commission, began to grow very lukewarm about peace in Russia, because they thought Kolchak would arrive in Moscow and wipe out the Soviet Government.[68]

A White success at once aroused hopes among many that they could crush Bolshevism instead of having to come to terms with it. At the same time, France and Britain could not amicably coordinate their policies in Russia any more than they could anywhere else. British complaints about French failure to give General Denikin, in South Russia, adequate support drew the usual excuse from the French Government about insubordination on the part of French officers on the spot and an assurance that they would be instructed to co-operate.[69] On 20 April, Lloyd George received a letter from G. N. Barnes, the Labour representative in his coalition Government, urging peace with the Bolsheviks,[70] but Kolchak's military successes encouraged those who wanted increased intervention against them to make the running.

On 30 April, with the German Treaty virtually complete, the Council of Four found time to turn its attention once more to the Russian problem. Lloyd George spoke of Kolchak's successes, but also said that Lenin's Government seemed inclined to behave in a more moderate fashion. Clemenceau said that his information was that the Bolsheviks were weakening, whereupon Lloyd George replied that his information was different, and all they could agree to do was to ask their General Staffs to report on the situation in Russia and suggest what were the possible courses of action.[71] The Council of Four were no nearer to developing an agreed policy on Russia, and the civil war was left to carry on without effective Allied intervention on either side.

# 10 Italy's Month: *April 1919*

One more aspect of the negotiations leading up to the presentation of the Treaty to the Germans remains: the efforts of various Allied Powers, especially Italy, to secure a share of the spoils of victory. Throughout the Conference many people had sought without success to persuade Italy to abate her demands, especially in relation to Yugoslavia, but such attempts had been met with an obstinacy and greed which had alienated everybody.* In April, Italy's determination to obtain her pound of flesh was to lead to one of the most famous incidents of the Conference – the open row between Orlando and Wilson which was finally to cause the Italians to withdraw from the Conference altogether.

At the beginning of April, Orlando began agitating for consideration of Italy's claims by the Council of Four. On the afternoon of 1 April, after a discussion of reparations, itself a matter which was then giving rise to much heated argument in the Council, Orlando said that

> From the Italian point of view it is essential that we should delay no longer in reaching a decision about Italy's eastern frontier. For the Italian people it is a question of national prestige as well as one of our national security. If the Italian people were to learn that all questions relating to Germany had been decided, while those relating to Italy had all been adjourned, that would produce a terrible impression.[1]

Lloyd George suggested that the matter might be discussed the following week.

* See pp. 115–20 above.

Two days later, however, this time after a discussion of Danzig, Orlando tried again. He said that Italy's demands were based upon the Treaty of London, but there was also the question of Fiume to consider: the dissolution of Austria–Hungary meant that there was no longer any need to assure that great Empire of an outlet to the sea, and if Fiume were left in the hands of the new Yugoslav state, the Italians living there would be at the mercy of the hated Croats. 'It is not just a case of not allowing an Italian city to unite with the rest of Italy, but of condemning the Italian character of the city to death.'[2] Italy would give Austria and Czechoslovakia use of the port. Lloyd George suggested that the same solution might be applied here as was proposed for Danzig – the creation of a free city state under the League of Nations – but Orlando refused to consider it. President Wilson supported Lloyd George's proposal. He had spoken to members of the city's administration, he said, and 'they told me that they did not want to be put under the government of either Italy or Yugoslavia, and had suggested a zone around the town which could be included to form an autonomous territory'.[3] Orlando then declared that he was compelled by national feeling to resist any such idea. 'For the Italians, the question of Fiume is a question of national pride; we cannot abandon our brothers whose liberation was the first object of our war effort.'[4] This Wilson would not accept, and he pointed out a fatal weakness in Orlando's argument, since by the terms of the Treaty of London Fiume would not have been ceded to Italy:

> You say you fought to liberate your compatriots in Fiume: why then did you declare war after having signed a treaty by which Fiume would have to remain outside Italy?[5]

Orlando faced considerable opposition to his claim for Fiume.

On 11 April, Orlando tried again to hasten a decision. Lloyd George had just received the 'Round Robin' telegram from his Parliamentary supporters on the subject of reparations,* and Orlando appealed to him, saying that 'I face the same difficulties as you do', and that the delay in considering the Italian case which must result from Lloyd George's absence 'would cause great trouble in Italy and must not be prolonged more than is necessary'.[6] He asked for a decision before the Italian Parliament was reopened later

* See pp. 205–6 above.

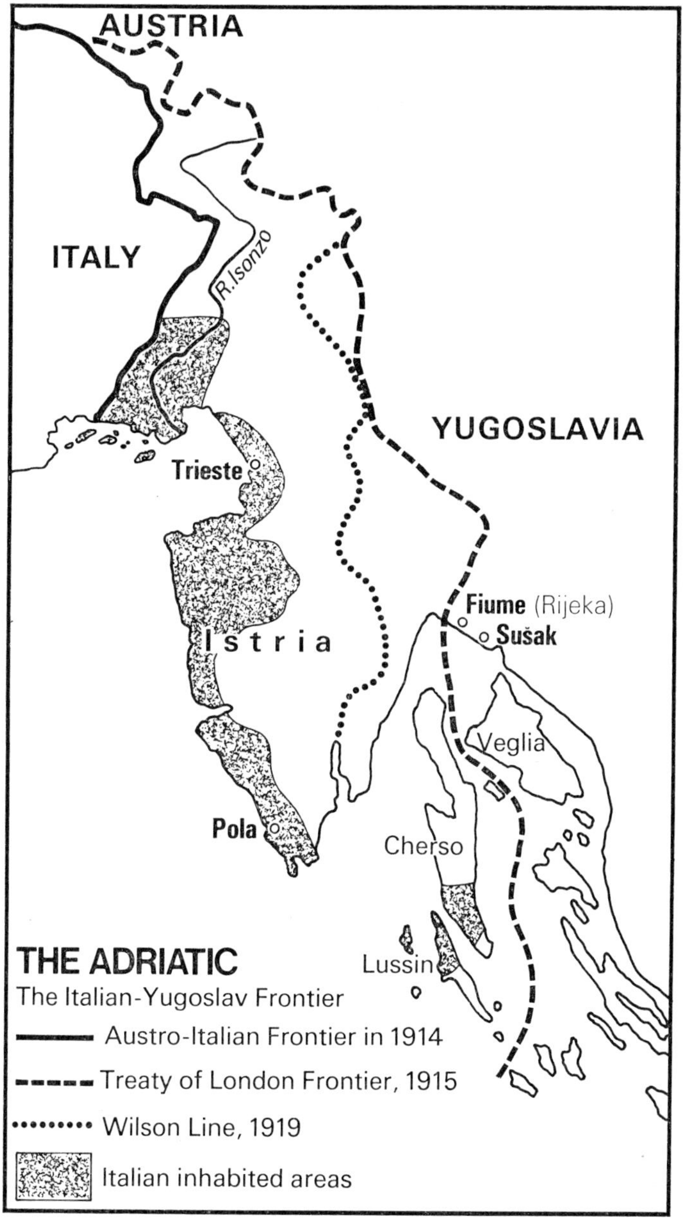
AUSTRIA
ITALY
R. Isonzo
YUGOSLAVIA
Trieste
Istria
Fiume (Rijeka)
Sušak
Veglia
Pola
Cherso
Lussin
THE ADRIATIC
The Italian-Yugoslav Frontier
Austro-Italian Frontier in 1914
Treaty of London Frontier, 1915
Wilson Line, 1919
Italian inhabited areas

that month. Lloyd George then pointed out that the matter was above all one for Orlando and Wilson, for Britain and France were bound by the Treaty of London.

The Council of Four's position was not made any easier by the fact that the Yugoslavs also felt strongly about Fiume,* as they had made clear to the Council of Ten, and again to the Council of Four on 3 April, when, in the absence of Orlando, Trumbič was given a hearing and claimed that the Italian nature of the city was purely a result of Hungarian endeavours to weaken the South Slavs, and Fiume was really a Slav city:

> . . . the Italians are only immigrants. . . . Rijeka – that is the ancient name of the city, translated into Italian as Fiume – belongs to Croatia, geographically. What is more it is surrounded on all sides by entirely Slav populations. . . .[7]

and he also said that the port would enjoy greater prosperity under Yugoslavia than under Italy, who had several other large ports. Clearly the Council of Four had a serious problem to face, since both Italy and Yugoslavia wanted Fiume and both could not have it, and there was no room for compromise.

Bound by the Treaty of London, Britain and France were caught in something of a cleft stick. They were bound to support Italy's claims to large parts of Dalmatia, though not Fiume, and it was clear that Wilson would object, although his position had been weakened by Colonel House's 'deviltry' of the previous November.† On 13 April A. J. Balfour met the Italian Ambassador in Paris, who warned him that any Italian Government which surrendered Fiume would fall and that such a decision might even provoke the army to revolt against the state. 'There was real ground for fearing that a decision on this subject adverse to Italy might probably produce a violent explosion of indignation in that country.'[8] Orlando raised the subject again that afternoon during a discussion of when the German delegates should be invited to come to Versailles to receive the terms. Orlando wished to delay this until his country's claims had been accepted in principle, since to receive the Germans before such a decision was made 'would create a disastrous impression in Italy'.[9] When President Wilson suggested inviting the Germans to attend

* See pp. 118–19 above.
† See p. 43 above.

ten days hence and that the Italian claims could be discussed meanwhile, Orlando was still reluctant. He wanted to hold up the whole business of the Conference until he had got what he wanted. He feared that unless he got a decision before he appeared before Parliament on 23 April, 'The least that will happen will be the fall of my Government'.[10] He won some measure of sympathy from Wilson, who offered to discuss the Italian claims with Orlando the next day.

The following day the Italians did indeed get a response from Wilson – a memorandum in which he rejected most of them. He stood firmly by his principles in this memorandum, dated 14 April:

> I feel myself obliged to adapt every conclusion at which I arrive as closely as possible to the fourteen principles of peace. . . . The Fourteen Points and the principles I laid down in my later speeches have been formally accepted as the basis of peace by all those Powers who have been associated with us in the war against Germany, except for one on which the Allies made a specific reservation.[11]

He therefore could not accept that the Treaty of London constituted a legitimate basis for the drawing of Italy's eastern frontier, and in any case that frontier as delineated in the Treaty of London had been designed to give Italy a secure defence against Austria–Hungary, which no longer existed. Hence the reasons for the Treaty of London frontier no longer existed. He would not cede Fiume either, since the new national states needed it as an outlet to the sea, and there was a need to secure a lasting peace:

> From the beginning, we must avoid making the mistake of making Italy's closest Eastern neighbours her enemies and of creating precisely that sentiment of injustice which has troubled Europe's peace for generations and which contributed not a little to the origins of the terrible struggle from which we have just emerged.[12]

The President thus flatly rejected Italy's whole case so far as the Adriatic was concerned. On 15 April, Wilson had what he described to A. J. Balfour as a 'most painful' interview with Orlando on the subject of Fiume,[13] and it was clear that a head-on clash was inevitable, which would be highly embarrassing for Britain and France, since they were bound by the Treaty of London and their freedom of manoeuvre was thus severely restricted. On 17 April Balfour wrote to the Marquis Imperiali, the Italian Ambassador in London, saying that he felt 'deep feelings of resentment at the suggestion that the British are animated on this or any other subject by hostility or even indifference to Italian interests', but urging that the Italian Government should recognise the desirability of in future having friendly relations with Yugoslavia, while reaffirming that Britain was still bound by the Treaty of London – 'We have already signed away our liberty of action.'[14] This seemed likely to prove a highly embarrassing commitment.

The Americans, for their part, were becoming more firm in their resolve to resist the Italian claims. At a meeting of the American Commissioners Plenipotentiary on 18 April, after some discussion as to whether Fiume should be constituted a Free City, the Secretary of State, Lansing, declared that he

> felt that the Italian threat of revolution, in case their claims were not granted, should not affect the American Delegation in the slightest in their determination as to what would be a just settlement. . . .

and Colonel House, agreeing with his colleagues that Fiume must be given to the Yugoslavs, said that 'it would be better to have the matter out with the Italians as soon as possible, preferably on the next day',[15] and this was in fact what happened. On the morning of 19 April, Orlando presented Italy's claims formally to the Council of Four, and the row began in earnest.

Orlando did this under three headings: the Brenner frontier with Austria; Fiume, an Italian city inhabited by Italians; and Dalmatia and the Adriatic islands, which Italy claimed chiefly for strategic reasons – 'the Eastern coast of Italy lies at the mercy of whoever is master of the other side of the Adriatic'.[16] The Treaty of London had been a compromise and he claimed as a minimum what was due under the terms of that treaty – 'we are thus moderate in our claims'.[17] President Wilson at once mounted his high horse to oppose the Italians:

> It was I who took the responsibility and the privilege of making the arrangements which led to the Armistice. At that time we all understood and accepted clearly defined principles which were to serve as the basis of peace with Germany. It is not possible for us now to say that we are making peace with Germany on the basis of certain principles, but that we are adopting other principles in making peace with Turkey, Bulgaria and with Austria.[18]

They were attempting to create a new order in international relations and must therefore reject certain kinds of claims,

> which would destroy precisely those principles on which the new order would be founded. For example, this makes it impossible for us to distribute territory on the basis of the idea of strategic frontiers.[19]

Fiume was also important to the new states. He then said, amazingly, that they had conformed to the principle of nationality in the case of Danzig. That might be so, but Wilson had only reluctantly accepted the Free City solution in that case. Because they had done so there they must do so in the case of Fiume. The League of Nations would, in any case, protect Italy against any threat from Yugoslavia. Then came a truly remarkable passage:

> We have sometimes spoken in this room as though we were the masters of Europe. We are not, we are responsible to the peoples of Europe and in their hands, and I am fearful of doing them wrong by making a tragic mistake.[20]

Whether one regards this as hypocrisy, or as Wilson's genuine reaction on this occasion, he was certainly claiming to speak for the world against the selfish ambitions which, as he saw it, governed European politics and diplomacy.

After this prolonged outburst, it was the turn of Orlando and his Foreign Minister, Baron Sonnino, to reply, and Sonnino did so in terms which had become familiar to the Council of Four. Italy wanted a guarantee of safety, in this case from attack from across the Adriatic Sea:

> The best League of Nations in the world could not give us a better guarantee of safety than the police in our towns, and the presence of the police in the streets did not make us feel that we need not lock our doors at night. That is what we want to be able to do in the Adriatic.[21]

He also spoke of Italy's war losses, and when Wilson offered an American Treaty of Guarantee, Sonnino said that American troops would arrive too late to protect Italy. All these arguments had become familiar to the Council of Four from other people and in other contexts. He would not trust the Yugoslavs – Italy would be faced by 'Balkan states which know neither good faith nor law and whom we will never see as anything other than enemies'.[22] The Italians were resolved to obtain what they claimed, whilst Wilson was determined they should not succeed.

At this point Clemenceau intervened. Britain and France were bound by the Treaty of London, he said, but he had been astonished at the claim for Fiume, which Italy had not demanded in the Treaty of London. He urged the Italians not to be obstinate: 'I fear that our Italian friends will commit a deplorable act which they will regret if they go to the point of breaking with the rest of us at the Conference. By so doing they will benefit neither the world nor themselves.'[23] Lloyd George affirmed that he intended to stick to the Treaty of London, under which Fiume must go to Croatia, but Wilson made things still more difficult by saying that he refused to accept the Treaty of London either, since it was 'one of those secret treaties against which we have declared ourselves', and to say that the Allies were determined to carry out that Treaty 'would put the United States Government in an impossible position'.[24] So the disagreement was now three-sided, with Italy demanding more than the Treaty of London had promised her, Britain and France prepared only to go as far as they were bound to by that Treaty, and President Wilson not prepared to accept the validity of the Treaty of London at all.

The discussion was resumed the following morning, Orlando saying that, although it would cause great discontent in Italy if she were not given Fiume, he would limit his demands to the provisions of the Treaty of London provided that the promises made therein were met in full. Wilson said this attitude was 'unbelievable', declaring that America had fought on behalf of certain principles, and these principles had been acclaimed by the peoples of great and small nations alike. If the principle of the self-determination of peoples were not adhered to, he said,

> We shall stir up an indignation and hatred which will be the most ready cause of perpetual conflicts. If Italy declares that she holds to the Treaty of London she will bar the way to peace. The United States could not associate herself with such a policy.[25]

Orlando protested that Italy had expressed reservations about the Fourteen Points. Lloyd George suggested that the signatories of the Treaty of London should discuss the matter before the Council met again, and, after warning that he could not agree to the cession of all the territory specified in the Treaty of London to Italy, Wilson agreed that it might help, and such a meeting was fixed for the morning of the next day, 21 April.

The British, French and Italians therefore forgathered that morning, to discuss the problems to which Wilson's stand had given rise. Britain and France were bound by the Treaty of London, but if it were implemented America might well refuse to sign the Austrian Treaty, and her cooperation would in any case be necessary, as Lloyd George pointed out, in the restoration of Europe, so he urged that some concession be made in order to enable agreement to be reached with the Americans, but if the Italians insisted on the execution of the Treaty of London he would stand by Britain's promise in the Treaty. Clemenceau suggested that if the Italians wanted Fiume so badly they should make a concession elsewhere, and pointed out how many of France's demands he had been compelled to give up in order to secure agreement.[26] The Italians, however, were obstinate. For Sonnino the League of Nations was irrelevant – 'Let it, if it can, restore order in Russia and regulate Balkan affairs! Not thus will you change human nature' – and he expressed great resentment at Wilson's attitude to the Italian claims:

> Having made concessions left and right to respectable interests, he now wants to recover the purity of his principles at our expense. How can we possibly accept that?[27]

The Italians were obdurate and no progress was possible, despite the efforts of Lloyd George and Clemenceau to secure a compromise. That afternoon Wilson refused to consider giving Italy the Adriatic islands on the ground that if this were done she would cause trouble in the Gulf of Fiume, and he also refused to consider compensating Italy for the loss of Dalmatia by giving her some territory in the Middle East: 'Italy has no experience in colonial administration. She is demanding territory only to satisfy her ambitions.'[28] Wilson plainly distrusted and disliked the Italians. It was not only a stand of principle that he was making, and he clearly wished to limit Italy's future influence as well. Lloyd George, however, felt that some concession must be made, otherwise Orlando and Sonnino would not be able to face the Italian Parliament.

At this point, President Wilson read a document which he said he proposed to publish the following day in which he repudiated the Treaty of London and said that his principles must be applied to the Austro-Hungarian territories as well as to Germany. Fiume must be an international port. Lloyd George urged that the Italians should be asked whether they would consider accepting territory in Asia Minor as a substitute for Dalmatia. Sir Maurice Hankey was sent out to ask them, and Wilson now agreed to envisage making Fiume a free city instead of giving it to Yugoslavia outright. Hankey returned and said that the Italians would not consider a proposal of the kind Lloyd George had made. Wilson declared that he would publish his document the next day, and both Clemenceau and Lloyd George appealed to him not to, since it would make any compromise impossible, and, Lloyd George said, it 'would release a storm in Italy. Everything would be overturned.'[29] Reluctantly, Wilson agreed to wait an extra day. The following day Lord Derby, the British Ambassador in Paris, told Lord Curzon in a letter that the Italian crisis was now 'very serious. They have set their hearts on Fiume,' and President Wilson was being 'very stiff with regard to their demands'. Moreover, the Italians believed that the British delegates were secretly supporting Wilson, which was making Britain's position highly embarrassing.[30]

The following day the crisis took several turns for the worse. The Council of Four were informed that the Italian delegation had withdrawn from the Conference in protest at Wilson's attitude, and Wilson himself said that he was now determined to publish his declaration on the following day, because he had been advised that it might bring the Italian delegates to their senses:

> When the Italian man in the street has read what we have to say, he will reflect that there could develop a new international relationship based on new principles. Thus publication could produce a reversal of Italian opinion.

Lloyd George believed that this view was not only over-optimistic but also dangerous: 'I am afraid that you will produce a crisis which no-one will be able to solve' in Italy, which might well bring Giolitti, known to be extreme on Italy's demands, to power.[31] The following day, nonetheless, Wilson published his appeal to the 'Italian people, in which he spoke of the new states, whose interests are henceforth to be as scrupulously safeguarded as the interests of the most powerful states', and of his principles – 'It was upon the explicit avowal of these principles that the initiative for peace was taken. It is upon them that the whole structure of peace must rest.' Fiume must be an international port, and disarmament and the

League would guarantee the safety of all. He ended with an open appeal to the people to support him:

> America is Italy's friend . . . and America was privileged by the generous commission of her associates in the war to initiate the peace we are about to consumate – to initiate it upon terms she had herself formulated and in which I was her spokesman. The compulsion is upon her to square every decision she takes part in with those principles. . . . She trusts Italy, and in her trust believes that Italy will ask nothing of her that cannot be made unmistakeably consistent with these sacred obligations.[32]

Wilson had publicly stated his position. The question now was how the Italians would react. Orlando issued a reply on 24 April in which he made clear his deep resentment at Wilson's attitude and action. Speaking of the self-determination of peoples, he said that

> I have great regret in calling to mind that this procedure, which until now has been used only against enemy governments, is today for the first time being used against a government which has been, and counts on remaining, a loyal friend of the great American republic – against the Italian Government.[33]

Allied Governments ought to be exempt from submitting their territorial claims to the self-determination of peoples, and Orlando flatly rejected the application of Wilson's principles to the Italian claims. In contradiction, he appealed for Fiume on the ground of self-determination, and he expressed astonishment that anyone could regard as excessive the Italian claim to the Dalmatian coast, 'this boulevard of Italy throughout the centuries, which Roman genius and Venetian activity have made noble and great, and whose Italianity . . . today shares with the Italian nation the same feelings of patriotism'.[34] The deadlock seemed to be so complete as to allow no room at all for manoeuvre.

On the morning of 24 April, Lloyd George reported to his colleagues in the Council of Four that he had discussed the crisis with Orlando, and had warned him that if he persisted in his demand for Fiume, he must give up the Treaty of London. This he had refused to do, and he had also told Lloyd George of his proposed reply to Wilson's declaration. Lloyd George urged that they should at least write to Orlando to ask him not to leave Paris altogether,[35] and this was agreed. In a note signed by Wilson, Lloyd George and

Clemenceau, they appealed to him not to break up the alliance over Fiume and to remain in Paris so that a solution could be sought.[36] That afternoon, the Council of Four again discussed the Italian question, with Orlando and Sonnino present. Orlando expressed his annoyance at Wilson's publication of his declaration, and said that certain consequences must follow from it:

> The publication of this document ... has given the public the impression that an appeal is being made to them in general. Even if this was not intended, the result has been to place my authority as the representative of the people of Italy in doubt. ... I must therefore return to the source of my authority.[37]

Wilson urged him to discuss the matter further and attempted to be conciliatory, but Orlando, while thanking him for his expressions of friendship, said that

> The fact is that the question of Fiume is a national question in Italy. Now, on this question, not only the United States but all our Allies oppose our claims, so it is useless to reopen the discussion; I must tell Italy this and see whether she is willing to resign herself to giving it up.[38]

Lloyd George offered the Free City solution and an exchange of this for Dalmatia, but Orlando refused and threatened that Italy would not sign the German Treaty, including the League Covenant: 'It will be very difficult for us to sign the Treaty of Peace with Germany if the questions concerning Italy are not settled first.'[39] Wilson stuck obstinately by his principles. Lloyd George then suggested that himself, Clemenceau and Wilson should prepare a joint proposal for the Italians to consider:

> I have had some experience of arbitration in industrial conflicts, and when I have had to play the role of arbiter I have always spoken to the parties to the dispute as follows: Will you take the responsibility, not of accepting my proposal, but of recommending to those whom you represent what seems to me to be reasonable?[40]

However, after further discussion, the gap between Wilson and the Italians was clearly so wide that this course of action had no hope of success, and at the end of the meeting Lloyd George said that nothing more could be done:

> Unhappily this dispute is a dispute of principle. I have nothing to say against President Wilson's principles; I have myself struggled on their behalf and we fought the war for them, but we also have the principle of respect for treaties, for which my country declared war.[41]

Lloyd George felt that he could not throw the Treaty of London overboard, and that Wilson had been unduly obstinate. There was clearly nothing to be done, however, and Orlando and Sonnino returned to Rome. On 30 April, the Council of Three, as it now was, discussed the problem anew, and Lloyd George expressed the opinion that further concessions would be useless, for in a speech in Italy Orlando had publicly declared that he would not relinquish his claim to Dalmatia in return for Free City status for Fiume, and Wilson said that he would only allow any territory at all to be ceded after a plebiscite.

Attitudes were now, in fact, hardening on both sides. On 29 April a member of the staff of the British Embassy in Rome informed Lord Curzon that Wilson's appeal to the people of Italy had had the reverse effect of what he had hoped for, since it had aroused the indignation of the Italian people and they were determined to get Fiume,[42] while in Paris the Council of Three resolved to carry on with the negotiations and preparations for the signing of the Treaty without Italy. On the morning of 1 May Lloyd George declared that 'Italy signed the Treaty of London, and by leaving the Conference she has torn it up',[43] and that evening it was agreed simply to inform the Italian Ambassador that negotiations with the Germans were to begin. The Italians could then do what they liked. On 2 May it was agreed not to publish the appeal that Wilson, Clemenceau and Lloyd George made to Orlando* lest it put him in a position where he could not compromise or return to the Conference, but that he should be informed that by walking out he was considered to have broken the Treaty of London, which would therefore lapse.[44] Next day they discussed the matter again, and confirmed this decision. Lloyd George felt bound to make a choice between Italy and America. 'To break with Italy was a grave decision, but to break with the United States would be a disaster for the peace of the world',[45] and the choice was necessary because the Italians were still insisting that they must be allowed to annex Fiume.

* See pp. 227-8 above.

That afternoon, Lloyd George told the Council that his Government had discussed the issue with the Italian Ambassador in London, who had complained that the Allies were making a separate peace with Germany, without Italy's participation despite the alliance. This complaint had been rejected, and Lloyd George said, 'Let us warn the Italian Government that if they are not here next Tuesday they will hear no more from us'.[46] Clemenceau agreed. If they threatened to scrap the Treaty of London, 'my impression is that we would receive proposals from them within twenty-four hours'.[47] Wilson said that he had told Italy that he would accept Free City status for Fiume, but he still could not accept the Treaty of London. On 5 May Clemenceau reported that he had heard that the Italians were considering returning to the Conference, and the following day Sir Rennell Rodd sent the Foreign Secretary a draft proposal from the Italian Government which proposed that Fiume should become Italian only after they had built a new port for Yugoslavia, and that Italy would relinquish her claims in Dalmatia except for the islands of Zebenico.[48] At the beginning of May, therefore, after all the drama and acrimony of April, there seemed to be some hope that an amicable solution might ultimately be found.

If the explosive crisis over the Italian claims was not enough for the Council of Four to have to deal with, they were faced with another issue of a similar kind at the same time, and which threatened to develop into just as bitter a quarrel. This was the dispute between Japan and China over the former German-controlled Chinese province of Shantung, which the Japanese wished to annex, they said, in order to return it to the Chinese. There had already been some preliminary discussions of this problem, and both sides had been heard,* but the problem had not yet been resolved. As in the case of Italy's claims, President Wilson was to figure strongly in the dispute by making an obstinate and high-handed stand on his principles which not unnaturally raised Japanese hackles, for, like the Italians, they knew only too well that he had betrayed his principles on other occasions, and they did not see why they should suffer when others had had their way despite the Fourteen Points. Again, as in the Italian case, Wilson's stand on his principles was partly inspired by dislike of the people who were making the claim.

The first signs that President Wilson was likely to oppose the

* See pp. 120–1 above.

Japanese claim came on 15 April, when Balfour had a discussion with him at which he found Wilson inclined to back the Chinese. Balfour had pointed out that for the Japanese it was a matter of honour, on which 'it would be very difficult for them to yield'. What was more, Britain was bound by a wartime agreement to support the Japanese.*[49] That same morning, the Council of Four discussed the Shantung question. At once President Wilson made it clear where his sympathies lay: 'As this region is one of those which evoke the most sacred memories in Chinese history and religion, she is particularly anxious to exclude all foreign influence.' Balfour tried to persuade him to show some sympathy for Japanese national pride,[50] but he refused, declaring openly that he was suspicious of Japanese motives: 'The Japanese are rather difficult to deal with. I know by experience that they are very ingenious in the interpretation of treaties.'[51] Wilson was clearly wary of the Japanese proposal and their promise to return Shantung to China if they were awarded it by the Conference.

That afternoon, the Council of Five had a brief discussion of the issue, with Robert Lansing opposing the Japanese claim and urging them to accept a proposal that the five Great Powers should jointly become trustees for Shantung, preparatory to its return to China. As they began to argue, the Chairman, Pichon, recalled the Council to the matter on the Agenda paper – a clause for the German Treaty whereby Germany was to 'renounce all rights, titles and privileges whatsoever' which she had held in territory outside Germany itself, and was to allow the Allies to dispose of such rights, titles and privileges as they saw fit. This was accepted.[52] Two days later the Council of Five agreed to allow the Japanese to present draft articles on Shantung for discussion.[53]

On 18 April, the matter came before the Council of Four, with a consideration of the resolution of the Council of Five three days earlier, which was adopted. President Wilson urged that pressure should be brought to bear on the Japanese to 'be generous toward China and . . . promise them, if they follow our advice, that we will facilitate their peaceful relations with the Chinese Republic'.[54] Wilson also expressed a fear that if care were not taken over the settlement in the Far East, they might sow the seeds of war there.

After this discussion, President Wilson had talks with the Japanese

* See p. 8 above.

delegates in Paris, putting to them Lansing's suggestion that the Great Powers should act jointly as trustees for Shantung. He told the Council of Four on 21 April that the Japanese 'had been very stiff about it',[55] and that 'they were absolutely set on obliging China to carry out the bond [the wartime treaties]. They insisted that Germany should resign the whole of her interests in Kiaou-Chow to the Japanese and that the Powers should trust Japan to carry out her bargain with China',[56] and return the territory, keeping only some economic concessions there. Lloyd George wanted to know what right the Japanese had to be treated differently from others in the matter of German colonies. Everyone else had been required to accept a mandate under the control of the League of Nations, and he insisted that the Japanese should be compelled to accept the same terms. Wilson, who had obviously weakened as a result of his talks with the Japanese delegates, said that 'to be perfectly fair to the Japanese he thought they would interpret that as a challenge to their good faith', and that they had 'expressed benevolent intentions' towards China.[57] Lloyd George would not have this: what had been good enough for the British Dominions was good enough for the Japanese, and if necessary he was prepared to see the Great Powers dictate a settlement to the Japanese. At this meeting, both Wilson and Lloyd George performed something of an about-turn, with Wilson weakening in the face of Japanese arguments and expressed good intentions, and Lloyd George increasingly for firmness, probably because of the resentment to which special treatment for Japan would give rise among the Dominions.

The Japanese now applied pressure for a speedy settlement of their claim, asking that they should be kept informed of all developments during the negotiations.[58] On 22 April the Council of Four met the chief Japanese delegates, who presented draft clauses for the German Treaty whereby Germany would cede all her rights in Shantung to the Japanese. They pointed out that theirs had been the military effort which had wrested the territory from the Germans, and once more confirmed their intention to return it to China. Lloyd George pointed out that if Japan were given anything more than a mandate, the Dominions would object to this favouritism, while Wilson expressed the view that peace in the Far East would depend on the development of good Sino–Japanese relations – at all events, China must be treated fairly, and once more he proposed that the Great Powers should jointly act as trustees for Shantung, since

> China must be put on the same footing as other nations, as sooner or later she must certainly be. He believed this to be in the interest of everyone concerned. There was a lot of combustible material in China and if the flames were put to it the fire could not be quenched, for China had a population of four hundred million people. . . . Shantung . . . was the most sacred Chinese province, and he dreaded starting a flame there because this reverence was based upon the very best motives and owing to the traditions of Confucius and the foundations of intellectual development.[59]

In the end it was agreed that the Council should give a hearing to the Chinese before deciding the matter. Wilson had become firm again, and that same day Lord Derby, writing, chiefly about Fiume,* to Lord Curzon, referred to Shantung, on which problem 'again President Wilson is very sticky'.[60] It looked as though President Wilson was about to have another clash with an ally, just when the row with Italy was at its height.

On the afternoon of 22 April, the Chinese, led by Wellington Koo, were heard. After Wilson had reviewed the history of Shantung and Lloyd George had explained why the Anglo–Japanese agreement of 1917, which included a commitment by Britain to support a Japanese claim to Shantung after the war, had been made – 'Japanese help was urgently required, and Japan had asked for this arrangement to be made. We had been very hard pressed and had agreed'[61] – Koo said that China had been compelled to concede the Twenty-One Points to Japan in 1915 under the threat of an ultimatum, and the other Treaties all arose from this agreement, which China had been forced to sign against her will. When the Twenty-One Points were submitted they 'caused absolute consternation to the Chinese Government, which eventually had to submit to *force majeure*'.[62] Japan already had extensive rights in Manchuria, arising out of her control of the South Manchurian Railway, and if she were given control over Shantung as well, 'Peking would be – as it were – caught in a pincers'.[63] Wilson said that the problem was how to escape from 'a position that was extremely difficult'.[64] Britain and France were obliged to respect the treaties they had made with Japan, but they did not wish to concede Shantung to the Japanese if it could be avoided. Lloyd George agreed, saying that 'It would be of no

* See p. 226 above.

service . . . to regard treaties as von Bethmann Hollweg had regarded them, as mere scraps of paper to be turned down when they were not wanted'.[65] There seemed to be an impasse, however. As in the case of Fiume there was little room for compromise. Either Japan must be given the territory or it must be returned to China. The members of the Council of Four would have to decide.

On 25 April they considered the matter afresh, and Lloyd George put to his colleagues a suggestion made by Balfour that they should attempt to lay down the conditions under which the Japanese would return Shantung to China, thus both ensuring that this would be done and defining the economic rights which Japan could retain in the area. On the whole, though, Lloyd George felt that they were obliged to support Japan in principle:

> Undoubtedly we should get the conditions which were best for China. He felt that he must point out that, if it had not been for Japanese intervention, the Germans would still have been in Shantung. The Chinese did nothing to help get rid of them. We must not forget that Japan had rendered considerable assistance in the war.[66]

Wilson accepted Lloyd George's suggestion that the terms for the return of Shantung to China by the Japanese should be discussed, and Lloyd George undertook to arrange talks with the Japanese delegates to this end. This solution bore some elements of compromise, but basically the Japanese had won on the strength of what they had done in the war.

Lloyd George asked Balfour to arrange a meeting between the Council of Four and the Japanese delegates as soon as possible,[67] and on 27 April Balfour discussed the issue with the Japanese, and reported to Lloyd George that 'their intention is fully to restore Chinese sovereignty within the leased territory', retaining only the economic rights granted to Germany in the original Chinese concession. Balfour concluded by saying of the Japanese that 'for reasons of national dignity which are easy to understand, [they] are unwilling to modify the letter of the treaties which they have made with China'.[68] By the assurances they had given, and by the nature of their arguments, the Japanese had clearly won Balfour's sympathy, and this was certain further to strengthen Lloyd George's support of their claim. He circulated Balfour's comments to the other members of the Council of Four, and they discussed Shantung further on the morning of 28 April. President Wilson was still dubious about the wisdom of conceding the Japanese claim. He now switched to a new argument: 'There was nothing on which the public opinion of the United States was firmer than on this question that China should not be oppressed by Japan. Public opinion expected him to take the same line for Japan as he had taken for Italy.'[69] The difficulty was the treaties between China and Japan, and between the Allies and the Japanese. Balfour was invited to attend, and when he came in he pressed for the Japanese to be allowed to annex the territory, pointing out that at Wilson's insistence the Japanese request that a declaration of racial equality should be written into the Covenant of the League of Nations had been rejected,* and that if her claim relating to Shantung were also rejected the Japanese would feel that they had come very badly out of the war and the Conference. The Japanese delegates had told him that if they were given Shantung before the Plenary session of the Conferencc which was to approve the Covenant of the League of Nations, they would confine themselves to a formal protest over the exclusion of racial equality from the Covenant, but if this were not done, 'he was unable to say what line the Japanese delegates might take'. This alarmed Wilson, who 'asked if they will go to the length of refusing to adhere to the League of Nations. His difficulty was that he could not possibly abandon China'.[70] However, if the Japanese would confine themselves to retaining economic rights in Shantung, and would agree not to demand the right to keep a garrison there, 'he would agree to what they desired',[71] and Balfour agreed to communicate this decision to Baron Makino.

The following morning the Council of Four met the Japanese again, and it must have seemed as though agreement was near, and that a public row would be avoided. However, the Japanese still insisted on a right to an extra-territorial railway across Shantung, to which Wilson objected. He regarded the form of this claim 'as an unwise one. It would give the impression of offending Chinese sovereignty. He himself was trying to get away from anything that would do this.'[72] There was an argument as to whether the Chinese had signed their treaties with Japan voluntarily or under duress, but eventually they agreed to consider confining their demands to police work on the railway to ensure the security of traffic. This they

* See p. 212 above.

accepted on 30 April, and the Council of Four agreed on these conditions that the territory should be ceded to Japan, although no mention was to be made in the Treaty of Japan's obligation to return the territory to China.[73] The Japanese had won the day.

The Chinese, for their part, were becoming increasingly anxious and disappointed at the turn events were taking. On 30 April one of the Chinese plenipotentiaries, Alfred Sze, wrote to Lloyd George urging him not to accede to the Japanese demand, and pointing out again that China had only signed the Twenty-One Points under duress: 'these Treaties and Notes are now before the Peace Conference for abrogation in a separate memorandum submitted by the Chinese delegation'. He was, however, prepared to allow Japan to hold the territory for a year.[74] He was, of course, too late. On 8 May Balfour wrote to Lord Curzon to tell him of the outcome of the Council of Four's discussion on Shantung. He dismissed the Chinese, saying that 'these gentlemen . . . do not seem to deserve much sympathy', and went on to speak of China's treaties with Japan, and other matters:

> They never could be got to understand that, whatever might be said of the Treaty of 1915,* the Treaty of 1918 between China and Japan was a voluntary transaction between sovereign states, and a transaction which gave important pecuniary benefits to China; nor did they ever adequately realise that by the efforts of Japan and her Allies, China, without the expenditure of a single shilling or the loss of a single life, had restored to her rights which she could never recover for herself.[75]

Thus, from Balfour, who had played an important role in the settlement of the Shantung issue, especially as a mediator between the 'Big Four' and the Japanese delegates, the Chinese got short shrift.

Nonetheless, the Chinese were bitterly disappointed at the outcome, and on 9 May they made a formal protest at the nature of the settlement:

> If the Shantung peninsula is to be restored in full sovereignty, according to the proposed settlement, to China, the reason does not appear clear why recourse should be had to two steps instead of one, why the initial transfer should be made to Japan, and then leave it to her to 'voluntarily engage' to restore it to China.

* The Twenty-One Points.

They expressed their fear of the Japanese and appealed to the Fourteen Points.[76] When the Council of Four considered this protest on 14 May, they agreed that if China felt that the Japanese were not treating her fairly she should appeal for redress to the Council of the League of Nations.[77] No concession could be made to her in the Treaty with Germany.

Another country which got little satisfaction from the Council of Four at the beginning of May was Belgium, whose Foreign Minister, Hymans, wrote to the Council of Four asking that she should be allowed to take over the German colonial territory in East Africa which had been conquered by Belgian troops. When the matter came up, on 2 May, President Wilson said that she could only be given a mandate by the League of Nations.[78] Next day Clemenceau raised the matter again, to try to get a better deal for Belgium. Wilson was firm and Lloyd George supported him, though he expressed the view that mandates should be allotted as quickly as possible. It was agreed that Belgium must submit to the mandate system.[79]

The crises over Italy's claim to Fiume and the Japanese claim to Shantung put the Council of Four in a most difficult position, since in both cases the scope for compromise was either non-existent or very limited. In both cases President Wilson was stubborn, although his support for China was perhaps less firm than his opposition to the Italians. Perhaps the greatest problem in interpreting the Peace Conference is that of explaining Wilson's inconsistency: he readily conceded major breaches of the principles of nationality and the self-determination of peoples in the case of the German–Polish frontier, and, somewhat less readily, in the case of the Rhineland. These apparent betrayals can be explained by the attitude of the American experts, especially in the case of Poland, and the activities of Colonel House, who undermined the stands of others and persuaded the President to accept compromise solutions which he may not entirely have liked. Above all, however, the explanation was his hatred of the Germans. Nevertheless, in view of these obvious breaches of his principles, there must be some sympathy for the Italians when Wilson made a firm stand of principle against them, and they were surely entitled to wonder why they should be singled out for this treatment. In the case of China and Japan, Wilson avoided a clash with the Japanese and his European allies by attempting to gain assurances about future Japanese conduct in relation to China, while granting, somewhat reluctantly, her immediate demands.

These solutions could not leave the unity of the Conference undamaged – the Italians had walked out and the Chinese were nursing a bitter sense of grievance. Nonetheless, the Treaty was now in the final stages of preparation, and would shortly be handed to the Germans.

This did not mean that everyone among the members of the major Allied Governments was happy at the way things had gone, or the way events were moving. On 25 April Churchill warned his Cabinet colleagues that the German Government might fall and Germany succumb to Bolshevism unless the 'terrible conditions' in parts of Germany were soon relieved. To this end the blockade must be relaxed and economic activity be allowed to resume there as soon as possible.[80] Others were becoming anxious at the nature of the peace terms, and Lord Robert Cecil, General Smuts and George Barnes all wrote to Lloyd George expressing concern at the severity of the terms to be imposed on the Germans, late in April or during May. Barnes warned the Prime Minister on 6 May of probable Labour opposition to the Treaty:

> What I am afraid of is that in Labour ranks in Great Britain a feeling of pity may be fostered for Germany. I have before pointed this out. I do hope that it won't be fostered by the little pin pricks which can do us no good. . . .

and he referred in particular to the occupation of the Rhincland.[81] Now that the Treaty was being assembled from all the Commissions and committees which had been at work on it for the last four months, it became possible for the first time to see it as a whole, and for many the first sight of the complete Treaty was a great shock. No-one until now had seen it complete. Now many disliked what they saw. Keynes wrote to his mother on 14 May that

> I've never been so miserable as for the last two or three weeks; the Peace is outrageous and impossible and can bring nothing but misfortune behind it. Personally I do not believe the Germans will sign. . . . Certainly if I was in the Germans' place I'd rather die than sign such a Treaty.[82]

Certainly the Treaty was severe, but it was a compromise between the conflicting views of the men who drew it up. It opened with the Covenant of the League of Nations, upon which many pinned their hopes for the future peace of the world. It contained a demand for the surrender and trial of the Kaiser: 'The Allied and Associated Powers publicly arraign William II of Hohenzollern, formerly German Emperor, for a supreme offence against international morality and the sanctity of treaties.'[83] It demanded that Germany admit her guilt for having started the war and accept responsibility for all the damage caused to the civilian population of the Allies by her aggression. Germany was to lose Silesia. She was also to lose Danzig, but it would become a Free City. She would have to submit to the creation of the Polish Corridor, splitting Prussia in two, but there would be a plebiscite in Marienwerder. The Rhenish provinces were to be occupied, but only for fifteen years, and they would not be separated from Germany. She could recover the Saar fifteen years hence if its people voted to return to Germany. Reparations were vast and indeterminate, but account would be taken of Germany's capacity to pay. Of most of the clauses of the Treaty statements of a similar kind could be made. It was certainly severe, but it was almost all less severe than some, especially the French, had wanted.

On 6 May, the Treaty was presented to the entire Conference for approval, before it was handed to the waiting German representatives. Those who spoke were either trying to further their own interests or seeking to stiffen the terms still further. Thus the Portuguese delegation protested at the proposed distribution of reparations, since they wanted the smaller Powers, including themselves, to have a larger share. The Chinese protested at the decision on Shantung, making a formal reservation on the clauses of the Treaty relating to this territory which, they said, had been prepared 'without sufficient account having been held of the considerations in regard to Right, Justice and the national security of China'.[84] Finally, Marshal Foch returned once more to the Rhine frontier, and protested that the settlement decided upon was virtually useless from France's point of view:

> The Treaty secures complete guarantees for a period of five years, during which Germany will doubtless not be in a position to do any harm; but from that moment onwards, in proportion as the strength of Germany may recover and the danger increase, the guarantees become less and less until they finally disappear after the lapse of fifteen years. . . . If you are master of the Rhine you are master of the whole country. But if you are not on the Rhine you have lost everything.[85]

To the last, Foch believed that only the Rhine frontier could adequately guarantee France against a new invasion, which he believed the Germans would inevitably attempt sooner or later. Now he had lost, however. The Preliminary Peace Conference of the Allied and Associated Powers had completed its work and was ready to present its terms for peace to the Germans. Those who had doubts or reservations now stood only a limited chance of obtaining changes in the Treaty, and the Germans themselves were only to be allowed to comment in writing upon it – there were to be no negotiations as such with the enemy. Next day, the Peace Congress would assemble for the first time in the Grand Trianon at Versailles.

# 11 The Peace Congress: *May 1919*

At three o'clock on the afternoon of 7 May 1919, the Peace Congress assembled for its first session in the Grand Trianon. Clemenceau was in the chair, and for him this was surely the greatest moment in his political career. He was to preside over the reversal of France's humiliation at the hands of Bismarck's Prussia in 1871, when on that same site she had been compelled to sign a peace treaty by which she had paid an indemnity of unprecedented size and had lost Alsace and Lorraine. His words in opening the Peace Congress of 1919 fitted the occasion of the reversal of that defeat: addressing the German plenipotentiaries, he said

> You see before you the accredited representatives of the Allied and Associated Powers, both small and great, which have waged without intermission for more than four years the pitiless war which was imposed on them. The hour has struck for the weighty settlement of our accounts. You asked us for peace. We are disposed to grant it to you.[1]

He then informed the Germans that they would be given fifteen days to submit, in writing, their observations on the Treaty, and during this time they could also ask questions if they felt uncertain about any of the terms. The Supreme Council would then reply to these questions and observations, setting also a time by which a final acceptance or rejection of the terms must be sent in. This procedure had been agreed by the Council of Four in the days before the Congress assembled.

For the Germans, who already knew unofficially a good many of the peace terms, Count von Brockdorff-Rantzau replied, attempting to preserve what shreds of dignity he could, and rejecting some of the accusations levelled against Germany by the Allies:

> We cherish no illusions as to the extent of our defeat or the degree of our impotence. We know that the might of German arms is broken. We know the force of hatred which confronts us here, and we have heard the passionate demand that the victors should both make us pay as vanquished and punish us as guilty.
>
> We are required to admit that we alone are war guilty: such an admission on my lips would be a lie.[2]

He claimed that imperialism on the part of all the Great European Powers had brought about the war, and that others besides the Germans had committed atrocities. Indeed he claimed that thousands of German civilians had perished since the Armistice thanks to the maintenance of the Allied blockade of Germany. He also protested at Germany's exclusion from the League of Nations, which was to prove a particularly sore point in the weeks to come:

> The lofty conception that the most terrible calamity in the history of the world should bring about the greatest advance in human progress has been formulated and will be realised. If that goal is to be attained, if the slain in this war are not to have died in vain, then the portals of the League of Nations must be thrown open to all peoples of goodwill.[3]

These were the points that Count Brockdorff-Rantzau made, but it was not the content of his speech so much as the fact that he delivered it sitting down that aroused the fury of many of those present. Commenting both on the speech and on Brockdorff-Rantzau's failure to rise, President Wilson commented angrily,

> What abominable manners! . . . The Germans are really a stupid people. They always do the wrong thing. They did the wrong thing during the war, and that is why I am here. They don't understand human nature. This is the most tactless speech I have ever heard. It will set the whole world against them.[4]

The depth of Wilson's detestation of the Germans is plain here, and this attitude goes far to explain his actions both during the previous four months and in the next two. Others took a more compassionate view of Brockdorff-Rantzau's apparent bad manners. Nicolson wrote in his diary of the Conference that

> There is a great row going on because Brockdorff-Rantzau failed to stand up at yesterday's ceremony when replying to Clemenceau. The *Daily Mail* calls his attitude 'impudent and unrepentant'. Hermann Norman, who was standing close to him, says that he was on the verge of collapse and could not have stood up even if he had wanted to. I ask A.J.B[alfour] whether he shares the general horror and indignation. 'What indignation?' he says. 'Oh, about Brockdorff-Rantzau's conduct yesterday'. 'What conduct?' 'His not standing up when replying to Clemenceau.' 'Didn't he stand up? I failed to notice. I make it a rule never to stare at people when they are in obvious distress.' A.J.B. makes the whole of Paris seem vulgar.[5]

For most people, however, this apparent piece of rudeness introduced a sour note into the proceedings from the beginning.

Two days later, the Germans sent in their first comments on the Treaty. In the first of two Notes dated 9 May, they protested at their exclusion from the League and asked 'whether, and if so under what conditions' they would be invited to adhere to the Covenant.[6] In their second Note the Germans made a general protest at what they considered to be the Treaty's departures from the Fourteen Points and Wilson's other declarations of principle, on the basis of which the Germans had signed the Armistice: they said that they

> have had to realise that on essential points the basis of the Peace of Right, agreed upon between the belligerents, has been abandoned. They were not prepared to find that the promise explicitly given to the German people and the whole of mankind is in this way to be rendered illusory.[7]

They added that they would submit detailed comments at a later date.

On 10 May the Council of Four considered these first complaints, and paid them little heed. Clemenceau opened the discussions, saying to Wilson: 'We shall have to reply to the German Delegation's Note: I propose to do so in five lines.' Wilson spoke of their complaint at their exclusion from the League and said that they should simply be referred to the article of the Covenant which said that the League was open to all truly democratic nations. He went on:

> We are obliged to wait to see what the true character of the German Government will be, and other Articles of the Covenant

lay down that there is no doubt about the conditions a new application for membership must meet.

M. CLEMENCEAU: We must tell them that the essential condition of a people's admission is that people's good conduct.

PRESIDENT WILSON: The Covenant expressly says so.[8]

President Wilson was as determined as Clemenceau to exclude the Germans from the League until there was a complete certainty that they would not again adopt a policy of militarism and aggression. The Council adopted two texts for replies to the German Notes which would bring no comfort to the German delegates. The first, in the sense of the discussion referred to above, referred the Germans to the Covenant of the League for the answer to their query about admission. In the second they rejected outright the German suggestion that the draft Treaty was not in accordance with the Allies' promises: the Allies replied that they

> wish to remind the German delegation that they have formed the Terms of the Treaty with constant thought of the principles upon which the Armistice and the negotiations for peace were proposed. They can admit no discussion of their right to insist upon the Terms of Peace substantially as drafted.[9]

The Allies refused to admit any departure from their principles and policies, and it looked as though the Germans could expect little in the way of concessions.

On 10 May, however, the report of a Commission under E. L. Dresel, which the Americans had sent to investigate conditions in Germany, became available to all the delegations at Paris. Dresel and his colleagues examined the political situation, the relative strength of revolutionary, moderate and reactionary forces, and predicted that the peace terms would be rejected, and that this might well cause the Government to collapse, either succumbing to the Bolsheviks or to reactionary forces.[10] Attached to the report were a number of interviews with prominent Germans, including one with Dr Carl Melchior, who warned that

> the result of refusing peace will be to plunge the country into Bolshevism, but [he] was quite clear that this was preferable to a dishonourable peace. He said if it were impossible to come to an understanding with the Western Powers obviously the only thing for Germany to do was to turn Eastwards.[11]

HONOUR SATISFIED.

GERMAN DELEGATE. "SIGN? I'D SOONER DIE! (*Aside*) AFTER WHICH PRELIMINARY REMARKS I WILL NOW SELECT A NIB."

From *Punch*, Vol. 156, p. 423.

Dresel therefore urged that if necessary the terms should be modified in order to ensure the survival of the present Social-Democratic Government in Germany, and partly as a result of the appearance of this report pressure for changes in the Treaty began to build up during May.

Meanwhile, the Germans made a number of specific objections to the terms. On 13 May Brockdorff-Rantzau sent three notes to Clemenceau outlining these objections. In the first of these he protested at the seizure of Germany's colonies and the cessions of territory demanded on Germany's eastern frontier, which would result in the loss of great parts of Germany's agricultural and mineral resources: 'Those who sign the Treaty . . . will sign the death warrant of millions of men.' There was also a protest at the War-Guilt Clause – 'the German people did not want the war and would never have engaged in a war of aggression'. Finally he entered a protest at the provisions relating to the Saar Valley, offering instead a guaranteed supply of coal to France.[12] The second Note contained a further protest at the War Guilt Clause, and claimed that under the terms of the Lansing Note the obligation to pay reparations had been accepted independently of any decision as to who was responsible for starting the war[13] – a shaky claim this, since the Lansing Note spoke of 'the aggression of Germany by land, by sea and from the air'. In the third note, Brockdorff-Rantzau protested at the severity of the Reparations and other economic clauses of the Treaty, saying that they would 'bring about the loss of several millions of persons in Germany. This catastrophe would not be long in coming about, seeing that the health of the population has been broken down during the war by the Blockade, and during the Armistice by the aggravation of the Blockade by famine. . . . Those who sign this Treaty will sign the death sentence of many millions of German men, women and children.'[14] Germany sought to preserve some dignity and to obtain some degree of mercy from the Allies. In a fourth Note Brockdorff-Rantzau protested once more at the infringements of the Fourteen Points made in the territorial settlement. The German Government considered it 'inadmissible that German territories should, by the Treaty of Peace, be made the subject of bargains between one sovereignty and another, as though they were mere chattels or pawns in a game, in order to ensure the satisfaction of the financial and economic claims of the adversaries of Germany'. Having thus echoed Wilson's speeches of 1918, they applied this protest particularly to the Saar, which contained 'a purely German population'.[15] The Germans, therefore, were protesting at being held responsible for starting the war, at the economic clauses which would result in poverty and starvation for the German people, and at the territorial settlements, especially the loss for fifteen years of the Saar Valley.

The Germans were not the only members of the Peace Congress to protest at the nature of the Treaty. On 14 May a member of the American Commission to Negotiate Peace, William C. Bullitt, resigned his post and wrote bitterly to President Wilson that

> I was one of the millions who trusted confidently and implicitly in your leadership and believed that you would take nothing less than 'a permanent peace' based upon 'unselfish and unbiased justice'. But our Government has consented now to deliver the suffering peoples of the world to new oppressions, subjections and dismemberments – a new century of war. And I can convince myself no longer that effective labour for 'a new world order' is possible as a servant of this Government. . . . I am sorry that you did not fight our fight to the finish and that you had so little faith in the millions of men like myself, in every nation, who had faith in you.[16]

General Smuts was another who was apprehensive at the nature of the terms. He wrote to Lloyd George on 14 May urging him to 'use your unrivalled power and influence to make the final Treaty a more moderate and reasonable document'.[17] He also wrote to President Wilson urging that the Treaty be modified, but received a reply which showed Wilson's feelings about his task – his hatred of the Germans was now, if possible, deeper than ever:

> I feel the terrible responsibility of this whole business, but inevitably my thought goes back to the very great offence against civilisation which the German State committed, and the necessity of making it evident once for all that such things can only lead to the most severe punishment.[18]

Could Bullitt and others have seen this letter, they might have understood the President's behaviour better, though, as we have seen, his feelings about the Germans had been clearly expressed in his speeches in 1918. Keynes was perhaps right to liken Woodrow Wilson to a Presbyterian minister, but the likeness was not to the inflexible theology of those churches, but to their belief in the rightness of retributive, Hellfire punishment.

On 20 May, the Council of Four adopted with little discussion replies to Brockdorff-Rantzau's first Note, relating to war-guilt, which they reaffirmed, saying that the abdication of the Kaiser could not absolve the present German Government of that burden.[19] That day, the Germans also requested more time to reply to the terms[20] and were granted until 29 May for this purpose.[21] On 22 May the question of the territorial clauses of the Treaty, and especially the Saar Valley, was taken up, and without dissent the Council of Four approved a text rejecting completely the German allegation that the Fourteen Points had been broken: 'The Allied and Associated Governments absolutely deny that any one of the provisions referred to in . . . the [German] letter may have a consequence to transfer peoples from one allegiance to another "as though they were but mere things or pawns",' the population of the Saar was mixed.[22] The Council did, however, agree to allow Germany to repurchase the mines if the plebiscite went in her favour, and not to hinder the transfer of sovereignty to Germany if she could not at once raise the money to buy them[23] – a reasonable concession. The Council also reaffirmed that Germany could not be admitted immediately to the League of Nations.[24] So far, the Germans had obtained very little indeed in the way of concessions.

Between 24 and 29 May, the German delegates sent three further Notes to Clemenceau, in which they set out in detail their objections to the terms presented to them, and their proposals for alterations in them. On 24 May, in the first of these Notes, Brockdorff-Rantzau protested yet again over the affirmation of German war guilt:

> The German nation never having assumed the responsibility for the origin of the war, has a right to demand that it be informed by its opponents for what reasons and on what evidence these conditions of Peace are based on Germany being to blame for all damages and all sufferings of this war. . . . This, a question of life or death for the German nation, must be discussed in all publicity.[25]

In a second Note, of 28 May, Brockdorff-Rantzau requested an impartial investigation of the origins of the war and sought to transfer the blame to Tsarist Russia and claimed that the defeat of Russia had been Germany's only war aim:

> Tsarism, with which any real understanding was completely impossible, constituted – until the Peace Treaty now before us –

> the most fearful system of individual and national slavery ever conceived. The German nation . . . only agreed to fight wholeheartedly and resolutely in 1914 in a war of defence against Tsarism. . . . The moment the object of overthrowing the power of Tsarism was attained the war lost its meaning.

Brockdorff-Rantzau ended with a further protest at the 'contradiction of solemn promises' contained in the Peace Terms.[26]

The third Note, entitled 'Observations on the Draft Conditions of Peace' and dated 29 May, was considerably longer than its predecessors and was a comprehensive review of the terms, and contained all Germany's proposals for changes in them. It opened with a claim that the Treaty was a breach of all the Allies' promises and, moreover, would be impossible to carry out.[27] The indeterminate provision for reparations, agreed by the Allies in the interest of moderation, was condemned as exposing the German people to limitless demands upon their resources – the German delegates were not to know what had passed in the Council of Four. Brockdorff-Rantzau declared that under the terms of the Reparations Chapter, 'the German people would . . . be condemned to perpetual slave labour'.[28] He also protested at Germany's exclusion from the League, and concluded that in sum the terms of the Treaty amounted to a demand for 'a whole people to sign the decree for its own proscription, nay, its own death-sentence'.[29] The Treaty appeared to the Germans to be extreme beyond all reason in its condemnation and its exactions.

The Note goes on to outline Germany's counter-proposals. It accepted disarmament to the level of an army of 100,000 men but demanded immediate admission to the League of Nations. On territorial questions, there should be a plebiscite in Alsace–Lorraine, the port of Danzig would be free while the city would remain in German hands, the Saar should remain German while Germany would guarantee a supply of coal to France. In addition, 'Germany demands that the right of self-determination shall . . . be respected where the interests of the Germans in Austria and Bohemia are concerned'.[30] On reparations they offered one hundred million gold marks to be paid without interest, the repair of damage in Belgium and France, and the supply of coal and other products to France and Germany to replace production lost as a result of this damage.[31] Finally, there should be an impartial investigation into the origins of the war.[32]

The Note ended with an appeal that the Peace should be both just and realistic:

> Germany is to put her signature to the Treaty laid before her and to carry it out. Even in her need, Justice is too sacred a thing to allow her to stoop to accept conditions which she cannot undertake to carry out. Treaties of peace signed by the Great Powers have, it is true, in the history of the last decades, again and again proclaimed the right of the stronger. But each of these Treaties of Peace has been a factor in originating and prolonging the World War. . . . The lofty aims which our adversaries first set before themselves in their conduct of the war, the new era of an assured peace of justice, demand a Treaty instinct with a different spirit.[33]

Thus the Germans sought to escape from terms which they regard as harsh and unrealistic. To some extent, they were naturally trying to obtain easier terms for themselves, and inevitably they misunderstood the Allies' intentions, especially over reparations, but their complaints that the Allies' promises, and especially those of President Wilson, had not been kept were in many cases justified.

This Note was accompanied by detailed comments and proposals, including a plebiscite in Upper Silesia instead of its cession outright to the Poles, immediate admission to the League of Nations, the redrawing of the Polish Corridor so as to reduce the number of Germans under Polish rule, the right of the Bohemian and Austrian-Germans to join Germany if they so wished, the proposals on reparations outlined earlier, evacuation of the Rhenish provinces six months after the signing of the Treaty, and the dropping of war pensions from the list of items for which reparations were to be claimed.[34] With this long and intricate set of proposals, the German case rested. It was now for the Allies to decide on their reaction.

The nature of the Treaty was already giving rise to concern among members of the Allied Delegations, and increasingly the Conference split between those who believed that the terms were just and should be imposed without substantial change, and those who believed that their demands were excessive and should be reduced. The development of views among the British delegates is of crucial importance, in view of what was to happen in early June. A. J. Balfour believed that the Treaty was substantially just. He wrote to Louis Botha on 27 May, in reply to a letter from Botha asserting that the Treaty was too severe, that

> Germany may long and deeply resent her defeat and its consequences.... Too often do unsuccessful wrongdoers remain embittered and unrepentant. But we firmly believe that ... all has been done to make wars in the future more difficult and peace easy.[35]

Balfour was on the whole moderate in his attitude towards Germany. Lord Cunliffe said that the German proposal on reparations 'should not be entertained', and believed that the Allies had been too moderate in their demands:

> It is unfortunately only too manifest to anyone connected with business that the demands of the Allies have fallen far short of the German capacity to pay and I am more than ever convinced that Germany can and will pay the whole of what is demanded, and that without nearly as much interference in her economic life as she so clearly merits.[36]

Others were uneasy, however. On 27 May Lord Robert Cecil wrote to Lloyd George saying that many people in Britain regarded the Treaty as 'out of harmony with the spirit, if not with the letter, of the professed war aims of the Allied and Associated Governments before and at the time of the Armistice' and that it would produce no 'lasting pacification of Europe'.[37] Bonar Law wrote to Lloyd George on 31 May to say that he felt that the final German reply to the Treaty 'is a very able one and in many particulars is very difficult to answer', and urged concessions, especially on Upper Silesia and reparations.[38]

Among the officials of the British delegation, there was more than unease – consternation would be a more accurate description. Harold Nicolson wrote to his wife on 28 May of the Treaty that

> The more I read it the sicker it makes me. The great crime is in the reparation clauses, which were drawn up solely to please the House of Commons, and which are quite impossible to execute. If I were the Germans, I shouldn't sign for a moment. You see it gives them *no* hope whatsoever, either now or in the future.[39]

He was 'working like a little beaver' to seek to make the Austrian Treaty, on which the experts were then working, better than the German one. This letter also shows that the British delegation was divided: talking of the reasons for the 'rottenness' of the German Treaty, Nicolson wrote

> The fault is that there is an old man called Lord Sumner and an old man called Lord Cunliffe – and they have worked away without consulting anyone – with the result that the Treaty is only worth the *Daily Mail* which it will be printed in.[40]

Certainly both Sumner and Cunliffe had supported extreme reparations demands, and Cunliffe believed that the Allies had been too lenient. The other notable malcontent was Keynes, who was moving towards resignation from his post with the delegation, and had told Nicolson of his intention.[41] He wrote to the Chancellor of the Exchequer, his immediate Ministerial superior, on 26 May expressing his intention to resign:

> If . . . the decision is taken to discuss the Treaty with the Germans with a view to substantial changes and if our policy is such that it looks as if I can be of real use, I am ready to stay another two or three weeks. But if the decision is otherwise, I fear that I must resign immediately. I cannot express how strongly I feel as to the gravity of what is in front of us, and I must have my hands quite free. I wish I could talk to you about the whole miserable business. The Prime Minister is leading us all into a morass of destruction. The settlement which he is proposing for Europe disrupts it economically and must depopulate it by millions of persons. The New States we are setting up cannot survive in such surroundings. Nor can the peace be kept or the League of Nations live. How can you expect me to assist at this tragic farce any longer, seeking to lay the foundation, as a Frenchman put it, 'd'une guerre juste et durable'.[42]

A depressing verdict indeed, but one that was shared by others both in the British and the American delegations. The resignation of Bullitt from the American delegation* was only one of a series by disillusioned men. Others had evidently been complaining, as Lord Robert Cecil told Lloyd George in his letter of 27 May:

> I am told that some of the American Delegation are already saying that if they have to defend themselves against popular criticism in America they are ready to say that they have struggled for milder terms, and that it was the English who made it impossible for that struggle to be successful.[43]

* See p. 247 above.

The Germans had proposed alterations to the Treaty and sought mercy, and clearly had the support of many Allied statesmen and officials. Whether all these pleas could secure any worthwhile alterations in the terms remained to be seen.

Other events occurred in May which undoubtedly influenced subsequent happenings. The Conference was by then also engaged in preparing the Austrian Treaty. The Council of Four discussed, on 14 May the question of whether Austria should be admitted to the League, though they did not reach any definite conclusion,[44] and they were also engaged in settling the future destiny of the Balkans.[45] During April and May also, Anglo–French relations were again soured by a squabble over Syria. It had been agreed that an inter-Allied Commission should be sent to the Middle East to determine the wishes of the inhabitants as to which of the Great Powers should act as mandatory over the various countries.* All that now remained was to appoint its members. The matter was raised in the Council of Four on 11 April by President Wilson, who enquired whether Britain and France had appointed their representatives yet. Lloyd George replied in the negative, and Clemenceau said that he wanted an Anglo–French understanding on mandates in the area before he did so, and that there were to be Anglo–French talks on Syria. Lloyd George supported Clemenceau, saying that it would be better to wait until agreement was reached, because he 'wants the Emir Feisal to understand that he must not count on a disagreement between France and England'. He also disavowed any British interest in Syria.[46] At that time all seemed well, and prospects for agreement seemed even better when Clemenceau and Feisal had an apparently friendly meeting at the Hotel Matignon, in Paris, on 13 April,[47] and subsequently exchanged letters which suggested the establishment of amicable relations. Certainly their letters gave this impression. Clemenceau wrote to Feisal on 17 April assuring him that the French rule over Syria would be 'a liberal régime according to the principles which have always inspired the deliberations of the Peace Conference', and declared that France 'recognised Syria's right to independence'. He also promised material aid and advice for the economic development of Syria.[48] In his reply Feisal described himself as 'a warm friend of France and of your administration', expressed his conviction of the need for a 'complete understanding'

* See pp. 162–3 above.

between France and Syria, and assured Clemenceau that when he returned there he would 'do my very best to assure my people of your kindly feelings towards us and will work to increase the friendly bonds between the French and the Arabs'.[49] It looked as though at least one Arab ruler would support the French in their claim to act as mandatory in Syria. On 22 April, according to Hankey's minutes of the Council of Four, Lloyd George expressed the opinion that the Inter-Allied Commission should leave as soon as possible, in view of the meeting between Clemenceau and Feisal and the correspondence between them.[50] Attached to the record of this meeting was a copy of Clemenceau's letter to Feisal.[51]

It is impossible to accept Dr Jukka Nevakivi's contention that Lloyd George made this proposal in revenge for Clemenceau's collusion with President Wilson in settling the Rhineland issue behind his back.[52] It arose naturally from the meeting and correspondence between Clemenceau and Feisal, and might be better explained in terms of anxiety on Lloyd George's part at the increasing amity between them, which might weaken Britain's position in negotiations over the Middle East. In fact, Lloyd George's suggestion evoked no dissent from Clemenceau or anyone else – indeed Professor Mantoux's record contains no reference to it whatever.[53] No row broke out between Britain and France until May, long after all details of the Rhineland and Saar settlements had been decided. The row which was to occur stemmed purely from conflicts in and over the Middle East itself.

What seems to have happened was that early in May, the French became impatient to realise their Syrian ambitions, at least in some degree. On 5 May, Cambon sent a letter to Lord Curzon informing him that the French intended to send military reinforcements to Syria and asked for British cooperation in this.[54] In reply, Lord Curzon requested time to consult General Allenby, in charge of the British forces in the Middle East, as to the wisdom of this course of action.[55] Also, on 3 May, Clemenceau said in the Council of Four that he had received 'very serious complaints' about the activities of British officers in Syria, and Lloyd George agreed that he would look into the matter if Clemenceau would let him have the details.[56] In early May, then, a niggling friction was developing, which was to erupt into a major row on 21 May, when Lloyd George presented a text and map of the proposed allocation of mandates in the Middle East under which France would not get the whole of Syria.[57]

Clemenceau refused to accept this and accused Lloyd George of breaking his promise to evacuate Syria so that French troops could move in,[58] and tempers rose on both sides. Lloyd George objected to being accused of breaking his word, and Clemenceau made a long and impassioned speech, accusing Lord Curzon of being the cause of British perfidy: he told Lloyd George that

> I believe all this has come about because of your talks in London with Lord Curzon. Lord Curzon is a very charming man and one of great stature, but he is anti-French.[59]

He went on,

> My constant policy has been to preserve the union between France, Great Britain and the United States. To that end I have made greater concessions than I would have believed possible before the Conference. I am happy to have made them. . . . Now you tell me that France cannot have a place in Asia Minor because that would annoy the Italians; what do you think it will do to the French public?[60]

There was much more in the same vein, and Clemenceau became very angry, challenging Lloyd George, according to one of his biographers, to a duel.[61] When President Wilson urged that the matter be resolved by the dispatch of the inter-Allied Commission to investigate the matter on the spot, Clemenceau retorted that he would only name his commissioners when French troops began to replace British troops in the occupation of Syria.[62]

The following morning, the argument was resumed. Clemenceau referred to the Sykes–Picot Agreement and expressed his resentment at the British attitude: 'You ask me today to make still more concessions – after all those I have already made – without negotiations, without even consulting me in advance.'[63] He also repeated his resolve not to cooperate in the Inter-Allied Commission until French troops were in Syria.[64] Lloyd George retorted by enquiring 'whether the French Government now demanded the execution of the entire Sykes–Picot Agreement, or whether it was only invoked to obstruct British claims', and pointed out that if the Agreement were put fully into effect France would lose Arab territory which it had already been agreed she should have. He also pointed out that the French had always refused to cooperate in the conquest of Syria:[65]

> During all the time when we asked France to help us to carry out the Sykes–Picot Agreement, the French Government was not disposed to make any effort to that end. M. Clemenceau himself told me that he thought the Agreement was of no value.[66]

After more recriminations on both sides, Lloyd George declared that if Clemenceau would not send Commissioners to the Middle East to determine the wishes of the inhabitants, which he accepted as the proper basis on which to settle the issue, neither would he. He would accept the conclusions of the American Commissioners,[67] and both Lloyd George and General Wilson, who was present, warned that the dispatch of French troops to Syria might cause serious trouble, in view of the opposition of the Arabs to a French occupation.[68] Neither side was prepared to yield. Balfour wrote in a memorandum on 22 May that British policy was to 'force the French into a more reasonable frame of mind',[69] while in London Cambon went to see Lord Curzon to tell him of the disagreement between Lloyd George and Clemenceau. Curzon wrote to Lord Derby in Paris displaying obvious distress that Clemenceau should think that Lloyd George's attitude was the result of 'my pernicious influence in Paris'.[70] Support for the British refusal to agree to the replacement of their troops by French troops came from General Allenby in a telegram to Balfour, in Paris, warning that any such move would provoke an Arab rising against the British and the French, and urging that unless the inter-Allied Commission was sent soon this might happen anyway:

> I look upon the situation as extremely grave. Unless you can at once enable me to reassure Feisal and tell him that the Commission is coming out and will decide the future of the country it is certain that he will raise the Arabs against the French and ourselves.[71]

Armed with this urgent appeal, Lloyd George once more appealed to the French to agree to send out their Commissioners. The American Commissioners had already left; if France could not agree to join Britain in sending theirs, the Americans should be authorised to decide the issues themselves.[72] Clemenceau again refused to co-operate until French troops began moving into Syria, and it was agreed to inform Allenby and Feisal of the position.[73] Accordingly, Balfour telegraphed Allenby to tell him that he could announce that the Commission would arrive 'almost immediately' as the American members were already on their way, and if Britain and France did not in the end send Commissioners the British Government would accord 'full weight' to the conclusions of Americans.[74] There the matter rested. Neither British nor French delegates were ever sent, and the Americans published their report on 28 August 1919 and advised that the Syrians' preference for a mandatory was America, followed by Britain. A French mandate was impossible – it would 'precipitate war between the Arabs and the French'.[75] The French, therefore, never got any satisfaction from the Conference as regarded Syria, and the importance of the row in late May from the point of view of the German Treaty was that it poisoned Anglo-French relations at a critical stage in the Conference.

Another problem which came before the Council of Four once more in May was the continuing civil war in Russia. All the members of the Council would welcome the overthrow of Lenin, but none of them had been able to see a way of achieving this end without spending large sums of money and sending large numbers of men to fight in Russia. Early in May, however, news came of victories by the White forces which made it appear as though this object might be achieved without the need for a large Allied commitment in Russia. On 7 May Lloyd George told his colleagues in the Council that

> I want to talk to you about Russia. The situation there has changed in a most extraordinary way; we are witnessing the final crushing of Bolshevism, and the British Cabinet therefore wants a decision from us on our policy in Russia. According to our reports, Kolchak is about to join up with the Archangel forces and may soon reach Moscow and establish a new Government there.[76]

This posed a number of problems for the Allies. First, Paderewski was alarmed by the possibility of Kolchak and Denikin gaining control in Russia, since he believed them to be pro-German and that they might join forces with Germany against Poland – a fear supported by the Government in Archangel, where the largest British force active in Russia was based, and with whom the British therefore had the closest contacts. Secondly, there was the Allied commitment not to permit the restoration of a reactionary Government in Russia: Lloyd George continued his remarks by saying that

> If these reports are correct, we must take without delay the decision as to what conditions we want to impose upon Kolchak

> and Denikin for our continued assistance to them. At present we have little in the way of guarantees from them; their supposedly liberal programme does not exist. It is the sort of programme which reactionaries always issue when they wish to give the appearance of being liberal. For example, they say that agricultural reform is necessary, without going into details.[77]

President Wilson agreed, but, before taking a decision, it was agreed to hear Tchaikovsky, the head of the Archangel Government, who was then in Paris, and get his opinion as to what should be done.

The matter was taken further two days later, when President Wilson said that the Japanese were giving extensive support to Kolchak, in whom he had no confidence – 'we must act to impose conditions on him or withdraw our aid'. Lloyd George said it was pointless to do this in isolation – such a move must be part of a general decision about policy in Russia. Sir Maurice Hankey informed the Council that Kolchak was still advancing, whereupon Wilson urged that the Allies should withdraw and leave the Russians to settle their own affairs. Lloyd George still wanted to hear Tchaikovsky, 'a liberal of really advanced ideas', and attempt to impose conditions on Kolchak. Wilson felt that such conditions could not be enforced, but agreed to defer a final decision until they had met Tchaikovsky.[78]

This meeting took place the following morning. After Tchaikovsky had been introduced to the members of the Council of Four, President Wilson explained the problem they faced:

> The reports we are receiving from Russia suggest that the Bolshevik Government is in danger of falling and that Admiral Kolchak may succeed in overthrowing them and taking their place. Whether he establishes a government in Russia or someone else does, we do not want to give our support to any government except one which undertakes to rule Russia truly democratically and to leave the land in the hands of the peasants.[79]

Tchaikovsky attempted to reassure the Council – Kolchak and Denikin had promised to call a Constituent Assembly, introduce agrarian reform and improve working conditions – but Wilson felt that these assurances were not sufficiently specific. Tchaihovsky insisted that Kolchak was not a reactionary and pointed out that he had the support of the Siberian people, who were democratically governed. Both Wilson and Lloyd George were still dubious, however, the latter saying that he had been given a report which

> indicates that as Kolchak advances disorder breaks out behind his front. The Bolsheviks have had some success in Eastern Siberia, thus might it not be said that the people believe that if Kolchak wins, the result will be a return to the past? Do people not believe that this is what the Allies are helping to bring about?[80]

Tchaikovsky sought to reassure them that a return to autocracy was 'absolutely impossible'[81] and that the Allies could safely continue to assist Kolchak. That afternoon, however, Wilson still hesitated to commit himself to supporting the White forces:

> If we decide to support Kolchak and Denikin, the world will not understand us if we later desert them, even if we do so because by their conduct they show themselves to be plainly reactionary. That is what I am afraid of, and that is why I hesitate to commit myself.[82]

The Council could only agree to consult experts further and consider the matter afresh later. They still could not make up their minds to act.

On 19 May, Lloyd George said that they must make up their minds within a week, and Wilson said that he had ordered the State Department to send a Note to Kolchak asking him about his intentions, especially in relation to agricultural reform and the calling of a Constituent Assembly, since his previous declarations were not enough to satisfy him, especially as other Russians, notably Kerensky, had expressed suspicions about Kolchak's intentions. He was determined to wait for Kolchak's reply before taking any decision on future policy.[83] In view of the uncertainty about policy in Russia, the British discouraged a Finnish proposal that, with Allied help, they should mount an attack on Petrograd,[84] but on 20 May Lenin did not endear himself to President Wilson or anyone else in the Council of Four by a refusal to agree to an armistice in order to allow a relief operation to be mounted to reduce the suffering being caused by the civil war. Wilson said that it seemed impossible to devise a policy to deal with the situation,[85] and Lloyd George agreed that it was very difficult:

> On the one hand there is a band of violent revolutionaries who were without scruples; on the other were people who claimed to be acting to restore order but whose intentions are suspect. . . .[86]

and it was decided to send a despatch to all the Russian Governments enquiring whether, if they were victorious, they intended to call a Constituent Assembly.[87] On 23 May the Council learned that the Japanese, impatient at the Allies' vacillation, had decided to recognise Admiral Kolchak's Government as the Government of Russia. Lloyd George said that the Allies must protect their interests by recognising him before the Japanese did, but Wilson refused.[88] That afternoon, however, Philip Kerr attended the Council to present a draft of a message to Kolchak asking him to promise to rule democratically and respect civil liberties if he governed Russia. The Archangel Government had already agreed to give these assurances, and a copy would be sent to Denikin.[89] Perhaps the replies they required would enable the Allies to break out of the miasma of irresolution into which the discussion of Russia always seemed to plunge them.

Next day, the Japanese resolved to take action. They sent a memorandum to the rest of the Allies announcing that they proposed to recognise Kolchak and urging them to follow suit.[90] What was more, Lord Curzon and the British Foreign Office had also decided that this was the right course to take, Curzon informing the British representative in Omsk on 24 May that the Foreign Office believed that the time to recognise Kolchak 'had arrived and were pressing this view upon the Allied representatives in Paris'. They were recommending that Kolchak be asked to promise to summon a Constituent Assembly as soon as possible and to adopt a friendly policy towards the states on Russia's borders.[91]

That afternoon, the Japanese were invited to discuss their intentions with the Council of Four. Wilson explained their desire to get assurances as to his future conduct from Kolchak before recognising him in order to ensure that he would not govern in a reactionary way if he was successful in overthrowing Lenin. If they received a satisfactory reply they would grant recognition.[92] A military adviser, Colonel Kisch, later informed the Council that, although Kolchak was advancing in some areas, he was retreating in others. Colonel Kisch was still optimistic about Kolchak's chances of success, however – 'The Bolshevik army is larger, but the morale of its troops is very low. In the areas they have occupied the Siberian troops have been well received.'[93] However, another problem was the behaviour of Denikin's troops, who were reported to be shooting all the Bolshevik prisoners they took.[94] No steps towards recognition could be taken without assurances, which were sought in the message approved by the Council of Four for despatch to Kolchak and the other Russian Governments. Informing Lord Curzon of the terms of the Note, Balfour wrote that the Council of Four 'are convinced by their experience of the last twelve months that it is not possible to attain these ends [democratic rule in Russia and the summoning of a Constituent Assembly as a first step towards this] by dealing with the Soviet Government of Moscow. They are therefore disposed to assist the Government of Admiral Kolchak.' He went on to outline the questions which the Allies were to pose to Kolchak: first, he must undertake to hold free elections for a Constituent Assembly as soon as his forces reached Moscow, or, if that were not possible, he must reconvene the Constituent Assembly set up by the Provisional Government after the February Revolution in 1917, which must sit until elections to a new Assembly could be held. He was to institute democratic rule in the territories he controlled at present and was not to attempt to revive the old class privileges which had existed under the Tsars. He was to promise friendship to Poland, Finland and the other border states and to join the League of Nations.[95] This was approved by the Council of Four and sent. Nothing more could now be done until his reply was received.

The problem of the dispute between Poland and the Ukraine over Eastern Galicia was still unsolved. Previous attempts to get the two sides to agree to an armistice had failed, and on 7 May the Council of Four decided to demand a cessation of hostilities in telegrams to be sent to Warsaw and Kiev.[96] The following day, President Wilson pointed out that they had not decided what the frontier between Poland and the Ukraine should be, whilst Lloyd George said that the Ukraine would sooner or later return to Russian domination anyway, so the issue would eventually have to be settled between Poland and Russia.[97]

Meanwhile, the Council of Foreign Ministers was also considering the question of the future attribution of Eastern Galicia. The expert Commission on Polish Affairs had not made any definite recommendation in view of the Council of Four's decision in March that neither side should be heard on the issue,* but said that if ethnographic considerations were to decide the issue it must go to the Ukraine, despite the presence of a large Polish minority. This information was given to the Council of Five on 26 April, who

* See p. 153 above.

decided that the Commission should examine the matter further, but that it would have to be decided by the Council of Four in the end.[98] On 14 May the Foreign Ministers discussed the issue again and decided to recommend that, since it was unlikely that the dispute between Poland and the Ukraine could be resolved before the Austrian Treaty was signed, Austria, whose Empire had included Galicia, should simply resign her rights in the territory to the Principal Allied and Associated Powers, who would decide its ultimate fate.[99] From the point of view of treaty-making, this took the urgency out of the situation.

The problem of the fighting between the Poles and the Ukrainians was still unsolved, however, and on 17 May President Wilson told the Council of Four that the Polish Diet had voted, against the advice of Paderewski, to send General Haller's army, which had been sent to Poland from France with Allied help to resist the Bolsheviks, to Lemberg. If this report was confirmed, 'we must inform the Poles that they must either accept the instructions of the Conference or recall their delegates and be prepared to do without our support'.[100] Even Wilson, who had supported the Polish case on her German frontier, was becoming exasperated by the Poles' behaviour. Lloyd George, who had always been suspicious of the Poles, urged that, if the report was true, they should cut off economic aid and, if that did not bring the Poles to heel, they should threaten not to resist the German objections to the German–Polish frontier as defined in the draft Treaty of Peace.[101]

Two days later, however, Wilson's attitude changed. On the morning of 19 May he informed his colleagues on the Council that Paderewski had again tried to persuade the Diet that the promise he had made to use Haller's army only against the Bolsheviks must be kept, as must his pledge not to interfere with the independence of Lithuania or Eastern Galicia. His appeals had been rejected, and to make matters worse, 'the situation in Warsaw is without doubt very dangerous. Public opinion is very heated and mixed with nationalist fervour are threats of a national railway and postal strike.' As a result, 'we have to choose between two alternatives: either to cede a certain amount to Polish public opinion in order to ensure that M. Paderewski remains in power, for we have some confidence in him, or to stand firm on the principles we have laid down and risk bringing about his fall'.[102] He believed that the crisis had been brought on by atrocities committed in Eastern Galicia by Ukrainian troops, and warned that intransigence on the part of the Conference would, in Paderewski's view, cause a revolution in Poland. Some concessions would therefore have to be made. Lloyd George was not sure:

> I have come to the conclusion that nowhere can we establish definite facts; on all sides we are surrounded by quicksands. If what we are told about Ukrainian atrocities is true, it would alter the whole basis of our policy.[103]

It was therefore agreed to enquire of an Allied Commission in Poland whether the reports were true.

In the main, however, Lloyd George was definitely anti-Polish, and he reverted to this position when it was reported to the Council on 21 May that the Poles and the Bolsheviks were attacking the Ukraine simultaneously: 'What the Poles are doing is a flagrant breach of their promises to us; they are doing nothing less than helping the Bolsheviks to crush the independence of the Ukrainian people.' He went on to denounce the Poles' entire attitude towards their neighbours:

> All these little nations will at once go to perdition if they behave like Poland. The time will come when we shall judge them as did the Prussians or the Russians; we shall conclude that they have no right to exist. After suffering terrible oppression themselves, the Poles can think of nothing other than oppressing others. Their attitude is the same as that of the Catholic Irish towards Ulster.[104]

An interesting parallel, perhaps. It was certainly true that the Poles were showing extreme intolerance towards people of different race and religious beliefs, and were determined to oppress them. Polish conduct aroused great indignation from Lloyd George.

That afternoon, the Big Four met a delegation from the Ukraine, who had come to state their side of the case. Their spokesman, Syderenko, said that they wanted friendly relations with Poland and were only seeking to defend the land of their fathers against both the Poles and the Bolsheviks, and denied committing atrocities in Eastern Galicia.[105] Later they assured Lloyd George that if they were given that territory, they would accord fair treatment to the Polish minority there.[106] From the subsequent discussion, it was clear that Lloyd George was looking for both guarantees of good behaviour from the Ukrainians and an effective ally against Bolshevism. He asked the Ukrainian delegates, 'If you were delivered from the Poles, would you be able to fight harder against the Bolsheviks?', to which one of the Ukrainians replied that this was what their soldiers wanted to do.[107] At present, Galicia was in a terrible condition:

> While we are defending our homes against the Bolsheviks, we have been attacked from the rear by the Poles. We had to turn around and resist the Poles, who, using the aid they had received from the Entente for other purposes, had invaded Galicia and were pillaging it. All our country is on fire.[108]

At this point the Allied Commission which had been sent to Poland to attempt to arrange an armistice between the Poles and the Ukrainians were admitted to the meeting and confirmed the truth of the Ukrainian allegations against the Poles. The head of the Commission, General Botha, said that the Poles must be forced to make peace, if need be by cutting off Allied assistance:

> Poland has received our assistance; she must therefore listen to us. . . . While you sit here making peace, the Poles, using the weapons you are sending them, are attacking people who are not our enemies. If they need our help to fight the Bolsheviks, we should be ready to continue helping them . . . but if we tolerate what Poland is doing today we shall ourselves push the Ukrainian people into the arms of the Bolsheviks.[109]

Wilson still feared that too strong a line with the Poles might bring about Paderewski's fall and his replacement by a more extreme Government in Warsaw, but in the end it was agreed to send a telegram commanding Poland to cease her aggression or Allied help would cease: Lloyd George said that 'we have the right thus to speak when we are about to have a struggle with the Germans in order to impose upon them acceptance of their new frontier with Poland'.[110] Lloyd George was now determined to curb the Poles.

A week later, however, evidence came to light that the Allies were not themselves acting as closely in concert to secure peace in Galicia as their discussions at Paris seemed to suggest. Although the intervention decided upon on 21 May seemed to be successful in producing an armistice, on 27 May Lloyd George reported that General

Botha, who had once more assumed the role of mediator, was still 'very dissatisfied' at the Polish attitude to the armistice, and suspected that they were being strengthened in this attitude by the French. Lloyd George reported that Botha

> had grounds for the belief that the French Minister in Warsaw had encouraged the Poles in their recent attack on the Ukrainians. A fact which had rather confirmed these suspicions was that General Botha reported that he had been unable to secure the attendance of the French representative at meetings of the Armistice Commission, and this had occurred so frequently that it was difficult to believe that it was not deliberate.[111]

The French wanted to strengthen Poland as much as possible as an ally against Germany and Bolshevism, and for the same reasons wanted to cement close links between themselves and the Poles and it would appear that to these ends they were sabotaging the Allied attempt to secure peace in Eastern Galicia. Clemenceau 'expressed incredulity, but promised to make the fullest possible enquiry',[112] and it was agreed to send a strong telegram to Marshal Pilsudski, President of Poland, warning him that

> The Council feel it their duty . . . in the most friendly spirit but with the most solemn earnestness, to say to the Polish authorities that, if they are not willing to accept the guidance and decisions of the Conference of Peace . . . the Governments represented in the Council of the Principal Allied and Associated Governments will not be justified in furnishing Poland any longer with supplies or assistance.[113]

It was thus made quite clear that the Allies were losing patience with the Poles, and would cease to help them unless they behaved reasonably. The following day, however, news reached the Foreign Office in London of renewed fighting in Galicia. The British Ambassador in Warsaw reported that Paderewski had told the Diet that the Ukrainians had attacked the Polish troops there on 12 May, and then 'nothing could stop our young soldiers'.[114] At the same time the French Chargé d'Affaires in Warsaw informed Clemenceau that the Poles now denied promising not to use Haller's troops in Galicia.[115] Such an attitude was bound to infuriate the Allies, and particularly Lloyd George, still further, especially as on 28 May it was reported that the Poles were advancing rapidly into Eastern Galicia.[116]

The report that General Haller and other Polish leaders now denied that they had ever promised not to use General Haller's troops against the Ukrainians re-awakened Lloyd George's suspicions of French good faith, and especially of that of Marshal Foch, who was supposed to have transmitted to the Poles the conditions for the transport of Haller's army to Poland. On 30 May Lloyd George said that Haller's failure to remember having made this promise 'raised the question as to whether Marshal Foch had ever carried out his instructions to notify General Haller that he was not to [fight the Ukrainians]. He recalled that Marshall Foch had, at one time, been exceedingly desirous of sending General Haller's army to Lemberg.'[117] Clemenceau promised to look into this, though such an accusation cannot have increased his liking for Lloyd George, especially coming, as it did, after their bitter dispute over Syria. President Wilson was now softening in his attitude to the Poles. He said that he had heard that Polish troops were behaving well in Galicia and had been welcomed by the local population.[118] Once more Lloyd George was alone in his enthusiasm for attempting to restrain the Poles. On 3 June the Allies received a conciliatory reply from Pilsudski to their Note demanding compliance with the Conference's decisions, in which he blamed his country's activities in Eastern Galicia on right-wing pressure.[119] For the moment, good relations between the Council of Four and the Poles seemed to have been restored, and an uneasy peace came to Eastern Galicia.

During May, the Italians took virtually no part in the Conference, after walking out over President Wilson's refusal to allow them to take Fiume. No-one wished to see the Italians make a separate peace with Germany or break with her wartime allies, but her obstinate insistence on being granted Fiume made it very difficult for the Allies to offer her an acceptable compromise which would allow Orlando to return. Lloyd George, Wilson and Clemenceau discussed the problem on 13 May, when Wilson proposed that plebiscites be held in Dalmatia, and pointed out that the Italians had offered to build Yugoslavia a new port if it was agreed to cede Fiume to Italy. Lloyd George thought that this was a bad solution – 'That would be to say to the inhabitants of Fiume that when you become Italian you will cease to exist and your trade will depart for a neighbouring town'[120] – and later insisted that if Italy wanted Fiume so much she should renounce Dalmatia, and he thought that the Yugoslavs would accept such a solution. Wilson did not agree.[121] On 25 May Orlando wrote to Lloyd George appealing for his support against President Wilson:

> I feel sure that you cannot fail to realise the absolutely intolerable situation which would arise in Europe if the peace which is about to be concluded were to give rise in the Italian people to the impression that its position is that of a conquered rather than of a victorious nation. . . . If we detach from the block on which the new European System will have to rely for support forty million Italians, and force them into the ranks of the malcontents, do you think that the new order will rest on a firm basis?[122]

Orlando was bound by public feeling to insist on Fiume; Lloyd George had been under similar pressure over reparations and would surely sympathise, Orlando thought.

On the afternoon of 26 May, Orlando met his former colleagues of the Council of Four to discuss the rift between them. The meeting began with Clemenceau making a 'last appeal' to Orlando to make concessions,[123] and Orlando replied that if he was unable to reach an honourable settlement, Italy must insist upon the execution of the Treaty of London. President Wilson insisted again that the Italian claims constituted a breach of the Fourteen Points, which the Italians had accepted at the time of the Armistice and which they could not break now. He could not countenance a settlement involving the execution of the Treaty of London: 'In insisting on the Treaty of London you are insisting on the very opposite of the ideal which caused the American people to enter the war, and on a principle utterly opposed to the new order which we are creating.'[124] Now, however, Orlando was faced with attacks from Clemenceau and Lloyd George as well as Wilson. Clemenceau criticised him for not making any proposals for settling the dispute: 'Italy has demanded Fiume in the name of the right of peoples to decide their own fate, and Dalmatia in defiance of that principle. Italy demands the execution of the Treaty of London, and Fiume contrary to the provisions of that Treaty.'[125] Lloyd George also subscribed to this view, which Orlando did not, of course, accept. They had got absolutely nowhere, and when Lloyd George replied to Orlando's letter requesting his support, he made it clear that he was entirely out of sympathy with Italy's position:

> What has the present trouble arisen out of? It is due entirely to the fact that Italy is claiming to annex to her dominion territories the overwhelming majority of whose peoples would prefer to attach themselves to another sovereignty.

He asked Orlando to accept the submission of Italy's claims to an independent Commission, and urged her not to persist in a course of action 'which will lead to disaster for her future. . . . Italy is . . . laying up a blood feud with the other two great races of Europe – the Germans and the Slavs.'[126] The same day as he wrote this letter, 28 May, Lloyd George had a meeting with Orlando at which the Italian offered to concede free city status for Fiume if he were allowed to annex Zara and Sebenico, but Lloyd George would only offer free city status for them too.[127] That afternoon Orlando met the Council of Four again, and Lloyd George introduced a new proposal made by Tardieu, that Fiume should be a free city under League of Nations rule for fifteen years, after which the people of the city would decide their fate by a plebiscite. Orlando offered to accept free city status for Zara and Sebenico too, if they were put under Italian mandates, but Wilson regarded this as an unacceptable breach of the self-determination of peoples.[128] There was no solution yet, but agreement seemed nearer than at any time since the dispute broke out in April.

It was not to be, however. On 3 June Orlando wrote again to Lloyd George insisting on the execution of the Treaty of London and attempting to escape from his acceptance of a plebiscite in Fiume.[129] He also wrote to Wilson stating that the frontiers of the free city had still to be decided, asking that Fiume should be autonomous even within the free state, and still claiming Zara and Sebenico. This Wilson refused to entertain. 'It is true that the majority of Zara's population is Italian, but would anyone suggest that we should give Milwaukee to the Germans?'[130] he asked the Council of Four on 6 June. Next day they met Orlando again, but it was no use.[131] Nothing could persuade either Wilson or Orlando to compromise further, and the breach with Italy remained unhealed.

Thus at the end of May the Conference was faced with increasing pressure to modify the Treaty in the light of the German complaints, which many of its members believed were justified, though others stoutly rejected any such view. Britain and France were at loggerheads over Syria, Italy was still sulking over Fiume, but the Council of Four had secured reluctant good behaviour from the Poles. The major decision of how far to modify the German Treaty had now to be taken, and in addition many other loose ends would have to be tidied up before the Council of Four's work would be at an end.

# 12 The Last Crisis: *June 1919*

The pressures within the British delegation for modification of the German Treaty had been building up throughout May, and at a meeting of the British Empire Delegation on 30 May, it became clear that there was fairly general agreement that the Treaty must be changed. Lloyd George opened this meeting by referring to General Smuts' view that the Treaty did constitute a breach of the Fourteen Points, and spoke of his particular concern at the proposed delineation of the frontier between Germany and Poland, and revealed that the expert advisers to the Conference now thought that there ought to be a plebiscite in parts of Silesia before it was decided to hand over the whole of that province to Poland. He spoke of his doubts about Polish competence and good will:

> He was glad to know that it was generally agreed that the Eastern provisions must be modified. Poland was an historic failure, and always would be a failure, and in this Treaty we were trying to reverse the verdict of history. He asked that the Allies should hesitate before guaranteeing frontiers for Poland such as were now proposed. . . . Perhaps a plebiscite would afford a solution.

A plebiscite would ensure that the Poles were not allowed to include too many Germans within their country: saying that 'the Poles were a difficult people to deal with', Lloyd George referred to the fact that 'at the present moment, the Poles were, in defiance of the Peace Conference, fighting the Ukrainians'. At the same time, the offer of a plebiscite in Upper Silesia would effectively meet the German objections – 'if the Germans refused a plebiscite, they would put themselves out of court'. Turning to a different matter, he deplored the unnecessary expense involved in the fifteen-year occupation of the Rhineland.[1]

On 1 June, the discussion was resumed, and Lloyd George opened the discussion on modifications in the Treaty, and 'said that he wished to put two questions to each individual member of the delegation: 1. Was he in favour of standing on the terms proposed in the present Draft Treaty, or was he in favour of making some concessions', and secondly, if they favoured concessions, the question then arose as to whether negotiations should be conducted in writing or orally. In response to the first question, every member of the delegation expressed support for modifications in the Treaty, for a variety of motives. General Smuts said that the Treaty was 'an impossible document, that to sign it would be a real disaster ... comparable in magnitude to the war itself', and that it was 'not a Wilson peace'. He attacked the occupation of the Rhineland, Germany's exclusion from the League, and the eastern frontier settlement, which was 'thoroughly bad'. Winston Churchill also spoke up for modifications, but for very different motives. He said that 'it was necessary to face the brutal facts' – if the Germans did not sign it would be necessary to renew the war which 'would be attended with the gravest military and political differences', and the Allies should therefore 'split the difference' with Germany. He was supported by Lord Birkenhead and Austen Chamberlain. William Hughes, the Australian Prime Minister, was the only dissentient, saying that the Germans 'had not a leg to stand on'. Hughes was against conciliation to the last.[2]

That afternoon, the discussion was resumed. Arthur Balfour agreed that the Treaty must be revised, especially where the German–Polish frontier was concerned, and he supported the proposal for a plebiscite in Upper Silesia. He was not as convinced that the Germans had a good case as Lloyd George was, however; he thought their statement that purely German areas had been included in Poland was 'impudent', and he felt that the Prime Minister had been too hard on the Poles and not hard enough on the Germans:

> He agreed that Poland had behaved quite abominably and had mismanaged her affairs, but he wished to point out that in discussion it had been assumed that Germany was repentant, that her soul had undergone a conversion and that she was now absolutely a different nation from the Germany which in the past

> had built up armaments and had caused the war. But why should there be faith in Germany altering her course, and no hope of Poland . . . behaving as a reasonably civilised state? He had no sympathy whatever with the attacks on the Eastern frontier. It was a very difficult problem and on the whole it had been well handled.

He would not, therefore, make any concessions beyond the plebiscite in Upper Silesia.

Lloyd George then summed up the meeting, and displayed complete mastery over his colleagues. He proposed that the British representatives at the Peace Conference should press for plebiscites in Upper Silesia and other disputed areas on Germany's Eastern frontier, where the nationality of the people was 'preponderantly German', and where 'territory had been added to Poland only on account of the existence of a railway'. He again attacked the occupation of the Rhineland on grounds of cost, and he also thought that Germany ought to be admitted to the League – 'if he thought that early admission to the League would make the difference of whether the Germans signed or not, he would take an indulgent view of the matter'. Finally, he proposed that the Germans should be given three months to make a better offer of reparations.

He then came to the most serious problem of all: how to secure these changes in the Treaty in the face of French opposition. Lloyd George said that

> we were confronted by a very grave issue. The French would give up nothing unless they were forced. As had already been remarked, the hatred of the French for the Germans was something inconceivable – it was savage – and he did not blame them for it . . . but he did not think that the British Empire would allow the future peace of the world to be tied to the chariot of French fury, however legitimate and justified though it might be.

He therefore proposed that the delegation should authorise him to tell the Council of Four that if alterations were not made in the Treaty along the lines they had agreed were necessary, he should refuse the assistance of the British Army in renewing the war, and of the Navy in enforcing the blockade of Germany, and this was agreed unanimously.[3]

Armed with this weapon, on the afternoon of 2 June, Lloyd George exploded his bombshell in the Council of Four. Without preamble, he stated the conclusion to which he and his colleagues had come.

> I feel that it is my duty to tell you of the situation in which the British delegation finds itself in relation to the Treaty of Peace. It is difficult. Our people wants peace above all and does not attach great importance to the terms. They would not support a Government which renewed the war unless the reasons for so doing were the best possible. That is why I invited all my colleagues in the British Government who could leave London to come here and confer with me. . . .
>
> At these meetings it became clear that if the Germans refuse to sign, they will not consent to renew the war or the blockade unless certain changes are made in the Treaty of Peace.[4]

He went on to outline the changes the delegation had decided to demand, beginning with the German–Polish frontier, where he requested a plebiscite in Upper Silesia and a number of other smaller areas. He spoke especially of Schneidemuhl, where, he said, 'a territory entirely inhabited by Germans had been given to Poland in order that the frontier might coincide with a river'; and nearby there was another German area which had been given to Poland because of a railway line.[5] These things should not be done except after plebiscites had been held. He went on to speak of the Saar, which had worried everyone, but 'I took a very energetic attitude on that and I think I persuaded them that we could not go back on what has been decided',[6] but they were not willing to support the occupation of the Rhineland:

> Since Germany will only have an army of one hundred thousand men, is it necessary, they ask, to have two hundred thousand on the left bank of the Rhine to stop the Germans invading France? They say that the occupation is just a way of feeding the French army at German expense.[7]

He also urged changes in the reparations settlement, and urged that Germany should be admitted to the League of Nations on signing the Treaty. He concluded by saying that these were the unanimous opinions of the British delegation, and urged the especial importance of making concessions on Germany's eastern frontier and on reparations.

He was met with hostility by Clemenceau and Wilson. Clemenceau remarked sarcastically that 'some of these little points that you have just been explaining to us are not without some importance',[8] and they both asked for time to consult their own colleagues. Clemenceau then stated his personal opposition to making any concessions to the Germans:

> I know that all the world is impatient for us to finish our task. In Britain you believe that the way to do this is to make concessions: in France we believe that it is necessary to be firm. Unhappily, we know the Germans better than anyone, and we believe that the more concessions we give them, the more they will demand.[9]

He rejected Lloyd George's views on the German–Polish frontier – Poland must form a barrier between Germany and Russia – and said that French public opinion was hostile to the reparations settlement because it did not compel Germany to pay all that she owed. He could make no further concession on the Rhineland either, for many Frenchmen believed that he had given away too much already. He then explained his reasons for making a stand for moderation against the wishes of many of his countrymen:

> My policy at the Conference, as I hope you realise, has been to seek a close link with Britain and the United States. I have not forgotten that you have great interests far from those which most concern us; I know something of the great American continent and of the vast British Empire. Because I have made this link with Britain and America the essential basis of my policy, I am attacked on all sides as feeble and inadequate. If I were to disappear, you would find yourselves faced with disagreements far greater than those which now divide us.[10]

He agreed to discuss ways of reducing the cost of the Army of Occupation, but nothing else. Lloyd George later outlined his proposal for giving the Germans time to make a new offer on reparations, but Wilson showed his hostility to the Germans and their complaints by saying that 'if the Germans had had the good sense to say to us, as the Austrians did, "We are in your hands, but we were not the only people responsible for the war",'[11] they could have been treated more leniently. The meeting closed to allow him and Clemenceau time to consult their colleagues.

Lloyd George's action caused a sensation among the other people present at the Conference. Keynes felt sympathetic towards the

Prime Minister's efforts, but believed them to be futile, writing to his mother on 3 June that

> The P.M., poor man, would like now at the eleventh hour to alter the damned Treaty, for which no-one has a word of defence, but it's too late in my belief and for all his wrigglings Fate must now march on to its conclusion. . . .[12]

and two days later he resigned his post with the British delegation, writing to tell Lloyd George that

> I ought to let you know that on Saturday I am slipping away from this scene of nightmare. I can do no more good here. I've gone on hoping even through these last dreadful weeks that you'd find some way to make of the Treaty a just and expedient document. But now it's apparently too late. I leave the twins* to gloat over the devastation of Europe and to assess to taste what remains for the British taxpayer.[13]

Keynes believed the battle for reason was lost, and opted out of the struggle, but not so Harold Nicolson, who wrote to his father that

> I have every hope that Lloyd George, who is fighting like a Welsh terrier, will succeed in the face of everybody in introducing some modification in the terms imposed upon Germany. Now that we see them as a whole we realise that they are much too stiff. They are not stern merely but actually *punitive*, and they abound with . . . 'pin-pricks' as well as dagger thrusts.[14]

Sir Robert Massey† wrote to Lloyd George supporting the action he had taken,[15] while General Smuts believed that he had not gone far enough.[16] Lord Sumner, by contrast, wrote to Lloyd George on 3 June, to say that the Reparations Chapter could not be modified without destroying the whole basis of the agreement reached between the Allies, and alleging that 'the supposed German offer is thoroughly insincere'.[17] He and Lord Cunliffe – Keynes' 'twins' – and William Hughes were the only members of the British Empire Delegation who did not support Lloyd George in his efforts to modify and moderate the terms of the Treaty.

* Lord Cunliffe and Lord Sumner.
† The New Zealand Prime Minister.

Lloyd George could only hope to succeed, however, if he could win some support from President Wilson. Clemenceau was obviously going to oppose virtually all of Lloyd George's proposals for modifications to the Treaty, and when the American Commissioners Plenipotentiary met on 3 June to consider the British proposals, it became clear that he could not hope for much support from Wilson either. After a discussion of reparations during which Wilson said that he felt that the present proposals were the only way out in view of the public hysteria on this issue,[18] and discussions of the other proposals made the previous day by Lloyd George, President Wilson launched into a tirade against the British:

> Well, I don't want to seem to be unreasonable, but my feeling is this: that we ought not, with the object of getting it signed, make changes in the Treaty, if we think that it embodies what we were contending for; that the time to consider all these questions was when we were writing the Treaty, and that it makes me a little tired for people to come and say now that they are afraid the Germans won't sign, and their fear is based upon things that they insisted upon at the time of the writing of the treaty; that makes me very sick. . . . Here is a British group made up of every kind of British opinion, from Winston Churchill to [H.A.L.] Fisher. From the reasonable to the unreasonable, all the way round, they are all unanimous, if you please, in their funk. Now that makes me very tired. They ought to have been rational to begin with and then they would not have needed to have funked at the end. . . . Though we tried to keep them from putting irrational things in the treaty, we got very serious modifications out of them. If we had written the treaty the way they wanted it, the Germans would have gone home the minute they read it.
>
> Well, the Lord be with us.[19]

Lloyd George was clearly going to have to fight his battle alone.

On the afternoon of 3 June, Lloyd George renewed his plea for a plebiscite in Upper Silesia, to find that his principal opponent was the President. Wilson and Lloyd George had never agreed closely in their attitudes towards Poland, and that afternoon they had a series of rows on the subject. The first was on the small region of Schneidemuhl, which Wilson said was sparsely populated and was partly marsh land, and the experts had considered the presence of a railway line to be the most important factor. Lloyd George retorted, 'The

Highlands of Scotland are also very thinly populated, but if it were proposed to cede them to Germany or Poland for that reason, you would find yourself in serious difficulties'.[20] Moving on to Upper Silesia, Wilson tried to argue that the difficulties involved in holding a plebiscite there were such as to render the idea impracticable. He was supported by Clemenceau, but Lloyd George would not accept such arguments.[21] Wilson then said that the people behind the German complaints about Upper Silesia were German capitalists who owned the province's industry, whereupon Lloyd George retorted that the Socialists were in a majority in the German Government.[22] To charges that the population would be intimidated, Lloyd George replied,

> I know what it is to be oppressed and intimidated by great landowners; I had experience of that in Wales, where one could make no appeal for outside help to throw off the yoke. In Upper Silesia the peasant population is small, and hence the number of people who can be thus intimidated is also small; most of the population of Upper Silesia are industrial workers, who are always difficult to intimidate.[23]

The argument went on for some time along such lines as these, and in the end Lloyd George became exasperated at Wilson's persistent obstruction:

> No-one has proclaimed more powerfully than you the right of people to decide their own fate. That means that the fate of peoples must be decided by the peoples themselves, and not by any Dr Lord* who believes that he knows better than the people themselves what they want. I am doing nothing other than abiding by your Fourteen Points; why, after deciding to insist upon plebiscites in Danzig, Klagenfurt and Fiume, and in the Saar Valley, do you have to reject this solution in the case of Upper Silesia?[24]

Lloyd George failed to comprehend why Wilson should be so inconsistent, and tried to appeal to him through his own principles. Wilson was not persuaded. When Lloyd George spoke of his fear of a Bolshevik revolution in Germany, 'I am afraid that Berlin may turn into another Moscow, and that there will be no-one there with whom

* The Chief American adviser on Polish Affairs.

we can sign peace,' Wilson retorted, echoing his remarks that morning to the American delegation that 'It is a bit late to say all that. The problem is to decide whether our earlier decisions were just or not.'[25] Lloyd George, however, continued to press for the adoption of his proposals for plebiscites.

Later the Council turned their attention to reparations, and Wilson once more made clear his opinion of the Germans: 'No injustice on our part would be involved in imposing complete reparations on the Germans, but we have recognised that that would be an impossible demand.'[26] Germany was totally guilty, and her duty to expiate her sin was only being lightened as an act of mercy. Both Wilson and Lloyd George agreed that the German complaints were exaggerated, though Lloyd George felt that their complaint that they would be left in a state of complete uncertainty as to the extent of their obligations was justified. Wilson pointed out, quite rightly, that the Americans had always favoured fixing a sum but after some discussion it was agreed that this was not possible. Lloyd George accepted that the Allies' reply should be that if Germany's obligations were undetermined, so was the extent of the damage they had caused. The Council was not disposed to make any change in the Reparations Chapter of the Treaty.

Finally, there was the question of Germany's admission to the League. Lloyd George wished to allow them to join at once, but neither Wilson nor Clemenceau would agree to this. Wilson said that they should only be admitted when the Allies were convinced that their democratic constitution was genuine and well-established, while Clemenceau argued that

> They only want to be in the League of Nations to cause trouble among us. I am not against the principle of admitting them . . . but we must first make sure that peace is firmly established and that Germany is prepared to respect it.[27]

Wilson and Lloyd George felt that the Germans should be given some assurance that they would be admitted, but Clemenceau did not wish to do so until they had given evidence of good behaviour. There the matter rested for the time being. The initial reactions to Lloyd George's proposals, then, were outright opposition from Clemenceau, and from Wilson either lukewarm support or opposition.

On the morning of 5 June, the question of the German–Polish

frontier was taken up again in the presence of Paderewski, the Polish Prime Minister. Paderewski and Lloyd George at once clashed over Eastern Galicia, where, according to reports Lloyd George had received, Polish troops were still advancing, and Paderewski said that Poland definitely claimed the whole of Galicia.[28] He then moved on to Silesia, and said that if the proposed changes were made here,

> I could not have anything more to do with politics, because it would be absolutely impossible to rule my country. You know that revolutions begin when people lose faith in their leadership. These people have belief in me now, because they were told by me, and most emphatically, that these things promised to them would be given to them. Well, now, if something is taken away from them, they will lose all faith in my leadership. They will lose faith in your leadership of humanity, and there will be revolution in my country.[29]

This intransigence caused Lloyd George to fly into a rage:

> The Poles had not the slightest hope of getting freedom, and they have only got their freedom because there are a million and a half of Frenchmen dead, very nearly a million British, half a million Italians, and I forget how many Americans. That has given them their freedom, and they say that they will lose faith in the leadership that has given them that, at the expense of millions of men of other races who have died for their freedom. If that is what the Poles are like, then I must say it is a very different Poland to any Poland I ever heard of.[30]

Later, harking back to his own boyhood experience of oppression by English landlords and his early career fighting that oppression, Lloyd George told Paderewski that

> You know, I belong to a small nation, and therefore I have great sympathy with all oppressed nationalities, and it fills me with despair, the way in which I have seen small nations, before they have hardly leaped into the light of freedom, beginning to oppress other races than their own. They are more imperialists, believe me, than either England or France, than certainly the United States. It fills me with despair, as a man who has fought all his life for little nations.[31]

Paderewski replied to this outburst by reverting to Eastern Galicia and alleging that the Ukrainians were committing atrocities against the Poles there and that the Poles of Lemberg, even the children, were fighting to defend themselves. He also alleged that the Germans and the Bolsheviks were conspiring together against the Poles. Paderewski was utterly opposed to Lloyd George's proposals, while Lloyd George was clearly disgusted with the Poles. That afternoon, he clashed with Clemenceau over the Polish advances in Galicia. Clemenceau said that the Poles were fighting for their lives, but Lloyd George rejected this outright: 'a country which has to raise an army to resist danger cannot also pursue an aggressive policy', as, in his opinion, the Poles were doing in Galicia. Wilson took Clemenceau's side, saying that his fears for Poland's safety had been aroused by a concentration of German troops on her border with Poland.[32]

On 7 June the Council returned to other problems which had been raised by Lloyd George. On reparations he said that Americans still wanted to fix a figure, but Loucheur, for France, still believed this to be impossible. Loucheur had, however, made a suggestion similar to Lloyd George's, that the Germans be given three or four months to undertake jointly with the Allies a review of the damage and the best means of making it good.[33] Later they discussed the question of Germany's admission to the League of Nations. Wilson proposed a paragraph for insertion in the Allies' reply to the German objections which would provide for the admission of Germany when her democratic government was seen to be stable and the German people were clearly of a mind to keep the peace, and added that the Allies 'hope this would be possible a few months from now', to which Clemenceau replied, 'Ah, that's saying a lot'. When Wilson said that alternatively they could say that they hoped Germany could be admitted 'in a short time', Clemenceau's reply was 'we shall see'.[34] Clemenceau could not bring himself to admit that the Germans might be trusted in the near future, and when Wilson said that he had always felt that it would be better to have Germany in the League than to leave her out, because it would be easier to keep a check on her, Clemenceau replied, 'You will never keep a check on them. I know them too well to believe that.'[35] When Lloyd George supported Wilson, Clemenceau accused him of being too much under the influence of Lord Robert Cecil, who was 'ready to open his arms to the Germans'.[36] Lloyd George, for his part, felt that this kind of clause would cause much annoyance in Germany, and was therefore better cut out, but

Clemenceau would not agree. German admission to the League must be delayed until her good faith and peaceful intentions were beyond doubt.

On the morning of 9 June, Lloyd George reported that the Commission on Polish Affairs had been unable to agree on how much time should elapse between the signature of the Treaty and the holding of a plebiscite in Upper Silesia. He then had an argument with Clemenceau about whether it would be necessary to eject the clergy from Upper Silesia while the voting took place.[37] After this they moved on to consider reparations again. Wilson, speaking on behalf of the committee of experts which had been charged with preparing the Allies' reply to the German objections to the Treaty, reported that both the British and the French financial experts were still opposed to any attempt to fix a figure to be named in the Treaty, for the same reasons as had brought about the original draft clauses: 'If the figure is too high, the Germans will be even more antagonised than before, but if it is too low there will be very great discontent in France and England.'[38] The Americans wanted to fix a figure, believing that this was essential for the re-establishment of international credit, but Lloyd George said that to do so was impossible: 'either the figure we fixed would frighten the Germans even more, or it would be impossible for Clemenceau and I to get our peoples to accept it'.[39] Wilson proposed that the Treaty should be left as it was, saying that at present no-one knew how much she owed; to this Lloyd George added that no-one knew the extent of her capacity to pay either. Wilson still felt, however, that the best solution would be to fix a figure so that world trade could be restarted on a firm basis – 'We must either renounce reparations by letting Germany sink to utter ruin, or, in order to obtain reparations, we must give her the means to re-establish her trade.'[40] He then proposed a figure of 120 million gold marks as the maximum capital figure above which the Reparations Commission would not be allowed to go in fixing Germany's indebtedness.[41] To this Lloyd George retorted,

> I like the crust and sauce of this pâté well enough, but not the meat.
>
> PRESIDENT WILSON: My dear friend. . . .
>
> M. CLEMENCEAU: I am always a bit afraid of you when you start off by calling us 'My dear friend'.
>
> PRESIDENT WILSON: Alright, if you prefer it: esteemed col-

leagues, it is necessary for you to prepare your stomach for a meat which will sustain you.

MR LLOYD GEORGE: Yes, on one condition, that you give me enough of it.

M. CLEMENCEAU: Yes, and above all I must be sure that it won't go into someone else's stomach.[42]

They could not agree, and it was decided to ask the financial experts whether they could make any further suggestions. The following morning, they discussed the issue again, and agreed to leave the Treaty as it was while allowing Germany four months from the date of the signing of the Treaty to make an improved offer of reparation. At the end of the discussion Clemenceau declared that 'All I want to say is that I am not in favour of the policy of begging pardon for our victory from the Germans: I have known them too well and for too long'.[43] He was also convinced that the German people now wanted peace and there would be no difficulty in getting the Treaty signed: 'if the delegates at Versailles refuse to sign, I am convinced that we shall still have peace within a fortnight; other delegates will be sent to sign'.[44] That afternoon Lloyd George reported to the British delegation on his progress so far since he dropped his bombshell in the Council of Four; he was having some success in securing plebiscites in Upper Silesia and elsewhere, but 'very great difficulties had been met in connection with the subject of compensation', and they had felt obliged to leave the Treaty unaltered, except for allowing Germany four months to make a better offer than that contained in their Note of 29 May. The French had refused to shorten the occupation of the Rhineland, but had agreed not to interfere with the civil administration of the province.[45] Some gains had been made, but it had been a hard struggle, especially in view of President Wilson's attitude to the German–Polish border question, and Clemenceau's obstinacy on every issue.

On 10 June, Lord Robert Cecil wrote to Lloyd George to say that he had been invited to attend the Council of Four when they discussed the Rhineland but would not do so. He believed the fifteen-year occupation to be 'a mistake', and after consulting colleagues from Italy and America he suggested that provision should be made for it to be reconsidered after two or three years.[46] Lloyd George was soon to act on this advice. Meanwhile, on 11 June the Council of Four at last agreed to the holding of a plebiscite in Upper Silesia, one or two years after the signing of the Treaty, provided that adequate steps were taken to ensure that German employers and priests could not have an undue influence on the vote.[47] Next morning, they discussed the German objection to being held solely responsible for the war, an objection which they had supported with evidence printed in a 'White Book'. Lloyd George felt that they ought to make some reply, but Clemenceau said that 'I do not think you can do that without examining their White Book. As far as French opinion is concerned there is no point, as we are entirely convinced of her guilt', and President Wilson agreed: 'All we need to do is to reject the German claim that Germany was not responsible for starting the war. We can just say that we do not believe a word of what the German Government says.'[48]

The Council went on to discuss Germany's admission to the League, and accepted without debate a new text for the reply to Germany simply reaffirming that at present the Allies could not trust her sufficiently to admit her, but must submit her to a period on trial:

> The duration of this period on trial will depend to a large extent on the actions of the German Government and it is that Government, by its attitude to the Treaty of Peace, that will be able to reduce the period of waiting that the League of Nations will think necessary without any thought of prolonging it unduly.[49]

In discussing disarmament immediately afterwards, Clemenceau said that he was quite prepared to see Germany admitted to the League, but would not say so at that time to the French people.[50]

Lloyd George then raised the issue of the occupation of the Rhineland, pointing out that the shorter the occupation was, the more strictly it could be enforced – 'for myself I would prefer a short but very rigorous occupation', in order, presumably, to deter the Germans of that region from again supporting militarism. Clemenceau refused to consider any reduction in the period of the occupation, but Wilson urged him to agree that it could be reconsidered at a future date, if in the meantime Germany had done all she could to comply with the terms of the Treaty.[51] Lloyd George urged him to consider this. The occupation would serve no useful purpose anyway, he said – 'It will not last beyond the time when Germany will be weakest, and will be a danger for France and for the peace of Europe. All we can do is to try and make it as inoffensive as possible.'[52] For Lloyd

George the way to a lasting peace was to conciliate Germany, not to oppress her. Clemenceau, however, was determined at least to avenge France's humiliation in 1871 – 'In 1871 the German army occupied French territory and stayed there until the indemnity was paid. It did not leave until the last sou was paid. The present situation is the same, only on a larger scale'[53] – and Lloyd George was forced to accept at least a temporary occupation, after Clemenceau pointed out that President Wilson was satisfied with the provisions of the Treaty as they stood.[54] On the morning of 13 June, Lloyd George asked Clemenceau to discuss the time at which the need for the occupation would be reviewed,[55] and that afternoon they discussed the matter again, Clemenceau refusing to countenance anything which might bring about the shortening of the period of occupation, saying that

> You ask me why I am so obstinate. I cannot act otherwise; our birthrate is low, we have lost a million and a half men. France's foremost need is security. . . . I have to take account of the feelings of my countrymen. That is not to say that I am afraid of being turned out of office; that is a matter of indifference to me, but I do not want to do anything that will break the spirit of our people.[56]

However, he did agree that the occupation should be reviewed when the military clauses of the Treaty had been executed and Germany was thus disarmed. This at least Lloyd George had managed to obtain.

Next day, the Council resumed its discussion of the German–Polish frontier, with Paderewski present once more. He described the decision to hold a plebiscite in Upper Silesia as a 'cruel blow' to the Poles, and warned that if the Germans won, it would be the Polish peasants and workers of Silesia who would suffer:

> They have suffered oppression for centuries and hoped at last to be able to live as free men in their own fatherland. If the results of the plebiscite go against us, it will be for us a calamity.[57]

President Wilson was sympathetic – 'Do not think your words have not moved me. I tell you now that I did not accept the decision you have just been discussing without grave reservations'[58] – but Lloyd George, while saying that Paderewski's words on 5 June had moved him, stated that the Allies had, after much thought, made up their minds on the issue.[59] In response to a request from Paderewski, however, the period that was to elapse between the signing of the Treaty and the holding of the plebiscite was shortened from between one and two years to between six and eighteen months. On 15 June the Bohemian Germans submitted a protest at their inclusion in the new Czechoslovak State, but no-one took any notice of them.[60]

On 16 June, the Allies sent the Germans their final reply to their observations on the draft Treaty. They began in a way not calculated to appease German bitterness about the nature of the terms: 'In the view of the Allied and Associated Powers the war which began on 1 August 1914 was the greatest crime against humanity and the freedom of peoples that any nation calling itself civilised has ever consciously committed.'[61] After more in this vein, and an affirmation that it was for this reason that the Allies considered the Reparations Chapter and the demand for the surrender of war criminals to be justified, they also repeated their refusal to admit Germany to the League of Nations:

> In the present temper of international feeling, it is impossible to expect the free nations of the world to sit down immediately in equal association with those by whom they have been so grievously wronged. To attempt this too soon would delay, not hasten that process of appeasement which all desire.[62]

After saying that this memorandum was their last word, the Allies went on to state the concessions they had seen fit to make and gave the Germans five days to accept the terms as now decided. The details of these concessions were contained in an appendix, which was also not written in a conciliatory tone. Speaking of the territorial settlement and the application of President Wilson's principles, they said that

> If in certain cases, not in all, the decision has in fact not been in favour of Germany, this is not the result of any purpose to act unjustly towards Germany. It is the inevitable result of the fact that an appreciable portion of the territory of the German Empire consisted of districts which had in the past been wrongfully appropriated by Prussia or Germany. It is a chief duty of the Allied and Associated Powers to rectify these injustices in accordance with the explicit statement of President Wilson.[63]

So Wilson's principles were regarded chiefly as of use in putting right the wrongs committed by Germany, not just in the war, but ever since Frederick the Great annexed Upper Silesia in 1742.

After much talk of the German demands they refused to meet, they revealed the concession of a plebiscite in Upper Silesia, while refusing to eliminate the Polish Corridor or return Danzig to the Germans. In the West, no concessions were made. They refused to accept the Germans' attempt to shuffle off responsibility for starting the war onto Tsarist Russia,* alleging instead that 'the series of events which caused the outbreak of war was deliberately plotted and executed by those who wielded the supreme power in Vienna, Budapest and Berlin'.[64] They were therefore determined to bring these men to trial and punishment. With the sending of this Note, the negotiations with the Germans came to an end, and the Germans now had to decide, within five days, whether to sign the Treaty or refuse and renew the war. The negotiations between the Allies over the terms of the Treaty were also concluded, although there was a last flurry over Upper Silesia on 24 June when Clemenceau told the Council of Four that the Polish authorities had captured a German dispatch containing plans for an armed rebellion there against the Poles.[65] The Germans were warned that they must not cause trouble in Upper Silesia.[66]

Lloyd George was also worried about the economic future of Europe. On 26 June he replied to President Wilson's letter, in which the President had rejected Keynes' proposal that the Americans should guarantee a bond issue by the central banks of the Central European Powers.† He pointed out that no-one had yet devised an adequate alternative solution, and that the American financial experts had never opposed the extraction from Germany of an initial reparations payment of £1,000 million, which Wilson had said was inadvisable and had made one of his reasons for rejecting Keynes' scheme. He pointed out that the Allies faced difficulties, and

> After all, it is not a question of deciding what amount can usefully be imposed on Germany by way of penalty for her crimes in plotting and starting the war; it is a question of compelling her to relieve, to the utmost of her powers, the intolerable burden which she has imposed upon her neighbours.

* See pp. 248–9 above.
† See pp. 208–10 above.

The Allies were in debt to the United States, which was the only country in a position to help. Lloyd George concluded his letter by saying that

> The responsibility for the reconstruction of the world . . . depends in an exceptional measure upon the United States, for the United States is the only country in the world which is exceedingly prosperous and is not overburdened, in proportion to her resources and population, by external or internal debts.[67]

The problem of inter-Allied indebtedness was to plague European Finance Ministers throughout the inter-war period, and failure adequately to solve this problem was not the least of the causes of the economic difficulties and disasters which occurred in those years. Woodrow Wilson never offered any constructive suggestions, despite Lloyd George's appeal.

There were a number of problems with which the Conference had to deal before the signing of the Treaty. Perhaps the most urgent of them was deciding what should be done about the two Allied countries who were in dispute with the Conference – Italy and China. In the case of Italy, a compromise had seemed fairly near in early June,* but there remained a stubborn disagreement between the Italians and President Wilson over Fiume and Dalmatia. On 7 June, President Wilson was still not willing to give Italy any of the Adriatic islands, although Lloyd George urged him to do so, since only a few people would be involved. Orlando said that he, for his part, could make no further concessions; in accepting autonomy for Fiume he had already gone far:

> We have not obtained satisfaction over Fiume; the city is to be submitted to the same kind of control as you have imposed on enemy or half-barbarian peoples. A highly civilised people which has emerged victorious at your side in a terrible war, is to be subjected to a system which you have regarded as appropriate for the Pacific Islands and the Saar Valley! To accept that has been a great sacrifice on our part.[68]

Orlando still believed that a victor Power was entitled to preferential treatment, but Wilson was still not satisfied, and no solution was reached. On 14 June, Orlando informed Wilson that unless the

* See pp. 261–8 above.

dispute between them was settled Italy could not sign the Treaty with Germany[69] and would thus remain in a state of war. On 23 June Orlando's Government fell, and he was replaced as Prime Minister by Signor Nitti, who, as the British Ambassador in Rome informed Lord Curzon, was unlikely to concede any more to Wilson than his predecessor.[70] However, the Council of Four decided to approach the new Government and get a settlement.[71] In fact the issue never was settled by the Peace Conference. In September 1919, dissident Italian forces under Gabriele d'Annunzio marched into Fiume and were applauded by most of the Italian people for doing so, and not all the objections and pressure of the Great Powers could get him to move out. In the end, Italy and Yugoslavia settled the issue between themselves by signing the Treaty of Rapallo in November 1920, by which the Italians gained Fiume and the surrounding area.[72] No-one ever found a middle road between the principles of President Wilson and the nationalism of d'Annunzio.

As far as the Chinese were concerned, their disgust at the decision to give Shantung to the Japanese was sufficient for them to consider not signing the Treaty. On 14 May the British Ambassador in Peking, Sir J. Jordan, informed Lord Curzon that the Chinese felt 'deeply aggrieved' at the decision and the Government was considering refusing to sign the Treaty.[73] In his reply a week later Curzon wrote, 'I sincerely hope that the Chinese Government will not do anything so foolish and likely to alienate sympathies of Allies such as refusing to sign the treaty'.[74] On 26 May the Chinese delegation wrote to Clemenceau as Chairman of the Peace Conference to say that the decision on Shantung 'is seen by the whole Chinese nation as a deception and has aroused voices of protest from the whole Chinese people'. The Chinese delegates could therefore only sign the Treaty if they were allowed to make a reservation on Shantung.[75] When Clemenceau reported this to the Council of Four, all were dubious about allowing this[76] but it was finally agreed on 26 June that the Chinese delegates should be allowed to make an oral protest 'at the last possible moment' during the signing ceremony.[77] In fact China did not sign the Treaty of Versailles, and made a separate peace with Germany in May 1921, under which Germany renounced all her former rights and possessions in China to the Chinese.[78]

The Poles also raised a problem, which was attended to by the Council of Foreign Ministers. On 18 June, this Council discussed the matter of Eastern Galicia on the basis of a memorandum from

Balfour urging that the Poles be allowed to occupy the area on a strictly temporary basis in order to defend it against the Red Army, and should be told that they were to obey the instructions of the League of Nations.[79] This was necessary, Balfour said, because the Bolsheviks were advancing into the area, but care must be taken not to prejudice the final disposal of the territory, and his proposal was accepted.[80] A week later it was also agreed that the Poles should temporarily administer the area under the supervision of a Commissioner appointed by the League of Nations, and that its final allocation should be decided by plebiscite.[81] This unpleasant problem was at last solved, at least for the time being.

The final stages of the process of making peace with Germany had now been reached. Although many Germans believed that, in the words of a Social-Democrat, Haase, 'Our nation has no choice but to make peace',[82] the terms still stuck in their throats and when the Cabinet received the final Allied Note it split and fell. On 20 June the German delegates at Paris raised a number of queries, and two days later offered to sign the Treaty with the exception of the war-guilt clauses:[83] this was the policy decided upon by the new Government in Germany and the reservation on the war-guilt clauses had been the only way of getting the Centre party to support the new government in the Reichstag. That evening, the Council of Four resolved, on a joint proposal by Wilson and Lloyd George, not to consider any alterations in the Treaty, and to allow the Germans only twenty-four hours to make up their mind, their attitude being hardened by the news, which reached Paris that day, of the scuttling of the German fleet interned at Scapa Flow.[84] Next morning, the Germans asked for forty-eight hours more, but Lloyd George told his colleagues that they ought not to grant any such request: he said that

> after carefully considering the matter he felt that the sinking of the German ships in the Orkneys weighted principally with him against granting the German request. . . . There was no doubt that the sinking of these ships was a breach of faith. If bridges were blown up and loss of life caused, and military operations hampered by these or similar measures the public would say that this was the reason for which time had been granted.[85]

By the scuttling of their fleet, the Germans caused Lloyd George to harden his attitude, and he had always been the most ardent advocate of moderation in the Council of Four. Wilson agreed that the request should be turned down – he 'did not trust the Germans'.[86] Clemenceau also agreed, and the German request was refused.

In Germany, the new Government resigned rather than sign the Treaty, but the President of the new German Republic, Ebert, refused to accept its resignation. He then demanded to know whether Germany could defend herself if she refused to sign, and Hindenburg walked out rather than give the humiliating reply, which was given by General Gröner: in the east the position was reasonable, but in the west quite hopeless.[87] Germany had no alternative but to sign the Treaty, and with only four hours of the Armistice left to run, the Germans informed the Allies that

> The Government of the German Republic has seen with consternation from the last communication of the Allied and Associated Governments, that the latter are resolved to wrest from Germany by sheer force even the acceptance of those conditions of peace which, though devoid of material significance, pursue the object of taking away its honour from the German people. The honour of the German people will remain untouched by any act of violence. The German people, after all the frightful suffering of the last few years, lacks all means of defending its honour by external action. Yielding to overwhelming force, but without on that account abandoning its view in regard to the unheard of injustice of the conditions of peace, the Government of the German Republic therefore declares that it is ready to accept and sign the conditions of peace imposed by the Allied and Associated Governments.[88]

With this last attempt to retain some shreds of dignity, this last protest at the severity of the terms, the Germans finally admitted defeat. When the Council of Four received this message, they gave instructions for guns to be fired, and adjourned. On 28 June all members of the Conference gathered in the Hall of Mirrors at Versailles for the second session of the Peace Congress. At three o'clock Clemenceau declared the session open and the Germans came up to sign. Robert Lansing has left us a vivid description of the scene:

> It was as if men were being called upon to sign their own death-warrants, fully realising that they were at the mercy of those whom they had wronged beyond the possibility of pardon. They seemed anxious to get through with it and be off. . . . With pallid faces and

THE END OF A PERFECT "*TAG.*"

(SCAPA FLOW, JUNE 21st.)

From *Punch*, Volume 157, p. 31.

> trembling hands they wrote their names quickly and were then conducted back to their places.[89]

The great task was over, and peace signed. There remained much more to do: there were three more peace treaties to prepare, and a myriad of old and new problems still to be solved, but the Treaty of Versailles now ended the war between the Allies and Germany. Clemenceau, introducing the Treaty to the Chamber of Deputies on 30 June, looked forward to a new age of French greatness now that 'the abominable attempt at universal oppression . . . has just been brought to nought',[90] while Lloyd George told the House of Commons on 3 July that the Treaty was designed

> to compel Germany, in so far as it is in her power, to restore, to repair and to redress. Yes, and to take every possible precaution of every kind that is within our power against the recurrence of another such crime. . . . That is not vengeance. It is discouragement.[91]

By his efforts to secure a more moderate Treaty, Lloyd George achieved a few useful changes, but with both Clemenceau and Wilson antagonistic towards his action, he could only achieve a limited degree of success, and his chances were not improved by the bitterness between Britain and France, and between himself and Clemenceau, that had been so much increased by the dispute over Syria in May. That problem remained unsolved, and so did many others, and we must look briefly at what was happening about them while the last stages of making peace with the Germans were being carried on.

## LEFT-OVER PROBLEMS: JUNE 1919

Two problems in particular remained to be considered and, if possible, solved by the Paris Peace Conference as the negotiations on the German Treaty came to a close: Russia and the Middle East. At the end of May, the Council of Four had at last resolved to offer recognition to Admiral Kolchak, if he gave certain guarantees.* This decision had resulted from Kolchak's military successes, but early in June evidence suggested that these successes might be only temporary. On 3 June a member of the British diplomatic mission in

* See pp. 259–61 above.

Vladivostok, Colonel Robertson, informed the Foreign Office that Kolchak's forces were suffering defeat, their morale was low, and soldiers were deserting to the Bolsheviks. The problem of morale and desertions arose from a low standard of living in the area controlled by the Omsk Government, and he warned that Allied help was essential if Kolchak were not to be replaced either by the Bolsheviks or by reactionary army officers.[92] That same day Lloyd George informed the Council of Four that he feared Kolchak might have suffered a serious defeat, and Clemenceau urged that he be granted immediate recognition by the Allies as he had made a speech in which he had made the promises demanded by the Allies. Lloyd George, however, was unwilling to grant him recognition until he replied to the Allied Note, and when Clemenceau said that some members of the Omsk Government were strongly opposed to the Allied demands, Lloyd George said 'I know that, and I have warned Admiral Kolchak that we shall withdraw our support from him if he does not give the guarantees we have asked for'.[93] Lloyd George was determined not to give aid or succour to anyone in Russia who, if they were victorious, would restore the old regime.

Equally, many felt that the constant failure of the Council of Four to make up its mind on a policy to combat Bolshevism was furthering the Bolshevik cause. A Foreign Office memorandum on the Bolshevik Government in Hungary asserted that Bela Kun could have been brought down long since if the Allies had acted decisively:

> Time and again during the past six weeks the Soviet Government [in Hungary] has been on the verge of falling, and on any of these occasions it only needed the smallest display of decision on the part of the Entente to ensure its overthrow. This, however, was never forthcoming.

Bela Kun was getting Russian and Italian support – the latter because the Italians saw this as a way of weakening Yugoslavia – and had strengthened his military position. The writer of the memorandum concluded with a warning that 'unless Bolshevism is eliminated from Hungary before peace is signed and the French armies withdrawn, it will most certainly spread all over Eastern Europe.'[94] Action must be taken, and soon. That same day, however, a resolution to back Kolchak seemed to come nearer when President Wilson read out in the Council of Four a speech Kolchak had made promising to call a Constituent Assembly and preserve civil liberties. This was welcomed by everybody present, and Clemenceau said that they would receive Kolchak's reply to their message that night as well.[95] At the same time, though, Lord Curzon received a report from Vladivostok that Bolshevism was increasing in Siberia as a result of low living standards there.[96]

The following day, however, Colonel Robertson reported from Vladivostok that Kolchak's reaction to the Allies' conditions for recognition of his régime was favourable, and his objections reasonable, especially his argument that he could not reconvene the Constituent Assembly of 1917, which had included Lenin and Trotsky.[97] On 11 June Kolchak's reply was received and he agreed to the Allies' demands, with few reservations, the most important being his objection to reconvening the 1917 Constituent Assembly.[98] Next day, the Council of Four met to consider the matter further. Lloyd George wanted to limit the Allied commitment to support Kolchak; he did not wish to commit himself to active intervention on his side.[99] This was agreed. However, it was becoming increasingly apparent that Kolchak's military successes, which had originally aroused Allied enthusiasm for recognising him, had been only temporary. Colonel Robertson reported on 15 June that Kolchak's position was now 'extremely bad', and more of his troops were deserting to the Bolsheviks.[100] This was discussed by the Council of Four on 17 June, and it became clear that Lloyd George's enthusiasm for recognising Kolchak was rapidly waning as he retreated:

> I do not believe that Admiral Kolchak will defeat Lenin. Rather there will come a time when the enemies will come together in order to put an end to anarchy. It seems that the Bolshevik armies are well run, but our reports indicate that the pure doctrine of Bolshevism is increasingly being abandoned and that in time Bolshevik Russia will be a state the same as any bourgeois state.[101]

Both Clemenceau and Wilson were sceptical, but Lloyd George stood firm and also believed that the Allies should establish contacts with the Soviet Government before the Germans did:

> MR LLOYD GEORGE: There is also a practical question to consider. If British traders ask me whether they may buy goods in Russia and I refuse, the Germans will buy the goods.
>
> PRESIDENT WILSON: We must tell our traders that they can trade with Russia at their own risk.[102]

Clemenceau and the Italians, for their part, were determined that the Allies should keep their promises to support and recognise Kolchak. The Allies were still in a state of almost complete confusion over their policy in Russia.

This chronic indecision was not only a problem for Admiral Kolchak. In the Baltic states there was still a large German army, which the Allies had allowed to go there in order to resist the Red Army. Now they were there and no policy relating to them had been decided. On 16 June A. J. Balfour wrote to Lloyd George to warn him of the possible consequences of leaving these troops where they were – 'These compacts with the Devil are apt to turn out ill in the end' – and he feared that the Germans would now try to keep these provinces firmly under their rule.[103] Another problem was the British force still stationed in Archangel. On 11 July the Secretary of State for War, Winston Churchill, told the Cabinet that the General Staff wished to mount an offensive there in order to weaken the Bolsheviks. This proposal aroused opposition in the Cabinet, E. S. Montagu pointing out that Parliament had been told that the garrison at Archangel had been strengthened only to ensure that it could be withdrawn safely. The Cabinet could not make up its mind about what to do in Russia either.[104] A week later Lord Curzon raised the matter again, saying that the defeats Kolchak had suffered made an offensive in the North more important as a means of relieving the pressure on the Siberian forces, but the chances of success now looked slim and the Cabinet was not willing to risk men and materials for a forlorn hope.[105] By 27 June Kolchak was even weaker, and the Cabinet was even less willing to order an offensive, especially as in Britain the Trades Unions were talking about launching a general strike to prevent aid being sent to the White forces in Russia. They were also worried about the activities of the German forces in the Baltic, but would not make up their minds what should be done about it.[106] No decision was ever made, and not surprisingly Admiral Kolchak became irritated at Allied tardiness in fulfilling their promise to recognise him,[107] and late in June attempted to blackmail them with a threat that if they did not do so, he would sign an alliance with Germany and Japan.[108] The Allies never did so, and were never able to decide on effective intervention against the Bolsheviks. In time the Whites were defeated and the Soviet Union became firmly established as the Government of all Russia.

The other unresolved problem was the Middle East. The departure of the King-Crane* Commission to investigate Arab opinion on the subject of who should act as mandatory for the various Arab nations† did not stop Anglo-French friction over Syria. On 11 June the French Ambassador in London, Paul Cambon, went to see Lord Curzon with a series of complaints about British activity in Syria, and, as Lord Curzon told Lord Derby, 'enlarged upon the French desire to secure and protect the independence of Syria'.[109] Next day, however, Lord Curzon received a despatch from General Allenby, in command of the British forces in Syria, warning that the Syrians would not accept a French mandate, although they would accept a British one.[110] Another problem was the Zionists, to whose demand for a national homeland in Palestine Britain had been committed by the Balfour Declaration of 1917. Among British politicians, Herbert Samuel, himself a Jew, had been pressing the Foreign Office to pursue a policy consistent with the Balfour Declaration, but was told in June that

> The Palestinians . . . desire their country for themselves and will resist any general immigration of Jews, however gradual, by every means in their power, not excluding armed resistance. They apparently consider that Great Britain is more systematically committed to the Zionist Programme than either the United States or France and both Arab and French propaganda are actually fostering this view.[111]

So, as a revenge for British activity in Syria, the French were using the Balfour Declaration to weaken the British position in Palestine, which, under the Sykes-Picot Agreement, was scheduled to be a British sphere of influence. Samuel's reply was that because Britain did not consistently follow the policy in Palestine indicated by the Balfour Declaration, they were raising Arab hopes of resisting Jewish immigration: the Balfour Declaration did not at the present time appear to embody

> the settled lines of British policy. As a consequence, there would naturally arise among the Arabs a feeling of doubt as to whether the establishment of the Jewish National Home in Palestine is really a decided issue, and a tendency to believe that if an agitation

* Named after the American representatives, who were in the event the only members of the Commission.

† See pp. 253–7 above.

> were set on foot and a threatening attitude adopted on their part, the British Government might well be ready to abandon the intentions it has just announced.[112]

The British must therefore stand firmly by the Jews. The King-Crane Commission soon became doubtful about the practicability of the Jewish National Home, however. On 20 June they sent a telegram to the American delegates in Paris advising them that 'we doubt if any British Government or American official here believes that it is possible to carry out Zionist programme except through support of a large army'.[113] On 10 July they reported that to impose a French mandate on Syria or a Zionist programme in Palestine would both be highly dangerous.[114] The Jews were not finally to get control of their homeland until after millions of them had perished in the gas chambers of the Third Reich, and even now its existence is not accepted by the Arabs. The Peace Conference failed to pacify the Middle East, and in fact changed very little there. It failed to take a firm line and impose solutions, because, as in the case of Russia, it could not make up its collective mind. There were too many conflicting interests and opinions at stake.

# 13 Portrait of a Decision

The Treaty of Versailles brought to an end the war between Germany and the Allied and Associated Powers, and in doing so laid the foundation for a re-ordering of world affairs. This was most obviously so in the case of the establishment of the League of Nations, whose Covenant formed the first section of the Treaty, together with the foundation of the International Labour Organisation. Much was hoped for from the League; it was to provide a permanent forum for the discussion and adjustment of international disputes, and it was hoped and expected that it would develop into a mechanism for the prevention of war, if need be by the application of the sanctions provided for by the Covenant, which culminated in joint military action by the League's members against any aggressor. The French hoped that it would be the ultimate guarantee of assistance if Germany should ever attack them again; in the meantime France would have the Treaties of Guarantee with Britain and the United States to protect her.

The League would also be responsible for administering many of the other provisions of the Treaty. When the time came it would conduct the plebiscites in Upper Silesia, the Saar Valley and elsewhere; it would supervise the administration of the former German colonies by the British Dominions and other states to whose care they would be entrusted, and it was to the League that China would have to look to ensure that Japan dealt fairly with her in the matter of Shantung. More generally, the work begun at Paris would have to be continued and modified in the light of subsequent events, in order that the Treaty might form a basis for a lasting peace.

In Europe, the effect of the Treaty was enormous. The creation of the new States of Eastern Europe out of the provinces of the old Austro-Hungarian Empire, and the inclusion in them of territory which had been regarded for up to two centuries as part of Germany, meant a major re-drawing of the political map of Europe. Many criticisms have been made of the territorial provisions of the Treaty of Versailles, but Winston Churchill was later to point out that it condemned only some four per cent of the population of Europe to live under a foreign allegiance, which, in view of the extent to which nationalities were mixed, especially in Eastern Europe, was no mean achievement. Alsace-Lorraine was restored to France, the Saar and Danzig were free states to be ruled by Commissioners to be appointed by the League, and Austria and Germany were obliged to remain as two separate and independent states – the Germans were forbidden to seek to realise the *Anschluss* which had been their ambition since the days of the Frankfurt Parliament.

Outside Europe too the effect was considerable, with the re-allocation of the German colonies to the Dominions and the ending of Germany's influence in China. Together with the subsequent Treaties with Austria, Bulgaria and Turkey, the Treaty of Versailles constituted a re-drawing of the map of the world.

Financially, the Reparations settlement was bound to be an important link in the chain of world credit. The Allied Powers were indebted to each other, and all were in debt to the United States and were dependent upon extracting money from Germany in order to meet these debts, and this was not the least reason for Allied obstinacy and apparent greed in the negotiations on this subject at Paris. The indefinite nature of the settlement was not, perhaps, the best means of creating security among the financiers and industrialists of Europe and America, even if it was the only means whereby the Conference could reach agreement, but Germany was to make a substantial down-payment and the uncertainty would last for at most two years, until May 1921, when the Reparations Commission was to prepare its report on the extent of the debt Germany owed and the limits of her capacity to pay. The demand for the trial of the Kaiser was to lead to a row with Holland, which refused to surrender him and sheltered him until his death. Germany was disarmed, but in later years managed to evade the terms of the Treaty. By that time, however, the system established by the Treaty of Versailles had already collapsed.

The immediate aftermath of the Treaty was a Europe seething

with unrest. The Conference's efforts at mediation in the various disputes which were raging within or between various countries met with little success. The Russian Civil War went on, and when the Conference laid down a boundary between Russia and Poland in September 1919, which became known as the 'Curzon Line' because the British Foreign Secretary was given the task of informing the Poles of the Conference's decision, the Poles rejected it and fought a war with Russia which did not end until March 1921, when by the Treaty of Riga the Poles and the Russians agreed on a boundary between them. In the aftermath of a Polish victory of arms, this frontier gave Poland considerably more than the Peace Conference had thought justifiable.[1] Elsewhere, d'Annunzio walked into Fiume and no Italian Government felt strong enough to order him out again, and the Greeks and the Turks quarrelled over Smyrna. Not until 1924 did Europe seem to settle down to a reasonably peaceful existence.

This is not the place for a comprehensive history of the years between the signing of the Treaty of Versailles and the outbreak of the Second World War – for this the reader must look elsewhere. In view of the frequency with which the provisions of the Treaty have been blamed for laying the foundations for the new war, it is, however, appropriate to consider two major misfortunes which befell the Treaty and Europe in the next decade, and destroyed whatever chances the Versailles settlement might otherwise have had of working.

The first and most immediate of these misfortunes was the withdrawal of America from participation in the settlement and in European affairs. President Wilson, when he returned home with the Treaty, faced a hostile partisan majority in the Senate. In American politics this in itself might not have proved an insuperable obstacle to the ratification of the Treaty, but coupled with two other factors it was so. The first was a growing feeling that America had been mistaken in getting involved in the affairs of Europe and should now withdraw from that involvement as soon as possible, and for ever. The second was that many of the men who now controlled the Senate were personal enemies of Woodrow Wilson. Senator Vandenberg, one of the chief opponents of the Treaty, justified his opposition to the Covenant by saying that it was essential that America should ensure 'the preservation of our absolute and untrammelled right of self-decision'.[2] Then, as since, the question of surrendering sovereignty to any international body was a powerful and emotive issue. This kind of suspicion also extended to other parts of the Treaty, as became clear while Wilson was answering questions put to him by members of a Senate Commission charged with examining the Treaty;

> SENATOR LODGE: I understand, Mr President, that war claims were not covered by the reparation clause.
> THE PRESIDENT: That is correct.
> SENATOR LODGE: I asked that question because I desired to know whether, under the Reparation Commission, there was anything expected to come to us.
> THE PRESIDENT: As I say, that remains to be decided.
> SENATOR LODGE: By the Commission?
> THE PRESIDENT: By the Commission.[3]

Not only did the Senators want to know whether America was going to get a share of the spoils, but they objected to that decision being taken by a Commission in which Americans would be involved with Europeans in making decisions which would affect American interests.

The chief sticking-point, however, was the Covenant. Senator Borah asked Wilson at this same hearing whether, if the League decided to apply military sanctions against an aggressor, there was any legal obligation upon the United States to go to war against that country. Wilson tried to reassure him that only a moral obligation was involved, but Borah was not easily convinced. Wilson said the same of the proposed Treaty of Guarantee for France – that too would involve only a moral obligation to fight.[4] Thus did Wilson try to assuage Senatorial fears that by signing the Covenant the Congressional power of decision as to war and peace might be restricted.

In the Autumn, anxiety in Europe at the turn events had taken in America increased. One criticism which had been made in the Senate was that the British Empire would have six votes in the Assembly of the League of Nations to the United States' one. On 24 October Lord Curzon wrote to the British Ambassador in Washington, Viscount Grey of Falloden, to suggest a way of reassuring the Senate on this point: it was the normal practice of international relations that a country involved in a dispute should not use its vote in reaching a decision at a Conference or other international gathering, and in this respect the British Dominions and Britain herself would operate as a unit in the League, and no British Empire vote would be used in such a case. In view of feelings in the Dominions, however, this representation must be maintained – 'we must stick by this absolutely'.[5] Grey replied that if need be further concessions must be made, and that in this he had the support of the Canadian Prime Minister:

> Sir R. Borden feels, and I entirely agree, that complete failure of treaty in Senate, followed by a separate peace between the United States and Germany, would be a calamity, and that nothing, however slight the chance, should be omitted which might help to avert it.[6]

Grey was clearly pessimistic about the Treaty's chances, and by mid-November the Americans were asking to be allowed to sign the Treaty on special terms, a request which the British were not disposed to grant, since to do so must give the impression 'that there is to be one rule for the United States and one rule for the rest of the world'. Complete Congressional control over American involvement in sanctions was also undesirable since this would destroy confidence in their effectiveness:

> The doctrine preached at Paris was that the small states must trust to the League to protect them, but the small states cannot trust to the League unless they know that the members of the League are pledged definitely to support them.[7]

These pleas were of no avail. The Senate refused to pass the Treaty, and at once one of the League's major props was knocked from under it: it would receive neither American delegates nor the support of the American armed forces. When the Senate also refused to ratify the French guarantee, the British claimed, justly but short-sightedly, that their own promise was dependent upon the fulfillment of the American one, and also refused to ratify the guarantee, while offering to discuss an alternative arrangement. France tried first to repress Germany and weaken her, but after the failure of the occupation of the Ruhr in 1923 France withdrew behind her own frontiers and into that spirit of negative self-protectiveness that was finally to lead to Vichy in 1940. American refusal to ratify the Treaty, then, was the first misfortune, in that the international system established by the Peace Conference broke up, and nations were left to fend for themselves. The world returned to the old ways of national rivalries, and the League was doomed to fail through weakness as soon as any major dispute broke out.

The second major misfortune which led to the collapse of world peace was the great economic slump of 1929–31. The privations suffered by the peoples of Europe, and especially the Japanese and the Germans, brought with them the political conditions which enabled the Dictators to seize and consolidate their power. To what extent the Treaty of Versailles was responsible for the Great Crash is almost impossible to determine. Certainly reparations were an unsound basis for credit, but there were others, and Professor Galbraith has argued that the cause of the Wall Street crash which started it all was the piling of company upon company, investment trust upon trust, with an inadequate backing of real assets. Professor Galbraith wrote of these investment trusts that

> Normally the securities of the trust were worth considerably more than the property it owned. Sometimes they were worth twice as much. There should be no ambiguity on this point. The only property of the investment trust was the common and preferred stocks and debentures, mortgages, bonds, and cash that it owned. . . . Yet, had these securities all been sold on the market, the proceeds would invariably have been less, and often much less, than the current value of the outstanding value of the investment company.[8]

If one major prop were knocked away, the whole edifice would collapse, and that, basically, is what happened on 'Black Friday', 24 October 1929, and the days that followed it. It is interesting that in this classic study of the Great Crash Professor Galbraith did not see fit to mention either the Treaty of Versailles or reparations. Perhaps they played a part in creating an unsound financial structure, but with better financial management, both private and public, the slump and what followed might have been avoided. The German elections between 1928 and 1933 show that the Nazi rise to power resulted from a desperate public turning to extremists who claimed that they could put an end to poverty, suffering and inflation, while the upper classes turned to Hitler in order to forestall the Communists, who were rising to power on the same tide.[9]

One other contemporary factor which was important both in weakening the authority of the Treaty and in distorting historical perspectives was the almost immediate expression of revulsion in many quarters against its terms. E. D. Morel, the founder of the Union for Democratic Control, said when the draft terms appeared that 'if this Treaty stands, your League of Nations . . . will be the most powerful engine of oppression the world has ever seen',[10] while more than a year later, a young major called Clement Attlee summed up the feelings of many when he said that

> When I was in the army I used to take occasion to chat with the men and with the officers, particularly with the men, and I have often asked the men what they went to fight for. I always got the same answer: they were fighting for something far bigger than the question of a King or Country. They believed, and we believed, that they were fighting for the good of the whole world. That is where the Government betrayal comes in.[11]

Such feelings were epitomised in Keynes' brilliant attack on the Treaty and the men who made it.* Such was the impact of this book, both in Britain and America, that when Britain and France were once more at war with Germany and fighting desperately, a young French historian, Etienne Mantoux, was moved to write a savage attack on Keynes' book entitled *The Carthaginian Peace: or the Economic Consequences of Mr Keynes.*[12] He pointed to the importance of the appearance of *The Economic Consequences of the Peace* in hardening American opposition to the Treaty and thus helping to destroy one of the essential supports of the Versailles system, and he went on to ask how it had come about that 'the days of Munich follow so insensibly after those of Versailles'.[13] His explanation was that, thanks to Keynes, most Europeans accepted as legitimate Hitler's proclaimed intention to abolish the Treaty of Versailles:

> For them this could only have meant the redress of a monstrous injustice. All that mattered was that it should be done 'by peaceful means'. *What* was to be done apparently did not matter. They could not imagine it might mean the destruction of free peoples. And yet, had not Hitler declared with the utmost precision that he aimed at Germany's expansion over European territory? . . . But all that could not be taken too seriously. Remember – he was in prison when he was thus writing – poor devil, he was pardonably excited; and even if he did still think so, surely he was confused by

* See pp. 1–3 above.

> some economic fallacy. That was not what could really be ailing the German people. Didn't you know? – 'the perils of the future lay not in frontiers and sovereignties, but in food, coal and transport'.[14]

With a polemic rivalling Keynes' own in brilliance, this young writer, who was killed on active service in 1945, laid at Keynes' door, and at those of others who thought like him both in 1919 and later, the blame for the destruction of the Treaty, and ultimately of peace. It was an unfair verdict, but certainly revulsion against the Treaty led to the British appeasement policy, just as the tales of the *Diktat* of Versailles and the 'stab in the back' were used by Hitler to arouse the Germans to a patriotic frenzy when the time was ripe.

It was not necessarily the faults in the Treaty which caused it to be ineffectual in preventing the outbreak of a new European war. Other factors intervened. Without them the League might have survived to make adjustments and smooth the rough edges of the settlement, and Europe and the world might have settled down to peace, as they seemed set fair to do between 1924 and 1929. The course of the Conference has been charted and how the Treaty was written in the way it was has been explained. The circumstances of the Conference have been examined: the pressure of inflamed public opinion represented in Parliaments to which the statesmen at Paris were responsible; the existence of both the secret treaties and Wilson's declarations, and the embodiment of the latter in the Armistice terms; the Russian Revolution and the fear that Bolshevism might spread into Eastern Europe.* The characters and activities of the chief characters in the drama can now be summed up, and then the nature of their interaction which produced the Treaty of Versailles can be stated once more.

## AMERICANS IN PARIS, 1919

Founded by emigrants who had fled from poverty, oppression or persecution in Europe, the United States of America had traditionally held aloof from involvement in European wars and diplomacy, and this aloofness had been confirmed in 1823 by the promulgation of the 'Monroe Doctrine', by which President Monroe, at the instigation of George Canning, proclaimed that America would not interfere in the affairs of other continents but would resist any

* See Chapters 1 and 2 above.

such interference with her own. Originally, Canning's object had been to prevent Spanish and French activity in South America, and to this end he called the New World into existence in order to redress the balance of the Old, but the long-term result was a century of isolation, as a result of which Americans and Europeans knew little of one another at political and diplomatic levels. When America did once more become involved in European affairs, when she entered the First World War, this led to misunderstandings on both sides. President Wilson's pronouncements led many Europeans to hope and expect that he could rescue them from the toils of secret diplomacy, nationalism and unjust frontiers, and Americans became involved in settling problems of whose detail and background they knew little.

Some Americans became anxious about their ignorance and lack of preparation for the peace negotiations as the opening of the Conference drew near. One such was General Tasker H. Bliss, whose series of questions about the territorial settlement, ending with 'How are we going to get the President's views or instructions on such questions?'* showed some agony of mind, both about the vagueness of the organisation of the American delegation and the lack of any idea of a detailed policy by which the Fourteen Points and President Wilson's other declarations could be applied to the realities of the European situation. Others, including Wilson himself, believed that statements of principle were enough, and that such declarations as 'Open covenants openly arrived at', or 'every territorial settlement involved in this war must be made in the interest and for the benefit of the populations concerned, and not as a part of any mere adjustment or compromise of claims among rival states', were self-explanatory and sufficient in themselves. This was a dangerous mistake, as Keynes afterwards pointed out, but the principles were also openly flouted, not least by Wilson himself.

People hoped for too much from President Wilson. Men like Keynes and Nicolson who journeyed to Paris 'not merely to liquidate the war, but to found a new order in Europe' had not noticed that mixed into the same speeches in which Wilson put forth his ideals was also the expression of a deep and increasingly vitriolic hatred of the Germans. In his Fourteen Points speech Wilson asserted that Germany must 'accept a place of equality among the peoples of

* See p. 58 above.

the world . . . instead of a place of mastery', and later he bitterly denounced the Treaty of Brest–Litovsk as the true and brutal German reply to his Fourteen Points. The Germans and their Allies were 'an isolated and friendless group of Governments', outlaws whose word could not be trusted, even when the promise they made would be to abide by the rules and decisions of that League of Nations which was Wilson's greatest hope for world peace. Hatred for the Germans was undoubtedly the main reason for Wilson's apparent inconsistency and his betrayal of his own principles. The evidence was there for contemporary observers to read, but they missed it – after all, it was only what all Allied politicians and soldiers were saying about the Germans at that time, and for that reason did not strike contemporary observers as in any way odd.

Again and again President Wilson's chief reason for his actions was hatred of Germany. He was reluctant to see the Kaiser tried because he did not want anyone to think that the Allies had gone beyond their rights – he did not want to take any chance that future generations might come to feel that the Kaiser had been unfairly treated and thus should become an object of sympathy. He thought Germany should be disarmed and humiliated, subjected to 'a generation of thoughtfulness', and equally he saw no reason, in terms of justice, why the Allies should not demand that Germany should pay for all the damage done to them and their peoples during the war. Germany's guilt, and thus her liability, were total. Above all, perhaps, he persistently resisted Lloyd George's efforts to have the Polish–German frontier redrawn more in accordance with the nationality of the population of the area and the self-determination of people, telling the Council of Ten on one occasion, for example, that Poland 'would have Germany on both sides of it, the Eastern fragment of Germany being one of a most aggressive character'. East Prussia was especially suspect, but all Germans were to be feared and distrusted. Little wonder that Wilson found it impossible to support the application of his principles in all cases. In the light of such emotions as are revealed in these and many other remarks, it is, if anything, surprising that Wilson was not even harder on the Germans than he was.

This point can be reinforced by remembering the stands of principle Wilson made when Germany was not involved: his imperious demand that in their dispute with the Ukrainians over Eastern Galicia the Poles, on whose behalf he had fought so stubbornly in the case of their western frontier, must 'either comply with the instructions of the Conference or renounce our support and recall their delegates';[15] and above all his obstinate resistance to the Italian demands for the execution of the Treaty of London and the cession to them in addition of the city of Fiume. He told the Council of Four on 19 April that 'We cannot possibly say that we have made peace with Germany on the basis of certain principles, but that we are invoking others to make peace with Turkey, Bulgaria and Austria'.[16] The Italians and the Allies could make no headway against Wilson and his principles on the Adriatic issue; he was perfectly capable of standing firm, but it was much easier to be saintly where the hateful Germans were not involved. Sometimes he felt that he could not countenance blatant annexation even where Germany was involved: the French were not to annex the Saar, nor the Belgians Malmédy, and equally the Belgians were only allowed a mandate in the Congo. But he went far to satisfy these demands in order to bring home to the Germans the enormity of their crime and the consequences which must in justice follow from it.

Another mistake often made in evaluating Woodrow Wilson's activities at Paris is to assume that he alone was responsible for the apparent betrayal of his principles. This was the work of others besides the President, and most important among them was Colonel House, Wilson's closest *confidant*, who claimed when Wilson sent him to Europe in 1918 as his Special Representative that their two minds thought as one.*

Basically, Colonel House was the eternal go-between. His first task, when he arrived in Europe, was to explain the Fourteen Points to the suspicious European Prime Ministers, and this he did in his 'Commentary' by explaining them, and in doing so modifying them, in a way calculated to soothe and please European ears.† The doctrines of Freedom of the Seas and free trade were emasculated to suit British tastes. There followed his 'deviltry' with Sonnino, an episode which reveals in House a considerable love of the diplomatic game for its own sake,‡ which led him not merely to compromise, but also to irresponsible behaviour. During the negotiations themselves, House played his go-between role on several occasions, most notably when he arranged the settlement of the dispute over the Rhineland

* See p. 28 above.
† See pp. 32–3 above.
‡ See p. 43 above.

between Clemenceau and Wilson behind Lloyd George's back. He also betrayed Wilson over the question of whether a Commission should be set up to inspect the German armed forces and their installations in order to ensure that the disarmament clauses of the Treaty were being kept. Wilson was opposed to this idea because it would irritate the Germans too much; House later told the Council of Four that he disagreed with Wilson's view and found the idea acceptable. When Wilson was ill or away from Paris, House took his seat in the Council of Four and on several occasions compromises were made which might not have been permitted had Wilson himself been putting the American case. What applied to the President also applied to other members of the delegation. After Robert Lansing made a firm stand against an angry Jules Cambon in the Council of Foreign Ministers against the attribution of the Bohemian Germans to Czechoslovakia on grounds of strategic necessity, Colonel House sold the pass which the Secretary of State had held so valiantly with what amounted to indifference when he agreed without demur in the Council of Four to Clemenceau's suggestion that the frontier be left as it was in 1914, with the Bohemian Germans in Czechoslovakia. Colonel House was fully capable of betraying both his leader and his colleagues if he saw fit.

It can occasion no surprise, in the light of the attitudes and activities of President Wilson and Colonel House, that other members of the American Commission to Negotiate Peace became anxious at what was happening to the President's principles. Lansing wrote to Wilson at the end of March to express his fears at the way the negotiations were going,* but got no response, and indeed, early in 1920, Wilson asked for Lansing's resignation as Secretary of State in very cruel terms:

> While we were still in Paris, I felt, and have felt increasingly ever since, that you accepted my guidance and direction on questions with regard to which I had to instruct you, only with increasingly reluctance. . . . I must say that it would relieve me of embarrassment, Mr Secretary, . . . if you would give your present office up and afford me an opportunity to select someone whose mind would more willingly go along with mine.[17]

Such was the fate of one fighter on behalf of the Fourteen Points.

* See p. 197 above.

Others did not wait for a Presidential dismissal but resigned, often expressing great bitterness at Wilson's failure to defend his principles. One such was William C. Bullitt.* Undaunted, however, others pressed on with the settlement, and accepted the compromises by which the Fourteen Points were modified or broken. Some shared Wilson's conviction of Germany's guilt and moral bankruptcy – John Foster Dulles spoke of 'the enormity of the crime committed by Germany',[18] while Dr Robert H. Lord, the chief American adviser on Polish affairs, was so convinced of the need to strengthen Poland and create in her as large and powerful a state as possible that he cared little about doing justice to the Germans. In doing so he aroused Lloyd George's wrath against him: 'The destiny of peoples should be determined by the peoples themselves and not by a Dr Lord who thinks he knows better than they do what they want.'[19] Lord was not a dispassionate adviser, and strengthened Wilson in his opposition to Lloyd George's efforts to obtain ethnic justice on the German–Polish frontier.

The American delegation was thus divided against itself. On the one hand were some almost fanatically devoted to the Fourteen Points, whilst on the other were people who did not care, or cared more for other things – vengeance upon Germany or the furtherance of other causes which interested them. One delegate undermined the work of another, and the influence of the opinions and interests of different advisers meant that American policy could never be consistent. What was more, these divisions and disagreements all had their place in the mind of the President himself, and he veered first one way and then another, depending on the circumstances of the case, the extent to which the Germans were involved, and the advice he was receiving. His chief colleagues in the Council of Four, David Lloyd George and Georges Clemenceau, both demanded vengeance upon Germany, and Clemenceau also wanted to weaken Germany to the point of dismembering her. With the first of these objectives Woodrow Wilson was in complete agreement. He was prepared to go further with Clemenceau in pursuit of the second than is generally realised, and at the last he stood against Lloyd George's final effort to secure a more moderate Treaty, a move which he attributed to 'funk'. The conflicts and divisions in his delegation were reflected in the mind and actions of the President.

* See p. 247 above.

President Wilson and his colleagues came to Paris with principles but no plan for applying them, and bearing in their hearts their own passions and concerns. Their coordination was poor, and as a result their policy was not consistent, but that inconsistency also reflected their beliefs and feelings.

### THE BRITISH DELEGATION

The British had been far more closely involved in the events leading up to the First World War than had the Americans. Even so, they had not been involved in the struggles over the Balkans, though Germany's colonial ambitions and the naval race which began with Admiral von Tirpitz's Navy Law of 1898 had concerned them. Like the Americans, therefore, the British approached the peace settlement, and especially the European territorial settlement, with a degree of detachment, and when the British Prime Minister, David Lloyd George, presented British war aims to the Trades Union Congress on 5 January 1918, he too spoke of the need for justice and regard for the wishes of the peoples involved in drawing up the territorial settlement. Above all, no injustice should be done which would give rise to a running sore of the kind created by Germany's seizure of Alsace–Lorraine in 1871 – there must be no new statues of Strasbourg, or anywhere else, in mourning. Later, in his election speeches, he had warned that there were limits to what might be extracted from Germany in the way of reparations, though some of his colleagues were less discreet. These were the pointers to Lloyd George's attitude to the future settlement: above all he wanted a peace which, so far as possible, would not sow the seeds of new wars and would allow the speedy re-establishment of European prosperity.

The chief issue is to what extent Lloyd George's actions were motivated by set objectives with which they were consistent. Keynes believed that Lloyd George had no principles, no objectives at all, that he played the games of politics and diplomacy for their own sakes and for the enjoyment he obtained from them, and that each of his actions was determined solely by the immediate balance of forces, the personalities around him, the possibility of scoring a *coup*. Keynes wrote that

> Lloyd George is rooted in nothing; he is void and without content; he lives and feeds on his immediate surroundings; he is an instrument and a player at the same time which plays on the company

> and is played on by them too; he is a prism, as I have heard him described, which collects light and distorts it and is most brilliant if the light comes from many quarters at once; a vampire and a medium in one.[20]

This portrait of Lloyd George as an unprincipled seducer, his earlier injunction to his readers to 'figure Mr Lloyd George as a *femme fatale*',[21] was the most unfair of his brilliant but cruel portraits of the principal statesmen at Paris and their roles. Lloyd George fought consistently and tenaciously to ensure that no new Alsace–Lorraines, as he himself put it, should be created by the Peace Treaty. For this reason he opposed the separation from Germany of the Rhenish provinces and French annexation of the Saar Valley, while being prepared to grant France what was justly hers – a guarantee of assistance should she once more be attacked, and the ownership of the Saar mines as compensation for the havoc wrought by German troops in the coalfields of north-eastern France. In preparing the Fontainebleau Memorandum, his chief object can be summed up in one sentence taken from it: 'The maintenance of peace will . . . depend upon there being no causes of exasperation constantly stirring up the spirit of patriotism, of justice, and of fair play.'[22] He fought the French wish to include provisions in the Treaty which he believed would inevitably create such causes of exasperation. When the French rejected the arguments of the Fontainebleau Memorandum, he threatened to withdraw his offer of a guarantee for France against aggression.* In the case of the Rhineland, Wilson and Clemenceau reached agreement behind Lloyd George's back. On the Saar Wilson supported him – the only major issue involving German territory where Wilson did not take the French side rather than Lloyd George's.

This policy of seeking a moderate territorial settlement in the interest of a secure peace is seen from another angle when Germany's eastern frontier is considered. Here Lloyd George faced the problem of preventing the new States, and especially Poland, from grabbing too much territory with the encouragement of the French. In the long struggle over the German–Polish frontier he got little help and much obstruction from Wilson, despite repeated appeals to the principle of the self-determination of peoples, of which the President had so often spoken in his war aims speeches. He also had to face the

* See p. 176 above.

Polish Prime Minister, Paderewski, whose emotional obstinacy must have been distressing for all present to behold. Lloyd George became more and more exasperated with the Poles: they were more imperialistic than the Great Powers, and were heading straight for perdition, and he appealed to Paderewski for understanding and support as a man who himself came from a small, oppressed nation and had fought for Welsh freedom and equality in the House of Commons in his political youth.[23] He got nowhere, and the modifications to the Polish settlement which he wrung from the Council of Four had to be imposed on the unwilling Poles.

Equally, however, he was determined that Germany and her rulers should be adequately punished for what they had done. Of the Kaiser he said that an example must be made: 'Whether he is sent to the Falkland Islands or to the island of the Devil matters not at all to me; let us do with him what we wish.'[24] He wanted to admit Germany to the League, but only because he thought it would be easier to keep an eye on her than if she were excluded. Germany must in future be watched – her former rulers must be punished, and vengeance wrought.

In Lloyd George's policy there was a third motive, which often caused him to refuse to agree to extreme actions of revenge – his fear that if the Treaty were too severe Germany might succumb to Bolshevism and might thus constitute a base from which the poison could be spread to the working classes of the rest of Europe. His failure, and that of his colleagues, to find anything effective they could agree to do to crush Russian Bolshevism served only to increase his anxiety that the Germans should not be driven by desperation into its arms. This was another reason for wanting to grant Germany admission to the League, and in the Fontainebleau Memorandum he asked whether admission might not be, for Germany, 'an inducement to sign the terms and to resist Bolshevism?'[25] At this time, Lenin and his colleagues were declaring their intention to spread Bolshevism throughout Europe, by the establishment of the Comintern in March. The Soviet revolutions in Hungary and Bavaria indicated that there was a real danger that, unless the starvation and suffering of Central Europe could quickly be alleviated and its peoples given some hope for the future, Lenin and Trotsky might succeed in their aim. Lloyd George asked the Council of Four later in March, 'If the Germans prefer the dangers of some years' anarchy to thirty-five years' slavery, what shall we do?'[26] For this reason, he sought a moderate reparations demand, but, caught between his fear of Bolshevism and demands from Parliament and public for a huge claim, he was obliged to insist on an indefinite provision in the Treaty. He always insisted, however, that the Commission which was to determine the extent of Germany's liability should take account of Germany's capacity to pay. He fought for this against French opposition, and when word of what he was doing reached the House of Commons he was forced to return home to quell fears and rout his enemies.*

Extremism had its advocates within the British delegation itself, notably in Lord Sumner and Lord Cunliffe, both of whom felt that Germany could and should make restitution for all the damage she had caused. They were supported by the Australian Prime Minister, Hughes, always an advocate of extreme penalties for Germany. Others, notably Keynes, were equally firmly on the side of moderation, and what he believed was the excessive severity of the terms as a whole finally drove Keynes to resignation. The British traditions of the collective responsibility of Ministers and of the loyalty of Civil Servants to Ministers meant that Lloyd George was far better able to coordinate the activities of his colleagues and his staff than was President Wilson, and there were none of the inconsistencies, the sabotaging of one delegate's work by another, that occurred in the American delegation.

Perhaps the biggest strain upon the British delegation was the dispute over the German colonies, which took place at the end of January, when the Dominion Prime Ministers clashed with President Wilson over their desire to be allowed to annex various former German territories of which they were then in possession. Tempers rose high for a time, but Lloyd George devised a compromise acceptable to all concerned. He was caught between an obligation to accede to the ambitions of the Dominions and a desire not to alienate President Wilson too far. In this, as in other issues, Lloyd George sought by compromise to secure the most moderate terms possible, given the circumstances such as public opinion, and the personalities which surrounded him. At the end of the Conference, moved by the German complaints and the comments of many of his colleagues on the severity and injustice of the terms, Lloyd George made a last attempt to moderate the Allies' demands, in which, despite

* See pp. 205–8 above.

Clemenceau's opposition and President Wilson's resentment, he enjoyed some measure of success. He was able to explode his bombshell on 2 June in the knowledge that he had the support of his Cabinet and that its members were bound to go along with him now, however much some of them disagreed with the line he was taking. He obtained the plebiscite in Upper Silesia and other concessions, but not German admission to the League or a shortening or the elimination of the Rhine occupation. He never got Wilson's support for the Keynes plan for the restoration of European credit, for the President's resentment was too deep, especially as Lloyd George felt obliged to insist on maintaining the indefinite reparations settlement, about which the Germans had complained bitterly and for which the Americans wished to substitute a fixed sum.* As the Conference wore on, relations between Wilson and Lloyd George got worse; between Lloyd George and Clemenceau they were seldom good, especially with the constant friction caused by the Anglo–French dispute over Syria.

Lloyd George thus had clear lines of policy, but he was not always able to implement them without making large concessions to other points of view. He made concessions where he thought the Germans would not be mortally offended at some deprivation, where the opposition to his point of view was too great to be overcome, or where his colleagues, his Parliament and the British public would not back his point of view. He was more able to control the activities of his colleagues at Paris, with the result that British actions were outwardly more consistent than American, the only major exceptions being the row over the German colonies and Churchill's intervention in February to urge a large-scale attack on the Bolshevik Government in Russia. In the main, Lloyd George was firmly in control, and was loyally supported by his colleagues. In the secret committee on Germany's frontiers his views were faithfully reflected by Philip Kerr,† and an example of the kind of support he received from his officials is this from Sir Roy Harrod's biography of Keynes:

> There was a very tangled question concerning shipping in the Adriatic, which had to be settled by the Council of Four one afternoon. Over lunch, Keynes and [Dudley] Ward reached the conclusion that they had briefed Lloyd George for the meeting in a

* See pp. 281–7 above.

† See pp. 146–8 above.

> sense diametrically opposed to British interests. They rushed round to the meeting. . . . Keynes . . . took up half a sheet of note-paper on which, having advised Lloyd George to reverse the British demand, he summarised with a brevity Ward would not have believed possible the arguments supporting this change. Keynes passed the paper to Lloyd George, who looked at it quickly and proceeded on the same lines as before. Ward was confirmed in his idea that it was too late to do anything. But gradually, as they listened, a gentle trickle of thought of a new kind began to appear in Lloyd George's pleadings. And then, slowly, as he took plenty of time in making his case, the whole trend was transformed, and he was soon using all Keynes' arguments on the opposite side; he added an admirable one of his own. He carried the day, and Ward is sure that the others did not perceive the change of front. It was the finest example which he ever knew of cooperation between two master minds to achieve what at first seemed quite impossible.[27]

With this kind of support, coupled with the collective responsibility of the Cabinet, Lloyd George was in a strong position, in relation both to his own countrymen and to his colleagues in the Council of Four, since it was unlikely that a colleague would openly attack him or sabotage something he was trying to achieve. British policy thus had a coherence which American policy often conspicuously lacked, even though within the British Empire Delegation disputes were frequent and violent: Keynes' and Nicolson's attempt to 'water down the Austrian financial clauses', when Nicolson was 'told by Sumner to mind my own business';[28] Churchill's efforts to get agreement to invade Bolshevik Russia; the opposition of Hughes, Sumner, Cunliffe, and to some extent even Arthur Balfour, to Lloyd George's desire to press for modifications in the Treaty in June. All these disputes were resolved in secret and never emerged to weaken Lloyd George's position in the Council of Four. Thus from the British traditions of Ministerial responsibility and the Civil Service habit of loyal service to Ministers, whatever their opinions,[29] stemmed the British Delegation's greatest strength – its apparent unity.

### THE FRENCH

To most writers about the Paris Peace Conference, the French position has seemed the simplest. Twice within half a century France had been invaded by Germany. On the first occasion Georges

Clemenceau had been Maire de Montmartre and had witnessed the Prussian siege of Paris in 1870–71; now, in 1919, he was Prime Minister of France, he had controlled her destiny when the victory had been won, and he was her chief representative at the Peace Conference, and its President. With his experience he naturally demanded above all that France should be made secure against a further attack, and in the Fontainebleau Memorandum Lloyd George recognised the justice of this demand. France was entitled to safety.

Many, however, saw Clemenceau as the chief architect of those elements in the Treaty which bore most heavily on Germany and were the greatest affronts to her national pride. Keynes wrote of Clemenceau that 'one could not despise Clemenceau or dislike him but only take a different view as to the nature of civilised man, or indulge, at least, a different hope',[30] and of Clemenceau's attitude to the Fourteen Points Keynes wrote that

> A peace of magnanimity or of fair and equal treatment, based on such 'ideology' as the Fourteen Points of the President, could only have the effect of shortening the interval of Germany's recovery and hastening the day when she will once again hurl at France her greater numbers and her superior resources and technical skill. Hence the necessity of 'guarantees'; and each guarantee that was taken, by increasing irritation and thus the probability of a subsequent *revanche* by Germany, made necessary yet further provisions to crush.[31]

Such a belief was an important motive of Georges Clemenceau's actions at the Conference – indeed, it can be plentifully illustrated from the discussions of the Council of Ten and the Council of Four. Replying to President Wilson's refusal to allow France to seize the Saar because this would be an infringement of the Fourteen Points which would exasperate the Germans, he said that

> It is a mistake to believe that the world is ruled by abstract principles. They are accepted by some people and rejected by others. . . . You want to do justice to the Germans. Do not imagine that they will ever forgive us; they will seek only the chance to obtain revenge.[32]

When Lloyd George sought to modify the proposals made by the expert Commission on Polish Affairs for the German–Polish frontier, Clemenceau reminded him of German persecution of the Poles and demanded that 'to make good the historic crime committed against the Polish nation, we are under an obligation, in bringing that nation back to life, to give her the means of life'.[33] Germany must be punished for all her crimes since at least the accession of Frederick the Great to the throne of Prussia.

Keynes' judgement is over-simplified, however, for Clemenceau had other policy aims which at times overrode his desire to crush the Germans. Speaking of the coming peace negotiations to the Chamber of Deputies at the end of 1918, he said that

> There was an old system, which stands condemned today, and to which I do not fear to say that I remain to some extent faithful at this time: countries organised their defence. It was very prosaic. They tried to have good frontiers. They went armed. It was a terrible burden to all peoples . . . this old system of alliances, which I am not for giving up. I tell you that openly.[34]

Clemenceau's system depended on security and alliances, and one of his main concerns at the Conference was to ensure the maintenance of the association of France, Britain and the United States which had won the war. For this reason, the proposal for a guarantee against aggression which Lloyd George and Wilson made in March was most welcome, and after Lloyd George had dropped his bombshell on 2 June Clemenceau said that his prime objective during the negotiations had been the maintenance of a close alliance between his country, Britain and America. To this end he had made concessions which had exposed him to attack as feeble. If his position were now made impossible and his Government fell, the gap between France and her allies could only widen.* On the issue of reparations, on this same occasion, Clemenceau said that

> France is the country which has suffered most of all from the war, and today her people are convinced that we are not demanding enough from Germany. . . . I am convinced that we have done what is reasonable but if I retreat even one step further I know that I will arouse a general revolt against myself.[35]

Clemenceau had made concessions of which few of his compatriots approved; even he could not go much further, or his Government

* See p. 274 above.

would fall, and it could only be replaced by one determined to be more severe with the Germans, whether or not this led to a rupture of the wartime alliance.

The attitude of many of his colleagues became clear in the negotiations over the Rhineland. Marshal Foch obstinately insisted that a frontier on the Rhine was the only sure guarantee of safety for France – any substitute must mean a devastating invasion, even if help eventually arrived with which the invader's forces could be thrown back. Again and again, he spoke of the need for '*une garantie d'orde physique*'.[36] Others agreed: Tardieu made the significant remark in the Committee of Three which sat on 11 and 12 March to consider the frontiers of Germany, and spent all its time discussing the Rhenish provinces,* that 'M. Clemenceau was the only man who could carry a moderate peace in France, but . . . it would be impossible for any French Government to leave France open to the same kind of attack as she had endured in 1914'.[37] Clemenceau in France, like Lloyd George in England, was strengthened by the enormous prestige of being the man who won the war, and no-one else, lacking that prestige, would have dared to go as far in the direction of compromise as he did. When, in the end, he compromised to the extent of agreeing to only a temporary occupation of the Rhenish provinces, because he believed the maintenance of the Alliance and securing the Anglo-American Guarantee against aggression were more important, he was bitterly rebuked by President Poincaré for failing adequately to protect the interests of France – 'the precious assistance which our friends will give us if we again suffer a German attack cannot, alas, arrive instantaneously. . . . It cannot, therefore, be seen as a replacement for the occupation.'[38] There was no love lost between Poincaré and Clemenceau anyway, and it was at the time of Poincaré's complaint, in late April, that Clemenceau whispered to Lloyd George, 'I wish you would lend me your George V!'[39] On this occasion, Poincaré was not alone: when Clemenceau presented the Treaty to the Chamber of Deputies, a young Socialist, on the opposite political wing to Poincaré, Vincent Auriol, cried: '*Garanties de paiement, ou de solidarité. . . . Ou sont-ils? Vous dites: garanties: moi, je dis: Incertitudes!*'[40] It took all Clemenceau's skill and prestige to carry a Treaty which fell so far short of satisfying the ambitions or allaying the fears of his country-

* See pp. 146–8 above.

men. Clemenceau, like Lloyd George, took great political risks in the interest of moderation.

The same was true for reparations. For Clemenceau, as for Lloyd George, the indeterminate settlement was a way of escape from an inflamed Parliamentary and public opinion without closing the door on moderation. Here too Clemenceau was more moderate than his colleagues. His Finance Minister, Klotz, again and again expressed his determination that the Germans should pay for all the damage they had caused – 'We only want what is due to us. What is not debatable is that the Germans owe us reparations,' he told the Council of Four at the end of March[41] – and he tried to resist proposals to limit the extent of Germany's liability to what she was capable of paying in thirty years; she should pay it all, however long it took: 'What is due is due, and the Commission shall not have the right to declare that Germany shall pay less.'[42] In the end, however, Clemenceau accepted a text which would allow the Permanent Commission on Reparations to take account of Germany's capacity to pay, despite the intransigence of his colleagues, 'in a spirit of conciliation'.[43] Once again, Clemenceau was more concerned with maintaining the unity of the Allies than with getting everything France wanted.

On other issues he stood firm, however. He would not agree to Germany's admission to the League of Nations, declaring that, in view of public and Parliamentary opinion in France, he dared not, and in any case he had President Wilson's backing. Lloyd George was alone in seeking her admission, and he gave in at the last: 'I understand M. Clemenceau's objection and the public feeling which it reflects.'[44] Clemenceau was the most moderate of Frenchmen in the discussions of the peace terms, but even he could and would only go so far. There were concessions he was not prepared to make even for the sake of the alliance.

The alliance with Britain and America was not, of course, the only alliance which Clemenceau was concerned to maintain and foster. With Russia in chaos and not to be relied upon in the forseeable future, there was an urgent need to ensure that the new states of Eastern Europe, especially Poland and Czechoslovakia, remained friends of France and enemies of Germany, both to create a military presence on Germany's eastern frontier and to act as a barrier to Russo-German collusion. To this end Clemenceau and France supported the territorial demands of these states, both to secure their friendship and, by giving them German territory, to ensure that they would remain in a state of hostility with Germany.* So it was that the greed of the Poles, to which Lloyd George took such violent objection, received support and encouragement from the French. Foch and Clemenceau urged Allied assistance for the Poles in the early months of the Conference, against British unwillingness arising from their suspicions of Polish motives, and later Clemenceau supported the Polish territorial claims, speaking often of German oppression and persecution of the Poles over the centuries. It was necessary for Poland to be able to defend herself against those who had killed and tortured her people in the past and would inevitably do so again if given the chance. Clemenceau was equally determined not to permit Germany to be strengthened by the addition to her numbers of the Germans of Austria and Bohemia. At the end of the Conference, he was able to resist many of Lloyd George's demands for modifications to the Treaty with President Wilson's assistance. Towards the end he appealed to his colleagues that he could not go too far in making concessions:

> You ask me: Why this obstruction? I cannot act otherwise. Our birthrate is low. We have lost a million men. France's first need is security. . . . I do not want to do anything that will destroy the spirit of our people.[45]

Clemenceau was sceptical about the extent of the change the League of Nations would bring in international relations, for, above all, Germany would remain a dangerous and treacherous neighbour, stronger than France. He had made concessions to maintain the wartime alliance, and within those concessions he sought as far as possible to guarantee his country's future safety. In that he had the support of all his countrymen, but many of them believed that he had conceded too much. Georges Clemenceau, so often painted as the seeker after a Carthaginian peace of vengeance and destruction, went further in preparing a moderate settlement than any other Frenchman would have dared or wished to go.

These, then, were the chief makers of peace: President Wilson, torn between his ideals and his hatred of Germany; Lloyd George, with his belief that moderation was the only way to secure lasting peace;

* See p. 11 above.

and Clemenceau, wanting vengeance, but wanting the continuation of the wartime alliance still more. In the end, these three men had to make the peace, because no-one other than heads of Governments could take the responsibility of making the compromises necessary if agreement was to be reached. The arguments, the discussions, the deadlock could not go on indefinitely, with millions in Central and Eastern Europe starving and an easy prey for Bolshevism; with chaos in Russia, with the Allied troops anxious to be demobilised and return to their homes, families and jobs. Someone had to take the responsibility for dropping the French demand for the permanent annexation of the Rhineland; for agreeing that the demand for reparations must be limited to Germany's capacity to pay; for refusing the fulfilment of many of the aspirations of the smaller Allied Powers; for deciding not to try the Kaiser on a charge of starting the war, and so on, and it was to take this responsibility that the Council of Four was brought into being. That above all, but also to put an end to the leaks to the Press that were a perpetual source of trouble in the Council of Ten. The essential compromises could only be made in the greatest secrecy, free from the pressures of Parliaments and public opinion, who must not have any inkling of what was going on – when rumours about reparations reached the House of Commons the result was the 'Round Robin' telegram to Lloyd George which was finally signed by the vast majority of his coalition supporters. The Council of Four was able to take effective decisions, despite the rows which occurred from time to time and the constant discord between Lloyd George and Clemenceau caused by their suspicions of one another over Syria. Three men made the peace, and their beliefs, ambitions and desires, and the interaction of their personalities, made the Treaty what it was: a mixture of revenge and appeasement, of brutality and consideration, of the Fourteen Points and demands for the destruction of the Germans and all their works. The settlement was more moderate than Clemenceau wished, and certainly than his colleagues and countrymen wished, but more severe than Lloyd George thought desirable. As for what President Wilson wanted, it is almost impossible to say, so inconsistent were his words and his actions. Certainly he was in no way bamboozled, and where his principles were used as a cloak for injustice and oppression this was done with his knowledge and often with his encouragement. He too wanted severity, and his principles were for use chiefly where the villainous Germans were not involved. In any case, the League of Nations was a cure-all for the future, and that helped to set his mind and his conscience at rest.

Only two further points remain to be made. First, Bolshevism was an important background factor, increasing the urgency of making peace, both so that Allied troops could be free for use in Russia if need be and, far more important, so that relief could be given to the hungry peoples of Europe. The Conference could never agree, however, on a course of action in Russia. Too many conflicting desires existed for agreement to be possible. No-one at Paris liked the Bolshevik Government much, but many of the statesmen were even less willing to support a reactionary Government which would restore autocracy and deprive the people of Russia of land and civil rights. Most of the statesmen at Paris were liberals who wanted to see the creation of a democratic government in Russia. In any case, they believed that ultimately the government of Russia was a matter for Russians, and if the people supported Lenin then the Allies could not legitimately overthrow him. Finally, the Allies not unnaturally wished to back the winner in order to gain his friendship and subsequent cooperation – hence their enthusiasm for the 'White' cause ebbed and flowed with the tide of their military successes or failures. With such uncertainty, the Allies had first tried to mediate at Prinkipo, and then, after the failure of that initiative, they had been paralysed by indecision, coming in May to the point of recognising Admiral Kolchak's government as the government of Russia when his troops were advancing, holding back because of doubts about his political and social beliefs and motives, and withdrawing when the Red Army turned the tide of battle against him. The Allies never took sides effectively in the Russian Civil War, and Bolshevism was only one among their many preoccupations.

Secondly, there is the question of whether the Treaty of Versailles was the product of the forces of History or of the thought and actions of individuals.

Throughout the century before Versailles, controversy had raged between those, like Hegel and Thomas Carlyle, who believed that the major turning-points of History were brought about by the actions of individuals, world-historical figures or heroes, and those like Karl Marx and Leo Tolstoy, who believed that free will and the apparent influence of thoughts and actions of individuals are illusory, and that decisions are really made by the clash of economic and social forces with which all men are swept along. The making of the Treaty of

Versailles was undeniably a major turning-point in History – by it the Europe of the eighteenth and nineteenth centuries was largely swept away and replaced by the world of the twentieth century, complete with the Third World, international arbitration, and nation states. The Treaty was the result partly of circumstances – the Allied victory, war-weariness, economic chaos and the threat of Bolshevism – but it was the work, ultimately, of three men. It is easy to forget, in these days when almost every major diplomatic dispute, move, or even armed conflict is expected to culminate in a 'summit' meeting between Heads of Governments, how novel was the procedure of the Council of Four, but it was essential, and from the personalities and attitudes of those three men emerged a settlement which affected most of the world, and indeed reshaped it. In this case, individual men were indeed the deciders of the world's destiny.

# Bibliographical References

# *Bibliographical References*


CHAPTER I.

1. *The Economic Consequences of the Peace* (London 1919. Hereafter cited as *E.C.P.*)
2. Ibid., p. 138.
3. Ibid., p. 26.
4. Ibid., p. 29.
5. Ibid., p. 46.
6. J. M. Keynes, *Essays in Biography* (Mercury Paper edition, London 1961), pp. 35–6.
7. Ibid., p. 34.
8. *E.C.P.*, pp. 40–2.
9. Keynes, *Essays in Biography*, p. 36.
10. Sir H. Nicolson, *Peacemaking, 1919* (University Paperback edition, London 1964), pp. 197–9.
11. *Encounter*, 1967, pp. 3–4.
12. Quoted in H. I. Nelson, *Land and Power* (London 1963), p. 326.
13. Ibid., p. 137.
14. A. J. Mayer, *The Politics and Diplomacy of Peacemaking* (London 1968).
15. For an effective selection, see A. J. P. Taylor, *The First World War: An Illustrated History* (London 1963).
16. D. Lloyd George, *The Truth about the Peace Treaties* (London 1938, hereafter cited as Lloyd George, *Truth*), Vol. I, pp. 466–7.
17. A. J. P. Taylor, *English History, 1914–1945* (London 1965), p. 129.

18. H. M. Pelling, *Social Geography of British Elections, 1885–1910* (London 1967), Chapter 1.
19. See R. Storry, *A History of Modern Japan* (London 1960), p. 151f., for details.
20. Ibid., p. 162. For the British guarantee see also *Documents on British Foreign Policy, 1919–1939* (London 1947, still appearing, hereafter cited as *D.B.F.P.*), First Series, Vol. VI, pp. 562–3.
21. *Papers Respecting Negotiations for an Anglo-French Pact*, Cmd 2169, hereafter cited by Command No. (London 1924), p. 2.
22. Ibid., pp. 5–8.
23. Ibid., p. 6.
24. Ibid., p. 7.
25. Ibid., pp. 3–4.
26. 19 December 1919. House of Commons *Debates:* Official Record, 5th Series, Vol. 100, col. 2017.
27. For a fascinating and detailed account of the *Revolutionierungspolitik*, see G. Katkov, *The February Revolution* (London 1967).
28. G. Clemenceau, *Grandeur and Misery of a Victory* (London 1930), pp. 190–2.
29. P. S. Wandycz, *France and her Eastern Allies* (Minneapolis 1962), pp. 11–14.
30. Ibid., p. 22.
31. Ibid., p. 14.
32. Lloyd George, *Truth*, Vol. II, pp. 925–6.
33. Sir H. Temperley, *History of the Peace Conference of Paris* (London 1920), Vol. V, p. 395.
34. Ibid., pp. 396–7.
35. Cabinet Papers: Public Record Office, GT Series, CAB 24, Vol. 67, No. 6050.
36. Ibid., Vol. 69, No. 6021.
37. Ibid., No. 6195.
38. Lloyd George, *Truth*, Vol. I, pp. 605–15.
39. Ibid., p. 606.
40. Quoted in L. E. Gelfand, *The Inquiry: American Preparations for Peace, 1917–1919* (New Haven, Connecticut and London 1963), p. 20.
41. Ibid., Chapter 1.
42. *Foreign Relations of the United States: The Paris Peace Conference, 1919* (13 volumes, Washington 1943–7, hereafter referred to as *P.P.C.*), Vol. I, p. 53.

43. Lloyd George, *Truth*, Vol. I, pp. 611–15.
44. D. Lloyd George, *War Memoirs* (London 1936), Vol. V, p. 2520.
45. Ibid., p. 2521.
46. Loc. cit.
47. Ibid., p. 2522.
48. Ibid., p. 2524.
49. Nicolson, op. cit., pp. 31–2.
50. *E.C.P.*, p. 34.
51. Ibid., p. 35.
52. Temperley, op. cit., Vol. I. Appendix I contains the texts of President Wilson's peace aims speeches. Quotation at p. 433.
53. A. J. P. Taylor, *The First World War*, pp. 161–3.
54. Temperley, op. cit., Vol. I, p. 441.
55. Ibid., p. 444.
56. Ibid., p. 446.
57. Loc. cit.
58. Ibid., p. 445.

CHAPTER 2.

1. A. J. Balfour Papers: Public Record Office, F.O. 800, Vol. 200, p. 147.
2. Ibid., p. 152.
3. Ibid., pp. 154–6.
4. Cabinet Minutes: Public Record Office, CAB 23, Vol. 14, No. 479A, Minute 1.
5. Cabinet Papers: Public Record Office, GT Series, CAB 24, Vol. 65, No. 5815.
6. Ibid., No. 5842.
7. Ibid., Vol. 66, No. 5950.
8. Cabinet Minutes: Public Record Office, CAB 23, Vol. 14, No. 482A, Minute 8.
9. Temperley, op. cit., Vol. I, pp. 448–9.
10. Ibid., p. 449.
11. Ibid., p. 450.
12. Colonel Repington, *The First World War, 1914–1918* (London 1920), Vol. II, p. 459.
13. Lord Hankey, *The Supreme Command* (London 1961), Vol. II, p. 850.

14. Cabinet Papers: Public Record Office, GT Series, CAB 24, Vol. 67, No. 6012.
15. Temperley, op. cit., Vol. I, pp. 450–1.
16. Cabinet Papers: Public Record Office, GT Series, CAB 24, Vol. 66, No. 5967.
17. Lloyd George Papers: Beaverbrook Library F/18/2/23.
18. Temperley, op. cit., Vol. I, pp. 451–2.
19. Ibid., pp. 452–3.
20. Lord Derby (British Ambassador in Paris) to A. J. Balfour, 17 October 1918. A. J. Balfour Papers, British Museum Add. MSS, Vol. 49744, p. 64.
21. Lloyd George Papers: Beaverbrook Library F/6/5/41.
22. Balfour Papers: British Museum Add. MSS, Vol. 49738, p. 232.
23. Balfour Papers: Public Record Office, F.O. 800, Vol. 202, pp. 320–2.
24. Balfour Papers: British Museum Add. MSS, Vol. 49738, p. 233.
25. Balfour Papers: Public Record Office, F.O. 800, Vol. 206, pp. 350–2.
26. Ibid., p. 354.
27. C. Seymour, *The Intimate Papers of Colonel House* (London 1928, hereafter referred to as *Intimate Papers*), Vol. IV, p. 87.
28. Ibid., p. 88.
29. Lloyd George Papers: Beaverbrook Library F/6/5/42.
30. Cabinet Papers: Public Record Office, GT Series, CAB 24, Vol. 67, No. 6018.
31. Temperley, op. cit., Vol. I, pp. 452–3.
32. Ibid., pp. 453–4.
33. Ibid., pp. 454–6.
34. Cabinet Papers: Public Record Office, GT Series, CAB 24, Vol. 67, No. 6068.
35. Ibid., No. 6069.
36. Cabinet Minutes: Public Record Office, CAB 23, Vol. 14, No. 489, Minute 3.
37. Ibid., No. 491A, Minute 2.
38. Ibid., No. 489B, Minute 2.
39. Ibid., Minute 1.
40. Ibid., No. 491A, Minute 5.
41. Ibid., Minute 6.

42. Temperley, op. cit., Vol. I, p. 456.
43. *Intimate Papers*, Vol. IV, p. 159.
44. Ibid.
45. *P.P.C.*, Vol. I, p. 285.
46. Colonel Repington, op. cit., Vol. II, p. 459.
47. *Intimate Papers*, Vol. IV, p. 167.
48. Lord Hankey, op. cit., Vol. II, p. 859.
49. *Intimate Papers*, Vol. IV, p. 168.
50. Ibid., p. 171.
51. See J. R. M. Butler, *Lord Lothian* (London 1960), pp. 72–3, on this point.
52. Hankey, op. cit., p. 862.
53. Cmd 2169, p. 9.
54. Butler, op. cit., pp. 72–3.
55. Temperley, op. cit., Vol. I, pp. 437–8.
56. Taylor, *The First World War*, p. 190.
57. Repington, op. cit., Vol. II, p. 474.
58. Cabinet Papers: Public Record Office, GT Series, CAB 24, Vol. 69, No. 6227.
59. Taylor, *The First World War*, p. 190.
60. Cabinet Papers: Public Record Office, GT Series, CAB 24, Vol. 69, No. 6265.
61. Balfour Papers: Public Record Office, F.O. 800, Vol. 200, pp. 153–4.
62. *P.P.C.*, Vol. XII, p. 784.
63. Cabinet Minutes: Public Record Office, CAB 23, Vol. 14, No. 500A.
64. Temperley, op. cit., Vol. I, pp. 459–76.
65. *P.P.C.*, Vol. I, p. 1.
66. Loc. cit.
67. Temperley, op. cit., Vol. I, p. 476.
68. Lloyd George Papers: Beaverbrook Library F/11/9/22. The text of this letter is somewhat uncertain, as Lord Curzon's handwriting is almost completely illegible.

CHAPTER 3.

1. Cabinet Papers: Public Record Office, GT Series, CAB 24, Vol. 69, No. 6269.
2. Ibid., No. 6201.

3. Ibid., Vol. 67, No. 6050.
4. Ibid., Vol. 70, No. 6311.
5. Ibid., No. 6302.
6. *P.P.C.*, Vol. I, p. 269.
7. Ibid., p. 270.
8. Ibid., pp. 130–1.
9. Ibid., pp. 134–5.
10. Ibid., p. 135.
11. Ibid., p. 132.
12. Balfour Papers: British Museum Add. MSS, Vol. 49744, pp. 123–8.
13. Quoted in V. S. Mamatey, *The United States and East Central Europe, 1914–1919* (Princeton, New Jersey, 1957), p. 361n.
14. Balfour Papers: Public Record Office, F.O. 800, Vol. 203, pp. 153–5.
15. Cabinet Papers: Public Record Office, GT Series, CAB 24, Vol. 70, No. 6337.
16. Ibid., Nos 6353–7.
17. Lloyd George, *Truth*, Vol. I, p. 94.
18. *P.P.C.*, Vol. I, pp. 303–4.
19. Ibid., p. 354.
20. Ibid., p. 490.
21. Cmd 2169, p. 10.
22. Cabinet Papers: Public Record Office, GT Series, CAB 24, Vol. 71, No. 6411.
23. Lloyd George Papers: Beaverbrook Library F/3/3/45.
24. *P.P.C.*, Vol. I, pp. 334–8.
25. Ibid., p. 339.
26. Ibid., pp. 340–2.
27. Ibid., p. 339.
28. Ibid., Vol. II, pp. 72–3.
29. Ibid., p. 73.
30. Ibid., p. 74.
31. Ibid., Vol. I, pp. 277–8.
32. Ibid., Vol. II, p. 582.
33. Ibid., p. 582f.
34. Ibid., Vol. I, p. 370.
35. Lloyd George, *Truth*, Vol. I, p. 320.
36. Ibid., p. 321.
37. Temperley, op. cit., Vol. I, p. 476.

38. Gelfand, op. cit., p. 171.
39. *Intimate Papers*, Vol. IV, pp. 291–4.
40. Gelfand, op. cit., pp. 173–4.
41. Keynes, *Essays in Biography*, p. 17.
42. See, for example, Cabinet Papers: Public Record Office, GT Series, CAB 24, Vol. 72, No. 6520.
43. Lord Curzon, a former Viceroy of India, was one. See ibid., Vol. 67, No. 6062.
44. Ibid., Vol. 71, No. 6507.
45. Balfour Papers: British Museum Add. MSS, Vol. 49744, pp. 184–90.
46. *P.P.C.*, Vol. II, pp. 326–7.
47. Ibid., Vol. I, pp. 294–6.
48. Ibid., pp. 296–7.
49. Keynes, *Essays in Biography*, p. 24.
50. Balfour Papers: British Museum Add. MSS, Vol. 49744, pp. 197–8.
51. Ibid., pp. 195–6.
52. *P.P.C.*, Vol. I, pp. 149–50. I am indebted to Professor Mayer's book at this point, although he underestimates the extent to which Clemenceau thought he had taken Wilson's measure.
53. Balfour Papers: British Museum Add. MSS, Vol. 49744, pp. 205–8.
54. Ibid., pp. 217–19.
55. Ibid., pp. 220–1.
56. Temperley, op. cit., Vol. III, pp. 52–3.
57. Cabinet Papers: Public Record Office, GT Series, CAB 24, Vol. 72, Nos 6549, 6550.
58. Ibid., Vol. 71, No. 6506.
59. Ibid., Vol. 72, No. 6508.
60. Quoted in P. S. Wandycz, op. cit., p. 14.
61. Loc. cit.
62. Lloyd George, *Truth*, Vol. I, pp. 324–30.
63. *P.P.C.*, Vol. I, pp. 585–6.
64. Ibid., p. 297.
65. Ibid., p. 300.
66. Balfour Papers: British Museum Add. MSS, Vol. 49744, pp. 228–32.
67. Balfour Papers: Public Record Office, F.O. 800, Vol. 203, pp. 242–3.

68. *P.P.C.*, Vol. I, pp. 487–8.
69. Lloyd George Papers: Beaverbrook Library F/3/4/2.
70. *P.P.C.*, Vol. I, pp. 381–5.
71. Cmd 2169, pp. 11–15.
72. Cabinet Papers: Public Record Office, GT Series, CAB 24, Vol. 74, No. 6757.

CHAPTER 4.

1. Cabinet Minutes: Public Record Office, CAB 23, Vol. 9, No. 515. Minute 5.
2. *P.P.C.*, Vol. III, p. 471.
3. Ibid., pp. 490–1.
4. Ibid., p. 491.
5. Foreign Office Papers, Public Record Office, F.O. 800, Vol. 153, No. 9.
6. Cabinet Papers: Public Record Office, CAB 29, Vol. 28, No. B.E.D. 1. (This volume contains the minutes of the meetings of the British Delegation during the Conference.)
7. *P.P.C.*, Vol. III, p. 533.
8. Lloyd George Papers: Beaverbrook Library F/8/3/2.
9. Cabinet Papers: Public Record Office, GT Series, CAB 24, Vol. 72, No. 6550.
10. *P.P.C.*, Vol. III, pp. 606–7.
11. Ibid., pp. 581–3.
12. Ibid., pp. 583–4.
13. Ibid., p. 584.
14. Ibid., p. 575.
15. Ibid., pp. 618–9.
16. Ibid., p. 164.
17. Lloyd George Papers: Beaverbrook Library F/3/4/7.
18. *P.P.C.*, Vol. III, pp. 623–6.
19. Cabinet Papers: Public Record Office, CAB 29, Vol. 28, No. B.E.D. 2.
20. *P.P.C.*, Vol. III, p. 635.
21. Ibid., p. 648.
22. Loc. cit.
23. Ibid., p. 649.
24. Ibid., p. 671.

25. J. Degras, *The Communist International: Documents* (London 1951), Vol. I, p. 3.
26. *P.P.C.*, Vol. III, p. 649.
27. Ibid., p. 642.
28. Ibid., pp. 670–1.
29. Ibid., p. 672.
30. Ibid., p. 673.
31. Ibid., p. 674.
32. Loc. cit.
33. Loc. cit.
34. Cabinet Papers: Public Record Office, CAB 29, Vol. 28, No. B.E.D. 3, Minute 9.
35. Ibid., Minute 10.
36. Lloyd George Papers: Beaverbrook Library F/45/9/28.
37. *P.P.C.*, Vol. III, pp. 718–19.
38. Ibid., pp. 721–2.
39. Ibid., pp. 722–3.
40. Ibid., p. 727.
41. Ibid., pp. 735–8.
42. Ibid., p. 741.
43. Ibid., p. 742.
44. Ibid., p. 745.
45. Ibid., p. 749.
46. Balfour Papers: Public Record Office, F.O. 800, Vol. 216, p. 138.
47. Cabinet Papers: Public Record Office, CAB 29, Vol. 28, No. B.E.D. 4.
48. Ibid., No. B.E.D. 5.
49. *P.P.C.*, Vol. III, pp. 765–6.
50. *Intimate Papers*, Vol. IV, pp. 308–9.
51. Lloyd George, *Truth*, Vol. I, p. 542, and Lord Hankey, *The Supreme Control at the Paris Peace Conference* (London 1963), p. 61. Neither of these sources establishes exactly when this incident took place, but the official minutes of the Council of Ten show that the most acrimonious discussion between Wilson and the Dominion Prime Ministers took place on the afternoon of 28 January, and this exchange probably took place during this meeting. The official minutes were a detailed but not completely *verbatim* record of the discussion.
52. *P.P.C.*, Vol. III, p. 786.

53. Loc. cit.
54. Ibid., p. 787.
55. Ibid., p. 801.
56. Ibid., p. 803.
57. Ibid., pp. 803–13.
58. Ibid., pp. 653–4, 677–82.
59. Ibid., pp. 682–3.
60. Ibid., p. 699.
61. Ibid., pp. 178–9.
62. Ibid., p. 182.
63. Ibid., p. 185.

CHAPTER 5.

1. House of Commons Debates, Official Record, 5th Series, Vol. 114, col. 2936.
2. Ibid., cols 2937–8.
3. Nicolson, op. cit., pp. 153–4.
4. Ibid., p. 188.
5. Ibid., p. 337.
6. Balfour Papers: British Museum Add. MSS, Vol. 49692, pp. 238–9.
7. Balfour Papers: Public Record Office, F.O. 800, Vol. 216, pp. 107–10.
8. Lloyd George Papers: Beaverbrook Library F/5/3/2.
9. Nicolson, op. cit., p. 142.
10. Cabinet Papers: Public Record Office, GT Series, Vol. 75, No. 6822.
11. I am indebted to Miss Elizabeth Dunn, of the University of Hull, for this information.
12. D. H. Miller, *The Drafting of the Covenant* (New York 1928), Vol. II, p. 229ff.
13. Ibid., p. 257.
14. Ibid., pp. 257–8.
15. Ibid., pp. 260–1.
16. Ibid., Vol. I, p. 164.
17. Ibid., p. 165.
18. Ibid., p. 167.
19. Ibid., p. 165.
20. Ibid., Vol. II, p. 278.

21. Ibid., pp. 263–8.
22. Ibid., pp. 268–9.
23. Lloyd George Papers: Beaverbrook Library F/6/6/8.
24. Miller, op. cit., Vol. II, pp. 272–3.
25. Ibid., pp. 278–9.
26. Ibid., p. 292.
27. Ibid., p. 294.
28. Ibid., pp. 296–7.
29. Ibid., p. 297.
30. Ibid., p. 299.
31. Loc. cit.
32. Ibid., p. 318.
33. Ibid., p. 320.
34. *P.P.C.*, Vol. III, pp. 212–13.
35. Ibid., p. 215.
36. Ibid., p. 222.
37. Lloyd George Papers: Beaverbrook Library F/8/3/7.
38. Ibid.
39. Ibid., F/8/3/8.
40. *P.P.C.*, Vol. III, pp. 635–6.
41. Cabinet Minutes: Public Record Office, CAB 23, Vol. 15, No. 532A.
42. Cabinet Papers: Public Record Office, GT Series, CAB 24, Vol. 75, No. 6808.
43. Ibid., No. 6861.
44. *P.P.C.*, Vol. III, p. 1042.
45. Loc. cit.
46. Ibid., p. 1043.
47. Ibid., Vol. IV, p. 13.
48. Ibid., pp. 16–17.
49. Cabinet Papers: Public Record Office, GT Series, CAB 24, Vol. 75, No. 6805.
50. Ibid., No. 6848.
51. Lloyd George Papers: Beaverbrook Library F/8/3/16.
52. Ibid., F/8/3/18. Also Lloyd George, *Truth*, Vol. I, pp. 371–2.
53. Balfour Papers: Public Record Office, F.O. 800, Vol. 216, p. 224.
54. Lloyd George Papers: Beaverbrook Library F/8/3/17.
55. Cabinet Papers: Public Record Office, CAB 29, Vol. 28, No. B.E.D. 8.

56. Foreign Office Papers: Public Record Office, F.O. 418, Vol. 53, No. 7.
57. Cabinet Papers: Public Record Office, GT Series, CAB 24, Vol. 76, No. 6935.
58. Repington, op. cit., Vol. II, pp. 498–9.
59. *P.P.C.*, Vol. III, pp. 774 and 779.
60. Ibid., p. 774.
61. Ibid., p. 775.
62. Ibid., p. 776.
63. Ibid., p. 780.
64. Ibid., p. 782.
65. Ibid., p. 877.
66. Ibid., p. 878.
67. Ibid., p. 879.
68. Ibid., p. 880.
69. Ibid., p. 881.
70. Ibid., p. 887.
71. Ibid., p. 903.
72. Ibid., p. 915.
73. Ibid., p. 904.
74. Ibid., p. 905.
75. Ibid., pp. 932–3.
76. Ibid., pp. 982–3.
77. Ibid., pp. 987–8.
78. Temperley, op. cit., Vol. I, p. 480.
79. *P.P.C.*, Vol. III, pp. 1007, 1014.
80. See W. M. Jordan, *Britain, France and the German Question* (London 1943), p. 37ff, and Mayer, op. cit., p. 179ff.
81. Cabinet Papers: Public Record Office, GT Series, CAB 24, Vol. 75, No. 6868.
82. *P.P.C.*, Vol. IV, p. 21.
83. Ibid., pp. 38–9.
84. Ibid., p. 25.
85. Ibid., pp. 104–7.
86. Ibid., p. 123.
87. Ibid., pp. 139–41.
88. *Intimate Papers*, Vol. IV, p. 344.
89. Ibid., p. 346.
90. Ibid., p. 345.
91. Ibid., p. 456.

92. Ibid., pp. 356–8.
93. Balfour Papers: British Museum Add. MSS, Vol. 49750, pp. 110–14.
94. Cmd 2169, p. 25.
95. Ibid., p. 32.
96. Ibid., pp. 36–7.
97. Ibid., p. 40.
98. Cabinet Minutes: Public Record Office, CAB 23, Vol. 15, No. 538A.
99. Balfour Papers: British Museum Add. MSS, Vol. 49734, p. 65.
100. Lothian Papers: Scottish Record Office, GD 40/17, No. 65.
101. See Cabinet Papers, Public Record Office, GT Series, CAB 24, Vol. 69, No. 6213, for examples of the arguments being advanced in Belgium for and against neutrality. The summary of these arguments which follows was based on this document.
102. Balfour Papers: British Museum Add. MSS, Vol. 49750, pp. 45–7.
103. *P.P.C.*, Vol. III, p. 959.
104. Ibid., p. 967.
105. Ibid., p. 968.
106. Ibid., p. 969.
107. Ibid., pp. 1006–7, 1014.
108. Balfour Papers: British Museum Add. MSS, Vol. 49750, pp. 110–14.
109. *P.P.C.*, Vol. IV, p. 195.
110. Balfour Papers: British Museum Add. MSS, Vol. 49750, pp. 48–52.
111. R. C. K. Ensor, *England, 1870–1914* (London 1936), pp. 244–5.
112. Ibid., pp. 366–9.
113. Balfour Papers: Public Record Office, F.O. 800, Vol. 216, pp. 156–9.
114. Jukka Nevakivi, *Britain, France and the Arab Middle East, 1914–20* (London 1969), p. 126. This monograph is essential reading for those concerned with the history or politics of this area in this period.
115. *P.P.C.*, Vol. III, p. 890.
116. Ibid., p. 1017. Dr Howard S. Bliss was President of the Syrian Protestant College in Beirut, and had been invited to Paris by the American Delegation. See Nevakivi, op. cit., p. 131.

117. *P.P.C.*, Vol. III, p. 1029.
118. Ibid., p. 1031.
119. Ibid., Vol. IV, pp. 2–5.
120. Foreign Office Papers: Public Record Office, F.O. 406, Vol. 41, No. 12.
121. Ibid., No. 17.
122. Ibid., No. 25.
123. Curzon Papers: Public Record Office, F.O. 800, Vol. 153, pp. 202–7.
124. For another example of this involving Lord Curzon, see Lord Beaverbrook, *The Decline and Fall of Lloyd George* (London 1963), pp. 251–2.
125. *P.P.C.*, Vol. IV, p. 162.
126. Lloyd George Papers: Beaverbrook Library F/3/4/18.
127. Nevakivi, op. cit., p. 135ff.
128. Cabinet Papers: Public Record Office, GT Series, CAB 24, Vol. 74, No. 6764.
129. *P.P.C.*, Vol. IV, pp. 44–53.
130. Ibid., p. 54.
131. Loc. cit.
132. Ibid., p. 85.
133. Ibid., p. 87.
134. Ibid., p. 89.
135. Ibid., pp. 89–90.
136. Ibid., Vol. XI, p. 72.
137. Ibid., pp. 77–8.
138. Ibid., p. 115.
139. Foreign Office Papers: Public Record Office, F.O. 425, Vol. 383, No. 3.
140. Ibid., F.O. 421, Vol. 297, No. 13.
141. Lloyd George, *Truth*, Vol. II, p. 293.
142. Ibid., p. 294.
143. *P.P.C.*, Vol. IV, p. 321.
144. Ibid., p. 322.
145. Ibid., p. 323.
146. Ibid., p. 325.
147. Ibid., Vol. III, pp. 735–7.
148. Ibid., pp. 738–40.
149. Ibid., p. 755.
150. Loc. cit.

151. Ibid., p. 756.
152. Loc. cit.

CHAPTER 6.

1. *P.P.C.*, Vol. III, p. 953.
2. Ibid., p. 954.
3. Cabinet Papers: Public Record Office, GT Series, CAB 24, Vol. 74, No. 6778.
4. Ibid., Vol. 75, No. 6822.
5. Balfour Papers: Public Record Office, F.O. 800, Vol. 216, pp. 250–3.
6. Lothian Papers: Scottish Record Office, GD40/17, Vol. 64.
7. A. Tardieu: *The Truth about the Treaty* (London 1921), pp. 286–7.
8. Ibid., pp. 287–8.
9. *Intimate Papers*, Vol. IV, p. 354.
10. *P.P.C.*, Vol. XI, p. 73.
11. Loc. cit.
12. *Intimate Papers*, Vol. IV, p. 360.
13. Ibid., p. 354.
14. Ibid., p. 372.
15. Lloyd George Papers: Beaverbrook Library F/40/2/38.
16. Ibid., F/30/3/27.
17. Lothian Papers: Scottish Record Office, GD40/17, Vol. 64.
18. *Intimate Papers*, Vol. IV, p. 368.
19. Balfour to Kerr, 10 March 1919. Lothian Papers, Scottish Record Office, GD40/17, Vol. 64.
20. Loc. cit.
21. Lloyd George Papers: Beaverbrook Library F/40/2/41.
22. Cabinet Papers: Public Record Office, CAB 29, Vol. 28, No. B.E.D. 13.
23. Lloyd George Papers: Beaverbrook Library F/40/2/42.
24. Lloyd George, *Truth*, Vol. I, p. 486.
25. Foreign Office Papers: Public Record Office, F.O. 425, Vol. 383, No. 15.
26. Lord Derby's Diary, 17 March 1919. Balfour Papers: British Museum Add. MSS, Vol. 49744, p. 261.
27. *Intimate Papers*, Vol. IV, p. 397.
28. Loc. cit.

29. Temperley, op. cit., Vol. I, p. 435.
30. *P.P.C.*, Vol. III, p. 952.
31. Ibid., p. 985.
32. Ibid., p. 986.
33. Ibid., p. 972.
34. Ibid., p. 975.
35. Ibid., p. 977.
36. Ibid., p. 979.
37. Ibid., p. 1002.
38. Ibid., p. 1005.
39. Ibid., p. 1009.
40. Ibid., Vol. IV, p. 103.
41. Ibid., p. 186.
42. Ibid., p. 187.
43. Ibid., p. 188.
44. Loc. cit.
45. Ibid., p. 189.
46. Ibid., pp. 215–6.
47. Ibid., p. 218.
48. Ibid., p. 219.
49. Ibid., p. 224.
50. Ibid., pp. 224–5.
51. Ibid., pp. 232–3.
52. Ibid., p. 263.
53. Ibid., p. 265.
54. Ibid., p. 295.
55. Ibid., p. 298.
56. Lloyd George Papers: Beaverbrook Library F/6/6/17
57. *P.P.C.*, Vol. IV, pp. 356–7.
58. Ibid., p. 358.
59. Ibid., p. 359.

CHAPTER 7.

1. The record of this meeting is in Cabinet Minutes: Public Record Office, CAB 23, Vol. 15, No. 538A.
2. The record of this meeting is in ibid., No. 541A.
3. Curzon Papers, Public Record Office, F.O. 800, Vol. 153, p. 212.
4. Ibid., p. 215.

5. Cabinet Papers: Public Record Office, GT Series, CAB 24, Vol. 76, No. 6978.
6. The only record of this meeting is a set of notes prepared afterwards by Lloyd George, which can be found in the Lloyd George Papers, Beaverbrook Library F/147/1.
7. The only such damage sustained by Britain was the result of raids by German cruisers on the east coast, resulting in four deaths in Bridlington, some broken windows in Scarborough, and damage to Whitby Abbey. Taylor, *English History*, p. 13.
8. Loc. cit.
9. *P.P.C.*, Vol. IV, pp. 307–8.
10. Ibid., pp. 299–300.
11. A record of the meetings of this Committee, in the form of notes kept by Kerr, are in Cmd 2169, pp. 59–65.
12. Ibid., p. 68.
13. Ibid., p. 69.
14. Quoted in J. B. Duroselle, *From Wilson to Roosevelt* (London 1964), p. 96.
15. Tardieu, op. cit., p. 176. This is the only account we have of this meeting; there is no record of it in the official documents of the Conference.
16. Ibid., p. 177.
17. *P.P.C.*, Vol. II, pp. 529–30.
18. Lloyd George Papers: Beaverbrook Library F/30/3/31.
19. Cmd 2169, pp. 70–2.
20. Lloyd George Papers: Beaverbrook Library F/3/4/19, and Balfour Papers, British Museum Add. MSS, Vol. 49751, pp. 230–3.
21. *Intimate Papers*, Vol. IV, p. 409.
22. Ibid., p. 405.
23. Cabinet Minutes: Public Record Office, CAB 23, Vol. 15, No. 545A.
24. *P.P.C.*, Vol. IV, p. 379.
25. Ibid., p. 381.
26. Ibid., p. 409.
27. Ibid., p. 410.
28. Ibid., p. 414.
29. Loc. cit.
30. Ibid., p. 415.
31. Ibid., p. 417.

32. Loc. cit.
33. Ibid., p. 418.
34. Ibid., p. 419.
35. Ibid., pp. 453–4.
36. Ibid., p. 449.
37. Ibid., p. 450.
38. Foreign Office Papers: Public Record Office, F.O. 418, Vol. 53, No. 9.
39. F. Borkenau, *World Communism* (Michigan 1962), p. 117ff.
40. *Intimate Papers*, Vol. IV, p. 405.
41. P. J. Mantoux, *Les Délibérations du Conseil des Quatre: Notes de L'Officier Interprète* (Paris 1955, hereafter cited as Mantoux, *Délibérations*), Vol. I, pp. 20–1.
42. *P.P.C.*, Vol. IV, p. 332.
43. Tardieu, op. cit., p. 54.
44. The only record of the early meetings of the Council of Four are the interpreter's notes published by Professor Mantoux in his *Les Délibérations du Conseil des Quatre*, cited above. To ensure secrecy, the Council of Four at first refused to employ a secretary to keep a record of its meetings, but since there was no language common to all four members an interpreter was essential from the beginning. Even so, there were some meetings before Professor Mantoux's record starts, on 24 March. For these we must rely on Tardieu, op. cit.
45. Mantoux, *Délibérations*, Vol. I, p. 14.
46. Ibid., pp. 15–16.
47. Ibid., p. 26.
48. Loc. cit.
49. Ibid., p. 27.
50. Ibid., p. 28.
51. Ibid., pp. 29–30.
52. Ibid., p. 35.
53. Curzon Papers: Public Record Office, F.O. 800, Vol. 153, pp. 212–15.
54. The minutes of this meeting are in *P.P.C.*, Vol. V, pp. 1–14.
55. Lothian Papers: Scottish Record Office, GD40/17, Vol. 60, p. 35ff.
56. Cabinet Papers: Public Record Office, GT Series, CAB 24, Vol. 78, No. 7037.
57. *P.P.C.*, Vol. XII, p. 747.

58. Balfour Papers: British Museum Add. MSS, Vol. 49745, p. 15.
59. Ibid., p. 16.
60. Foreign Office Papers: Public Record Office, F.O. 421, Vol. 297, No. 14.

CHAPTER 8.

1. Lloyd George Papers: Beaverbrook Library F/23/4/39.
2. Lord Hankey, *The Supreme Control*, pp. 100–1.
3. See the Lothian Papers, Scottish Record Office, GD40/17, Vol. 60, for these drafts.
4. The text has been printed several times; those used here were in Lloyd George, *Truth*, Vol. I, p. 404ff., Temperley, op. cit., Vol. IV, p. 544ff, and Cmd 2169, p. 76ff.
5. Lloyd George, *Truth*, Vol. II, p. 990.
6. Ibid., p. 991.
7. Mantoux, *Délibérations*, Vol. I, pp. 49–51.
8. Ibid., p. 43ff.
9. Lloyd George Papers: Beaverbrook Library F/45/9/29.
10. *Intimate Papers*, Vol. IV, p. 410.
11. Mantoux, *Délibérations*, Vol. I, pp. 50–1.
12. Ibid., p. 58f.
13. Quoted in Jordan, op. cit., p. 103.
14. *P.P.C.*, Vol. V, p. 19.
15. Mantoux, *Délibérations*, Vol. I, p. 83.
16. Lloyd George, *Truth*, Vol. I, p. 494.
17. Ibid., p. 496.
18. Mantoux, *Délibérations*, Vol. I, p. 85.
19. Cmd 2169, p. 89.
20. Loc. cit.
21. Ibid., p. 90.
22. Ibid., p. 87.
23. Mantoux, *Délibérations*, Vol. I, pp. 92–5.
24. Ibid., p. 108.
25. Cmd 2169, p. 91.
26. Ibid.
27. See, for example, his speech to the Chamber of Deputies on 29 December 1918, quoted in Mayer, op. cit., pp. 184–5, and Jordan, op. cit., p. 37.
28. Mantoux, *Délibérations*, Vol. I, pp. 62–5.

29. Ibid., p. 68.
30. Ibid., pp. 69–70.
31. Ibid., pp. 71–2.
32. Ibid., p. 73.
33. Ibid., p. 89.
34. See J. Headlam-Morley, *A Memoir of the Paris Peace Conference 1919*, ed. A. Headlam-Morley, R. Bryant and A. Cienciala (London 1972).
35. Tardieu, op. cit., p. 180.
36. Mantoux, *Délibérations*, Vol. I, p. 181.
37. Ibid., p. 182.
38. Ibid., p. 193.
39. Ibid., p. 194.
40. Loc. cit.
41. Ibid., p. 196.
42. Ibid., pp. 203–4.
43. Ibid., p. 204.
44. Loc. cit.
45. Lloyd George Papers: Beaverbrook Library F/51/1/16.
46. Mantoux, *Délibérations*, Vol. I, pp. 208–13.
47. Ibid., pp. 224–8.
48. Ibid., pp. 353–4.
49. Ibid., pp. 96–7.
50. Curzon Papers: Public Record Office, F.O. 800, Vol. 152, p. 231.
51. Mantoux, *Délibérations*, Vol. I, p. 146.
52. Ibid., p. 147.
53. Loc. cit.
54. Loc. cit.
55. Foreign Office Papers: Public Record Office, F.O. 425, Vol. 383, No. 70.
56. Mantoux, *Délibérations*, Vol. I, p. 238.
57. Ibid., p. 246.
58. Loc. cit.
59. Ibid., p. 247.
60. Ibid., p. 260.
61. Loc. cit.
62. Curzon Papers: Public Record Office, F.O. 800, Vol. 152, p. 237.
63. *P.P.C.*, Vol. V, p. 309.

64. Ibid., p. 339.
65. Foreign Office Papers: Public Record Office, F.O. 425, Vol. 383, No. 89.
66. Ibid., No. 46.
67. Mantoux, *Délibérations*, Vol. I, p. 144.
68. Ibid., pp. 144–5.
69. Ibid., p. 145.
70. Loc. cit.
71. Tardieu, op. cit., p. 184.
72. *Intimate Papers*, Vol. IV, p. 422.
73. *P.P.C.*, Vol. XI, p. 550.
74. Lloyd George, *Truth*, Vol. I, p. 422.
75. Mantoux, *Délibérations*, Vol. I, p. 319.
76. Loc. cit.
77. *P.P.C.*, Vol. V, p. 112.
78. Ibid., pp. 376–86.
79. Cmd 2169, p. 98.
80. Ibid., p. 99.
81. Loc. cit.
82. *D.B.F.P.*, First Series, Vol. VI, p. 1, n. 3.
83. Loc. cit.
84. *P.P.C.*, Vol. IV, p. 543.
85. Balfour Papers: Public Record Office, F.O. 800, Vol. 216, pp. 10–12.
86. *P.P.C.*, Vol. IV, p. 544.
87. Loc. cit.
88. Loc. cit.
89. Ibid., p. 546.
90. Mantoux, *Délibérations*, Vol. I, p. 149.
91. See R. A. C. Parker, *Europe, 1919–45* (London 1969), pp. 13–16.
92. Mantoux, *Délibérations*, Vol. I, pp. 109–10.
93. Ibid., pp. 110–11.
94. Ibid., p. 111.
95. Loc. cit.
96. Loc. cit.
97. Ibid., p. 112.
98. Ibid., p. 197.
99. Ibid., p. 198.
100. Ibid., p. 199.

101. Ibid., p. 200.
102. Ibid., pp. 201–2.
103. Ibid., p. 231.
104. Ibid., p. 249.
105. Ibid., pp. 271–2.
106. Ibid., p. 120.
107. Loc. cit.
108. Ibid., pp. 247–8.
109. Ibid., p. 312.
110. *P.P.C.*, Vol. IV, pp. 624–5.
111. Ibid., Vol. V, p. 114.
112. Mantoux, *Délibérations*, Vol. I, p. 461.
113. Ibid., p. 494.
114. *P.P.C.*, Vol. XI, pp. 547–8.
115. Repington, op. cit., p. 513.
116. *P.P.C.*, Vol. XI, pp. 548–9.
117. A. J. Sylvester, *The Real Lloyd George* (London 1942), pp. 30–1.
118. Lord Riddell, *My Intimate Diary at the Peace Conference and After* (London 1933), p. 50.
119. Op. cit., p. 31.
120. See D. Lloyd George, *War Memoirs* (2–volume edition, London, 1938), Vol. I, pp. 580–4, 643–4, and H. Daalder, *Cabinet Reform in Britain, 1914–63* (London 1964), pp. 42–53.
121. Balfour Papers: Public Record Office, F.O. 800, Vol. 216, pp. 84–7.

CHAPTER 9.

1. Lloyd George Papers: Beaverbrook Library F/30/3/39.
2. *Intimate Papers*, Vol. IV, p. 417.
3. Lothian Papers: Scottish Record Office, GD40/17, Vol. 71.
4. See Borkenau, op. cit., p. 148ff.
5. Mantoux, *Délibérations*, Vol. I, p. 114.
6. Ibid., p. 120.
7. Ibid., pp. 120–1.
8. Ibid., p. 121.
9. Ibid., p. 123.
10. Ibid., p. 124.
11. Loc. cit.

12. Ibid., p. 186.
13. Ibid., p. 187.
14. Ibid., p. 189.
15. Ibid., pp. 151–2.
16. Ibid., p. 154.
17. Ibid., p. 155.
18. Ibid., p. 158.
19. Ibid., p. 161.
20. Loc. cit.
21. *Intimate Papers*, Vol. IV, p. 417.
22. Ibid., pp. 418–9.
23. Ibid., p. 418.
24. Mantoux, *Délibérations*, Vol. I, p. 169.
25. Lloyd George Papers: Beaverbrook Library F/41/8/31.
26. Lloyd George, *Truth*, Vol. I, Chapter 11.
27. Lloyd George Papers: Beaverbrook Library F/30/3/43.
28. Mantoux, *Délibérations*, Vol. I, p. 216.
29. Ibid., p. 219.
30. Ibid., pp. 223–4.
31. Ibid., p. 61. See pp. 172–3 above.
32. Lloyd George Papers: Beaverbrook Library F/28/3/26 and 27.
33. Cabinet Papers: Public Record Office, CAB 29, Vol. 28, No. B.E.D. 19A.
34. Mantoux, *Délibérations*, Vol. I, p. 235.
35. House of Commons Debates: Official Record, 5th Series, Vol. 114, col. 2950.
36. Loc. cit.
37. Lloyd George Papers: Beaverbrook Library F/6/6/30.
38. Ibid., F/7/2/27.
39. Ibid., F/7/2/34.
40. Loc. cit.
41. Sir Roy Harrod, *The Life of John Maynard Keynes* (London 1951), p. 246.
42. Ibid., p. 247.
43. Ibid., p. 250.
44. Miller, op. cit., Vol. II, p. 344. See pp. 119, 161 above.
45. Ibid., p. 345.
46. Ibid., p. 358.
47. Balfour Papers: Public Record Office, F.O. 800, Vol. 216, pp. 390–2.

48. Lloyd George Papers: Beaverbrook Library F/6/6/25.
49. Miller, op. cit., Vol. II, p. 366.
50. Loc. cit.
51. Ibid., p. 367.
52. Ibid., p. 372.
53. Ibid., p. 374.
54. Ibid., p. 379.
55. Ibid., p. 391.
56. Mantoux, *Délibérations*, Vol. I, p. 369.
57. Ibid., p. 398.
58. *P.P.C.*, Vol. III, pp. 285–319.
59. Mantoux, *Délibérations*, Vol. I, p. 56.
60. Loc. cit.
61. Foreign Office Papers: Public Record Office, F.O. 418, Vol. 53, No. 10.
62. Cabinet Minutes: Public Record Office, CAB 23, Vol. 9, No. 552.
63. Cabinet Papers: Public Record Office, GT Series, CAB 24, Vol. 77, No. 7074.
64. Quoted in E. H. Carr, *The Bolshevik Revolution* (London 1953), Vol. III, p. 129.
65. Cabinet Papers: Public Record Office, GT Series, CAB 24, Vol. 78, No. 7117.
66. Ibid., No. 7128.
67. Foreign Office Papers: Public Record Office, F.O. 418, Vol. 53, No. 12.
68. Carr, op. cit., p. 113 n.2.
69. Foreign Office Papers: Public Record Office, F.O. 418, Vol. 53, No. 13.
70. Lloyd George Papers: Beaverbrook Library F/4/3/11.
71. Mantoux, *Délibérations*, Vol. I, p. 430.

CHAPTER 10.

1. Mantoux, *Délibérations*, Vol. I, p. 114.
2. Ibid., p. 128.
3. Ibid., p. 129.
4. Ibid., p. 130.
5. Ibid., p. 131.
6. Ibid., p. 223.

7. Ibid., p. 234.
8. Balfour Papers: British Museum Add. MSS, Vol. 49751, pp. 51–5.
9. Mantoux, *Délibérations*, Vol. I, p. 237.
10. Ibid., p. 243.
11. Temperley, op. cit., Vol. V, Appendix III.
12. Loc. cit.
13. Balfour Papers: Public Record Office, F.O. 800, Vol. 216, pp. 93–8.
14. Curzon Papers: Public Record Office, F.O. 800, Vol. 155, pp. 63–76.
15. *P.P.C.*, Vol. XI, pp. 156–7.
16. Mantoux, *Délibérations*, Vol. I, p. 280.
17. Loc. cit.
18. Ibid., p. 281.
19. Loc. cit.
20. Ibid., p. 285.
21. Ibid., p. 286.
22. Loc. cit.
23. Ibid., p. 287.
24. Ibid., p. 290.
25. Ibid., p. 293.
26. Ibid., p. 301.
27. Ibid., p. 302.
28. Ibid., p. 308.
29. Ibid., p. 315.
30. Curzon Papers: Public Record Office, F.O. 800, Vol. 152, pp. 220–1.
31. Mantoux, *Délibérations*, Vol. I, p. 329.
32. Temperley, op. cit., Vol. V, Appendix III.
33. Loc. cit.
34. Loc. cit.
35. Mantoux, *Délibérations*, Vol. I, p. 347.
36. Foreign Office Papers: Public Record Office, F.O. 425, Vol. 383, No. 90.
37. Mantoux, *Délibérations*, Vol. I, p. 355.
38. Ibid., p. 357.
39. Ibid., p. 361.
40. Ibid., p. 364.
41. Loc. cit.

42. Foreign Office Papers: Public Record Office, F.O. 425, Vol. 383, No. 100.
43. Mantoux, *Délibérations*, Vol. I, p. 437.
44. Ibid., pp. 450–1.
45. Ibid., p. 473.
46. Ibid., p. 477.
47. Ibid., p. 478.
48. Foreign Office Papers: Public Record Office, F.O. 421, Vol. 297, No. 35.
49. Lothian Papers: Scottish Record Office, GD40/17, Vol. 55, p. 135.
50. Mantoux, *Délibérations*, Vol. I, p. 250.
51. Loc. cit.
52. *P.P.C.*, Vol. IV, p. 556.
53. Ibid., p. 570.
54. Mantoux, *Délibérations*, Vol. I, p. 274.
55. *P.P.C.*, Vol. V, p. 109
56. Ibid., p. 110.
57. Ibid., p. 111.
58. Lothian Papers: Scottish Record Office, GD40/17, Vol. 74.
59. *P.P.C.*, Vol. V, p. 130.
60. Curzon Papers: Public Record Office, F.O. 800, Vol. 153, pp. 220–1.
61. *P.P.C.*, Vol. V, p. 139.
62. Ibid., p. 141.
63. Ibid., p. 142.
64. Ibid., p. 143.
65. Ibid., p. 147.
66. Ibid., pp. 245–6.
67. Balfour Papers: British Museum Add. MSS, Vol. 49692, p. 333.
68. Lothian Papers: Scottish Record Office, GD40/17, Vol. 74.
69. *P.P.C.*, Vol. V, p. 316.
70. Ibid., p. 317.
71. Ibid., p. 318.
72. Ibid., p. 329.
73. Ibid., p. 367.
74. Lothian Papers: Scottish Record Office, GD40/17, Vol. 74.
75. *D.B.F.P.*, Vol. VI, pp. 565–6.
76. Foreign Office Papers: Public Record Office, F.O. 405, Vol. 206, No. 30.

77. *P.P.C.*, Vol. V, p. 607.
78. Mantoux, *Délibérations*, Vol. I, p. 459.
79. Ibid., p. 482.
80. Cabinet Papers: Public Record Office, GT Series, CAB 24, Vol. 78, No. 7149.
81. Lloyd George Papers: Beaverbrook Library F/4/3/14.
82. Quoted in Harrod, op. cit., p. 249.
83. Temperley, op. cit., Vol. III, p. 212 (Article 227 of the Treaty of Versailles).
84. *P.P.C.*, Vol. III, pp. 383–4.
85. Ibid., pp. 385–6.

CHAPTER 11.

1. *P.P.C.*, Vol. III, p. 415.
2. Ibid., p. 417.
3. Ibid., p. 419.
4. Duroselle, op. cit., p. 106.
5. Nicolson, op. cit., pp. 329–30.
6. *P.P.C.*, Vol. V, pp. 563–4.
7. Ibid., p. 564.
8. Mantoux, *Délibérations*, Vol. II, p. 21.
9. *P.P.C.*, Vol. V, p. 564.
10. *P.P.C.*, Vol. XII, pp. 88–123, and Lothian Papers, Scottish Record Office, GD40/17, Vol. 72.
11. Lothian Papers, loc. cit.
12. *P.P.C.*, Vol. V, pp. 672–3.
13. Ibid., p. 727.
14. Ibid., pp. 739–40.
15. Ibid., pp. 817–9.
16. Ibid., Vol. XI, pp. 573–4.
17. Lloyd George Papers: Beaverbrook Library F/45/9/34.
18. Quoted in H. I. Nelson, op. cit., p. 326.
19. *P.P.C.*, Vol. V, pp. 742–3.
20. Ibid., p. 767.
21. Ibid., p. 773.
22. Ibid., pp. 827–8.
23. Mantoux, *Délibérations*, Vol. II, pp. 165–7.
24. Ibid., p. 132.
25. *P.P.C.*, Vol. VI, p. 38.

26. Ibid., pp. 781–94.
27. Ibid., p. 795.
28. Ibid., p. 796.
29. Loc. cit.
30. Ibid., pp. 797–8.
31. Ibid., p. 798.
32. Ibid., p. 799.
33. Ibid., pp. 799–800.
34. Ibid., pp. 800–913.
35. Lothian Papers: Scottish Record Office, GD40/17, Vol. 58.
36. Note by Lord Cunliffe, 1 June 1919. Lothian Papers, Scottish Record Office, GD40/17, Vol. 62.
37. Lloyd George Papers: Beaverbrook Library F/6/6/47.
38. Ibid., F/30/3/71.
39. Nicolson, op. cit., p. 350.
40. Loc. cit.
41. Ibid., p. 351.
42. Harrod, op. cit., p. 251.
43. See note 37 above.
44. Mantoux, *Délibérations*, Vol. II, p. 75.
45. Nicolson, op. cit., p. 326ff.
46. Mantoux, *Délibérations*, Vol. I, pp. 228–9.
47. J. Nevakivi, op. cit., pp. 141–4.
48. *D.B.F.P.*, First Series, Vol. IV, p. 252.
49. Ibid., pp. 252–3.
50. *P.P.C.*, Vol. V, p. 112.
51. Ibid., p. 115.
52. Op. cit., p. 149.
53. Mantoux, *Délibérations*, Vol. I, p. 318.
54. Foreign Office Papers: Public Record Office, F.O. 406, Vol. 41, No. 39.
55. Ibid., No. 40.
56. *P.P.C.*, Vol. V, p. 460.
57. Mantoux, *Délibérations*, Vol. II, pp. 133–6.
58. Ibid., pp. 137–8.
59. Ibid., p. 138.
60. Ibid., pp. 138–9.
61. G. Suarez, *Clemenceau* (Paris 1930), p. 287n.
62. Mantoux, *Délibérations*, Vol. II, p. 143.
63. Ibid., p. 160.

64. Loc. cit.
65. Ibid., pp. 160–1.
66. Ibid., p. 161.
67. Ibid., p. 163.
68. Ibid., p. 164.
69. Balfour Papers: British Museum Add. MSS, Vol. 49152, pp. 4–10.
70. *D.B.F.P.*, First Series, Vol. IV, p. 254.
71. Ibid., p. 256.
72. Mantoux, *Délibérations*, Vol. II, p. 263.
73. Ibid., p. 264.
74. *D.B.F.P.*, First Series, Vol. IV, p. 259.
75. *P.P.C.*, Vol. XII, pp. 795–8.
76. Mantoux, *Délibérations*, Vol. I, p. 505.
77. Loc. cit.
78. Ibid., Vol. II, pp. 16–18.
79. Ibid., p. 27.
80. Ibid., p. 29.
81. Ibid., p. 30.
82. Ibid., p. 36.
83. Ibid., pp. 123–4.
84. Foreign Office Papers: Public Record Office, F.O. 418, Vol. 53, No. 18.
85. Mantoux, *Délibérations*, Vol. II, p. 127.
86. Loc. cit.
87. Ibid., p. 128.
88. Ibid., p. 178.
89. Ibid., p. 190.
90. Foreign Office Papers: Public Record Office, F.O. 418, Vol. 53, No. 19.
91. Ibid., No. 20.
92. Mantoux, *Délibérations*, Vol. II, pp. 200–2.
93. Ibid., p. 203.
94. Ibid., p. 204.
95. Foreign Office Papers: Public Record Office, F.O. 418, Vol. 53, No. 25.
96. Mantoux, *Délibérations*, Vol. I, p. 505.
97. Ibid., Vol. II, p. 7.
98. *P.P.C.*, Vol. IV, pp. 624–6.
99. Ibid., p. 711.

100. Mantoux, *Délibérations*, Vol. II, p. 90.
101. Loc. cit.
102. Ibid., p. 108.
103. Loc. cit.
104. Ibid., pp. 130–1.
105. Ibid., p. 147.
106. Ibid., pp. 149–50.
107. Ibid., p. 150.
108. Loc. cit.
109. Ibid., p. 153.
110. Ibid., p. 156.
111. *D.B.F.P.*, First Series, Vol. III, pp. 326–7.
112. Ibid., p. 327.
113. Ibid., p. 328.
114. Foreign Office Papers: Public Record Office, F.O. 418, Vol. 53, No. 23.
115. *D.B.F.P.*, First Series, Vol. III, pp. 334–5.
116. Ibid., p. 333.
117. Ibid., p. 334.
118. Loc. cit.
119. Ibid., p. 337.
120. Mantoux, *Délibérations*, Vol. II, p. 54.
121. Ibid., p. 55.
122. Lloyd George, *Truth*, Vol. II, pp. 882–3.
123. Mantoux, *Délibérations*, Vol. II, p. 220.
124. Ibid., p. 223.
125. Ibid., p. 226.
126. Lloyd George, *Truth*, Vol. II, p. 883.
127. Mantoux, *Délibérations*, Vol. II, p. 238.
128. Ibid., pp. 242–4.
129. Lloyd George, *Truth*, Vol. II, p. 886ff.
130. Mantoux, *Délibérations*, Vol. II, p. 326.
131. Ibid., pp. 345–6.

CHAPTER 12.

1. Cabinet Papers: Public Record Office, CAB 29, Vol. 28, No. B.E.D. 32.
2. Ibid., No. B.E.D. 33.
3. Ibid., No. B.E.D. 34.

4. Mantoux, *Délibérations*, Vol. II, pp. 265–6.
5. Ibid., p. 267.
6. Loc. cit.
7. Loc. cit.
8. Ibid., p. 268.
9. Ibid., p. 269.
10. Ibid., p. 271.
11. Ibid., p. 273.
12. Harrod, op. cit., p. 252.
13. Ibid., p. 253.
14. Nicolson, op. cit., p. 359.
15. Lloyd George Papers: Beaverbrook Library F/36/4/17.
16. Ibid., F/45/9/39.
17. Ibid., F/46/2/9.
18. *P.P.C.*, Vol. XI, pp. 200–2.
19. Ibid., p. 222.
20. Mantoux, *Délibérations*, Vol. II, p. 276.
21. Ibid., p. 277.
22. Loc. cit.
23. Ibid., p. 278.
24. Loc. cit.
25. Ibid., p. 280.
26. Ibid., p. 283.
27. Ibid., p. 286.
28. *D.B.F.P.*, First Series, Vol. III, pp. 348–9.
29. Ibid., p. 351.
30. Ibid., pp. 351–2.
31. Ibid., p. 352.
32. Mantoux, *Délibérations*, Vol. II, p. 321.
33. Ibid., p. 338.
34. Ibid., pp. 346–7.
35. Ibid., p. 348.
36. Loc. cit.
37. Ibid., pp. 351–2.
38. Ibid., p. 354.
39. Ibid., p. 355.
40. Ibid., p. 356.
41. Ibid., p. 357.
42. Ibid., p. 358.
43. Ibid., pp. 362–4.

44. Ibid., p. 366.
45. Cabinet Papers: Public Record Office, CAB 29, Vol. 28, No. B.E.D. 35.
46. Lloyd George Papers: Beaverbrook Library F/6/6/54.
47. Mantoux, *Délibérations*, Vol. II, pp. 383–4.
48. Ibid., p. 391.
49. D. H. Miller, op. cit., Vol. I, p. 547, and Mantoux, *Délibérations*, Vol. II, p. 392.
50. Mantoux, op. cit., Vol. II, p. 392.
51. Ibid., p. 393.
52. Loc. cit.
53. Loc. cit.
54. Ibid., p. 394.
55. Ibid., pp. 405–7.
56. Ibid., p. 410.
57. Ibid., p. 421.
58. Ibid., p. 422.
59. Loc. cit.
60. Lloyd George, *Truth*, Vol. II, p. 228.
61. *P.P.C.*, Vol. VI, pp. 927–8.
62. Ibid., p. 934.
63. Ibid., p. 938.
64. Ibid., p. 959.
65. Mantoux, *Délibérations*, Vol. II, p. 499.
66. Ibid., p. 515.
67. Lloyd George Papers: Beaverbrook Library F/7/2/34, No. 3.
68. Mantoux, *Délibérations*, Vol. II, pp. 345–6.
69. Lothian Papers: Scottish Record Office, GD40/17, Vol. 66.
70. Foreign Office Papers: Public Record Office, F.O. 425, Vol. 383, Nos 171, 172.
71. *D.B.F.P.*, First Series, Vol. IV, pp. 5–6.
72. See ibid., Nos 1–168, R. Albrecht-Carrié, *Italy at the Paris Peace Conference* (New York 1938), and V. S. Mammatey, op. cit.
73. Foreign Office Papers: Public Record Office, F.O. 405, Vol. 206, No. 33.
74. Ibid., No. 34.
75. Ibid., No. 43.
76. *P.P.C.*, Vol. VI, pp. 674–5.
77. Ibid., p. 710.

78. Ibid., Vol. XIII, p. 64.
79. Ibid., Vol. IV, pp. 838–9.
80. Ibid., pp. 831–2.
81. Ibid., pp. 848–9.
82. Eric Eyck, *History of the Weimar Republic* (London 1962), Vol. I, p. 98.
83. *P.P.C.*, Vol. VI, pp. 609–11.
84. Ibid., pp. 605, 612.
85. Ibid., p. 613.
86. Loc. cit.
87. Taylor, *The First World War*, p. 207.
88. *P.P.C.*, Vol. VI, p. 664.
89. Ibid., Vol. XI, p. 600.
90. Temperley, op. cit., Vol. III, p. 80.
91. House of Commons Debates: Official Record, 5th Series, Vol. 117, col. 1220.
92. *D.B.F.P.*, First Series, Vol. III, pp. 339–40.
93. Mantoux, *Délibérations*, Vol. II, pp. 286–7.
94. Lothian Papers: Scottish Record Office, GD40/17, Vol. 68.
95. Mantoux, *Délibérations*, Vol. II, pp. 334–5.
96. *D.B.F.P.*, First Series, Vol. III, p. 356.
97. Ibid., pp. 357–61.
98. Ibid., pp. 361–4.
99. Mantoux, *Délibérations*, Vol. II, p. 395.
100. *D.B.F.P.*, First Series, Vol. III, p. 384.
101. Mantoux, *Délibérations*, Vol. II, p. 453.
102. Ibid., p. 455.
103. Balfour Papers: British Museum Add. MSS, Vol. 49750, pp. 31–40.
104. Cabinet Minutes: Public Record Office, CAB 23, Vol. 15, No. 578A.
105. Ibid., No. 580A.
106. Ibid., No. 585B.
107. *D.B.F.P.*, First Series, Vol. III, pp. 392–3.
108. Ibid., p. 402.
109. Foreign Office Papers: Public Record Office, F.O. 899, Vol. 15B, No. 47.
110. *D.B.F.P.*, First Series, Vol. IV, pp. 275–6.
111. Ibid., p. 283.
112. Ibid., p. 284.

113. *P.P.C.*, Vol. XII, p. 749.
114. Ibid., pp. 749–50.

CHAPTER 13.

1. See H. J. Elcock, 'Britain and the Russo-Polish Frontier, 1919–1921', in *Historical Journal*, Vol. XII, 1969, pp. 137–154, for a more detailed account of the Conference's decisions and the Russo-Polish War of 1920.
2. Quoted in F. R. Dulles, *America's Rise to World Power* (London 1955), p. 145.
3. Temperley, op. cit., Vol. III, p. 68.
4. Ibid., p. 69.
5. Foreign Office Papers: Public Record Office, F.O. 414, Vol. 245, No. 6.
6. Ibid., No. 7.
7. Ibid., No. 8.
8. J. K. Galbraith, *The Great Crash* (London, Penguin edition, 1961), p. 79.
9. See A. Bullock, *Hitler: A Study in Tyranny* (London 1952), Chapters 3, 4.
10. A. J. P. Taylor, *The Trouble-Makers* (London 1957), p. 160.
11. Ibid., p. 166.
12. London 1946.
13. E. Mantoux, *The Carthaginian Peace* (London 1946), p. 13.
14. Ibid., pp. 13–14.
15. Ibid., Vol. II, p. 90.
16. Ibid., p. 284.
17. R. Lansing, *The Peace Negotiations: A Personal Narrative* (London 1920), p. 3.
18. Tardieu, op. cit., p. 287.
19. Mantoux, *Délibérations*, Vol. II, p. 278. See p. 277 above.
20. Keynes, *Essays in Biography*, p. 36.
21. Ibid., p. 34.
22. Cmd 2169, p. 76.
23. See K. O. Morgan, *David Lloyd George: Welsh Radical as World Statesman* (Cardiff 1963).
24. Mantoux, *Délibérations*, Vol. I, p. 186.
25. Lloyd George, *Truth*, Vol. I, p. 405.
26. Mantoux, *Délibérations*, Vol. I, p. 26.

27. Sir R. Harrod, op. cit., p. 240.
28. Nicolson, op. cit., p. 359.
29. For an excellent account of this tradition see C. H. Sisson, *The Spirit of British Administration* (London 1959).
30. *E.C.P.*, p. 26.
31. Ibid., pp. 31–2.
32. Mantoux, *Délibérations*, Vol. I, p. 70.
33. Ibid., p. 44.
34. Jordan, op. cit., p. 37.
35. Mantoux, *Délibérations*, Vol. II, p. 270.
36. Cmd 2169, p. 36.
37. Ibid. p. 61.
38. Ibid., p. 100. See pp. 187–8 above.
39. Lord Riddell, op. cit., p. 52.
40. E. Weill-Raynal, *Les Réparations allemandes et la France* (Paris 1938), Vol. I, p. 132.
41. Mantoux, *Délibérations*, Vol. I, p. 58.
42. Ibid., p. 161.
43. Ibid., p. 219.
44. Ibid., p. 14.
45. Ibid., Vol. II, p. 410.

# Appendices
# Bibliography
# Index

N*

# Appendix I

## *Main Events in the Making of Peace, September 1918 - June 1919*

1918

| | | |
|---|---|---|
| September: | 15 | Austria-Hungary requested armistice, the first of the Central Powers to do so. |
| | 27 | President Wilson made his 'Five Particulars' speech, the last of his speeches defining American war aims. |
| October: | 4 | Germany requested President Wilson to arrange an armistice on the basis of the Fourteen Points. |
| | 12 | The Irish ferry boat *Leinster* was sunk by a German U-boat in the Irish Sea with the loss of 450 lives. |
| | 14 | Wilson sent a severe Note to Germany demanding the cessation of inhumane war practices and the destruction of arbitrary government in Germany and Austria-Hungary. |
| | | Wilson appointed Colonel E. M. House as his Personal Representative in Europe. |
| | 27 | Germany and Austria-Hungary accepted President Wilson's demands. |
| | 29 | Colonel House met Lloyd George and Clemenceau to explain the Fourteen Points and to reassure them. |
| November: | 4 | The Allies accepted the Fourteen Points as a basis for peace with reservations accepted by the Americans. |
| | 5 | The American Secretary of State offered an armistice to Germany on the basis of the Fourteen |

Points as modified by the Allies; the 'Lansing Note'.

9 Britain and France issued a declaration promising eventual self-government to the Arabs and to abstain from excessive interference with the Arab states in the meantime.
Kaiser Wilhelm II abdicated.

11 The Armistice signed at Compiègne.
American mid-term Congressional elections. The Republican Party won a sweeping victory over Wilson's Democrats.

December: 1 The Allied Prime Ministers (Lloyd George, Clemenceau and Orlando) met to discuss peace terms. No American representative was present.

14 President Wilson arrived in Europe.
British General Election – the 'Coupon Election'. Lloyd George's coalition won a massive victory.

16 President Wilson and Clemenceau met for the first time. Clemenceau suddenly ceased to oppose Wilson's intention to attend the Peace Conference.

1919

January: 18 Peace Conference formally opened in Paris.

22 The Council of Ten agreed to summon the parties to the Russian Civil War to a conference at Prinkipo and to call for a truce between them during this meeting.

25 Plenary Session of the Peace Conference agreed to the establishment of a League of Nations. Commissions were appointed to draft the Covenant and prepare other sections of the Treaty.

30 Dispute between Wilson and the British Dominions over the former German colonies was resolved.

February: 3 First Meeting of the League of Nations Commission, with Wilson in the chair.

4 The Soviet Government accepted the Prinkipo

proposal with conditions unacceptable to the Council of Ten.

20 Admiral Kolchak, Head of the Siberian Provisional Government, rejected the Prinkipo proposal.

25 France appealed for British support in her effort to secure a frontier on the Rhine.

March: 11 J. M. Keynes proposed that the total Germany should pay in reparations should be left out of the Treaty and should be determined later.

11–12 Meetings of a Secret Committee on the Frontiers of Germany. Deadlocked by British opposition to French demands for a Rhenish buffer state.

14 First meeting of the Council of Four. Wilson and Lloyd George offered France a guarantee against aggression if she would give up the Rhine frontier.

17 The Council of Ten reached agreement on German disarmament.

19 The Committee of experts on the frontiers of Poland presented its report to the Council of Ten. Lloyd George rejected these proposals as unfair to the Germans.

26 Lloyd George issued his Fontainebleau Memorandum urging a peace of moderation and justice.

April: 1 Lloyd George proposed that Danzig should become a Free City under the government of the League of Nations.

4 The King of the Belgians attended the Council of Four to plead his country's case.

The Council of Four decided that the Bohemian Germans must remain in Czechoslovakia despite their claim on grounds of nationality for inclusion in Germany.

7 President Wilson threatened to leave the Conference unless the Allies were more moderate in their demands for reparations.

8 The Council of Four decided that the ex-Kaiser should be prosecuted for breaking the Treaty of 1839 which guaranteed Belgian neutrality.

Lloyd George received a telegram from his supporters in the House of Commons protesting at his apparent weakness on reparations.

10 The Council of Four agreed on reparations clauses which left the total sum to be determined in 1921.

14 Wilson and Clemenceau settled the Rhineland issue while Lloyd George was in London to defend himself in the House of Commons. France was to occupy the territory for up to fifteen years.

President Wilson declared his opposition to the Italian demands for the cession to them of Fiume and most of Dalmatia.

16 Lloyd George defended his policy at Paris in the House of Commons and won a large vote of confidence.

19 Orlando formally presented the Italian claims to the Council of Four and met fierce opposition from Wilson.

22 The Italians withdrew from the Conference in protest at Wilson's attitude to their claims.

23 Wilson published an appeal to the Italian people not to persist with their claims.

25 Plenary Session of the Conference accepted the final draft of the Covenant of the League of Nations.

30 The Council of Four decided to cede the Chinese province of Shantung to Japan.

May: 2 The Council of Four agreed that German Austria must not seek unity with Germany.

6 Plenary Session of the Conference accepted the draft of the peace treaty with Germany.

7 First Session of the Peace Congress: the draft terms were presented to the Germans.

20 Admiral Kolchak was asked by the Council of Four to give assurances as to his liberal and democratic intentions prior to the granting of Allied recognition of his Government. At this point it seemed that Kolchak stood a chance of conquering the whole of Russia.

June: May 30–1 June: The British Empire Delegation discussed their reservations about the peace terms and decided to threaten not to renew the war unless concessions were made to the Germans.

2 Lloyd George informed the Council of Four of his Delegation's decision and met with resentment from Clemenceau and Wilson.

5 J. M. Keynes resigned from the British Delegation in protest at the peace terms.

9 The Council of Four decided that a plebiscite should be held in Upper Silesia instead of ceding it to the Poles outright.

16 The Allies informed the Germans of their final peace terms, giving them five days to accept them.

21 The German battle fleet scuttles itself at Scapa Flow.

The Allies allow the Germans a further twenty-four hours to accept the Peace Treaty.

22 Germany accepts the Treaty four hours before the expiry of the Armistice.

28 Second Session of the Peace Congress: signing of the Treaty at Versailles.

# Appendix II

## *Principal Participants in the Paris Peace Conference*

Note: details are given as follows: name, dates of birth and death, office held in 1919, then brief details.

BALFOUR, Arthur J. — (1848–1930) British Foreign Secretary. Leader of the Conservative Party 1902–11, Prime Minister 1902–5. Became first Earl of Balfour 1922. Philosopher.

BONAR LAW, Andrew — (1858–1923) Leader of the House of Commons and Acting Head of the British Government during Lloyd George's absence in Paris. Leader of the Conservative Party 1911–23, Prime Minister 1922–3.

CHURCHILL, Winston S. — (1874–1965) British Secretary of State for War. President of the Board of Trade 1908–10, Home Secretary 1910–11, First Lord of Admiralty 1911–15. Prime Minister 1940–5 and 1951–5. Led his country to victory in the Second World War.

CLEMENCEAU, Georges — (1841–1929) President of the French Council of Ministers (Prime Minister). President of the Peace Conference.

| | |
|---|---|
| | His experiences as Maire de Montmartre during the Prussian siege of Paris in 1871 left him with an abiding hatred of all things German, yet was the most moderate Frenchman at the Conference. Was President of the Council of Ministers 1906–9 and 1917–20. His biting tongue was feared by all. |
| CURZON, George N. (Marquis) | (1859–1925) British Lord President of the Council, and in charge of the Foreign Office during Balfour's absence in Paris. Viceroy of India 1899–1905, Foreign Secretary 1919–24. His decision to resign in 1922 precipitated the collapse of Lloyd George's coalition Government. |
| FOCH, Ferdinand (Marshal) | (1851–1929) Supreme Allied Commander, Western Front. Marshal of France 1918, Field Marshall in the British Army 1919. The military architect of victory. |
| HANKEY, Sir Maurice | (1877–1963) British Cabinet Secretary. Secretary of the Supreme War Council, the Council of Ten and the Council of Four. Collaborated with Lloyd George in setting up the War Cabinet system in December 1916, when he became Cabinet Secretary, which post he retained until 1938. Held minor Ministerial offices 1939–41. |
| HOUSE, Edward M. (Colonel) | (1858–1938) President Wilson's deputy at the Peace Conference and his *confidant*. Previously Wilson's |

Special Representative in Europe, October-December 1918. Tended to interpret Wilson's policies and instructions freely.

HUGHES, William — (1864–1951) Australian Prime Minister. Born in Llandudno, North Wales, emigrated to Australia in 1884 and was Federal Prime Minister from 1915 until 1923. A stout champion of the British Empire and Commonwealth and a stern opponent of leniency towards Germany. Deaf and obstinate.

KERR, Philip H. — (1882–1940) Private Secretary to Lloyd George, became 11th Marquis of Lothian in 1930. Was probably Lloyd George's closest *confidant* in 1919 and his chief assistant in trying to moderate the peace terms. In 1936, when Hitler reoccupied the Rhineland in defiance of the Treaty of Versailles, he declared that 'they are only walking into their own back garden'. Became British Ambassador in Washington in 1939 and died there the following year.

LANSING, Robert — (1864–1928) American Secretary of State, 1915–20. A firm believer in the Fourteen Points, was abruptly dismissed by Wilson in 1920.

LLOYD GEORGE, David — (1863–1945) British Prime Minister. Born in Manchester, brought up in North Wales. President of the Board of Trade 1906–8, Chancellor of the Exchequor 1908–15, Minister of Munitions 1915-16, Prime Minister 1916–22. Great administrative innovator. Wanted a stable peace in Europe.

| | |
|---|---|
| ORLANDO, Vittorio E. | (1860–1952) Italian Prime Minister. Minister of Education 1903–5, Minister of Justice 1907–9 and 1914–16, Minister of the Interior 1916–17, Prime Minister 1917–19. A Liberal who sought better relations between the Vatican and the Italian state before the war, and as Prime Minister agreed to the creation of a sovereign Vatican state. He favoured the creation of a Yugoslav state and was opposed to intervention against the Bolsheviks in Russia.* |
| PADEREWSKI, Jan Ignace | (1860–1941) Polish Prime Minister 1918–19. Renowned concert pianist, made brief excursion into politics to re-establish his country's place in Europe. |
| SMUTS, Jan C. (General) | (1870–1950) South African Prime Minister. Member of the British War Cabinet and Imperial War Cabinet 1917–18. For a Boer he was a man of liberal views. |
| SONNINO, Sidney (Baron) | (1847–1922) Italian Foreign Minister. A wealthy Tuscan conservative, son of a Jewish father and a Scottish Presbyterian mother. Anti-clerical despite his conservatism, he opposed efforts at a rapprochement with the Vatican. Served as Minister of the Treasury 1893–6, Prime Minister and |

*I am indebted to Dr Robert Baxter, of the University College of Wales, Swansea, for information on Orlando and Sonnino.

Minister of the Interior 1906 and 1909–10, Foreign Minister 1914–19. Before the war was a warm supporter of the Triple Alliance with Germany and Austria-Hungary, but after the German defeat on the Marne he moved to favouring an alliance with the Entente Powers, especially when offered territorial gains for Italy if he joined the Entente and they were victorious. He sold his country to the highest bidder, when he concluded the Treaty of London with Britain and France in 1915. Opposed the creation of a Yugoslav state, supported intervention against the Bolsheviks.

WILSON, T. Woodrow (1856–1921) President of the United States of America. History professor, became President of Princeton University 1902, Governor of New Jersey 1911, President of the United States 1912–21. Author of the Fourteen Points but could never forget his hatred of all things German when trying to apply them.

# *Bibliography*


DOCUMENTARY SOURCES

*Printed Documents*

*Foreign Relations of the United States: The Paris Peace Conference, 1919* (13 volumes) (Government Printing Office, Washington, DC, USA, 1942–7)

D. H. MILLER, *The Drafting of the Covenant* (2 volumes) (Government Printing Office, Washington, DC, 1928)

BANE and LUTZ, *The Blockade of Germany after the Armistice, 1918–1919* (Hoover Library, Stanford University, USA, 1942)

P. J. MANTOUX, *Les Délibérations du Conseil des Quatre: Notes de l'Officier Interprète* (2 volumes) (Centre National de la Recherche Scientifique, Paris, 1955). See also Mantoux, *Paris Peace Conference, 1919: Proceedings of the Council of Four, March 24th–April 18th* (Droz, Geneva, 1964), for English translation of Mantoux's minutes where they constitute the only record taken of the meeting.

*Documents on British Foreign Policy, 1919–1939*, First Series (Her Majesty's Stationery Office, 1947)

SIR H. V. TEMPERLEY, *A History of the Peace Conference of Paris* (4 volumes) (Royal Institute of International Affairs, London, 1920–4)

J. DEGRAS, *Soviet Documents on Foreign Policy*, Volume I (Royal Institute of International Affairs, London, 1951)

———, *The Communist International: Documents*, Volume I (Royal Institute of International Affairs, London, 1951)

*Papers Respecting Negotiations for an Anglo-French Pact*, Cmd 2169 (Her Majesty's Stationery Office, London, 1924)

Parliamentary Debates, Official Record: House of Commons, 5th Series

*Unpublished sources*

In the Public Record Office, London:

Cabinet Minutes: CAB 23, Volumes 9–15

Cabinet Papers: GT Series, CAB 24, Volumes 65–82
Also CAB 29, Volume 28
CAB 63, Volume 25 (Hankey Papers)

Foreign Office Correspondence: F.O. 414–245
405–206
406–41
418–53
421–297
425–383
899–15B

Papers of Lord Curzon of Kedleston: F.O. 800, Volumes 150, 152–3, 155, 157

Papers of A. J. Balfour: F.O. 800, Volumes 200–3, 206–7, 212, 216–7

In the British Museum, London:

Papers of A. J. Balfour, Add. MSS, Volumes 49692, 49704, 49734, 49738, 49744–5, 49750–2

In the Scottish Record Office, Edinburgh:

Papers of the Eleventh Marquess of Lothian (Philip Kerr), GD40/17, Volumes 54–5, 58, 60–6, 68, 70–5

In the Beaverbrook Library, London:

Papers of David Lloyd George (catalogued individually, references indicated in bibliographical references)

MEMOIRS AND CONTEMPORARY RECORDS

G. CLEMENCEAU, *Grandeur and Misery of a Victory* (Harrap, London, 1930)

LORD HANKEY, *The Supreme Command*, Volume II (G. Allen and Unwin, London, 1961)

——, *The Supreme Control at the Paris Peace Conference* (G. Allen and Unwin, London, 1963)

J. HEADLAM-MORLEY, *A Memoir of the Paris Peace Conference 1919*, ed. A. Headlam-Morley (Methuen, London, 1972)

J. M. KEYNES, *The Economic Consequences of the Peace* (Macmillan, London, 1920)

———, *Essays in Biography* (Mercury paper edition, London, 1961)

———, *Two Memoirs* (Hart Davis, London, 1949)

———, *A Revision of the Treaty* (Macmillan, London, 1922)

R. LANSING, *The Peace Negotiations: A Personal Narrative* (Houghton Mifflin, Boston, USA, 1920)

D. LLOYD GEORGE, *War Memoirs* (6 volumes) (Odhams, London, 1936)

———, *The Truth About the Peace Treaties* (2 volumes) (Gollancz, London, 1938)

H. NICOLSON, *Peacemaking, 1919* (Methuen, London, 1964)

COLONEL REPINGTON, *The First World War*, Volume II (Constable, London, 1920)

LORD RIDDELL, *My Intimate Diary of the Peace Conference and After, 1918–1923* (Gollancz, London, 1933)

C. SEYMOUR, *The Intimate Papers of Colonel House*, Volume IV (Benn, London, 1928)

G. SUAREZ, *Clemenceau* (Paris, 1930)

F. STEVENSON, *Lloyd George: A Diary*, edited by A. J. P. Taylor (Hutchinson, London, 1971)

A. J. SYLVESTER, *The Real Lloyd George* (Cassell, London, 1947)

A. TARDIEU, *The Truth about the Treaty* (Hodder and Stoughton, London, 1921)

SECONDARY WORKS

R. ALBRECHT-CARRIÉ, *Italy at the Paris Peace Conference* (University of Columbia Press, New York, 1938)

R. S. BAKER, *Woodrow Wilson and the World Settlement* (3 volumes) (Doubleday, New York, 1922)

LORD BEAVERBROOK, *The Decline and Fall of Lloyd George* (Collins, London, 1963)

F. BORKENAU, *World Communism* (Ann Arbor, Michigan, USA, 1962)

A. BULLOCK, *Hitler: A Study in Tyranny* (Odhams, London, 1952)

J. R. M. BUTLER, *Lothian* (Macmillan, London, 1960)

E. H. CARR, *The Bolshevik Revolution*, Volume III (Macmillan, London, 1953)

J. B. DUROSELLE, *From Wilson to Roosevelt*, translated by N. L. Roelker (Harvard University Press, USA, 1963)

H. J. ELCOCK, 'Britain and the Russo-Polish Frontier, 1919–1921', *Historical Journal*, Volume XII, 1969, pp. 137–154

R. C. K. ENSOR, *England, 1870–1914* (Oxford University Press, London, 1936)

E. EYCK, *History of the Weimar Republic*, Volume I, translated by H. P. Hanson and R. G. L. Waite (Oxford University Press, London, 1962)

L. E. GELFAND, *The Inquiry: American Preparations for Peace, 1917–1919* (University of Yale Press, New Haven, Connecticut, USA, 1963)

SIR ROY HARROD, *The Life of John Maynard Keynes* (Macmillan, London, 1953)

W. M. JORDAN, *Great Britain, France and the German Question* (Royal Institute of International Affairs, London, 1943)

T. KOMARNICKI, *Rebirth of the Polish Republic: A Study in the Diplomatic History of Europe, 1914–1920* (Heinemann, London, 1957)

I. J. LEDERER, *Yugoslavia at the Paris Peace Conference* (Yale University Press, 1963)

V. S. MAMMATEY, *The United States and East Central Europe, 1914–1919* (Princeton University Press, New York, 1957)

E. MANTOUX, *The Carthaginian Peace, or The Economic Consequences of Mr Keynes* (Oxford University Press, London, 1946)

F. S. MARSTON, *The Peace Conference of 1919* (Oxford University Press, London, 1944)

A. J. MAYER, *The Politics and Diplomacy of Peacemaking* (Weidenfeld and Nicolson, London, 1968)

K. O. MORGAN, *David Lloyd George: Welsh Radical as World Statesman* (University of Wales Press, Cardiff, 1963)

H. I. NELSON, *Land and Power: British and Allied Policy on Germany's Frontiers, 1916–1919* (Routledge and Kegan Paul, London, 1963)

J. NEVAKIVI, *Britain, France and the Arab Middle East, 1914–1920* (University of London: The Athlone Press, London, 1969)

R. A. C. PARKER, *Europe, 1914–1945* (Weidenfeld and Nicolson, London, 1969)

S. D. SPECTOR, *Rumania at the Paris Peace Conference: A Study of the Diplomacy of Ioan I. C. Bratianu* (Brookman Associates, New York, 1962)

K. R. STADLER, *The Birth of the Austrian Republic, 1918–1921* (Sijthoff-Leyden, 1966)

R. STORRY, *A History of Modern Japan* (Penguin Books, London, 1960)

A. J. P. TAYLOR, *English History, 1914–1945* (Oxford University Press, London, 1965)

———, *The First World War: An Illustrated History* (Hamish Hamilton, London, 1963)

———, *The Trouble-Makers: Dissent over Foreign Policy, 1792–1939* (Hamish Hamilton, London, 1957)

———, *The Struggle for Mastery in Europe, 1848–1918* (Oxford University Press, London, 1954)

S. P. TILLMAN, *Anglo-American Relations at the Paris Peace Conference* (Princeton University Press, New York, 1962)

J. M. THOMPSON, *Russia, Bolshevism and the Versailles Peace* (Princeton University Press, New York, 1966)

P. S. WANDYCZ, *France and her Eastern Allies* (University of Minneapolis Press, Minneapolis, 1962)

E. WEILL-RAYNAL, *Les Réparations Allemandes et la France*, Volume I (Nouvelles Editions Latines, Paris, 1938)

J. W. WHEELER-BENNETT, *The Treaty of Brest-Litovsk and Germany's Eastern Policy* (Oxford University Press, London, 1939)

# Index